Ayu
Watanabe

L♥DK

10

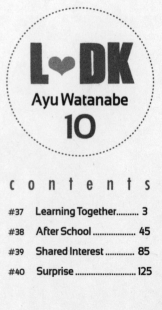

L♥DK

Ayu Watanabe

10

c o n t e n t s

#37	Learning Together	3
#38	After School	45
#39	Shared Interest	85
#40	Surprise	125

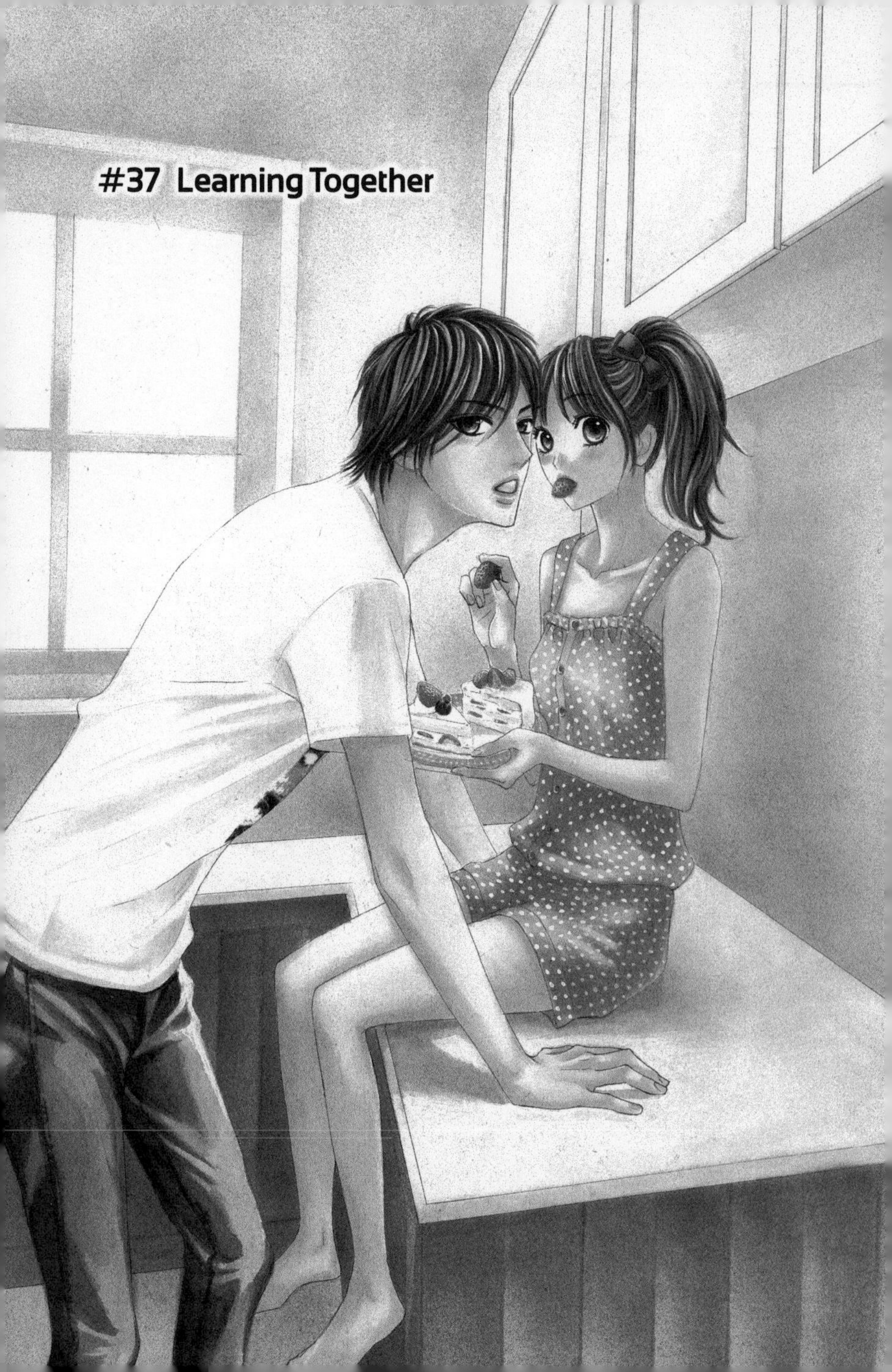
#37 Learning Together

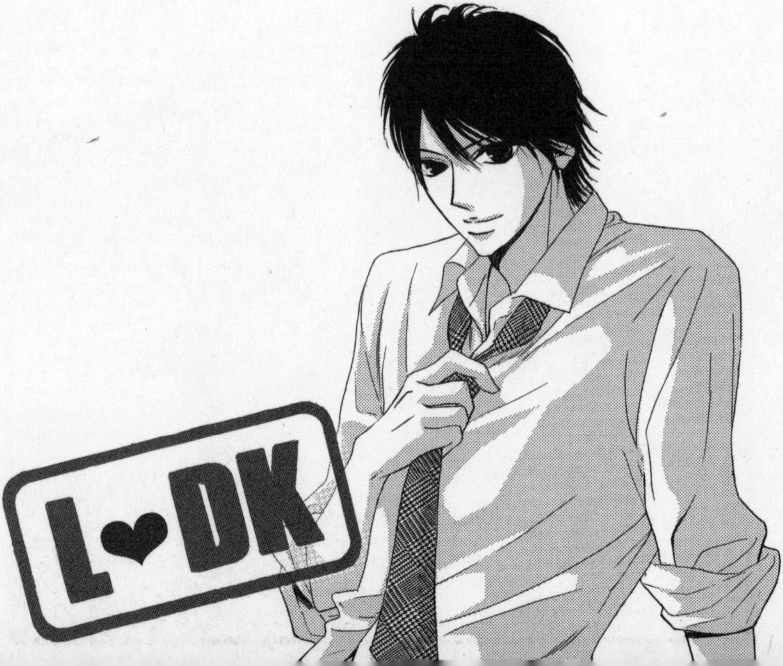
L♥DK

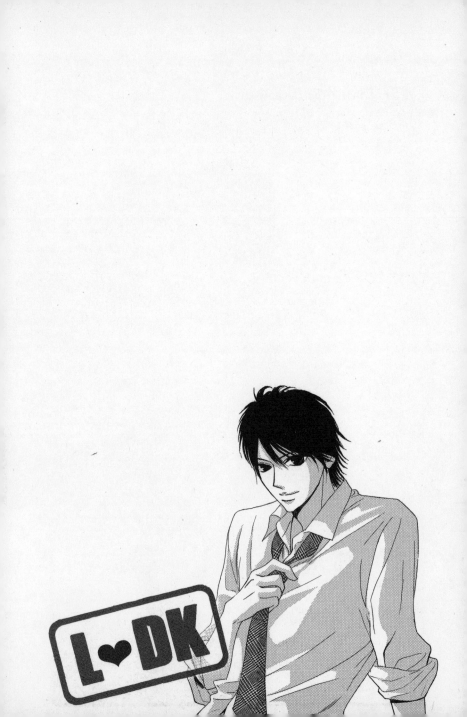

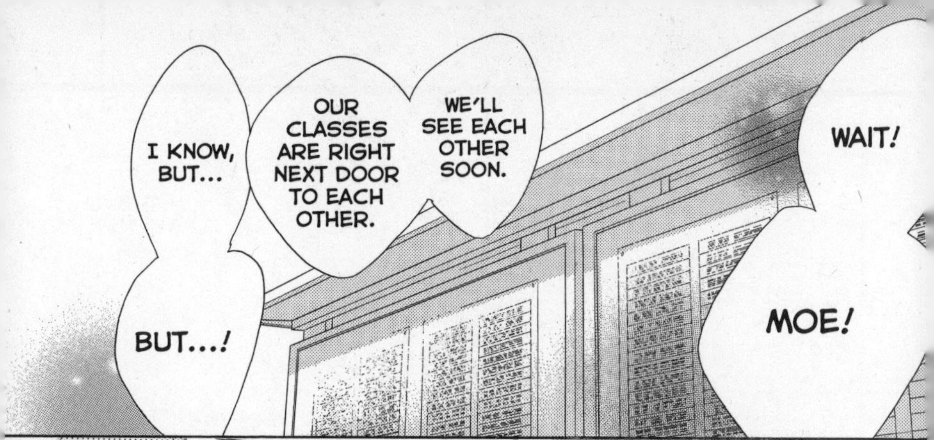
WAIT!
MOE!
WE'LL SEE EACH OTHER SOON.
OUR CLASSES ARE RIGHT NEXT DOOR TO EACH OTHER.
I KNOW, BUT...
BUT...!

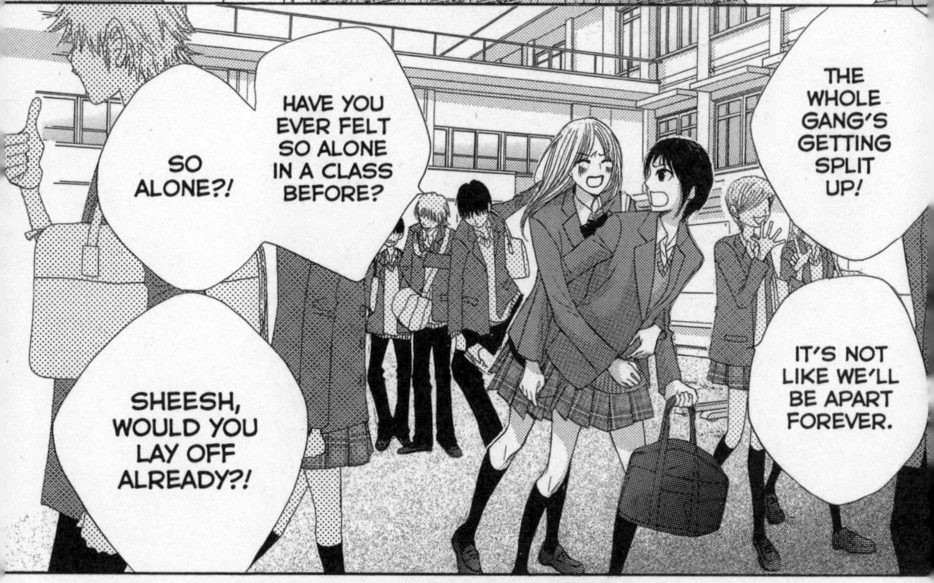
THE WHOLE GANG'S GETTING SPLIT UP!
IT'S NOT LIKE WE'LL BE APART FOREVER.
HAVE YOU EVER FELT SO ALONE IN A CLASS BEFORE?
SO ALONE?!
SHEESH, WOULD YOU LAY OFF ALREADY?!

Story So Far

L♥DK

Story

High schooler Aoi is living in the secret arrangement of sharing an apartment with the school's hottest student Shusei. Things couldn't be happier when they realize they feel the same way about each other...but when their situation gets leaked to Aoi's dad, the two are in for a world of trouble! Thankfully, her father changes his mind upon seeing how strongly Shusei cares about Aoi and when she tells him that "because you always protected me, I want to protect someone too." He agrees to let them live together. But under the one condition: "No sexual relations until graduation!"

Cast

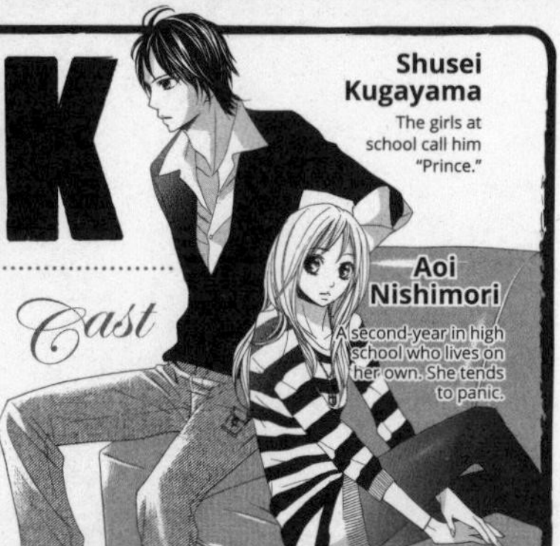

Shusei Kugayama
The girls at school call him "Prince."

Aoi Nishimori
A second-year in high school who lives on her own. She tends to panic.

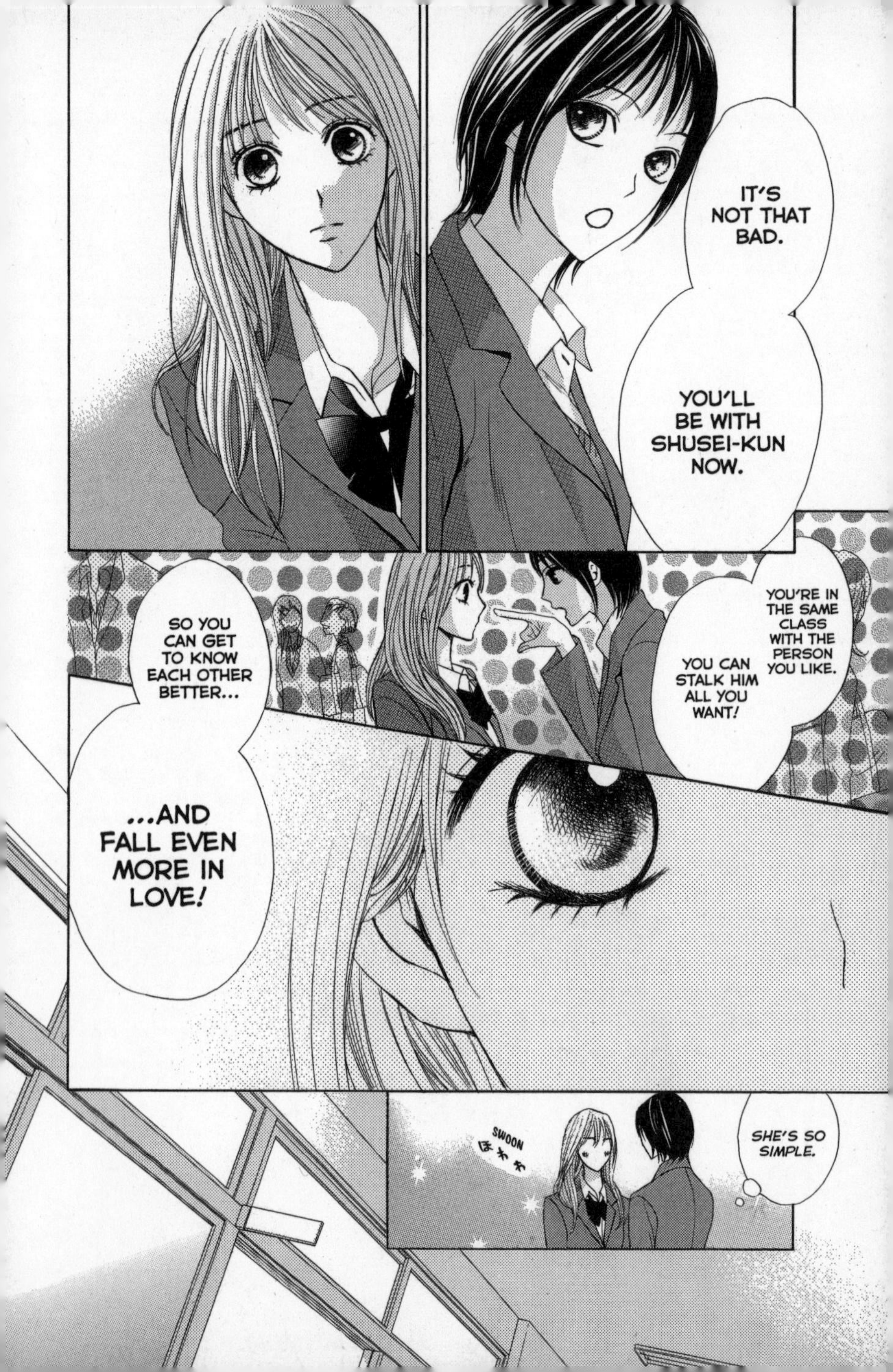
IT'S NOT THAT BAD.
YOU'LL BE WITH SHUSEI-KUN NOW.
YOU'RE IN THE SAME CLASS WITH THE PERSON YOU LIKE.
YOU CAN STALK HIM ALL YOU WANT!
SO YOU CAN GET TO KNOW EACH OTHER BETTER...
...AND FALL EVEN MORE IN LOVE!
SHE'S SO SIMPLE.
SWOON

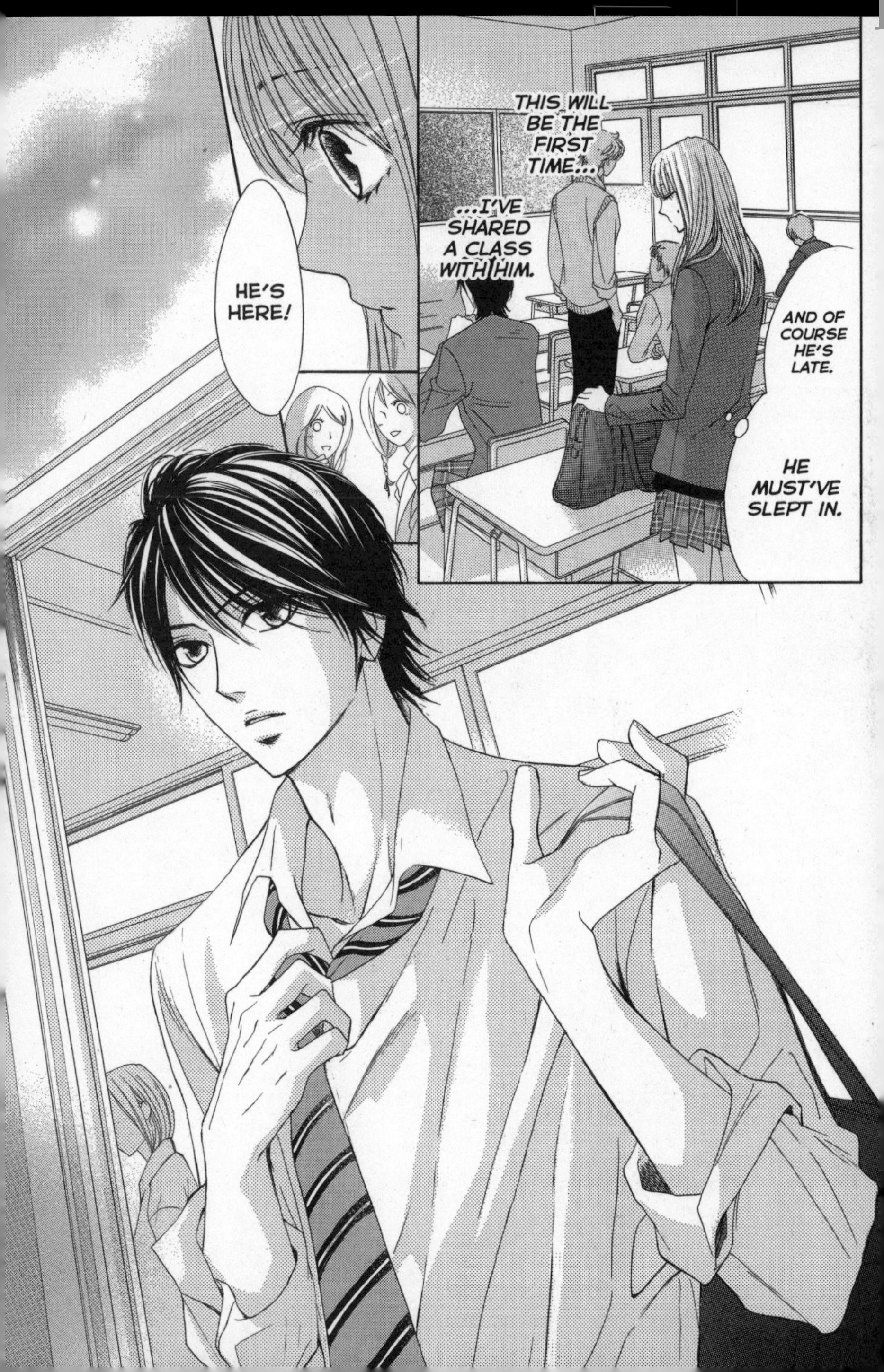
THIS WILL BE THE FIRST TIME...
...I'VE SHARED A CLASS WITH HIM.
AND OF COURSE HE'S LATE.
HE MUST'VE SLEPT IN.
HE'S HERE!

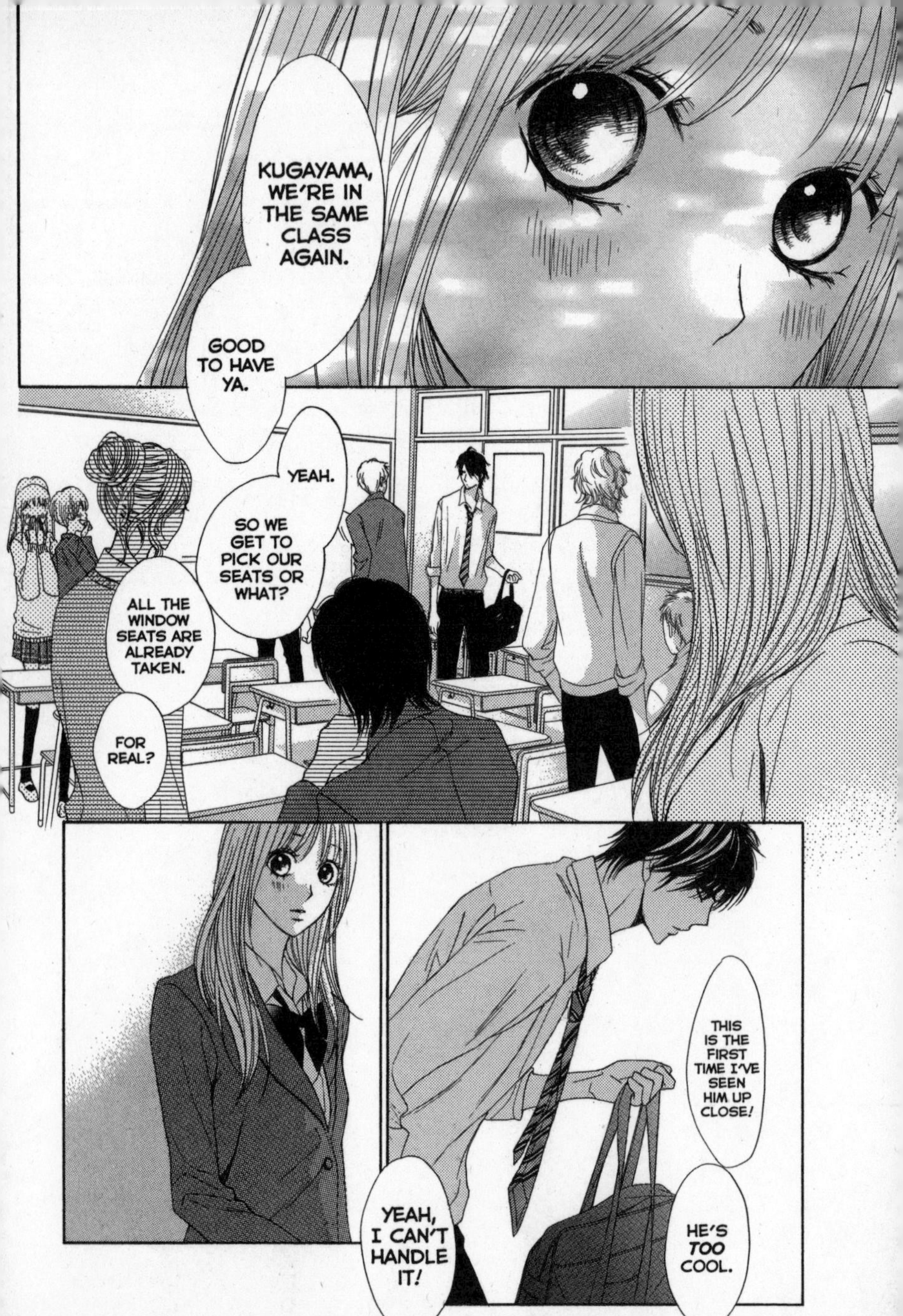
KUGAYAMA, WE'RE IN THE SAME CLASS AGAIN.
GOOD TO HAVE YA.
YEAH.
SO WE GET TO PICK OUR SEATS OR WHAT?
ALL THE WINDOW SEATS ARE ALREADY TAKEN.
FOR REAL?
THIS IS THE FIRST TIME I'VE SEEN HIM UP CLOSE!
HE'S *TOO* COOL.
YEAH, I CAN'T HANDLE IT!

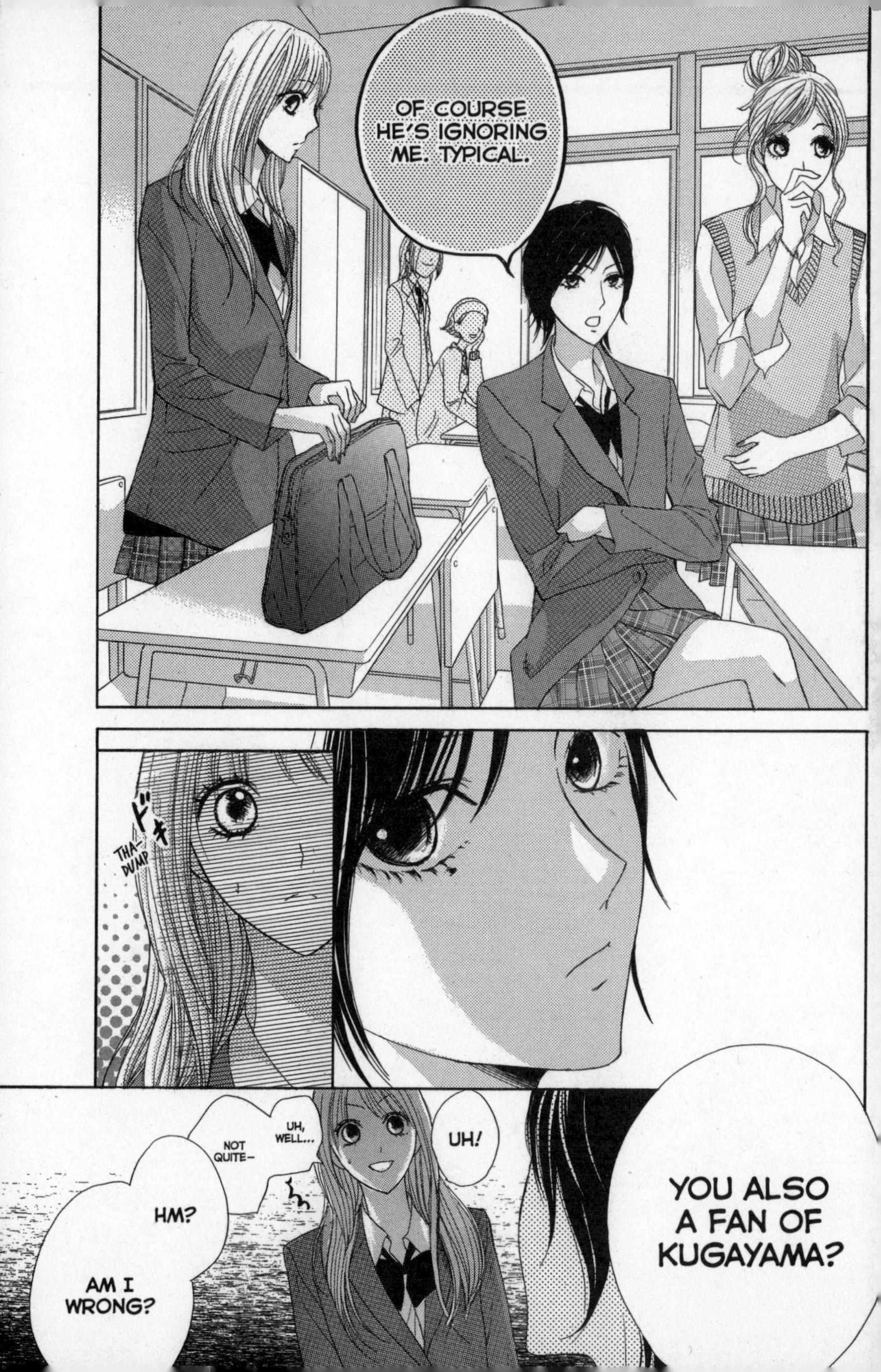
OF COURSE HE'S IGNORING ME. TYPICAL.
ドキ
THA-DUMP
YOU ALSO A FAN OF KUGAYAMA?
UH!
UH, WELL...
NOT QUITE–
HM?
AM I WRONG?

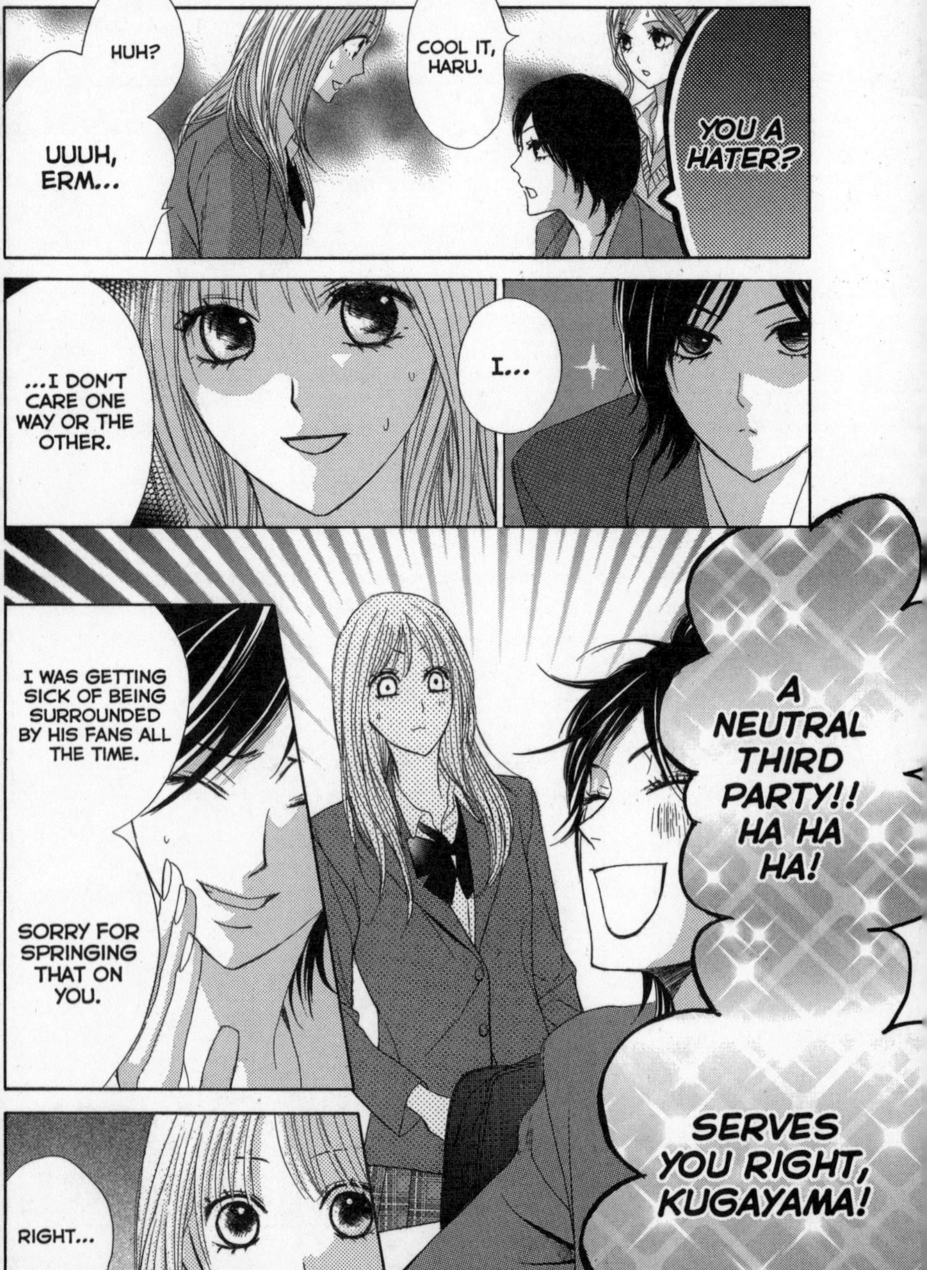
YOU A HATER?
COOL IT, HARU.
HUH?
UUUH, ERM...
I...
...I DON'T CARE ONE WAY OR THE OTHER.
A NEUTRAL THIRD PARTY!! HA HA HA!
I WAS GETTING SICK OF BEING SURROUNDED BY HIS FANS ALL THE TIME.
SORRY FOR SPRINGING THAT ON YOU.
SERVES YOU RIGHT, KUGAYAMA!
RIGHT...

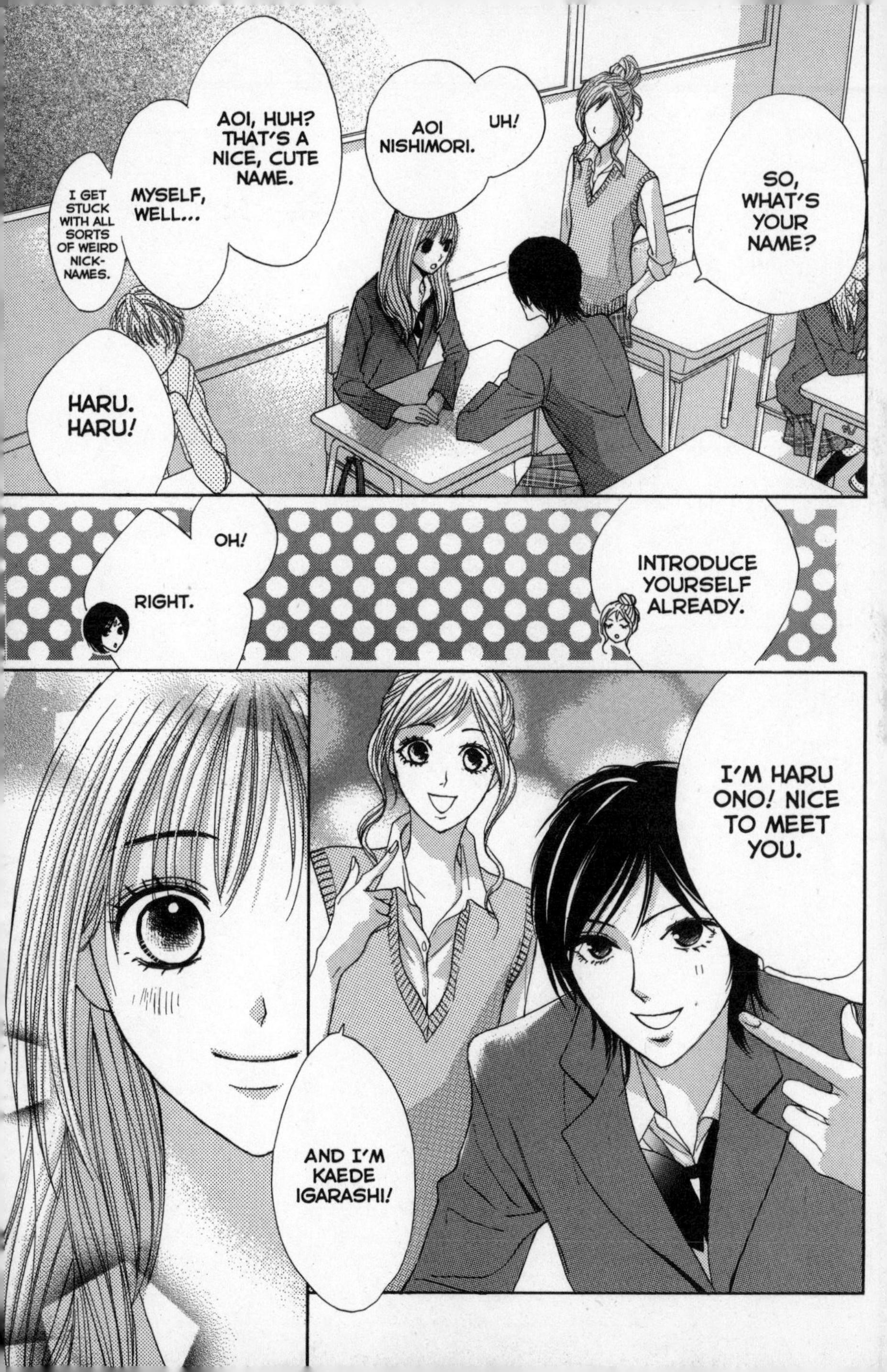
SO, WHAT'S YOUR NAME?
UH!
AOI NISHIMORI.
AOI, HUH? THAT'S A NICE, CUTE NAME.
MYSELF, WELL...
I GET STUCK WITH ALL SORTS OF WEIRD NICK-NAMES.
HARU. HARU!
INTRODUCE YOURSELF ALREADY.
OH!
RIGHT.
I'M HARU ONO! NICE TO MEET YOU.
AND I'M KAEDE IGARASHI!

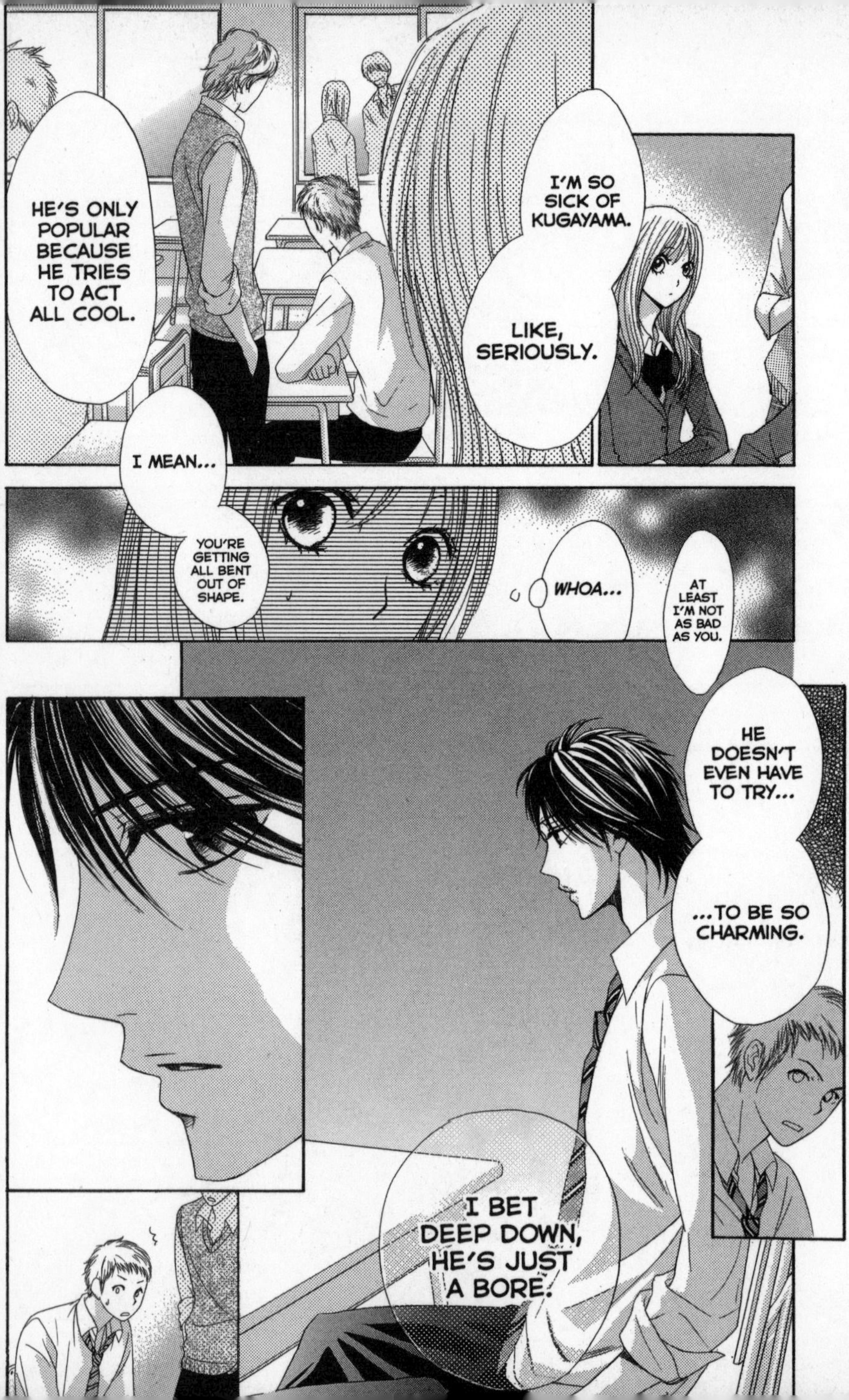
I'M SO SICK OF KUGAYAMA.
LIKE, SERIOUSLY.
HE'S ONLY POPULAR BECAUSE HE TRIES TO ACT ALL COOL.
I MEAN...
YOU'RE GETTING ALL BENT OUT OF SHAPE.
WHOA...
AT LEAST I'M NOT AS BAD AS YOU.
HE DOESN'T EVEN HAVE TO TRY...
...TO BE SO CHARMING.
I BET DEEP DOWN, HE'S JUST A BORE.

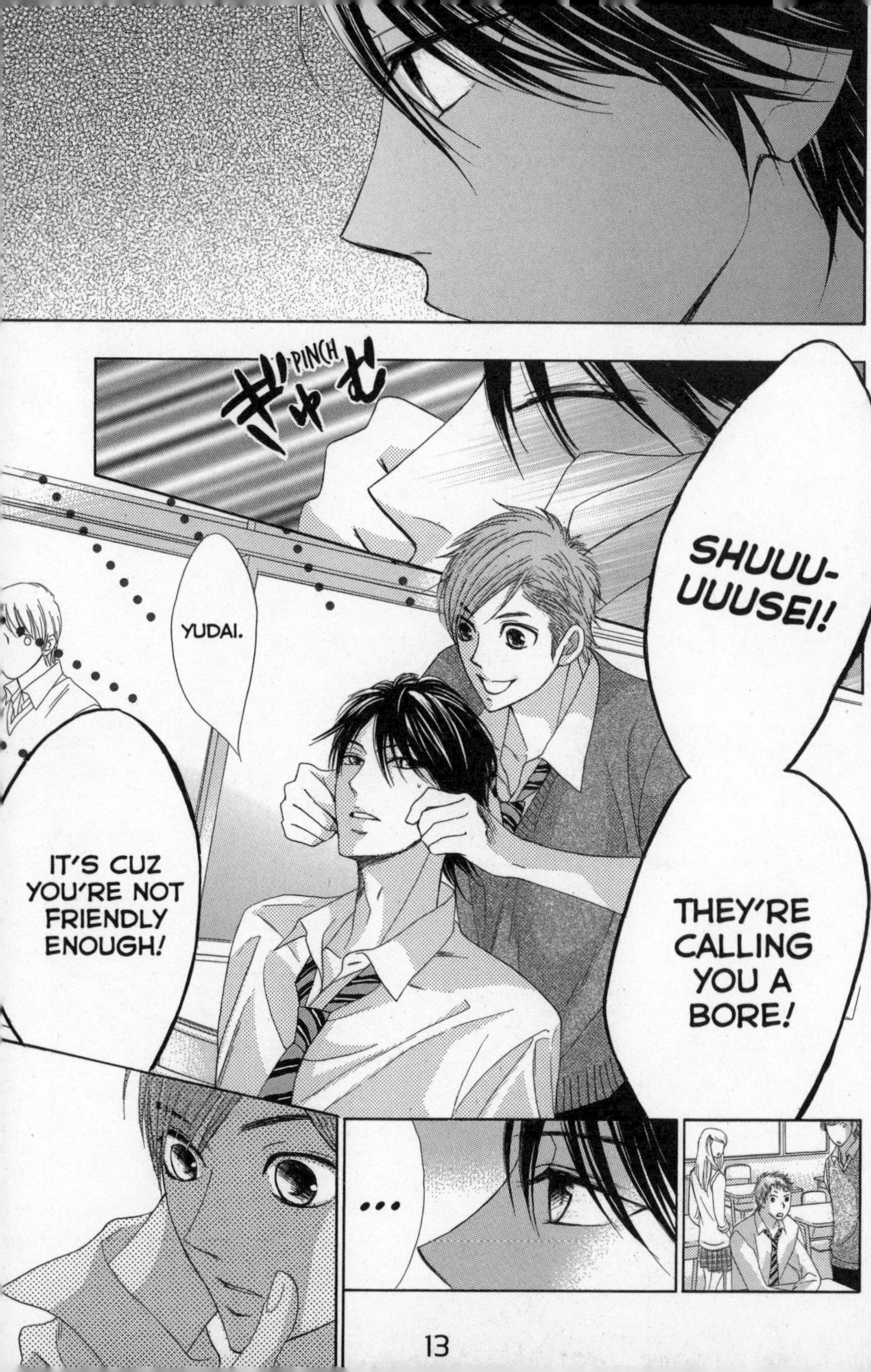
ぎゅむ PINCH
SHUUUU-UUUSEI!
THEY'RE CALLING YOU A BORE!
YUDAI.
IT'S CUZ YOU'RE NOT FRIENDLY ENOUGH!
...

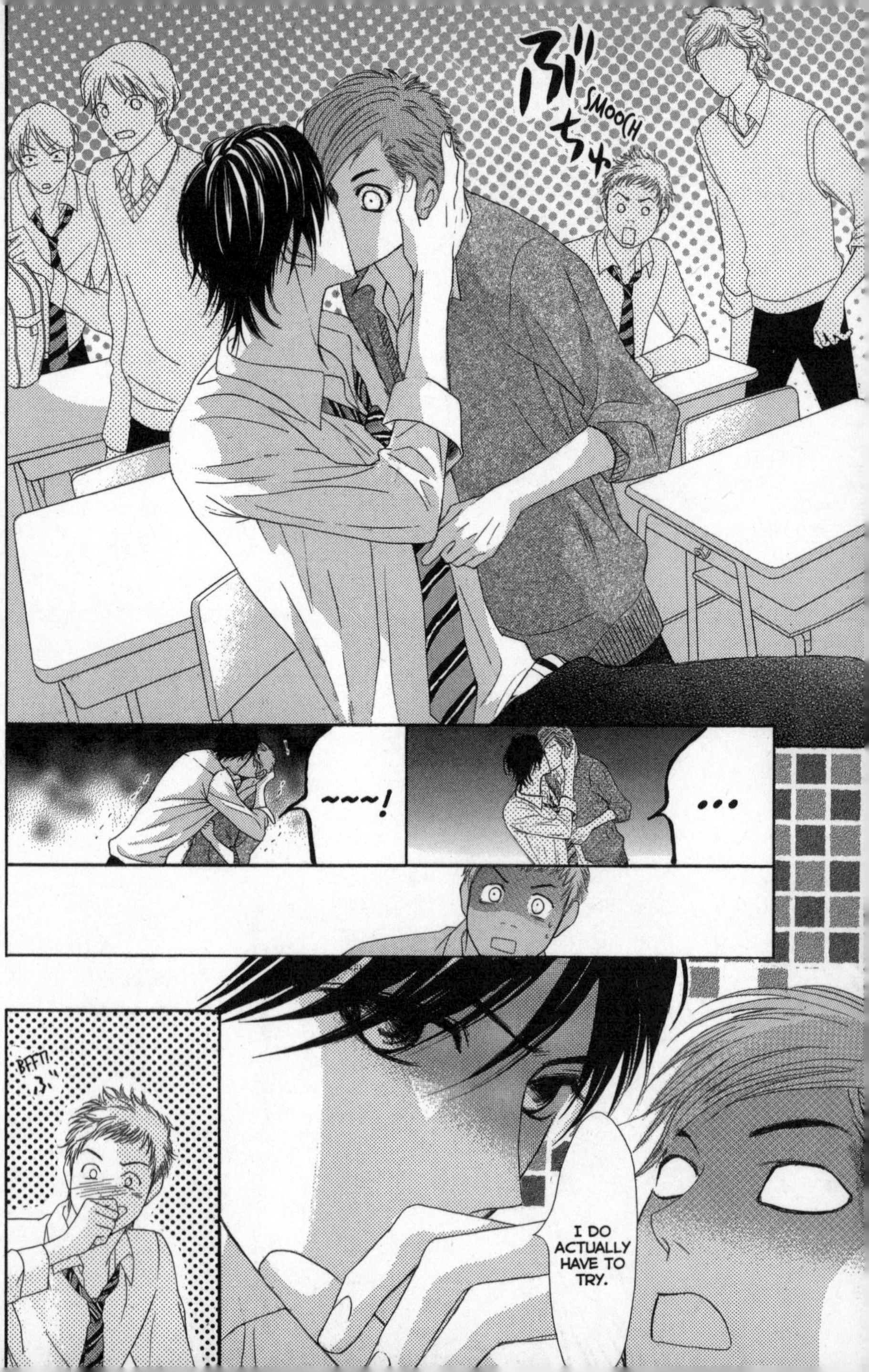
ぶちゅ
SMOOCH
...
~~~!
I DO ACTUALLY HAVE TO TRY.
BFFT!
ふ
~~~

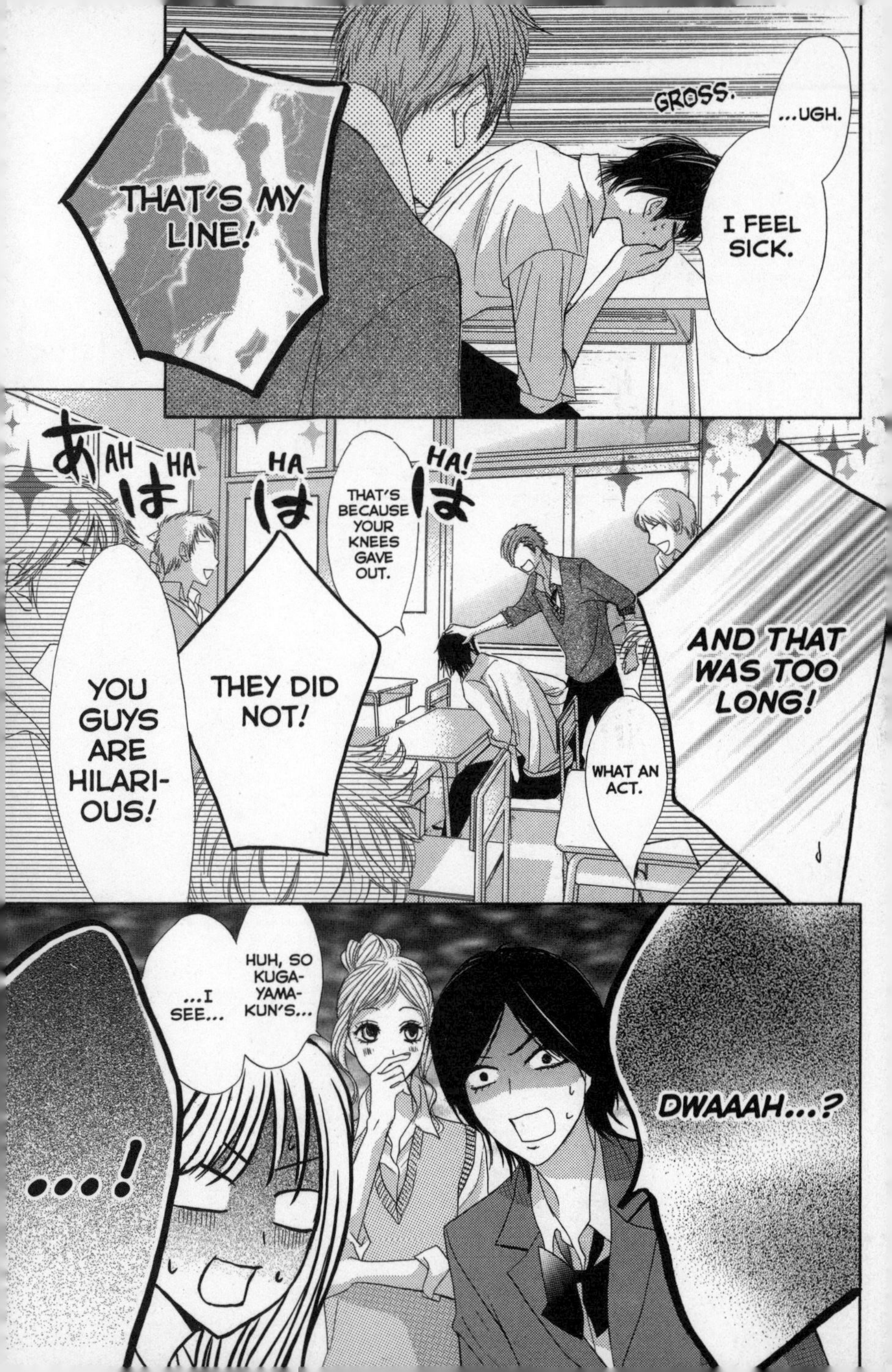

...UGH.
I FEEL SICK.
GROSS.
THAT'S MY LINE!
AND THAT WAS TOO LONG!
HA! は
THAT'S BECAUSE YOUR KNEES GAVE OUT.
HA は
THEY DID NOT!
あ AH は HA
YOU GUYS ARE HILARIOUS!
WHAT AN ACT.
DWAAAH...?
HUH, SO KUGA-YAMA-KUN'S...
...I SEE...
...!

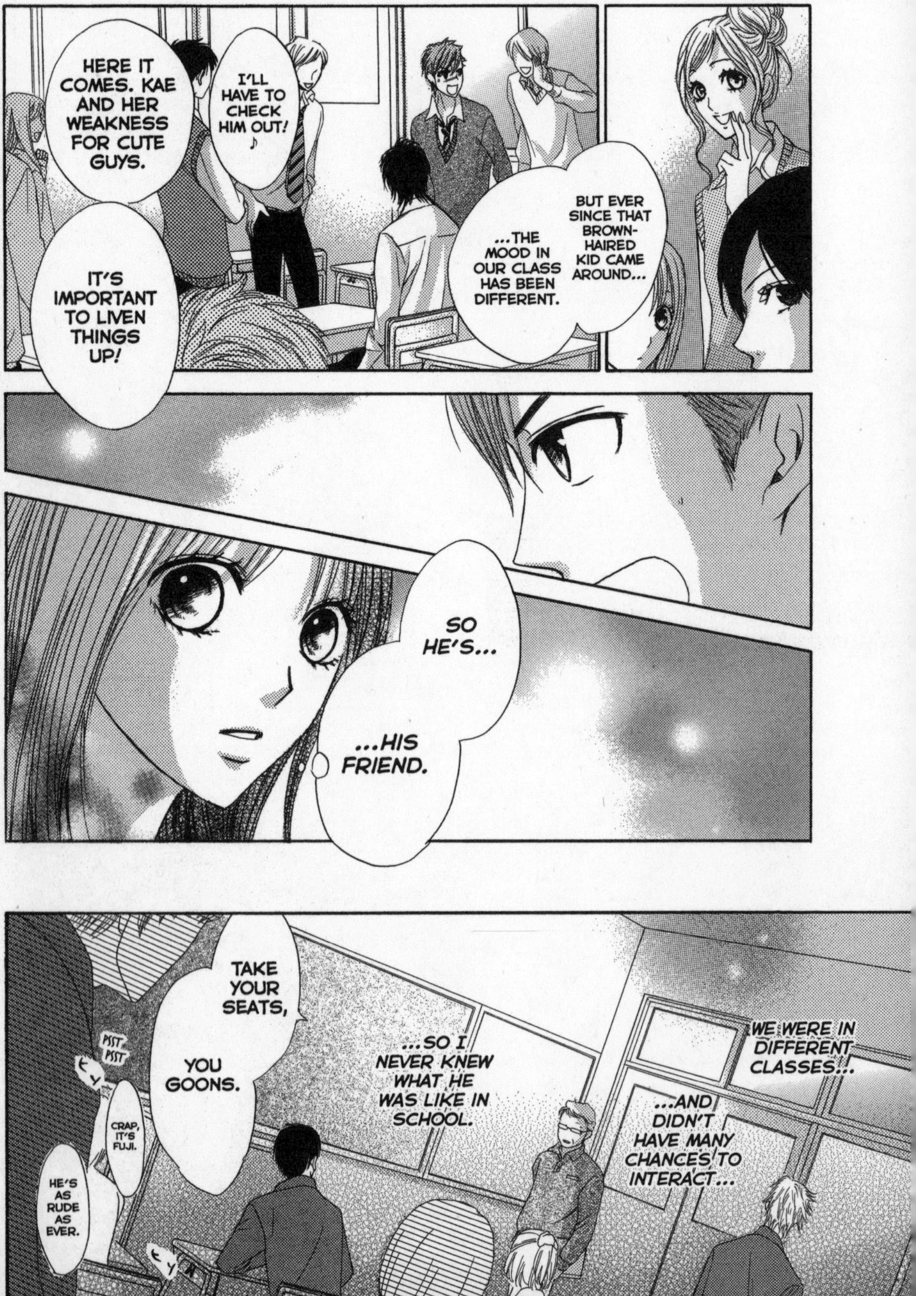
BUT EVER SINCE THAT BROWN-HAIRED KID CAME AROUND...
...THE MOOD IN OUR CLASS HAS BEEN DIFFERENT.
I'LL HAVE TO CHECK HIM OUT! ♪
HERE IT COMES. KAE AND HER WEAKNESS FOR CUTE GUYS.
IT'S IMPORTANT TO LIVEN THINGS UP!
SO HE'S...
...HIS FRIEND.
WE WERE IN DIFFERENT CLASSES...
...AND DIDN'T HAVE MANY CHANCES TO INTERACT...
...SO I NEVER KNEW WHAT HE WAS LIKE IN SCHOOL.
TAKE YOUR SEATS,
YOU GOONS.
PSST PSST
CRAP, IT'S FUJI.
HE'S AS RUDE AS EVER.

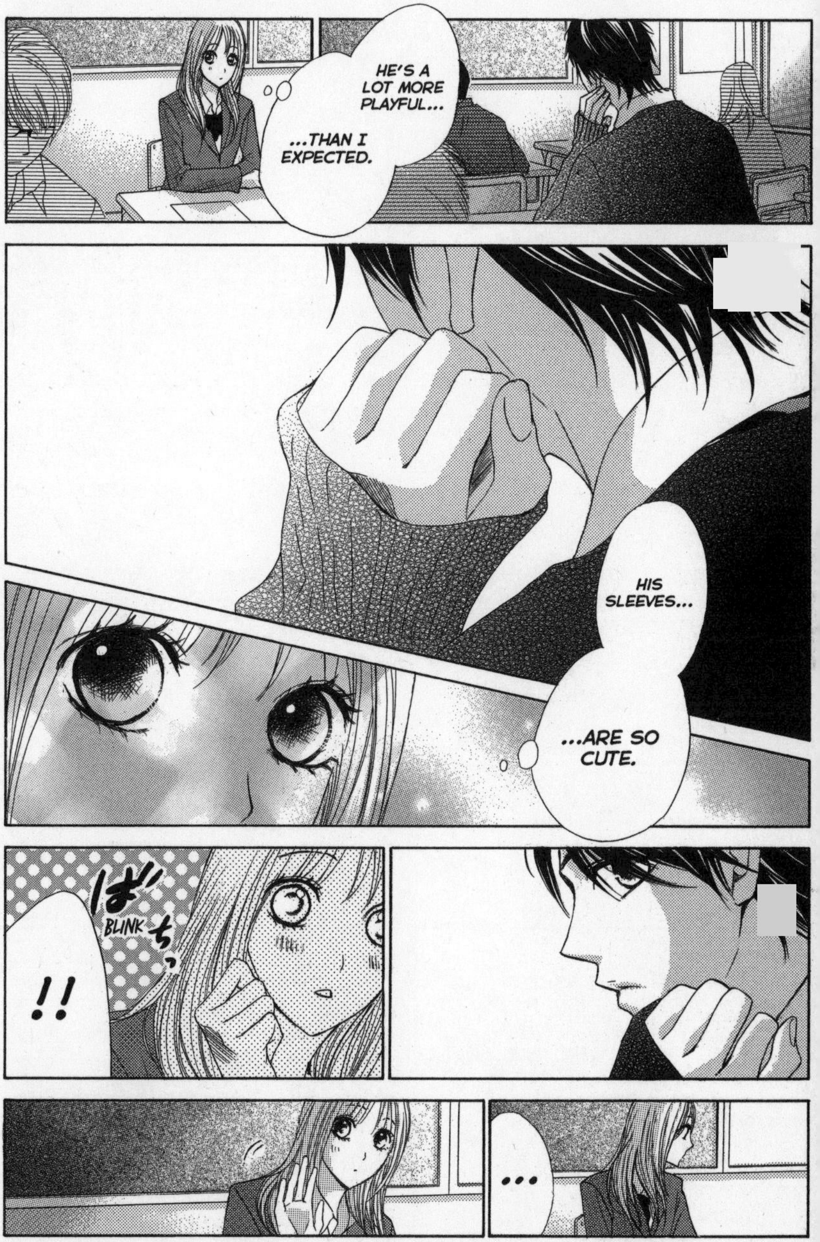
HE'S A LOT MORE PLAYFUL...
...THAN I EXPECTED.
HIS SLEEVES...
...ARE SO CUTE.
ぱちっ
BLINK
!!
...

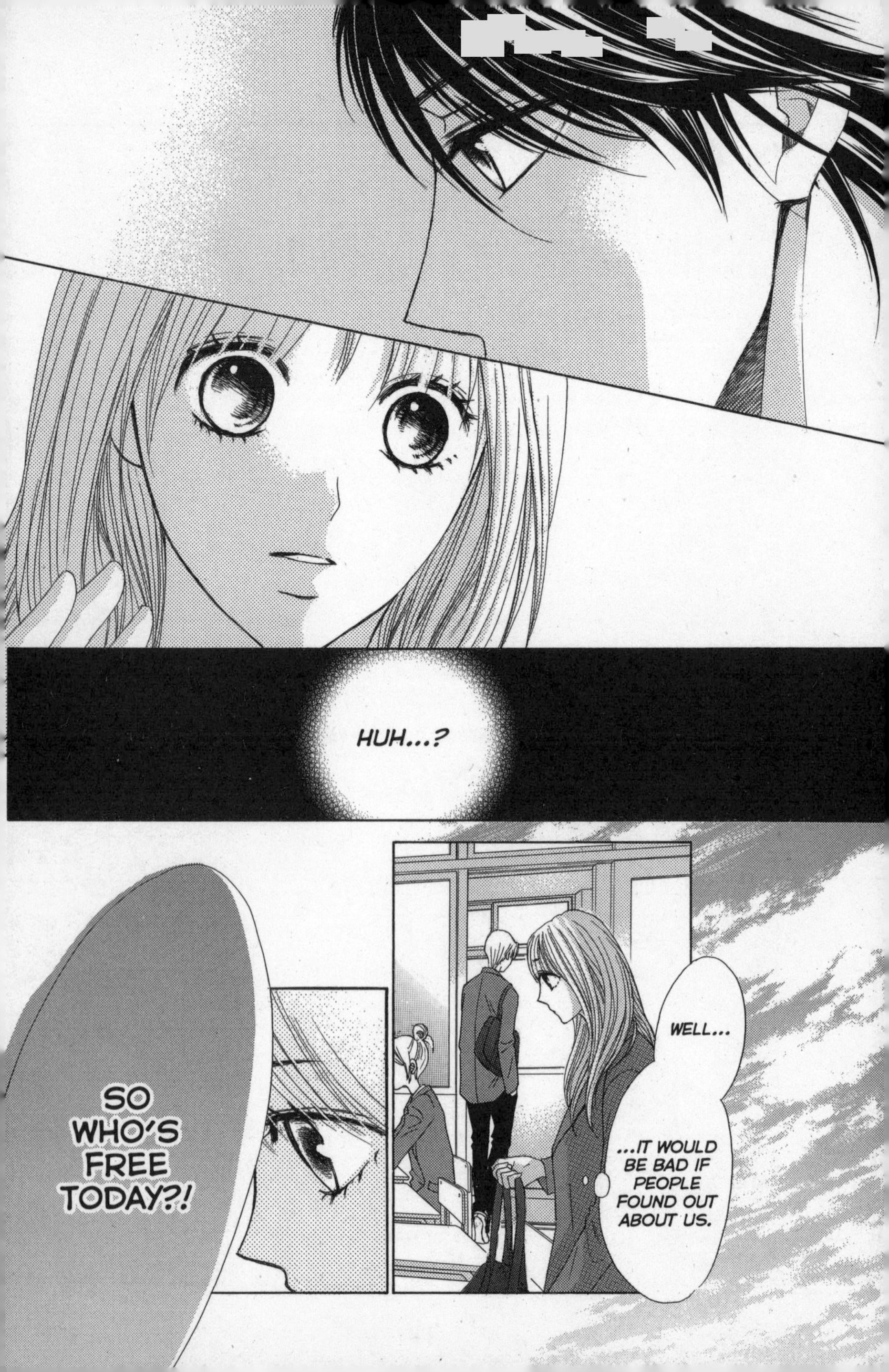
HUH...?
WELL...
...IT WOULD BE BAD IF PEOPLE FOUND OUT ABOUT US.
SO WHO'S FREE TODAY?!

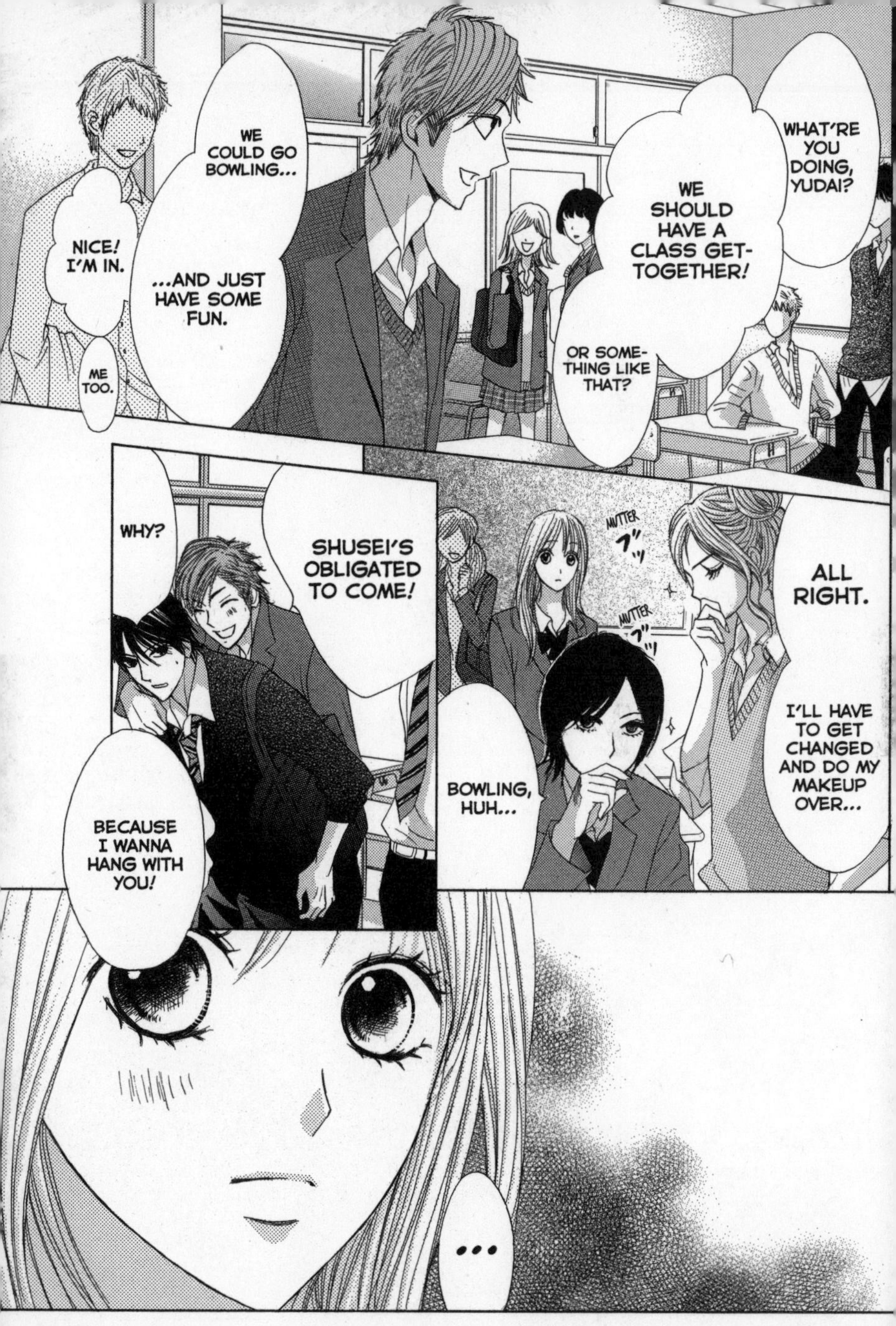
WHAT'RE YOU DOING, YUDAI?
WE SHOULD HAVE A CLASS GET-TOGETHER!
OR SOME-THING LIKE THAT?
WE COULD GO BOWLING...
...AND JUST HAVE SOME FUN.
NICE! I'M IN.
ME TOO.
ALL RIGHT.
MUTTER
MUTTER
I'LL HAVE TO GET CHANGED AND DO MY MAKEUP OVER...
BOWLING, HUH...
SHUSEI'S OBLIGATED TO COME!
WHY?
BECAUSE I WANNA HANG WITH YOU!
...

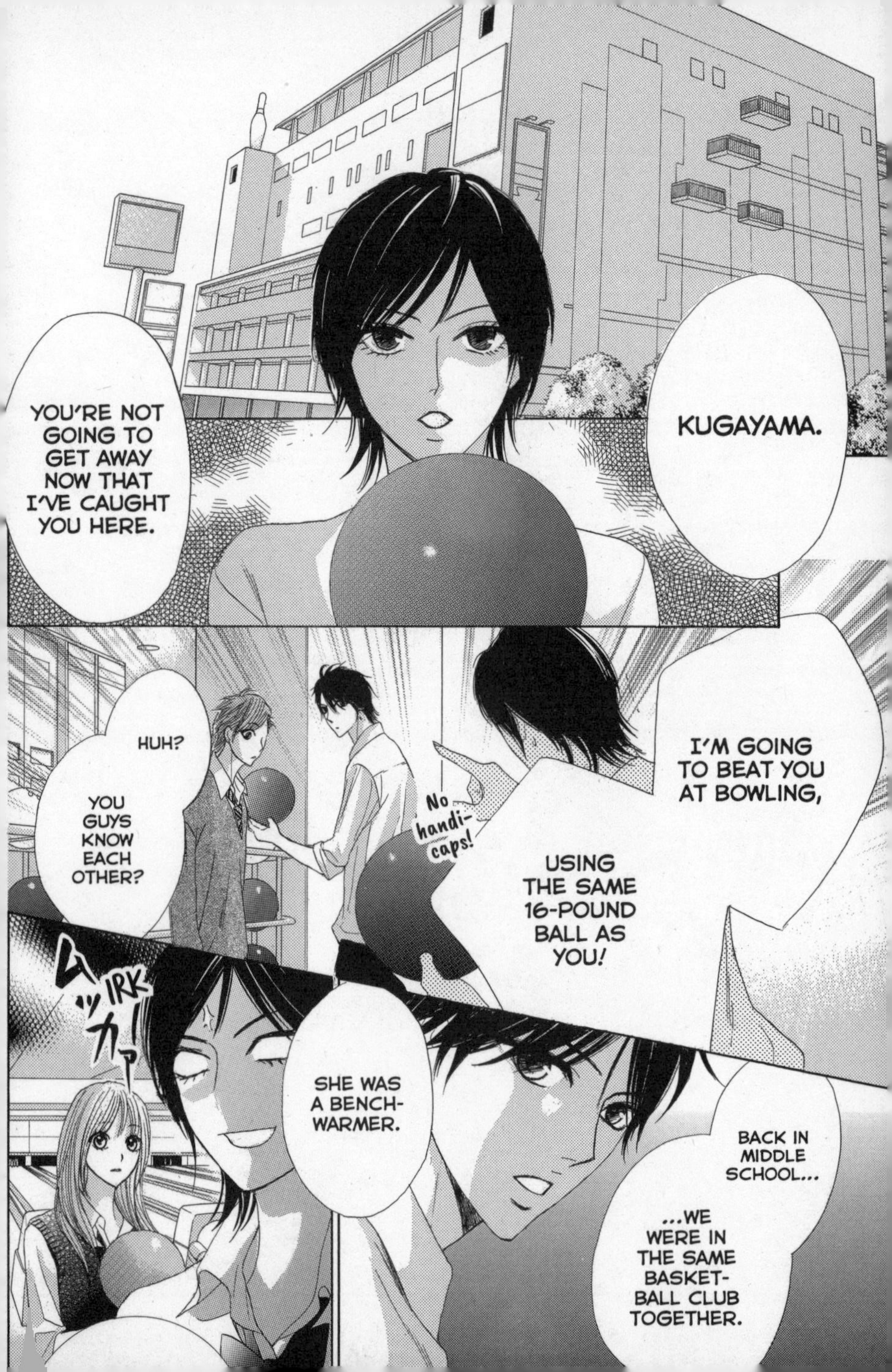
KUGAYAMA.
YOU'RE NOT GOING TO GET AWAY NOW THAT I'VE CAUGHT YOU HERE.
I'M GOING TO BEAT YOU AT BOWLING,
USING THE SAME 16-POUND BALL AS YOU!
No handi-caps!
HUH?
YOU GUYS KNOW EACH OTHER?
BACK IN MIDDLE SCHOOL...
...WE WERE IN THE SAME BASKET-BALL CLUB TOGETHER.
SHE WAS A BENCH-WARMER.
ムッカァ
IRK

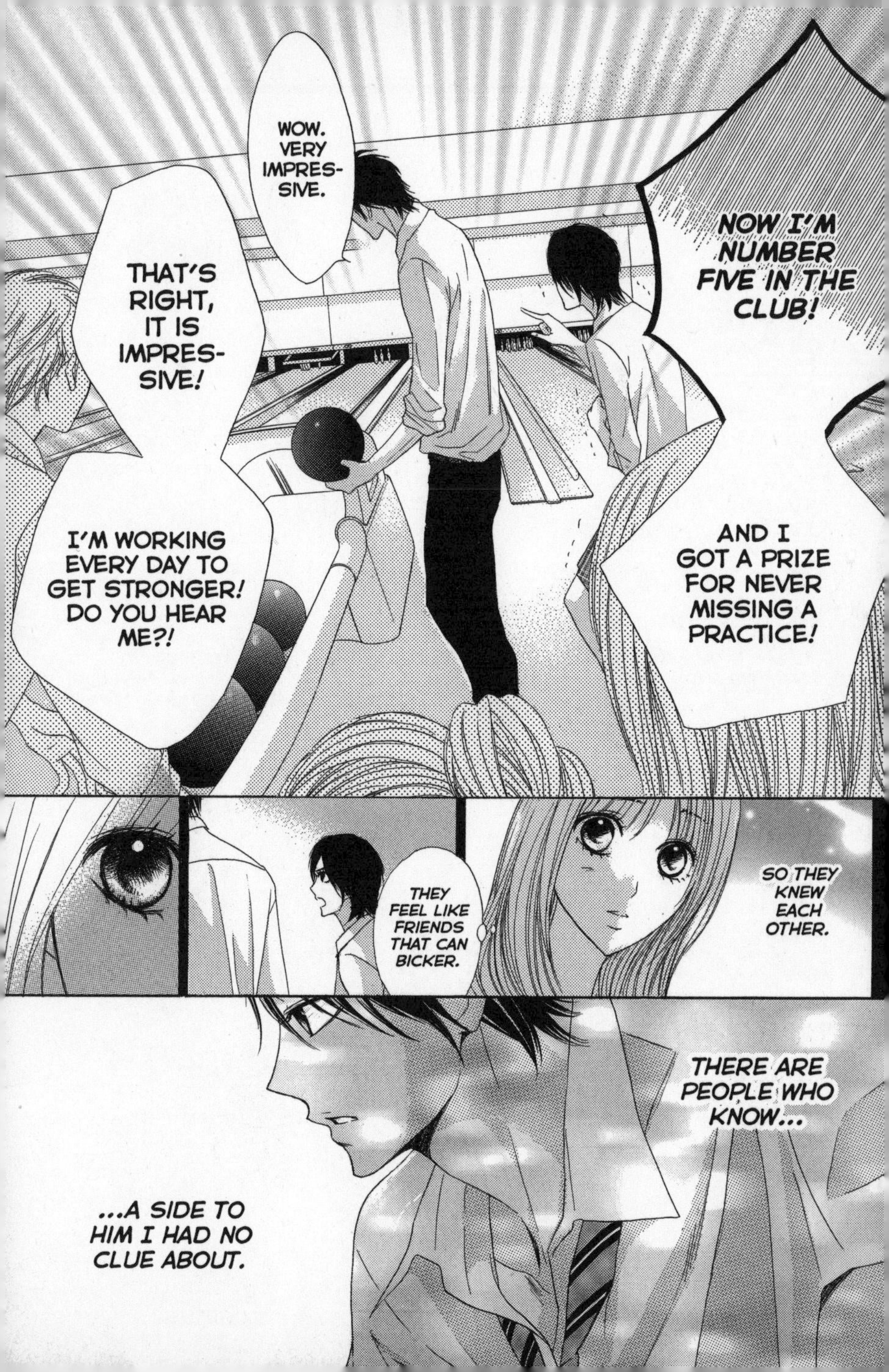
NOW I'M NUMBER FIVE IN THE CLUB!
AND I GOT A PRIZE FOR NEVER MISSING A PRACTICE!
WOW. VERY IMPRES-SIVE.
THAT'S RIGHT, IT IS IMPRES-SIVE!
I'M WORKING EVERY DAY TO GET STRONGER! DO YOU HEAR ME?!
SO THEY KNEW EACH OTHER.
THEY FEEL LIKE FRIENDS THAT CAN BICKER.
THERE ARE PEOPLE WHO KNOW...
...A SIDE TO HIM I HAD NO CLUE ABOUT.

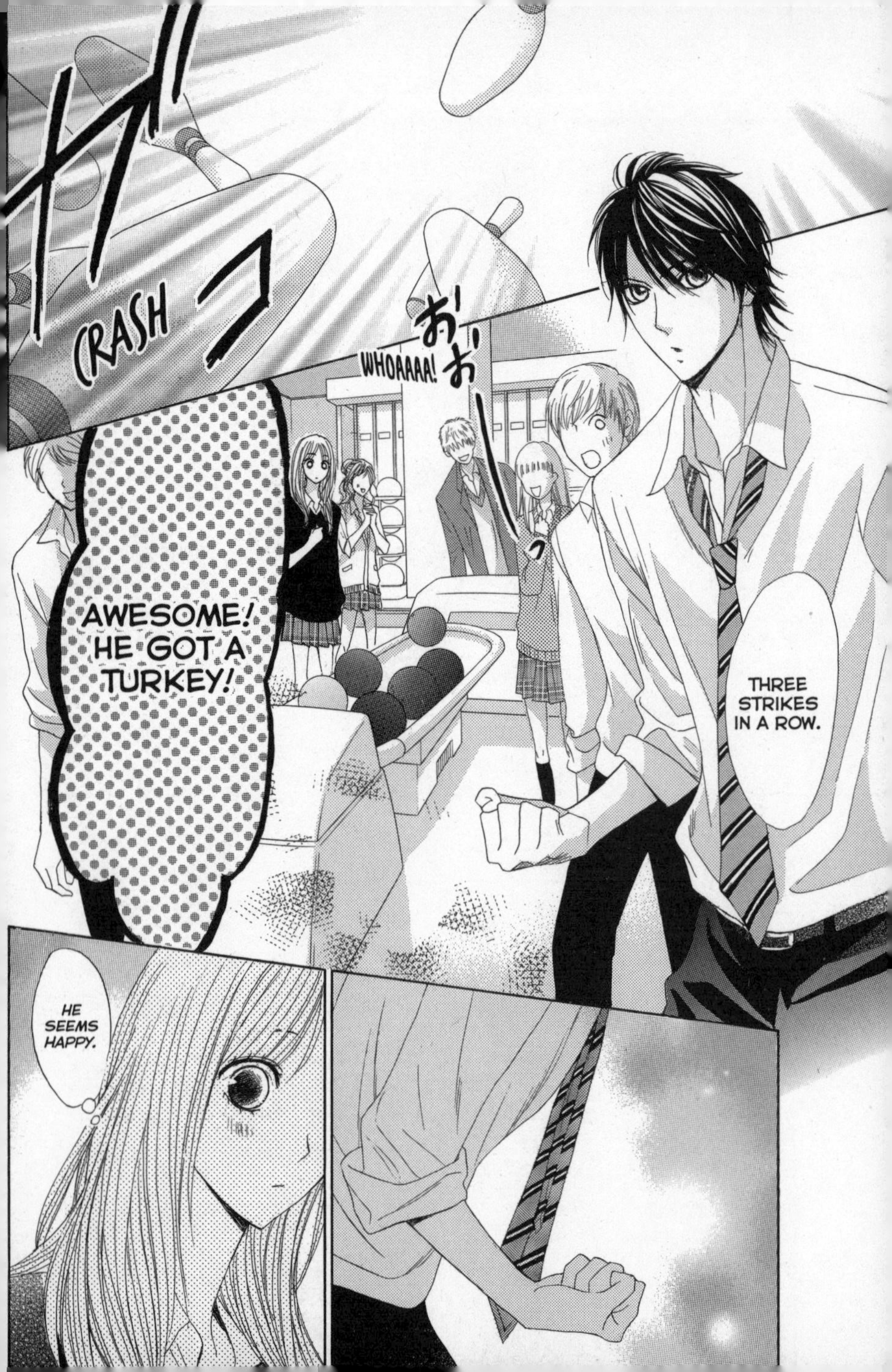
CRASH
WHOAAAA!
THREE STRIKES IN A ROW.
AWESOME! HE GOT A TURKEY!
HE SEEMS HAPPY.

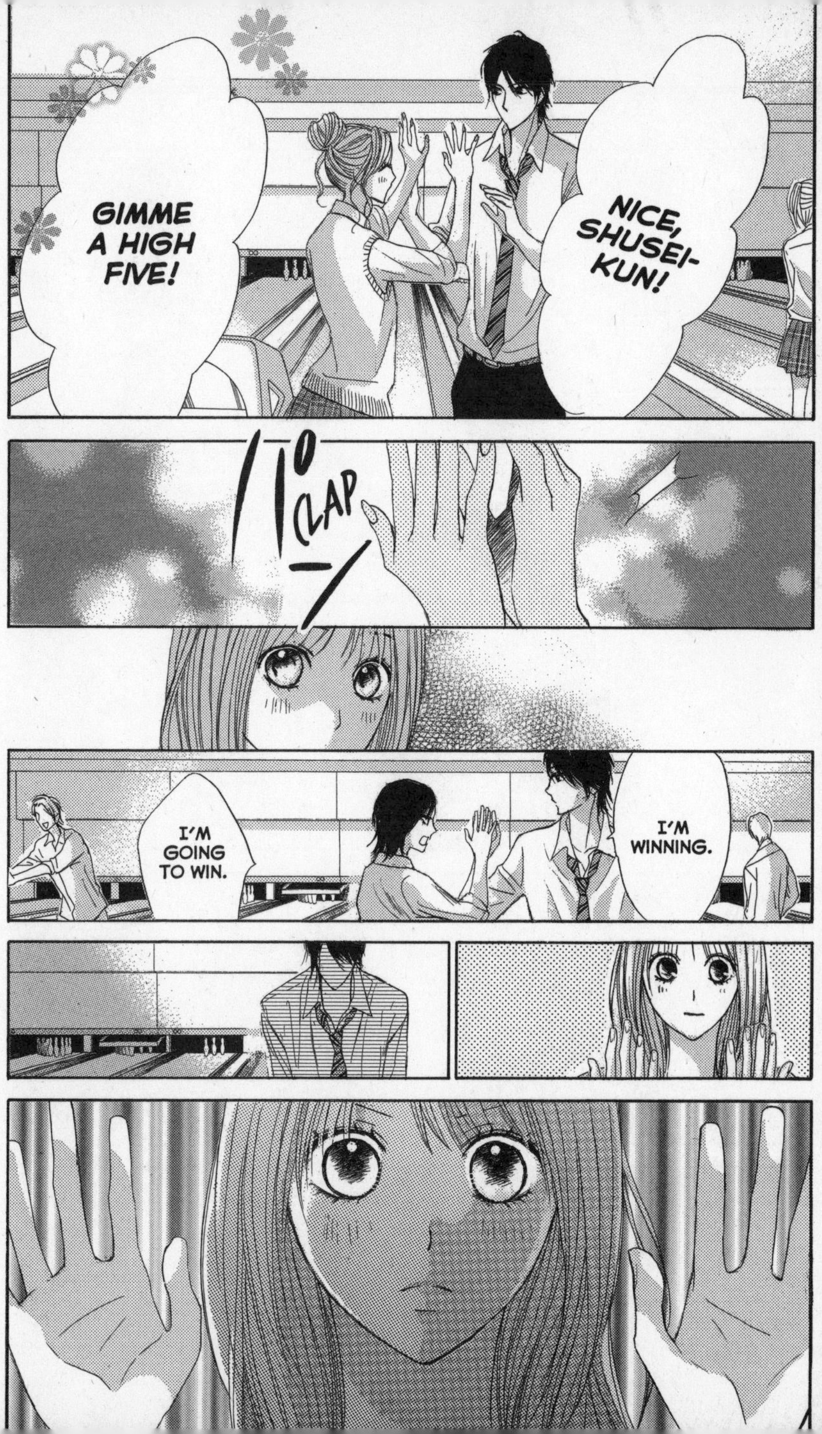
NICE, SHUSEI-KUN!
GIMME A HIGH FIVE!
CLAP
I'M WINNING.
I'M GOING TO WIN.

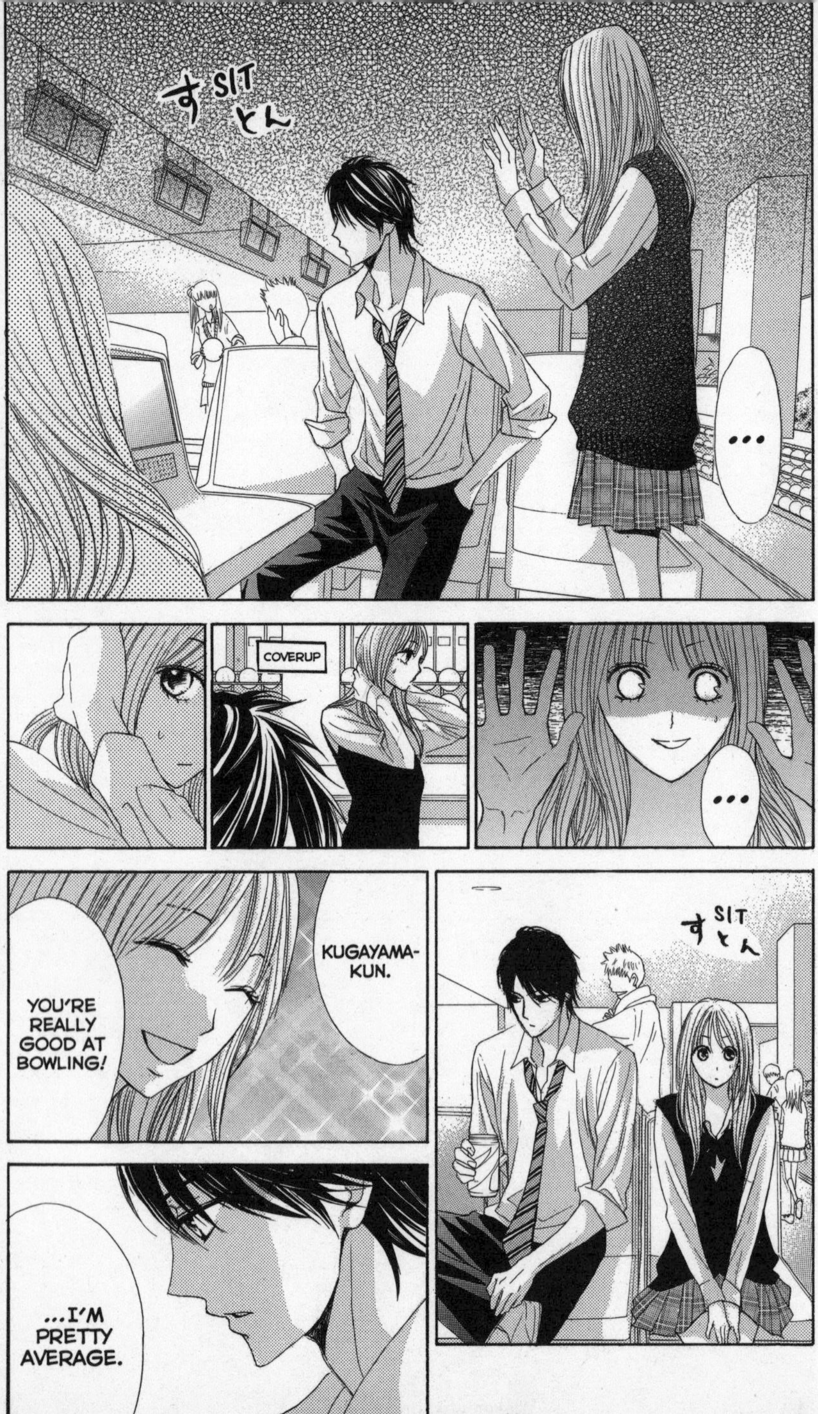
すとん
SIT
...
...
COVERUP
すとん
SIT
KUGAYAMA-KUN.
YOU'RE REALLY GOOD AT BOWLING!
...I'M PRETTY AVERAGE.

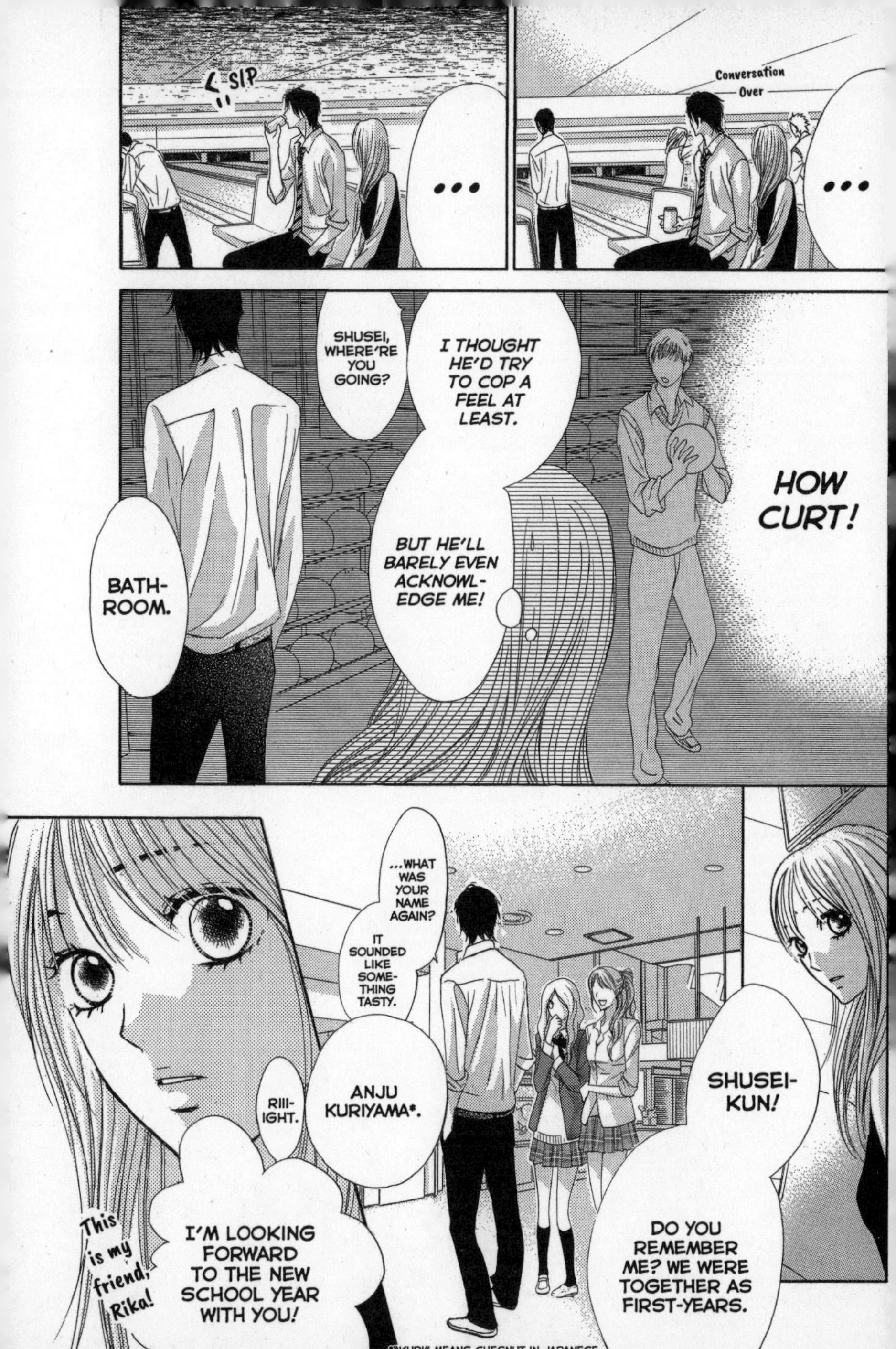
Conversation Over
...
SIP
...
HOW CURT!
I THOUGHT HE'D TRY TO COP A FEEL AT LEAST.
BUT HE'LL BARELY EVEN ACKNOWL-EDGE ME!
SHUSEI, WHERE'RE YOU GOING?
BATH-ROOM.
SHUSEI-KUN!
DO YOU REMEMBER ME? WE WERE TOGETHER AS FIRST-YEARS.
...WHAT WAS YOUR NAME AGAIN?
IT SOUNDED LIKE SOME-THING TASTY.
ANJU KURIYAMA*.
RIII-IGHT.
I'M LOOKING FORWARD TO THE NEW SCHOOL YEAR WITH YOU!
This is my friend, Rika!

*"KURI" MEANS CHESNUT IN JAPANESE.

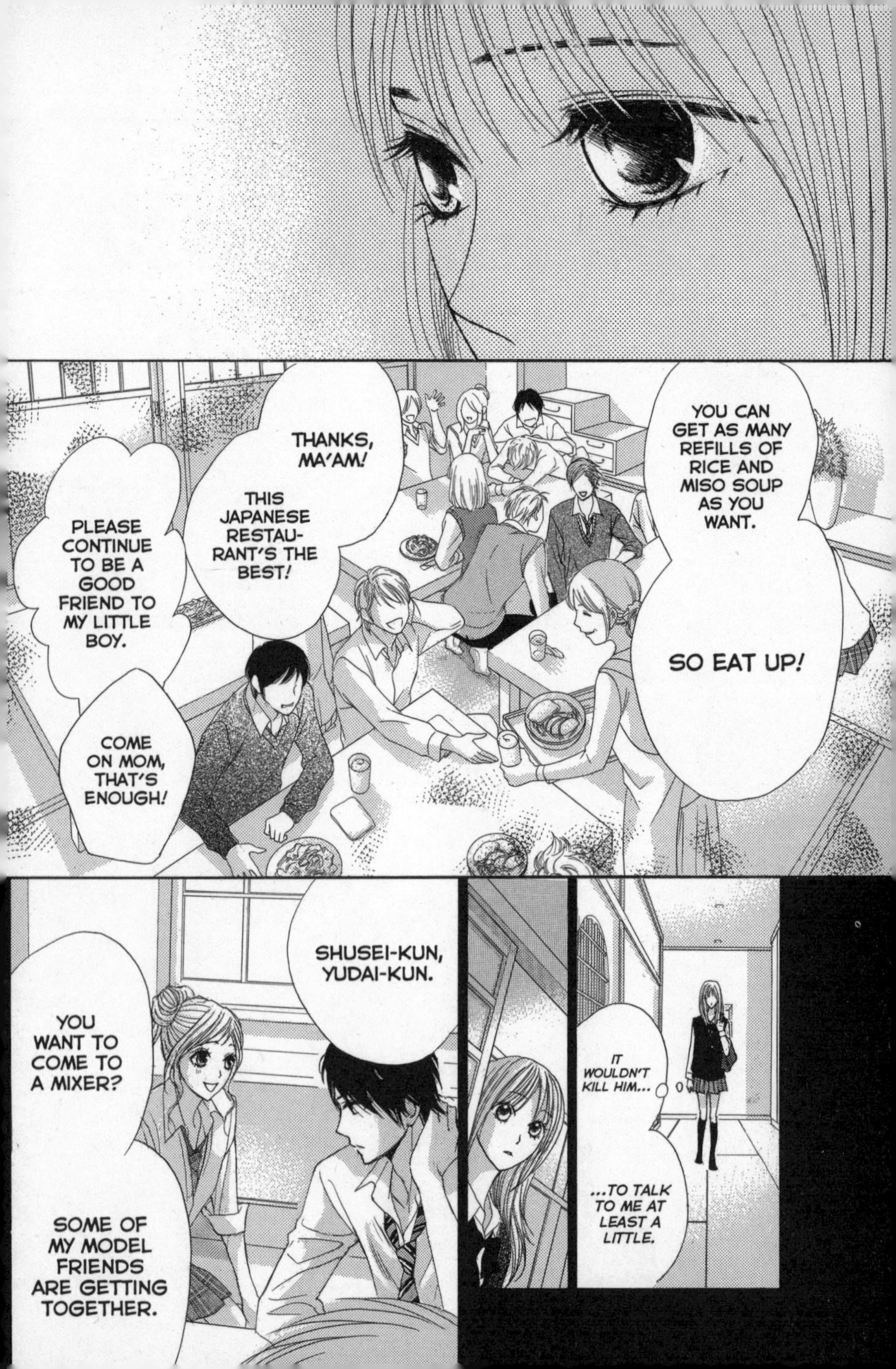
YOU CAN GET AS MANY REFILLS OF RICE AND MISO SOUP AS YOU WANT.
SO EAT UP!
THANKS, MA'AM!
THIS JAPANESE RESTAU-RANT'S THE BEST!
PLEASE CONTINUE TO BE A GOOD FRIEND TO MY LITTLE BOY.
COME ON MOM, THAT'S ENOUGH!
IT WOULDN'T KILL HIM...
...TO TALK TO ME AT LEAST A LITTLE.
SHUSEI-KUN, YUDAI-KUN.
YOU WANT TO COME TO A MIXER?
SOME OF MY MODEL FRIENDS ARE GETTING TOGETHER.

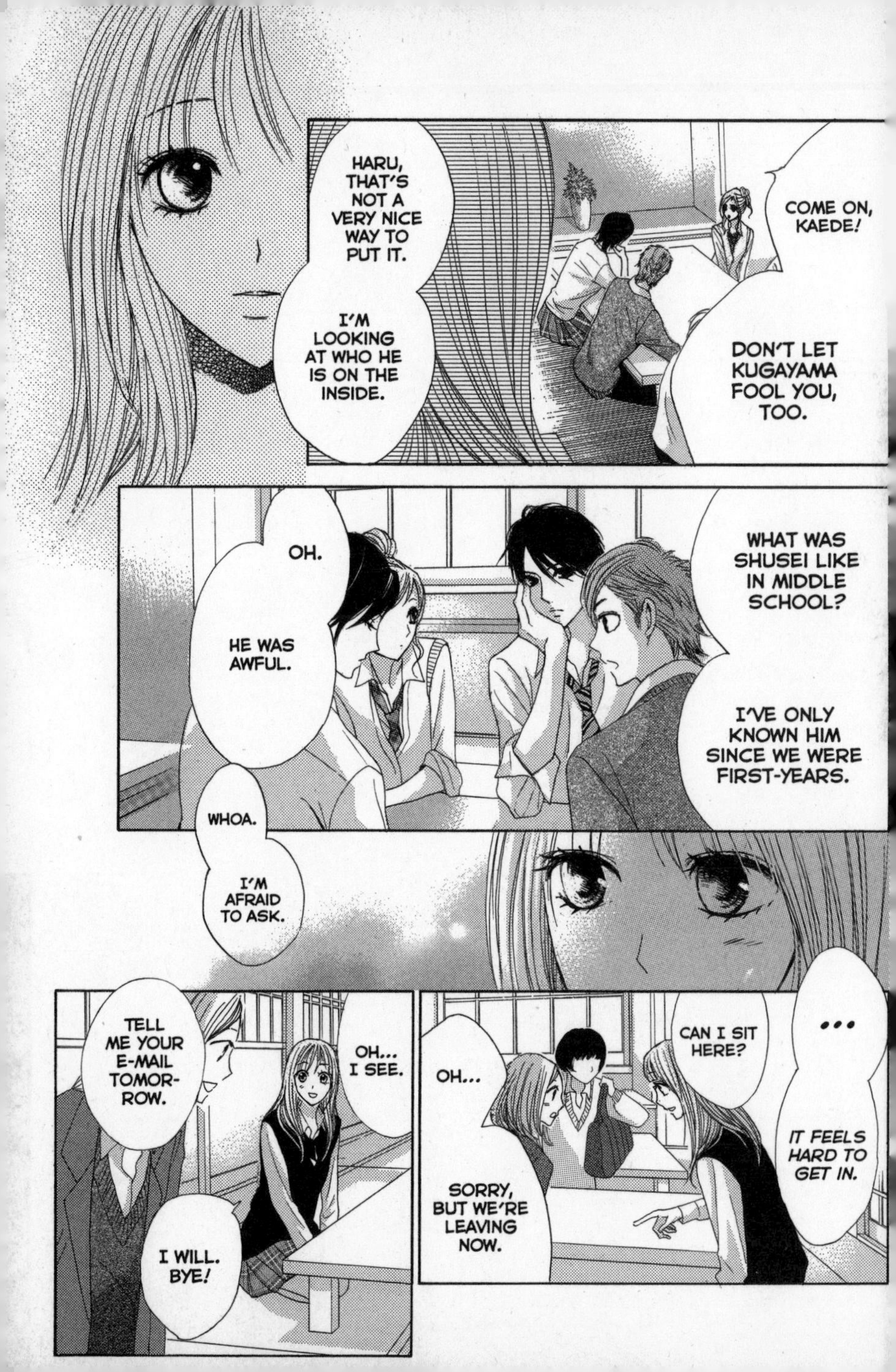
COME ON, KAEDE!
DON'T LET KUGAYAMA FOOL YOU, TOO.
HARU, THAT'S NOT A VERY NICE WAY TO PUT IT.
I'M LOOKING AT WHO HE IS ON THE INSIDE.
WHAT WAS SHUSEI LIKE IN MIDDLE SCHOOL?
I'VE ONLY KNOWN HIM SINCE WE WERE FIRST-YEARS.
OH.
HE WAS AWFUL.
WHOA.
I'M AFRAID TO ASK.
...
IT FEELS HARD TO GET IN.
CAN I SIT HERE?
OH...
SORRY, BUT WE'RE LEAVING NOW.
OH... I SEE.
TELL ME YOUR E-MAIL TOMORROW.
I WILL. BYE!

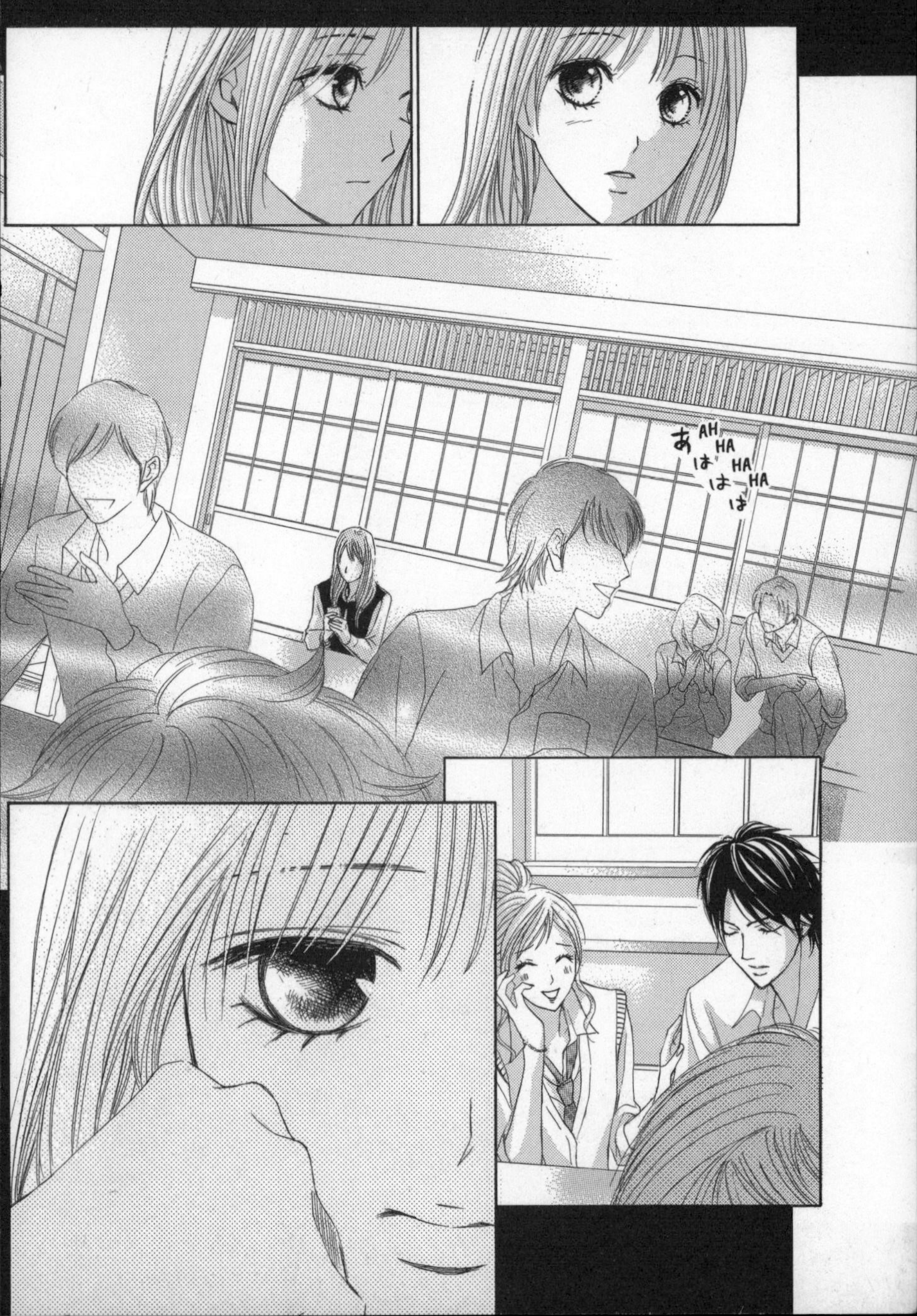
あははは
AH HA HA HA

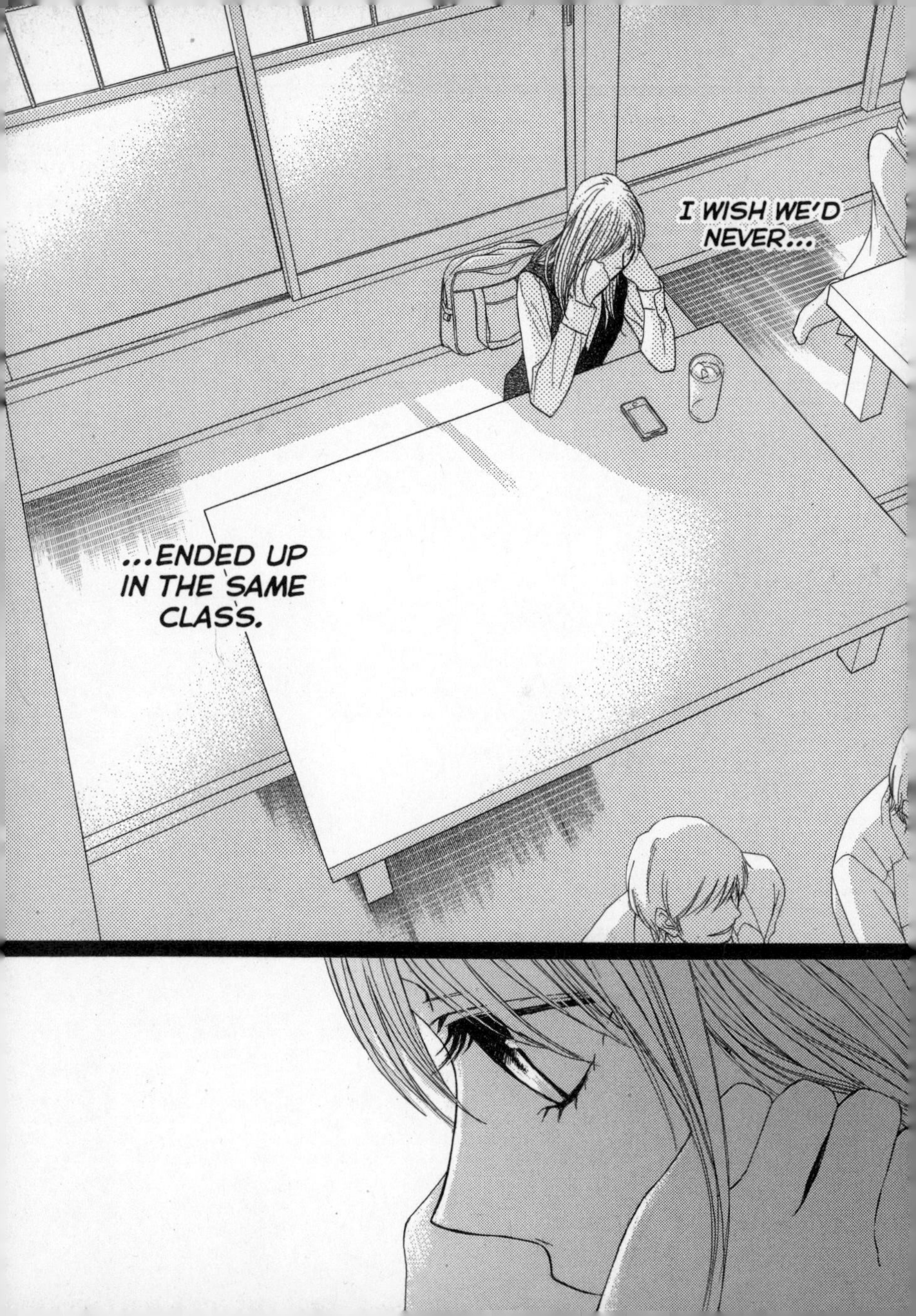
I WISH WE'D NEVER...
...ENDED UP IN THE SAME CLASS.

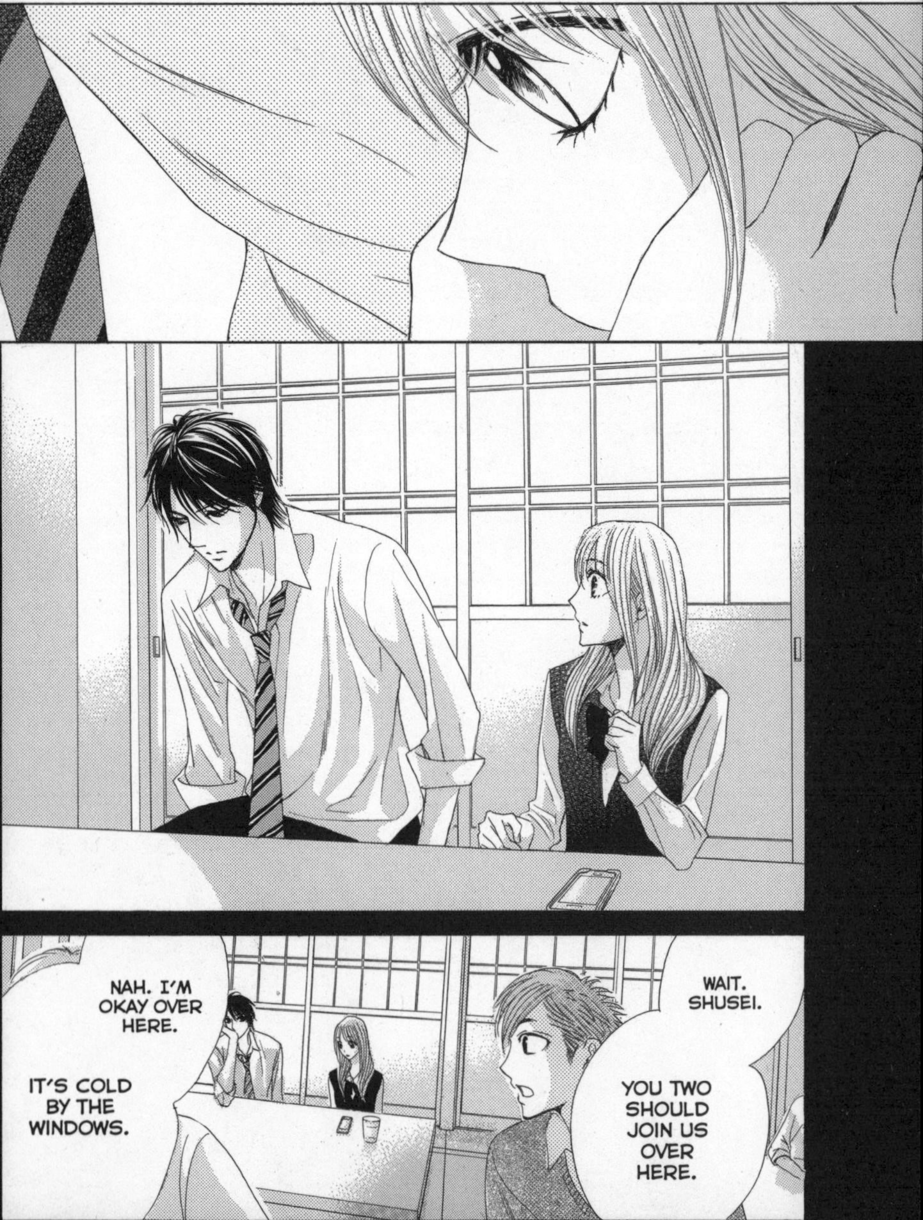
WAIT. SHUSEI.
YOU TWO SHOULD JOIN US OVER HERE.
NAH. I'M OKAY OVER HERE.
IT'S COLD BY THE WINDOWS.

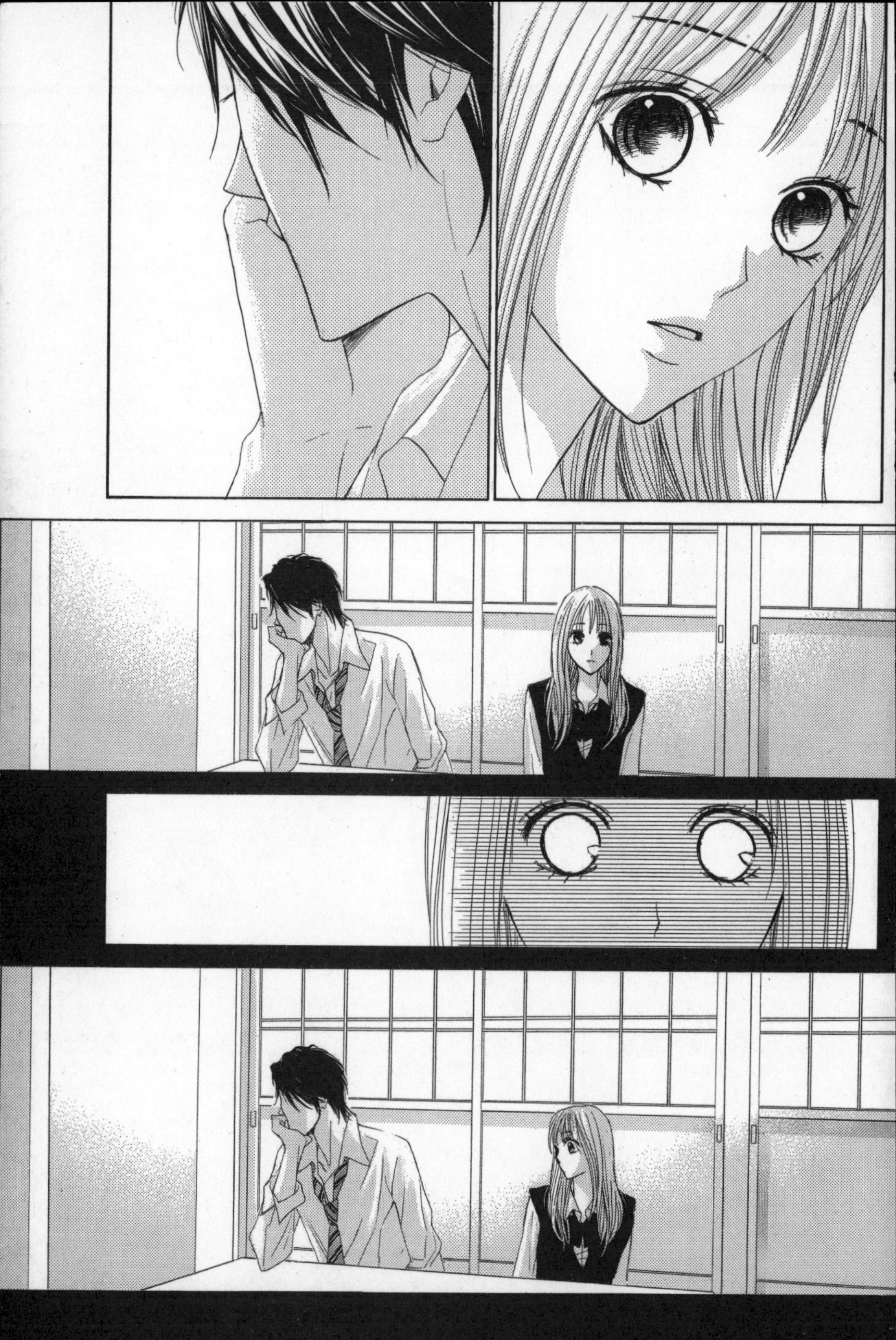

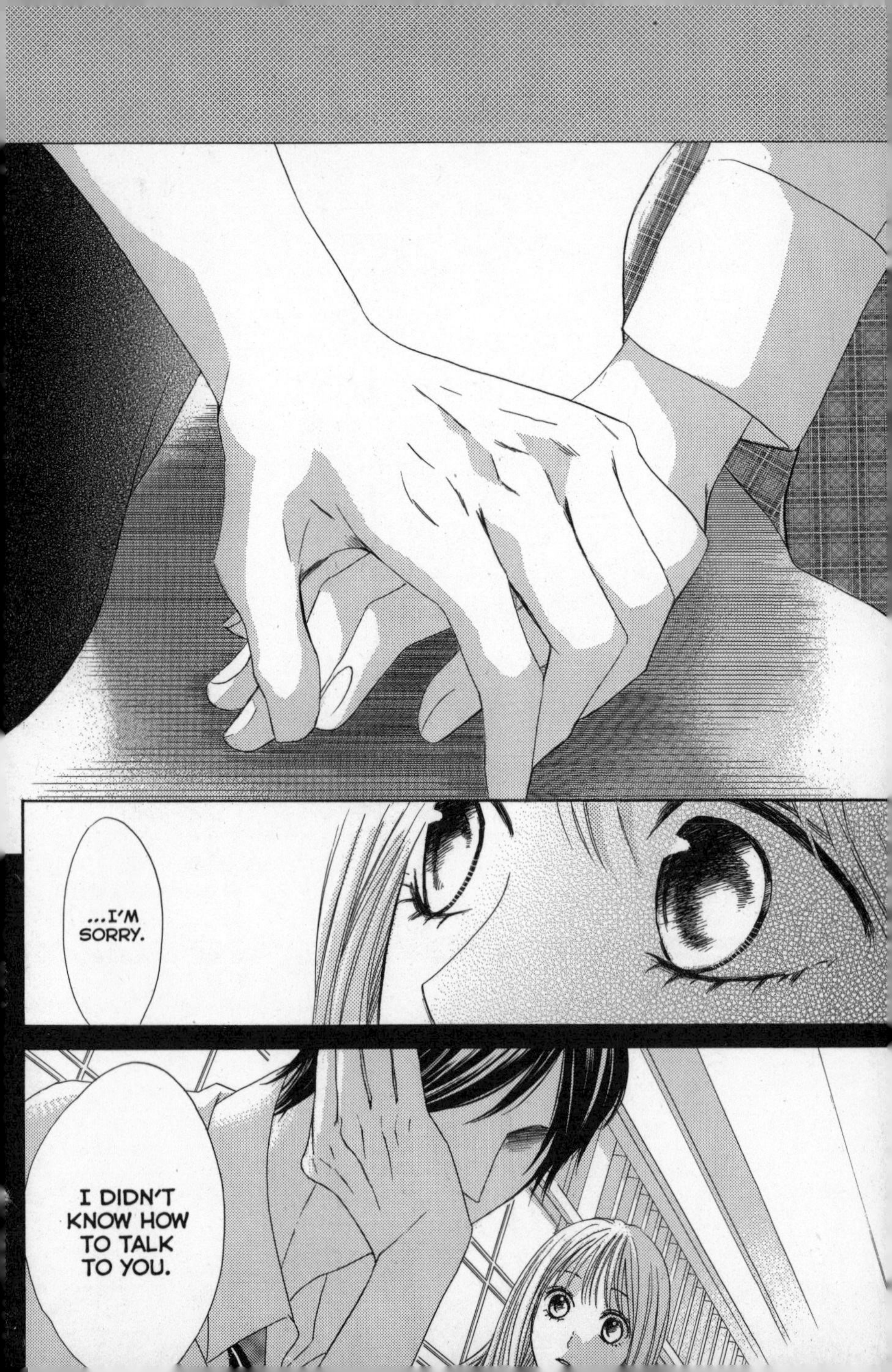
...I'M SORRY.
I DIDN'T KNOW HOW TO TALK TO YOU.

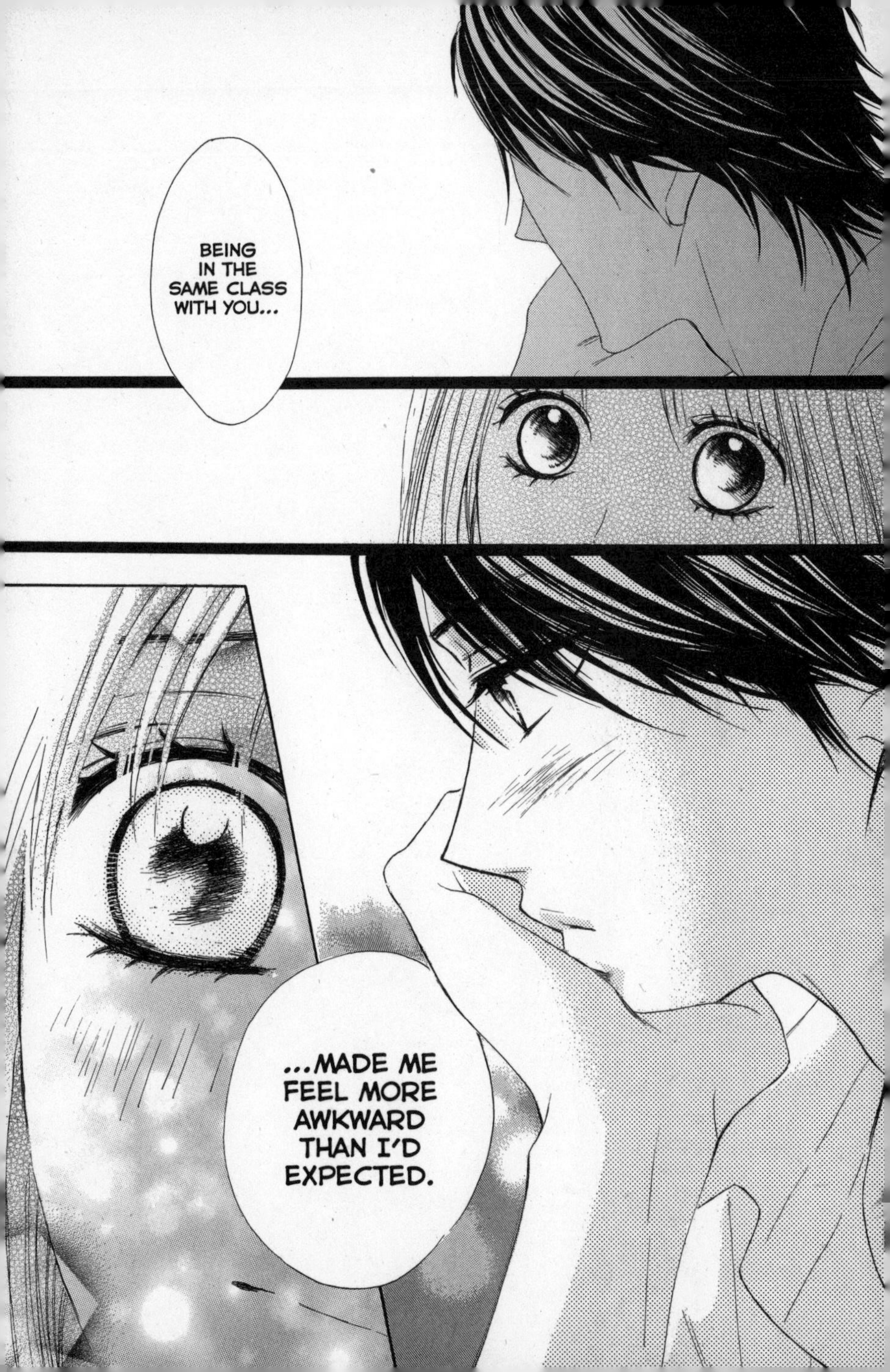
BEING IN THE SAME CLASS WITH YOU...
...MADE ME FEEL MORE AWKWARD THAN I'D EXPECTED.

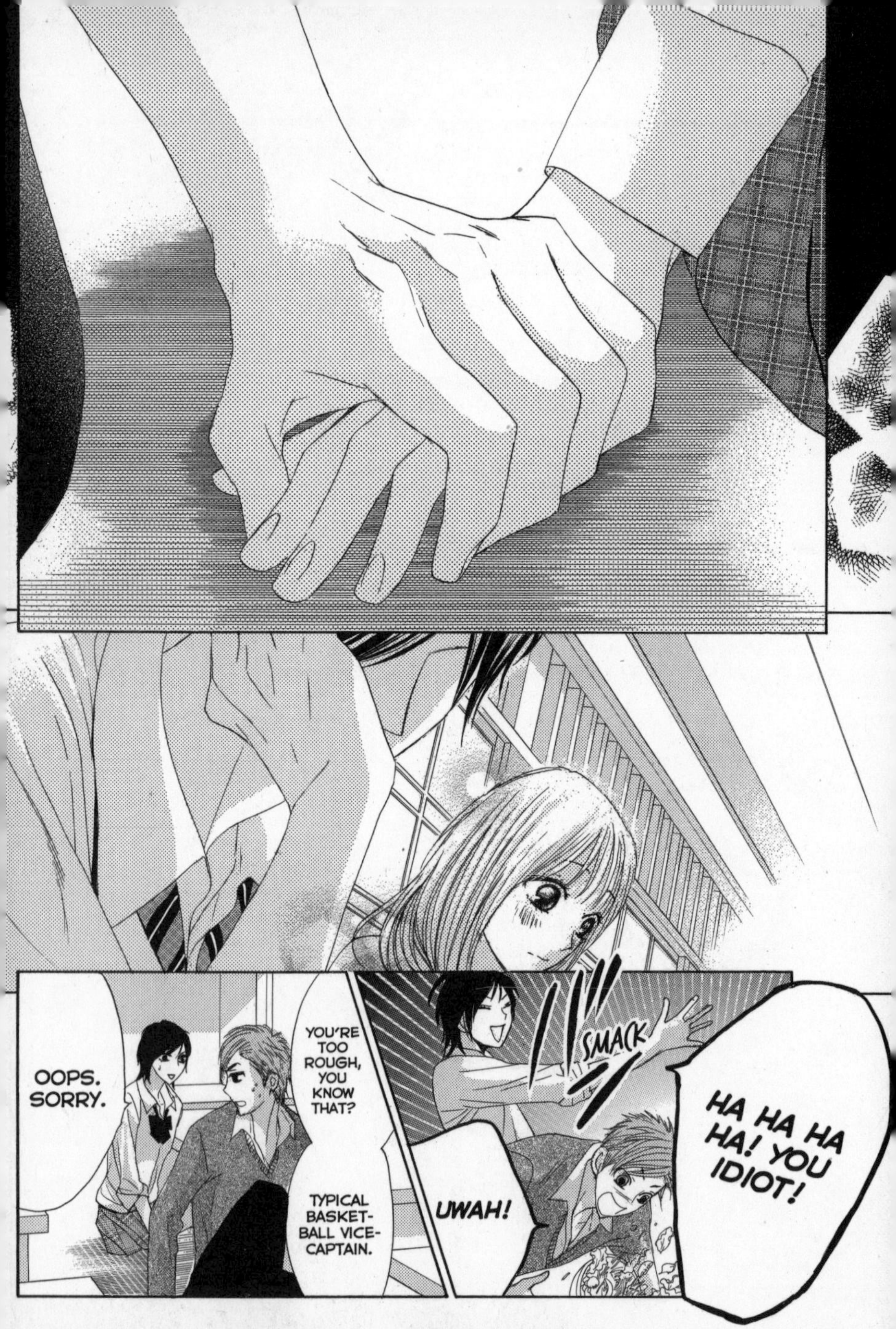
HA HA HA HA! YOU IDIOT!
SMACK
UWAH!
YOU'RE TOO ROUGH, YOU KNOW THAT?
TYPICAL BASKET-BALL VICE-CAPTAIN.
OOPS. SORRY.

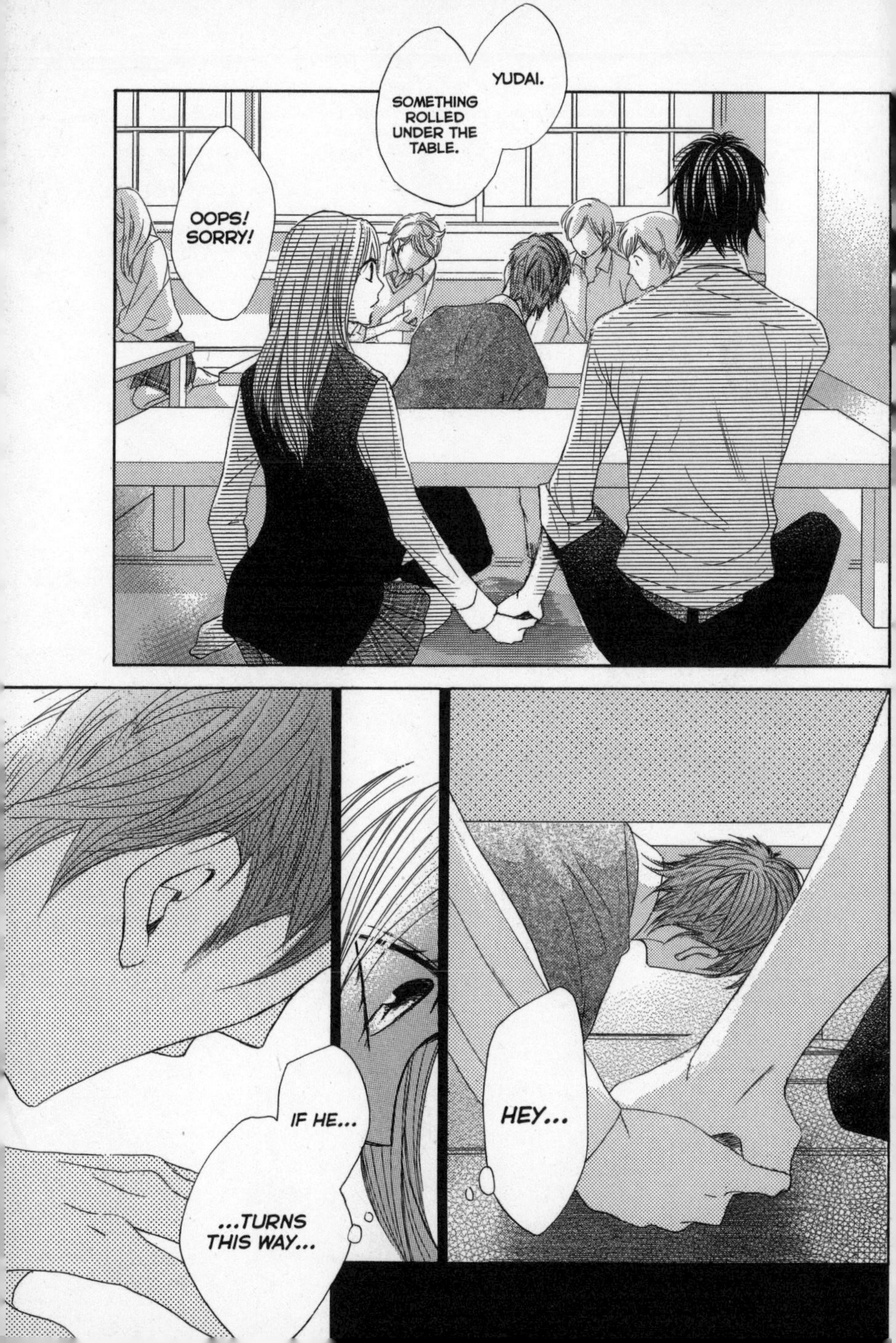
YUDAI.
SOMETHING ROLLED UNDER THE TABLE.
OOPS! SORRY!
HEY...
IF HE...
...TURNS THIS WAY...

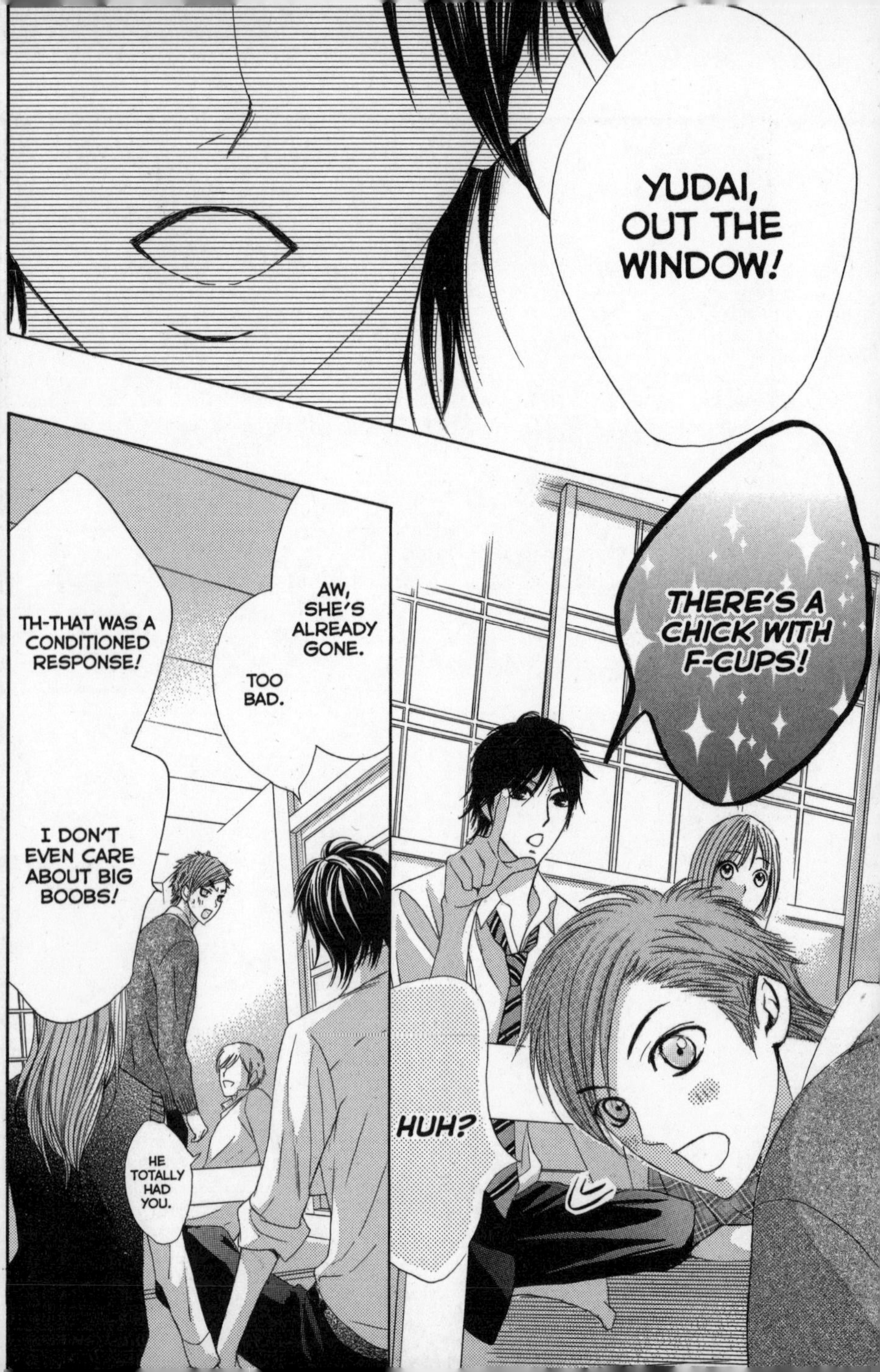
YUDAI, OUT THE WINDOW!
THERE'S A CHICK WITH F-CUPS!
HUH?
AW, SHE'S ALREADY GONE.
TOO BAD.
TH-THAT WAS A CONDITIONED RESPONSE!
I DON'T EVEN CARE ABOUT BIG BOOBS!
HE TOTALLY HAD YOU.

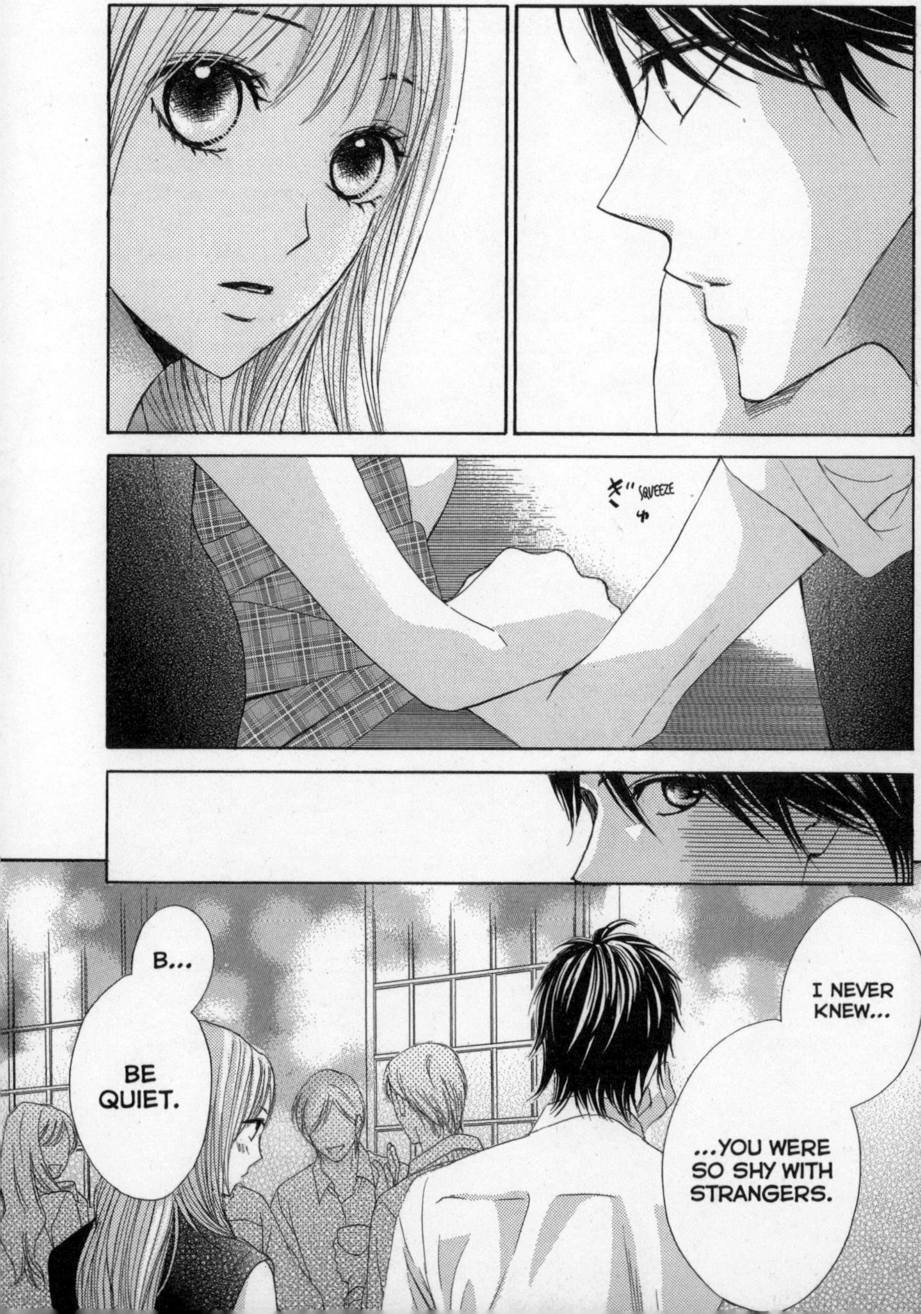
SQUEEZE
I NEVER KNEW...
...YOU WERE SO SHY WITH STRANGERS.
B...
BE QUIET.

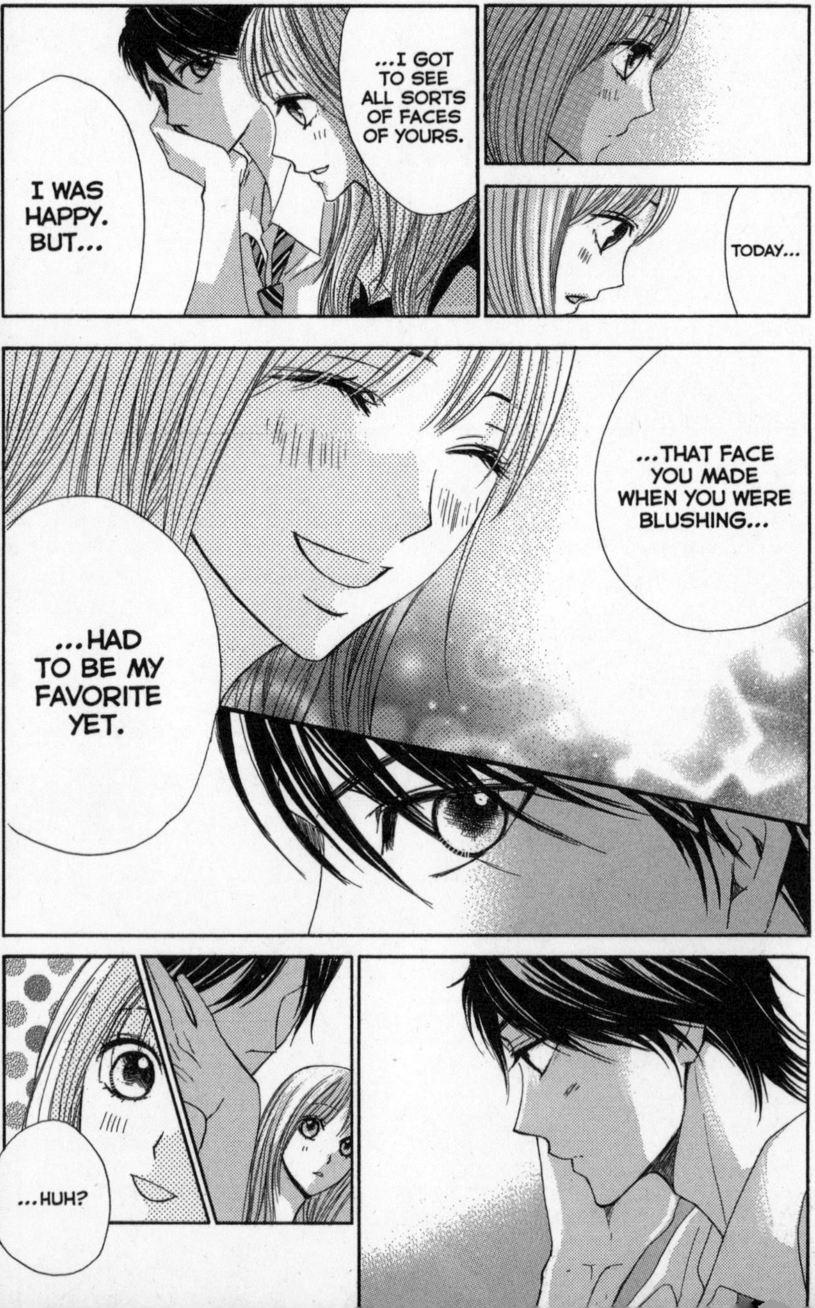
TODAY...
...I GOT TO SEE ALL SORTS OF FACES OF YOURS.
I WAS HAPPY. BUT...
...THAT FACE YOU MADE WHEN YOU WERE BLUSHING...
...HAD TO BE MY FAVORITE YET.
...HUH?

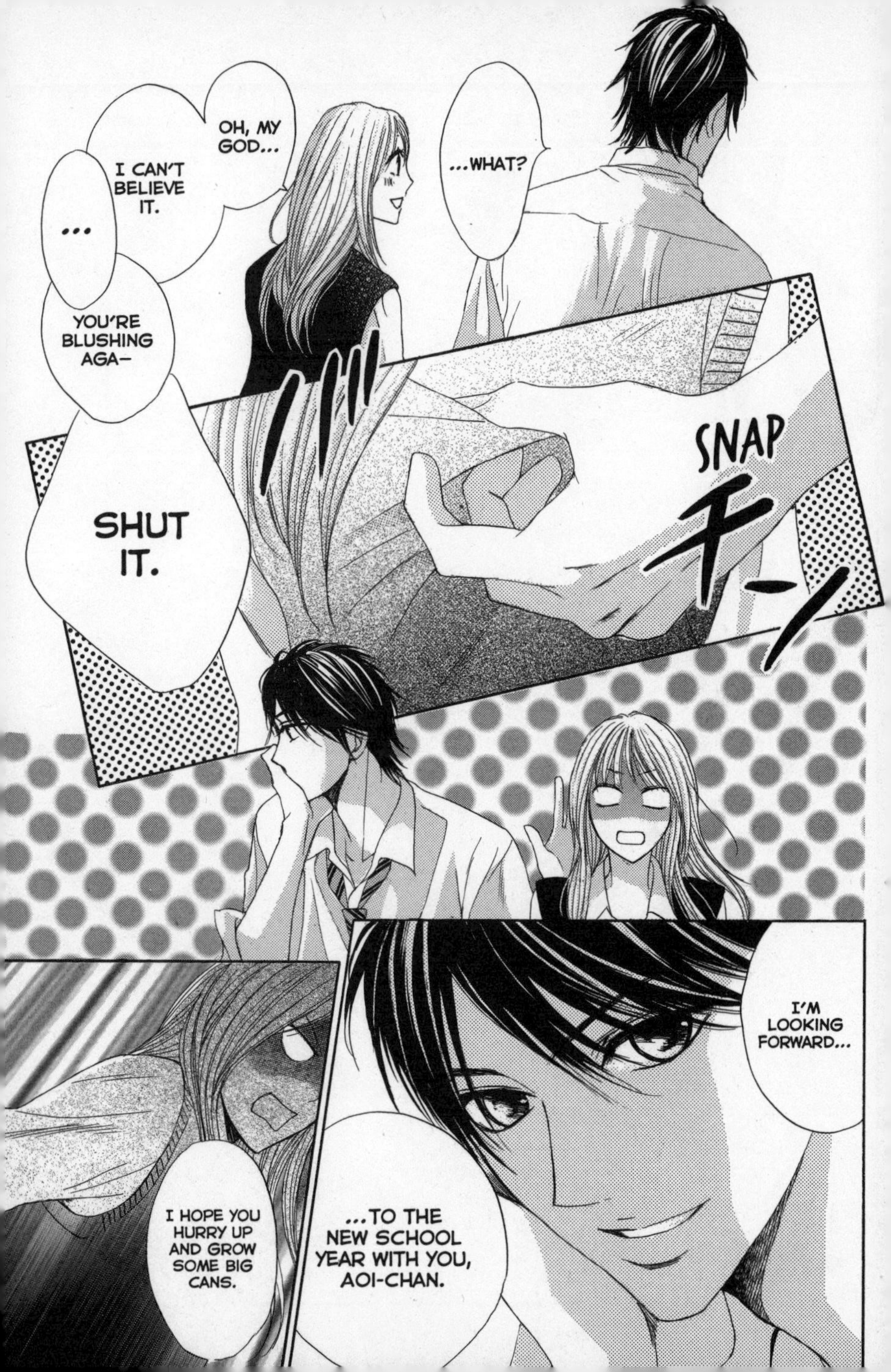
...WHAT?
OH, MY GOD...
I CAN'T BELIEVE IT.
...
YOU'RE BLUSHING AGA—
SNAP
チーン
SHUT IT.
I'M LOOKING FORWARD...
...TO THE NEW SCHOOL YEAR WITH YOU, AOI-CHAN.
I HOPE YOU HURRY UP AND GROW SOME BIG CANS.

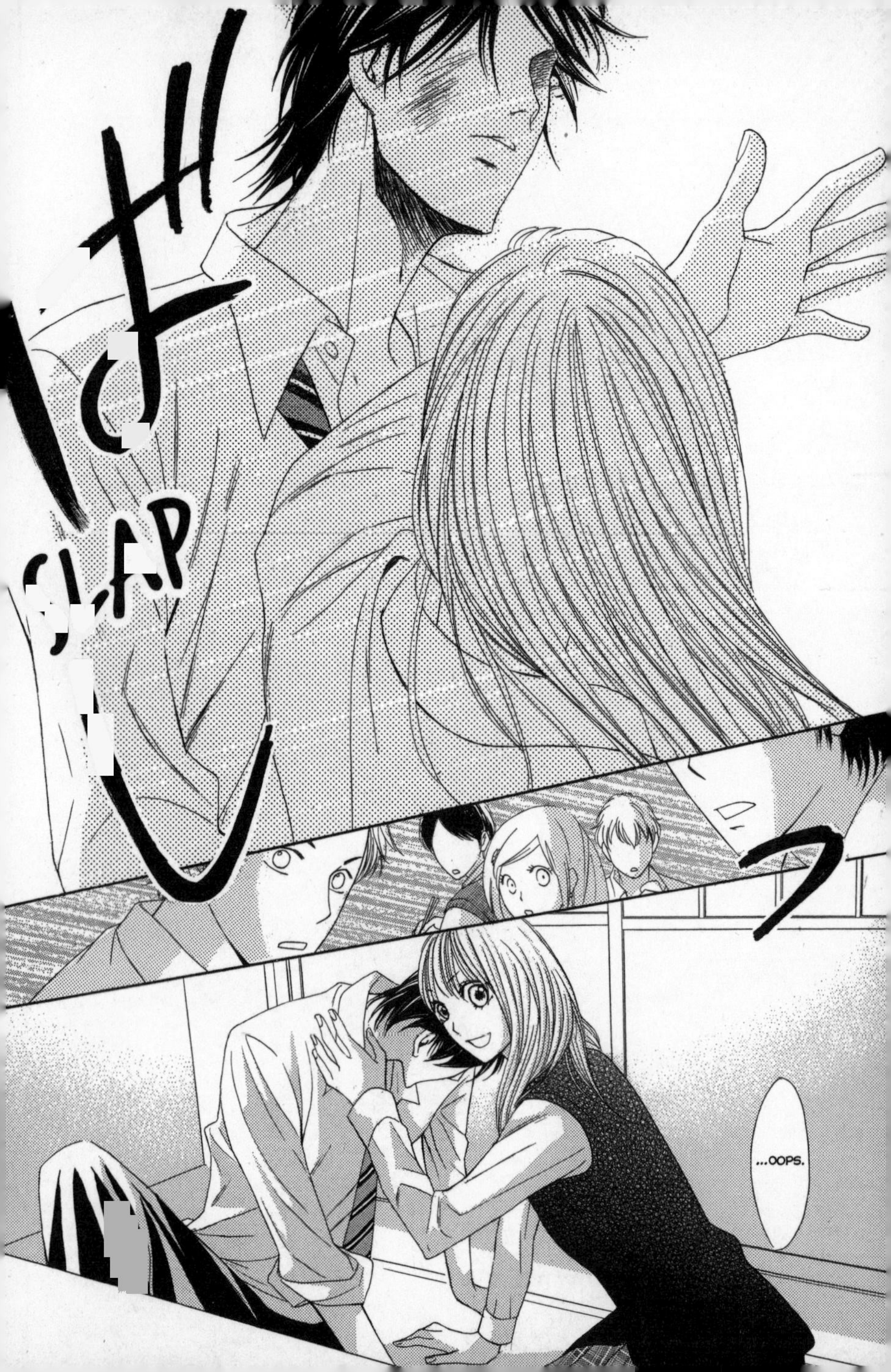
SLAP
...OOPS.

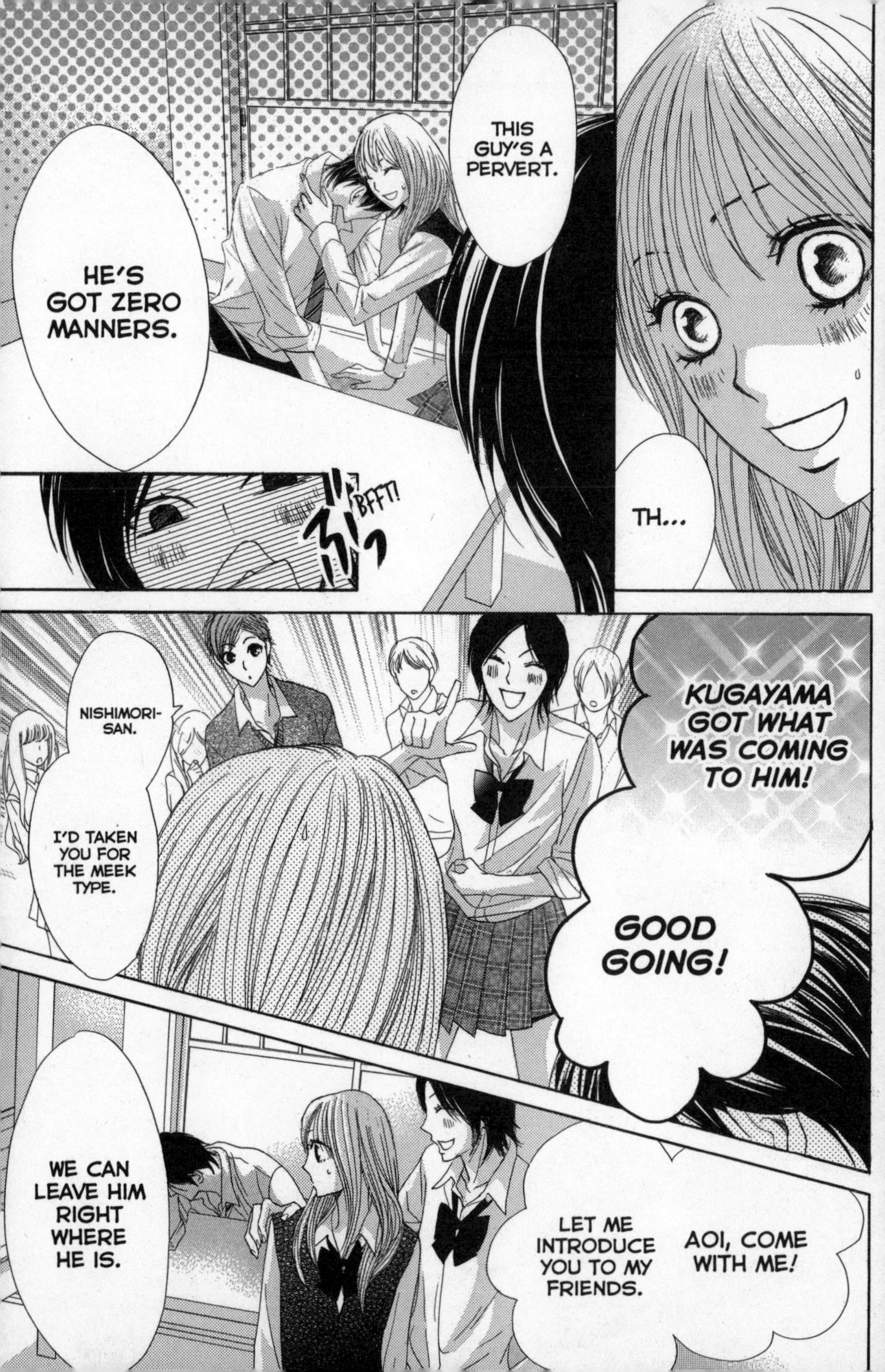
TH...
THIS GUY'S A PERVERT.
HE'S GOT ZERO MANNERS.
BFFT!
KUGAYAMA GOT WHAT WAS COMING TO HIM!
GOOD GOING!
NISHIMORI-SAN.
I'D TAKEN YOU FOR THE MEEK TYPE.
AOI, COME WITH ME!
LET ME INTRODUCE YOU TO MY FRIENDS.
WE CAN LEAVE HIM RIGHT WHERE HE IS.

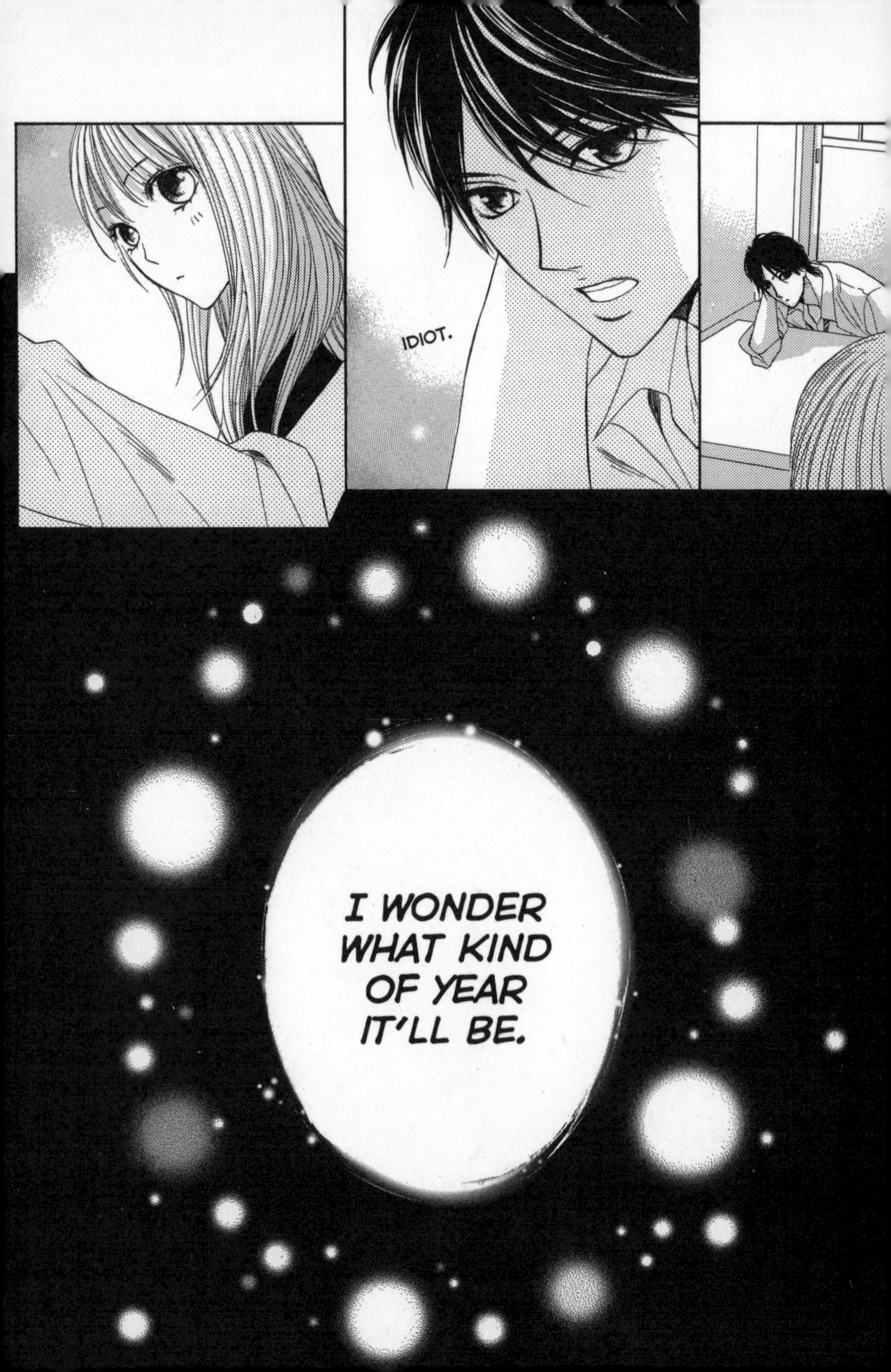
IDIOT.
I WONDER WHAT KIND OF YEAR IT'LL BE.

L♥DK

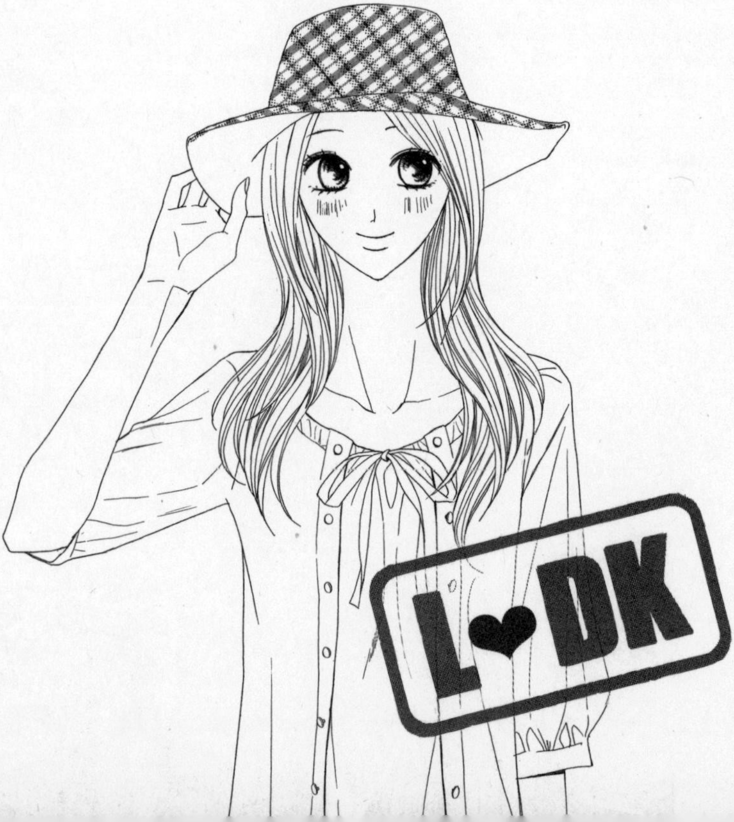
L♥DK

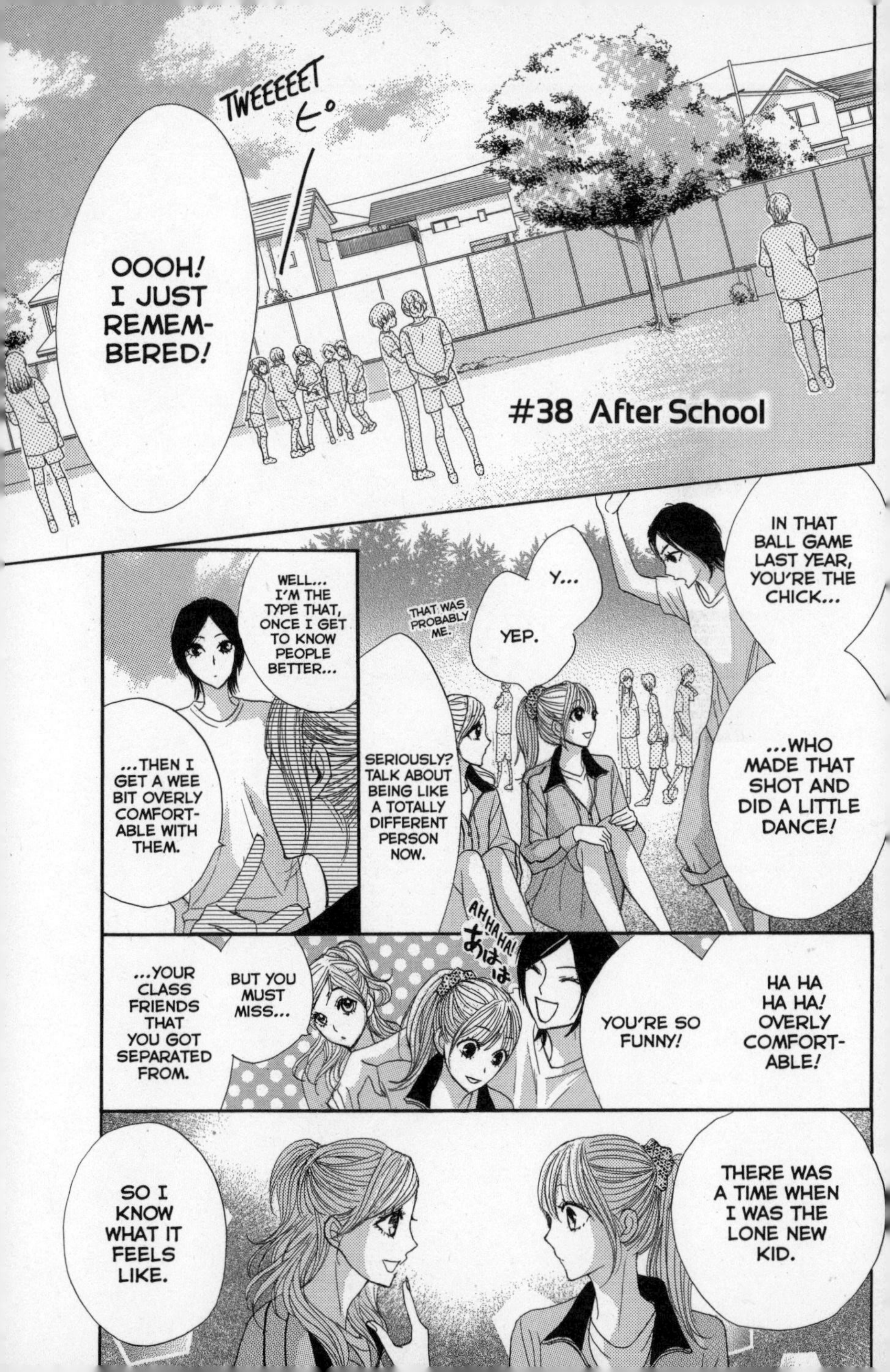
#38 After School
TWEEEEET ピ
OOOH! I JUST REMEM-BERED!
IN THAT BALL GAME LAST YEAR, YOU'RE THE CHICK...
...WHO MADE THAT SHOT AND DID A LITTLE DANCE!
Y...
YEP.
THAT WAS PROBABLY ME.
SERIOUSLY? TALK ABOUT BEING LIKE A TOTALLY DIFFERENT PERSON NOW.
WELL... I'M THE TYPE THAT, ONCE I GET TO KNOW PEOPLE BETTER...
...THEN I GET A WEE BIT OVERLY COMFORT-ABLE WITH THEM.
HA HA HA HA! OVERLY COMFORT-ABLE!
YOU'RE SO FUNNY!
AHAHAHA! あはは
BUT YOU MUST MISS...
...YOUR CLASS FRIENDS THAT YOU GOT SEPARATED FROM.
THERE WAS A TIME WHEN I WAS THE LONE NEW KID.
SO I KNOW WHAT IT FEELS LIKE.

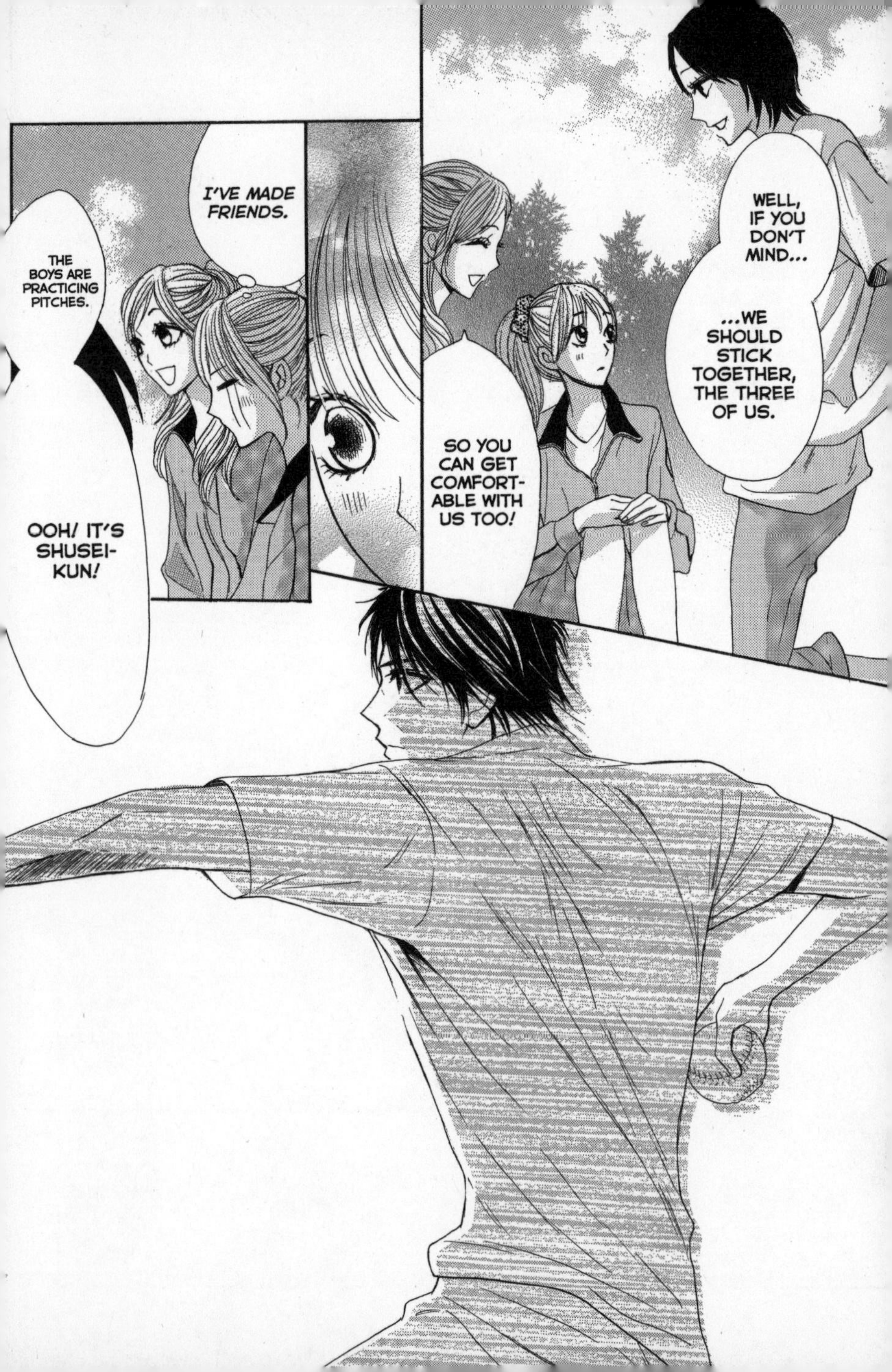
WELL, IF YOU DON'T MIND...
...WE SHOULD STICK TOGETHER, THE THREE OF US.
SO YOU CAN GET COMFORT-ABLE WITH US TOO!
I'VE MADE FRIENDS.
THE BOYS ARE PRACTICING PITCHES.
OOH! IT'S SHUSEI-KUN!

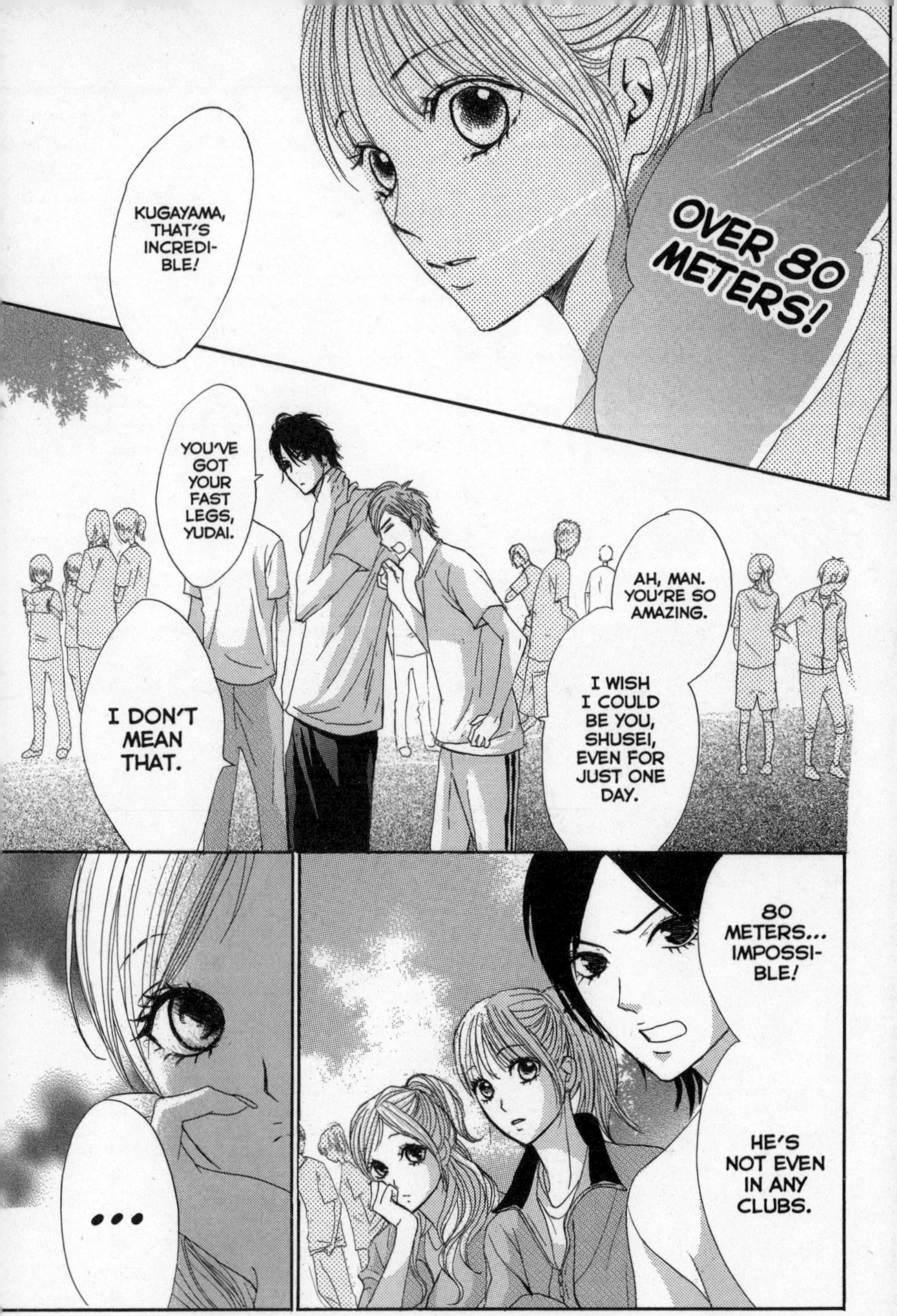
OVER 80 METERS!
KUGAYAMA, THAT'S INCREDI-BLE!
AH, MAN. YOU'RE SO AMAZING.
I WISH I COULD BE YOU, SHUSEI, EVEN FOR JUST ONE DAY.
YOU'VE GOT YOUR FAST LEGS, YUDAI.
I DON'T MEAN THAT.
80 METERS... IMPOSSI-BLE!
HE'S NOT EVEN IN ANY CLUBS.
...

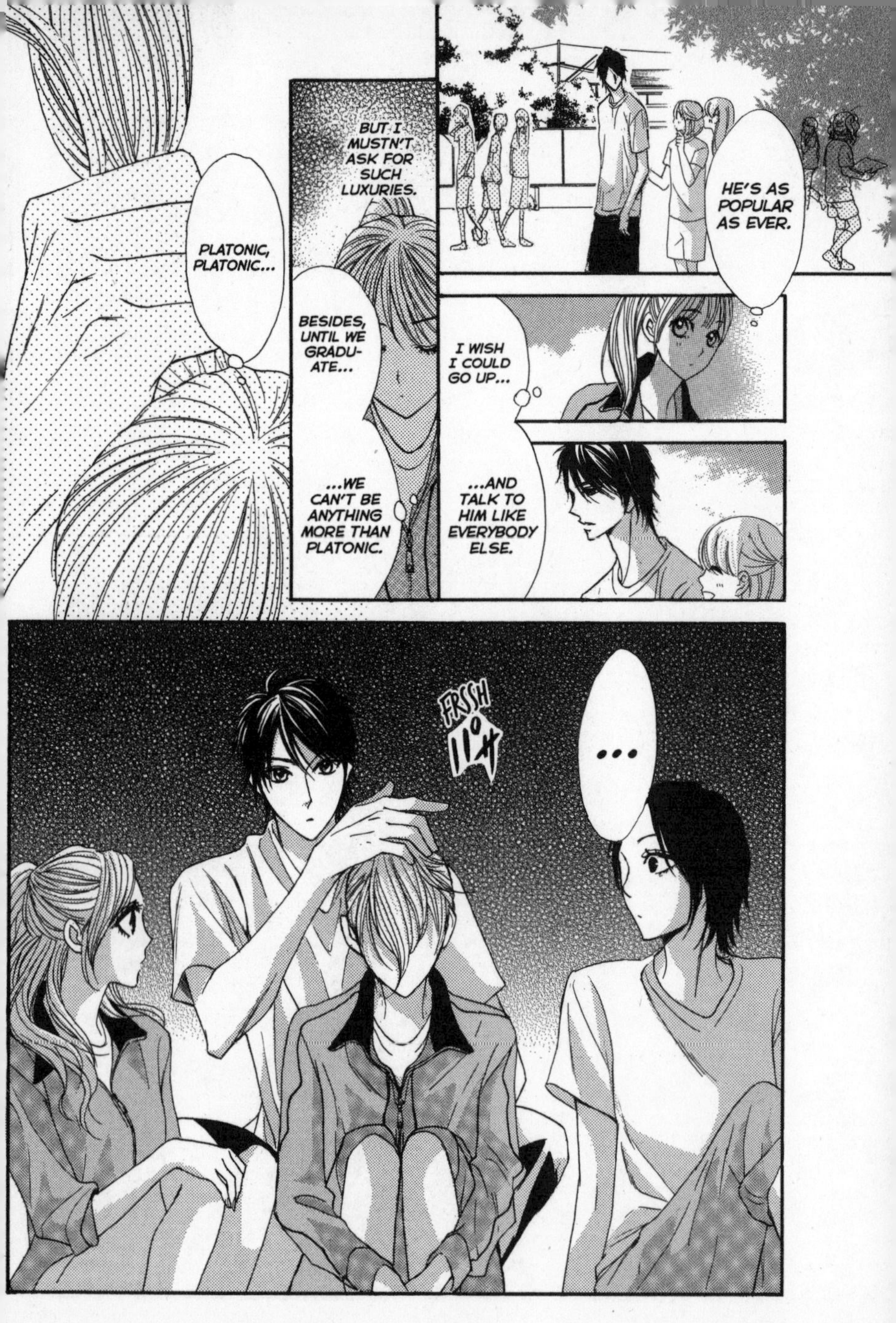
HE'S AS POPULAR AS EVER.
I WISH I COULD GO UP...
...AND TALK TO HIM LIKE EVERYBODY ELSE.
BUT I MUSTN'T ASK FOR SUCH LUXURIES.
BESIDES, UNTIL WE GRADU-ATE...
...WE CAN'T BE ANYTHING MORE THAN PLATONIC.
PLATONIC, PLATONIC...
FRSSH
...

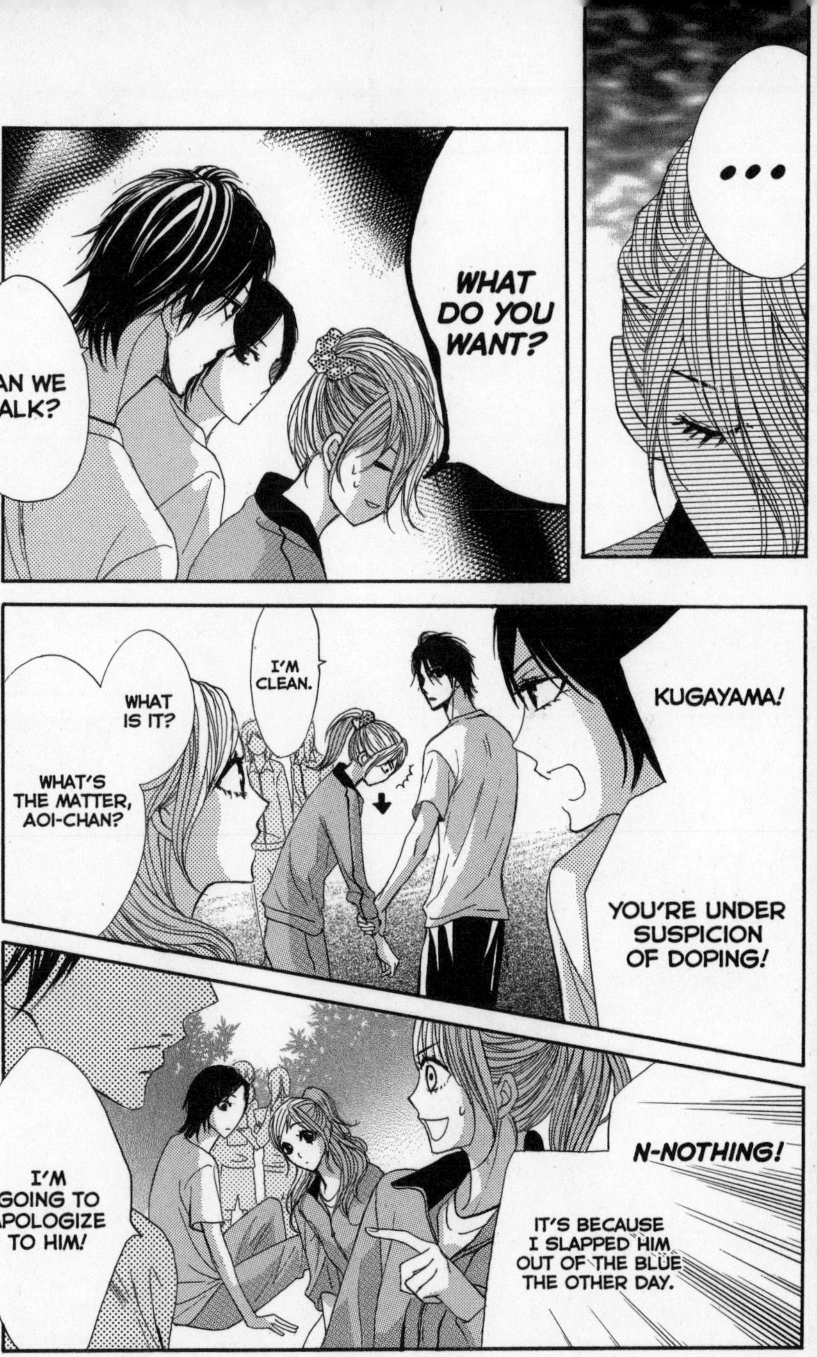
...
WHAT DO YOU WANT?
CAN WE TALK?
KUGAYAMA!
YOU'RE UNDER SUSPICION OF DOPING!
I'M CLEAN.
WHAT IS IT?
WHAT'S THE MATTER, AOI-CHAN?
N-NOTHING!
IT'S BECAUSE I SLAPPED HIM OUT OF THE BLUE THE OTHER DAY.
I'M GOING TO APOLOGIZE TO HIM!

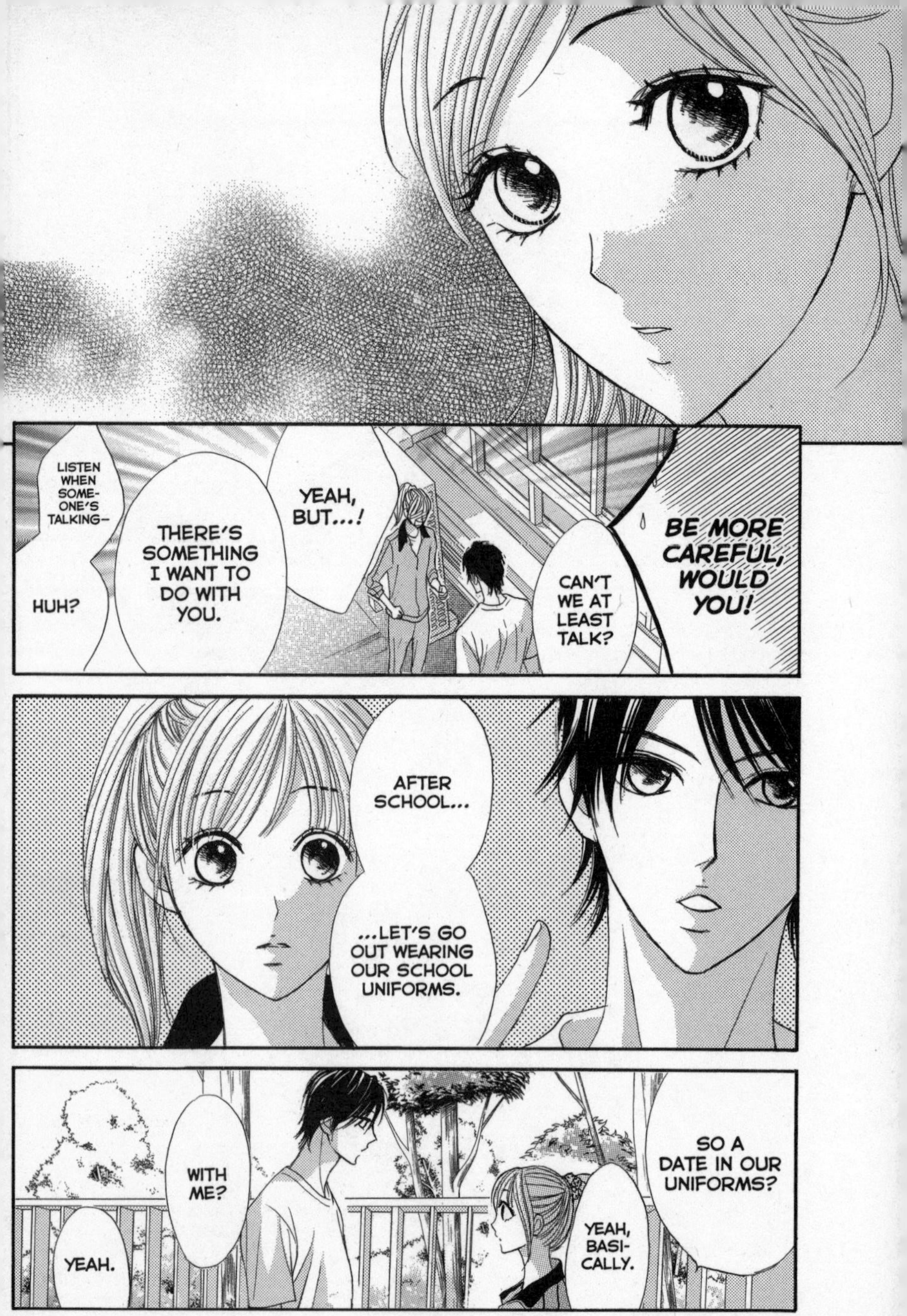
BE MORE CAREFUL, WOULD YOU!
CAN'T WE AT LEAST TALK?
YEAH, BUT...!
THERE'S SOMETHING I WANT TO DO WITH YOU.
LISTEN WHEN SOME-ONE'S TALKING—
HUH?
AFTER SCHOOL...
...LET'S GO OUT WEARING OUR SCHOOL UNIFORMS.
SO A DATE IN OUR UNIFORMS?
YEAH, BASI-CALLY.
WITH ME?
YEAH.

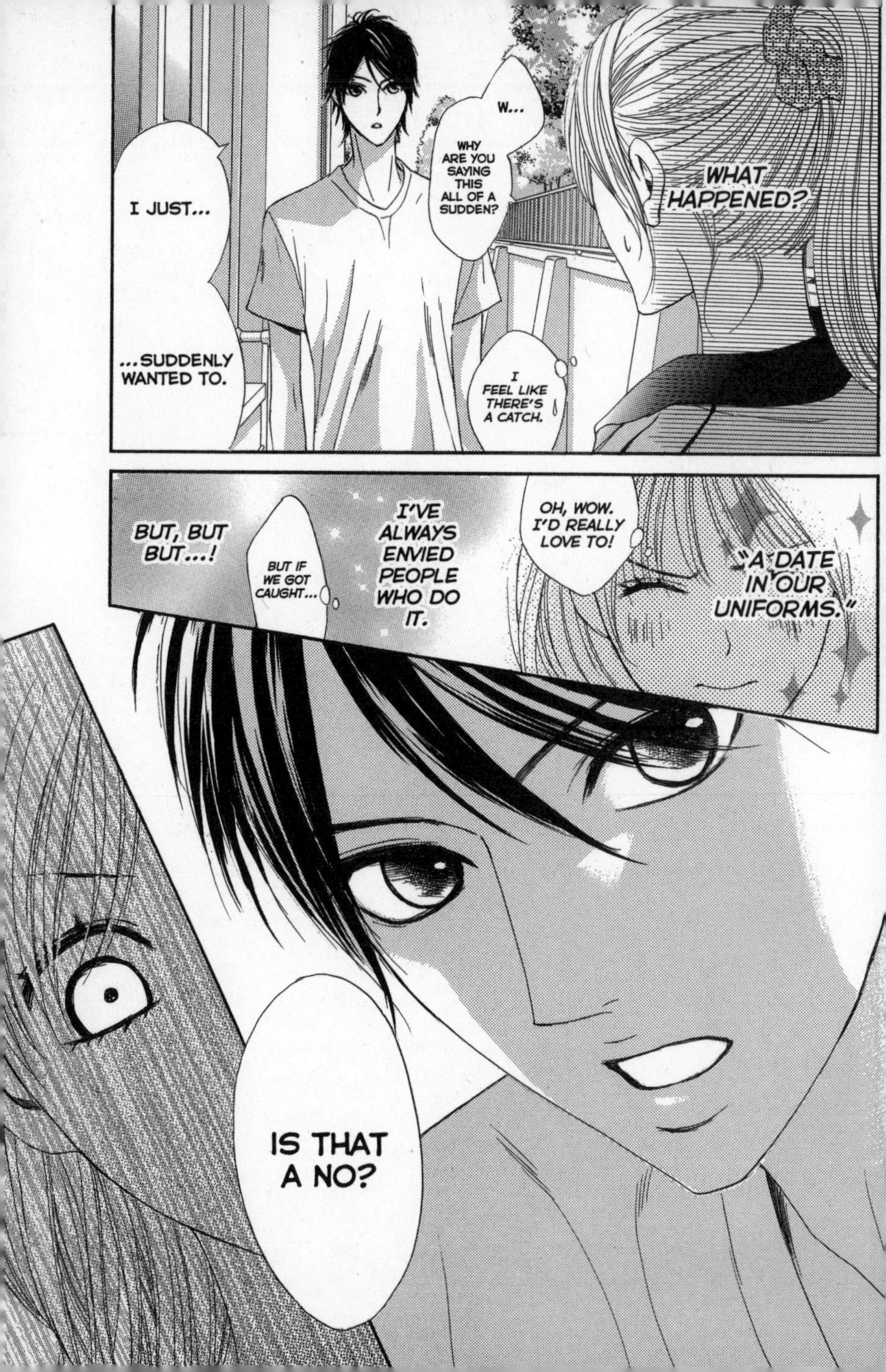
WHAT HAPPENED?
W...
WHY ARE YOU SAYING THIS ALL OF A SUDDEN?
I FEEL LIKE THERE'S A CATCH.
I JUST...
...SUDDENLY WANTED TO.
"A DATE IN OUR UNIFORMS."
OH, WOW. I'D REALLY LOVE TO!
I'VE ALWAYS ENVIED PEOPLE WHO DO IT.
BUT IF WE GOT CAUGHT...
BUT, BUT BUT...!
IS THAT A NO?

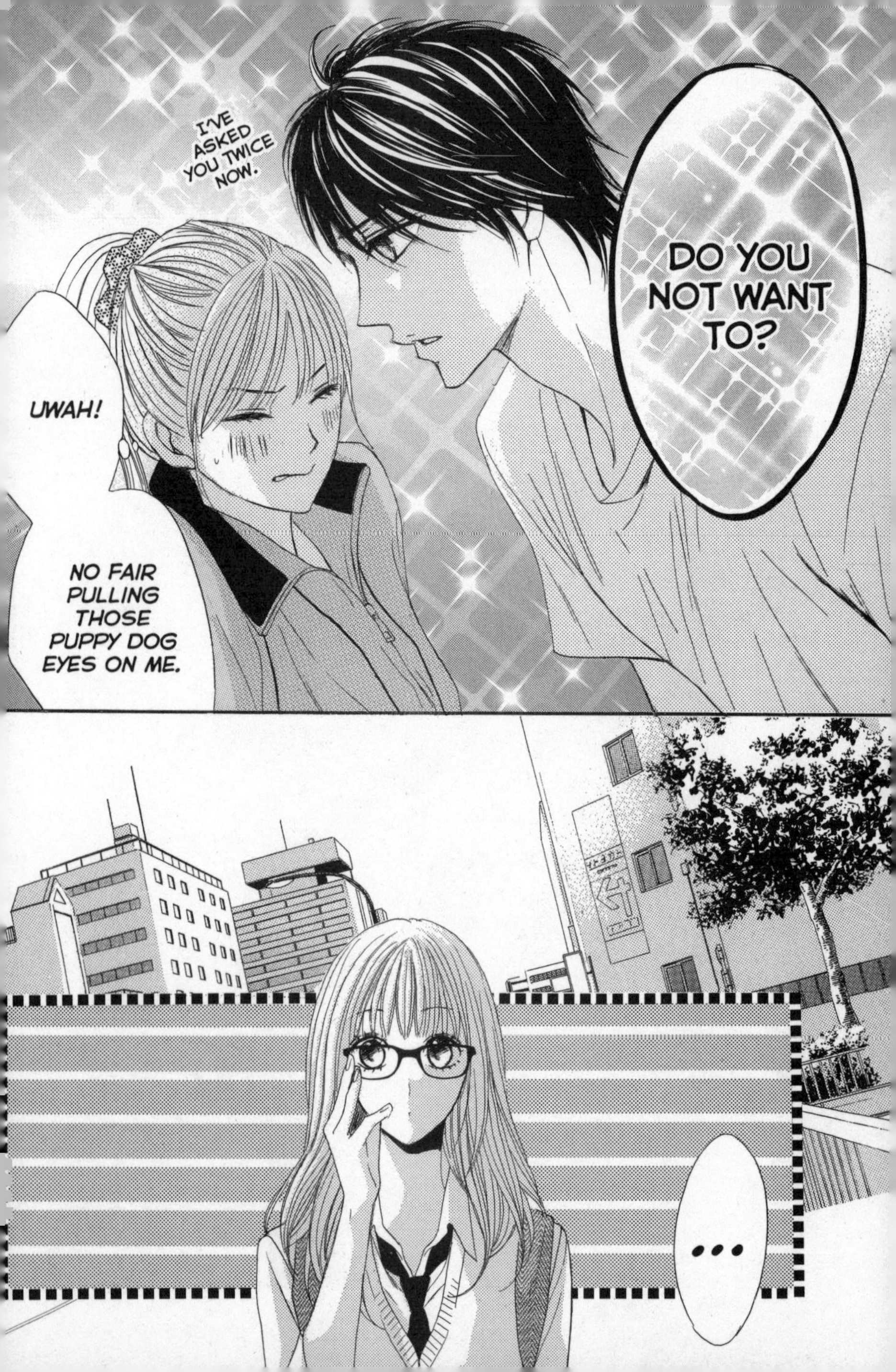
DO YOU NOT WANT TO?
I'VE ASKED YOU TWICE NOW.
UWAH!
NO FAIR PULLING THOSE PUPPY DOG EYES ON ME.
...

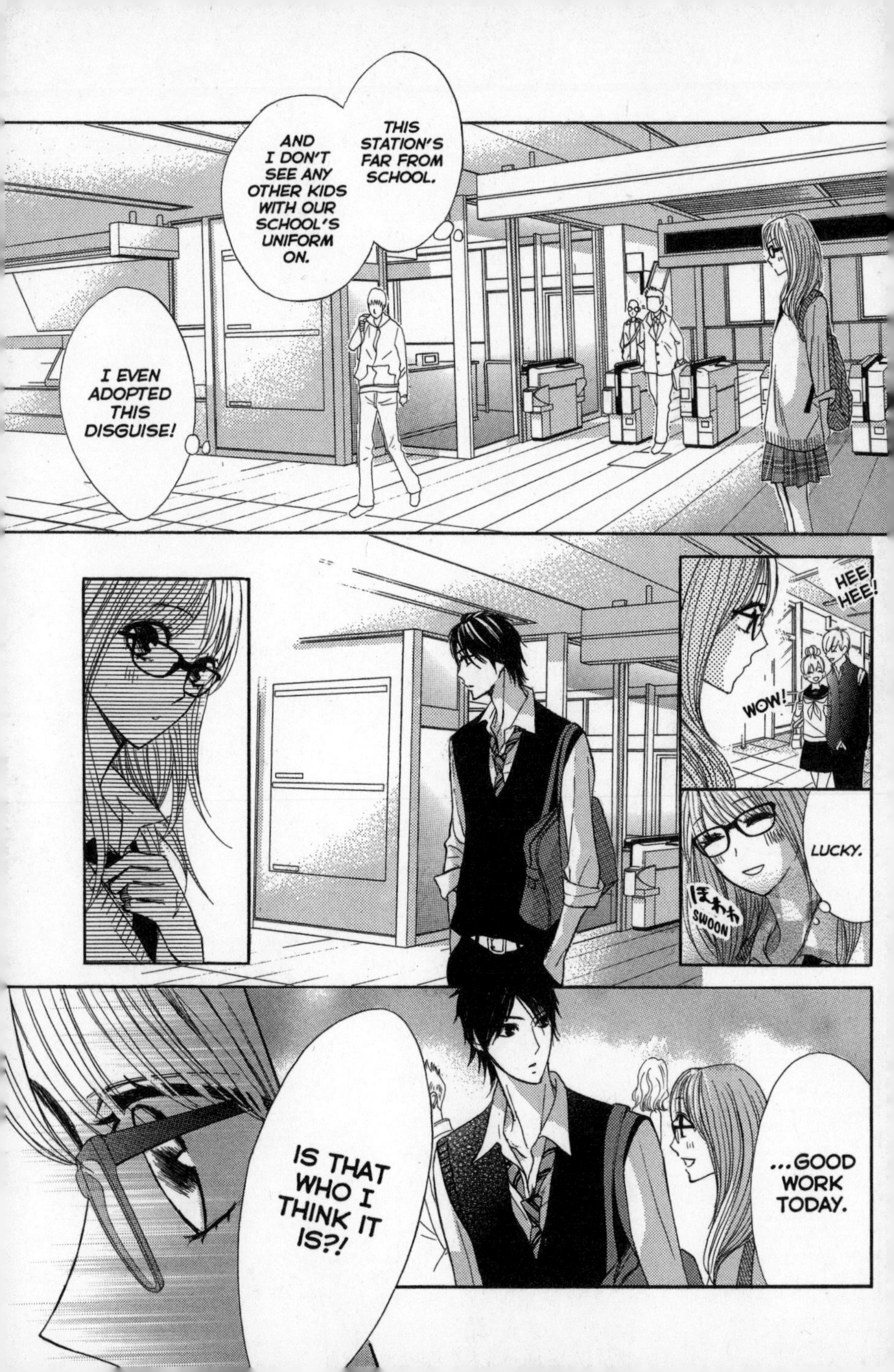
THIS STATION'S FAR FROM SCHOOL.
AND I DON'T SEE ANY OTHER KIDS WITH OUR SCHOOL'S UNIFORM ON.
I EVEN ADOPTED THIS DISGUISE!
HEE HEE!
WOW!
LUCKY.
ほわわ
SWOON
...GOOD WORK TODAY.
IS THAT WHO I THINK IT IS?!

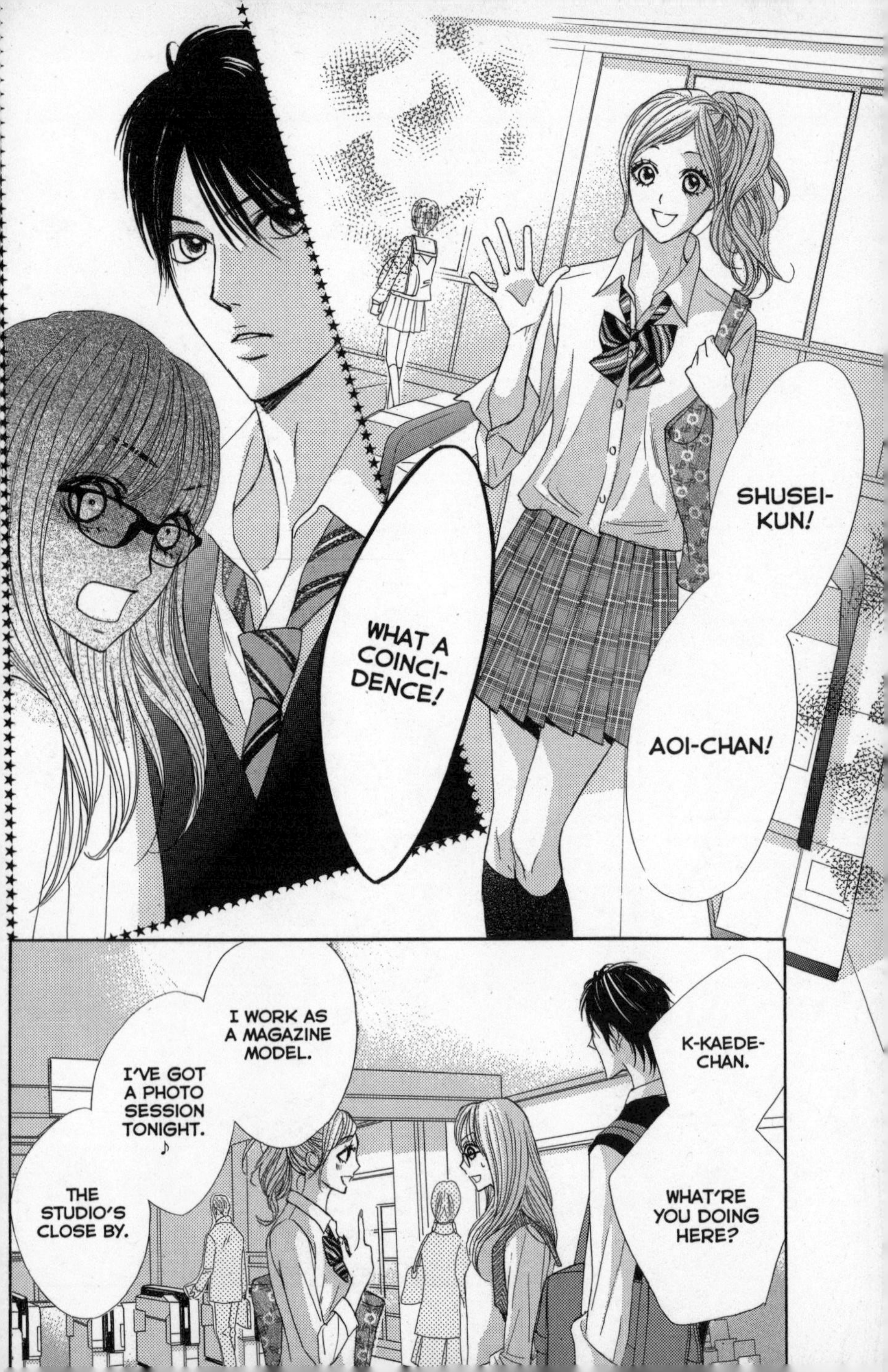
SHUSEI-KUN!
AOI-CHAN!
WHAT A COINCI-DENCE!
K-KAEDE-CHAN.
WHAT'RE YOU DOING HERE?
I WORK AS A MAGAZINE MODEL.
I'VE GOT A PHOTO SESSION TONIGHT. ♪
THE STUDIO'S CLOSE BY.

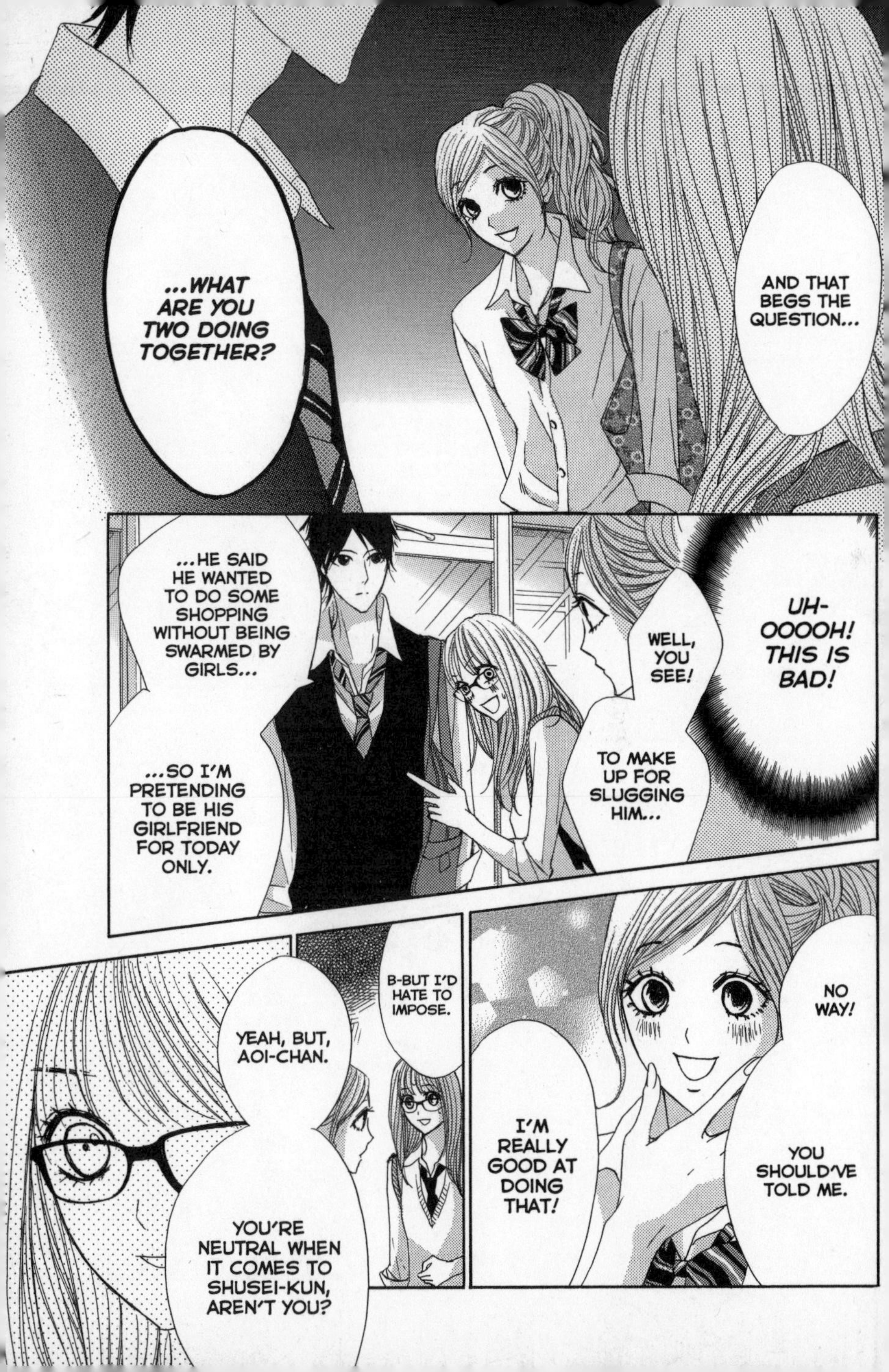
AND THAT BEGS THE QUESTION...
...WHAT ARE YOU TWO DOING TOGETHER?
UH-OOOOH! THIS IS BAD!
WELL, YOU SEE!
TO MAKE UP FOR SLUGGING HIM...
...HE SAID HE WANTED TO DO SOME SHOPPING WITHOUT BEING SWARMED BY GIRLS...
...SO I'M PRETENDING TO BE HIS GIRLFRIEND FOR TODAY ONLY.
NO WAY!
YOU SHOULD'VE TOLD ME.
I'M REALLY GOOD AT DOING THAT!
B-BUT I'D HATE TO IMPOSE.
YEAH, BUT, AOI-CHAN.
YOU'RE NEUTRAL WHEN IT COMES TO SHUSEI-KUN, AREN'T YOU?

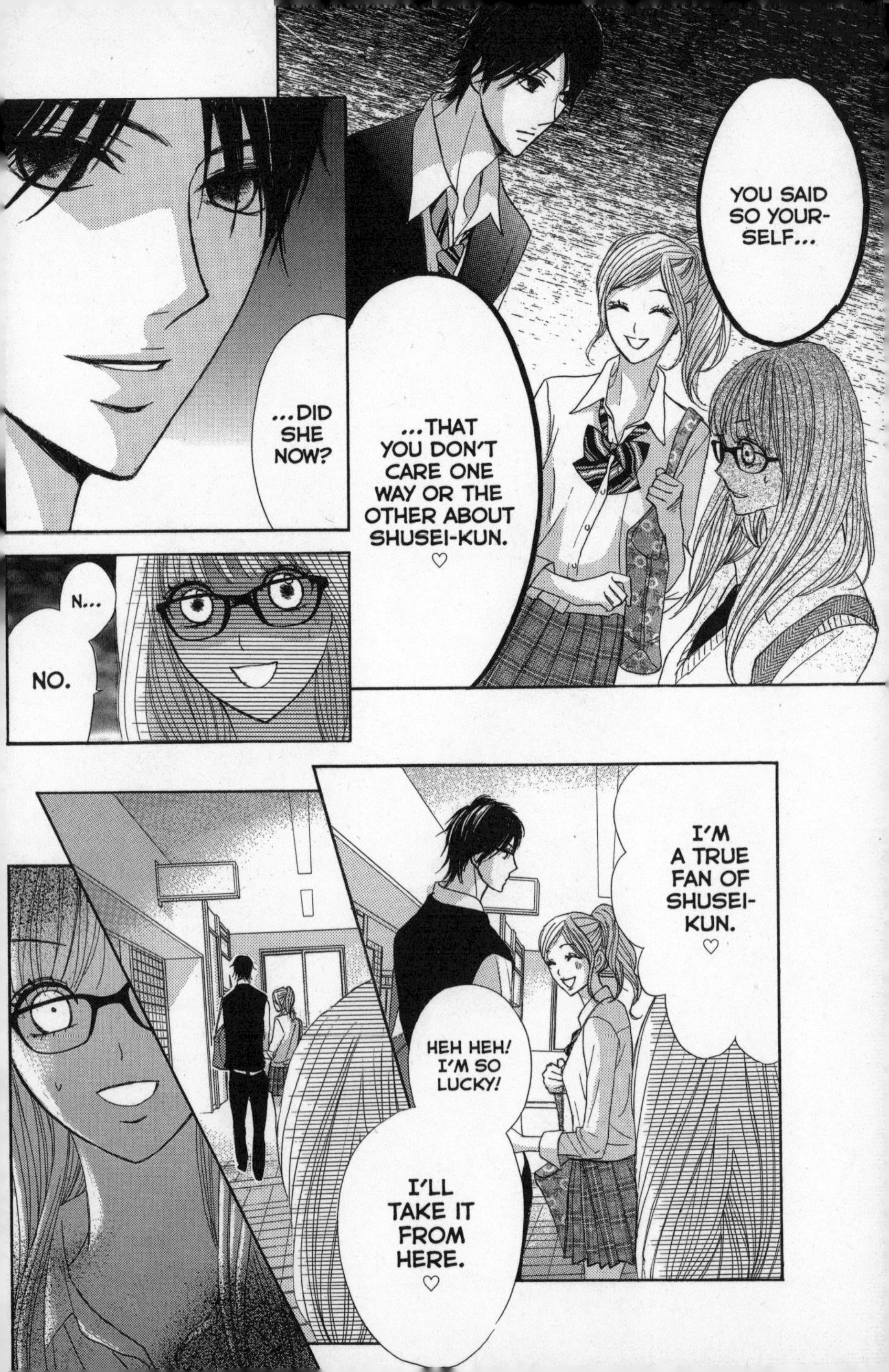
YOU SAID SO YOURSELF...
...THAT YOU DON'T CARE ONE WAY OR THE OTHER ABOUT SHUSEI-KUN. ♡
...DID SHE NOW?
N...
NO.
I'M A TRUE FAN OF SHUSEI-KUN. ♡
HEH HEH! I'M SO LUCKY!
I'LL TAKE IT FROM HERE. ♡

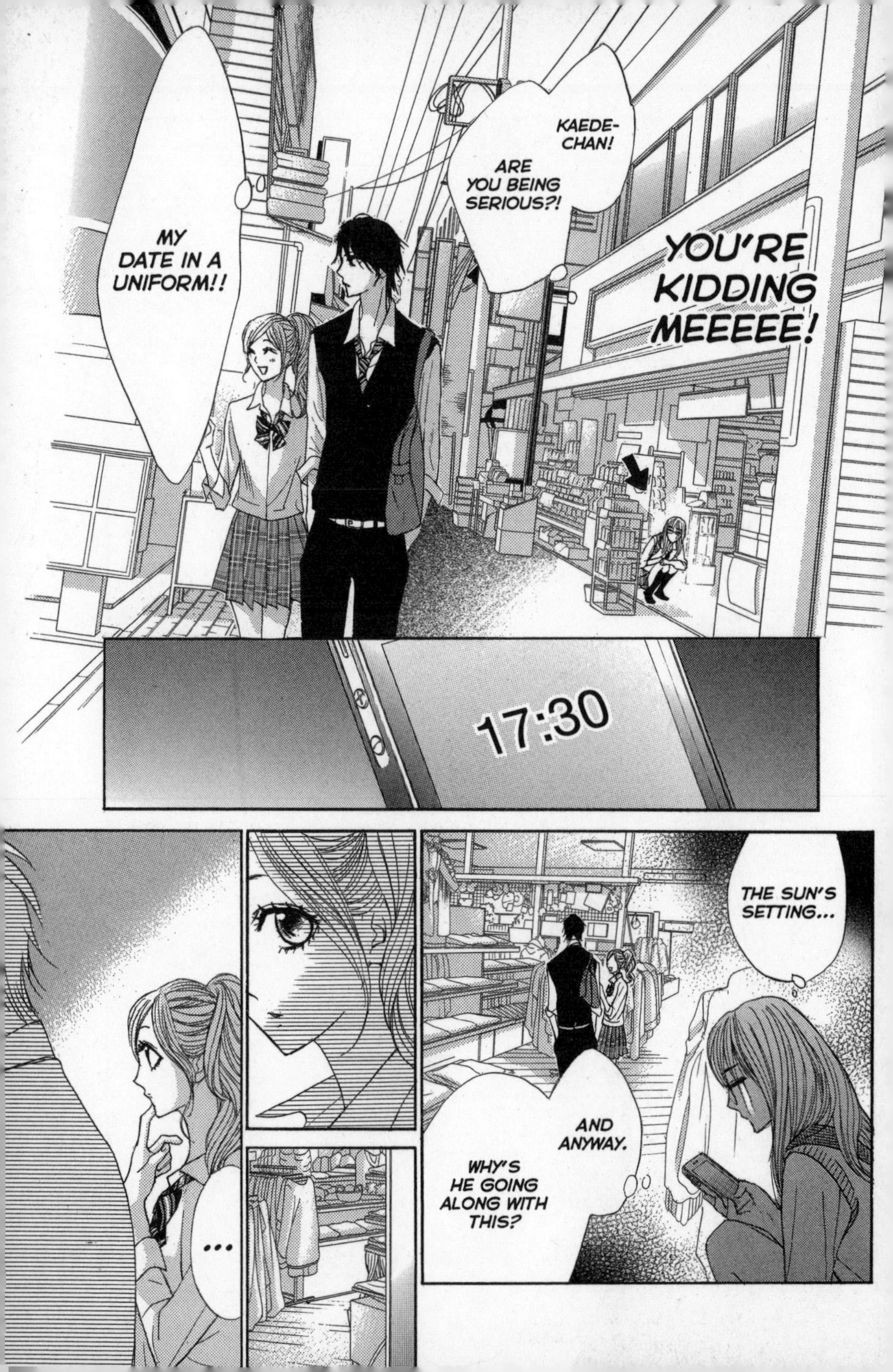
KAEDE-CHAN!
ARE YOU BEING SERIOUS?!
YOU'RE KIDDING MEEEEEE!
MY DATE IN A UNIFORM!!
17:30
THE SUN'S SETTING...
AND ANYWAY.
WHY'S HE GOING ALONG WITH THIS?
...

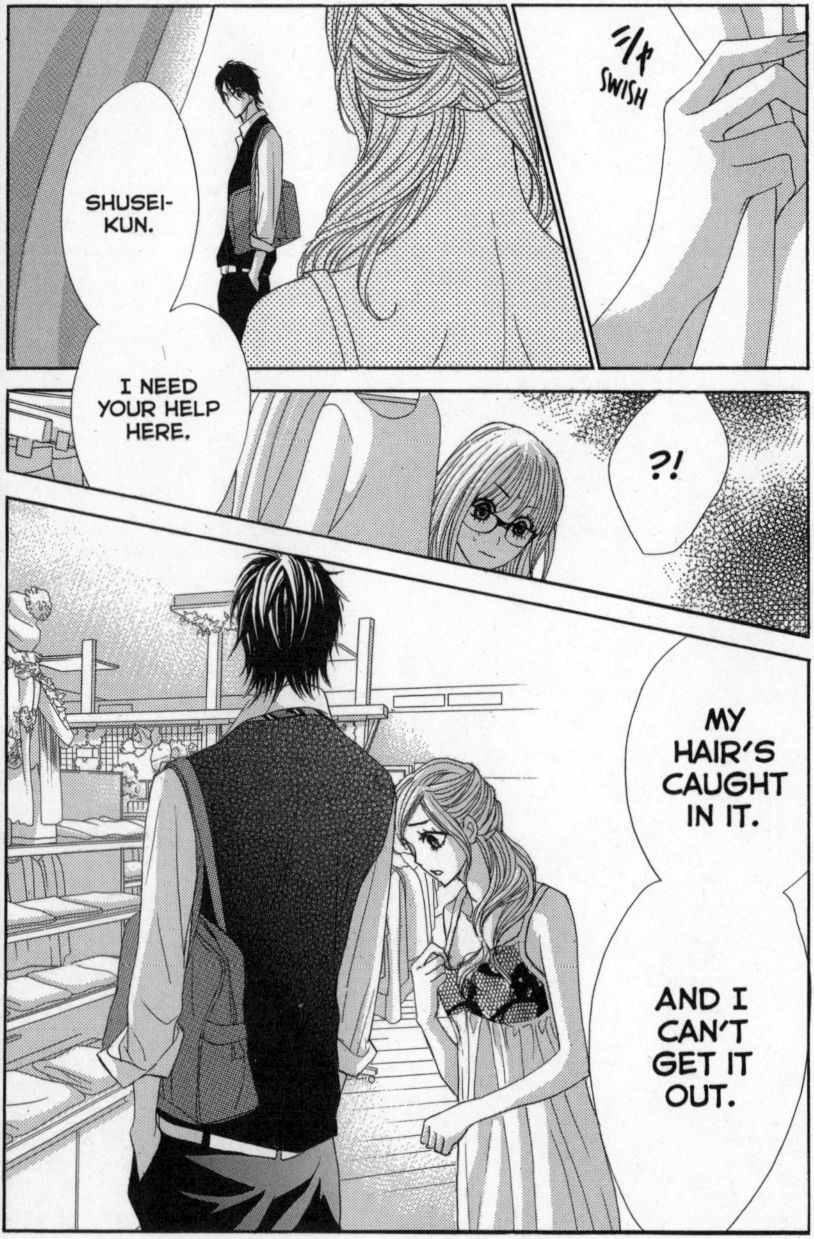
シャ
SWISH
SHUSEI-KUN.
I NEED YOUR HELP HERE.
?!
MY HAIR'S CAUGHT IN IT.
AND I CAN'T GET IT OUT.

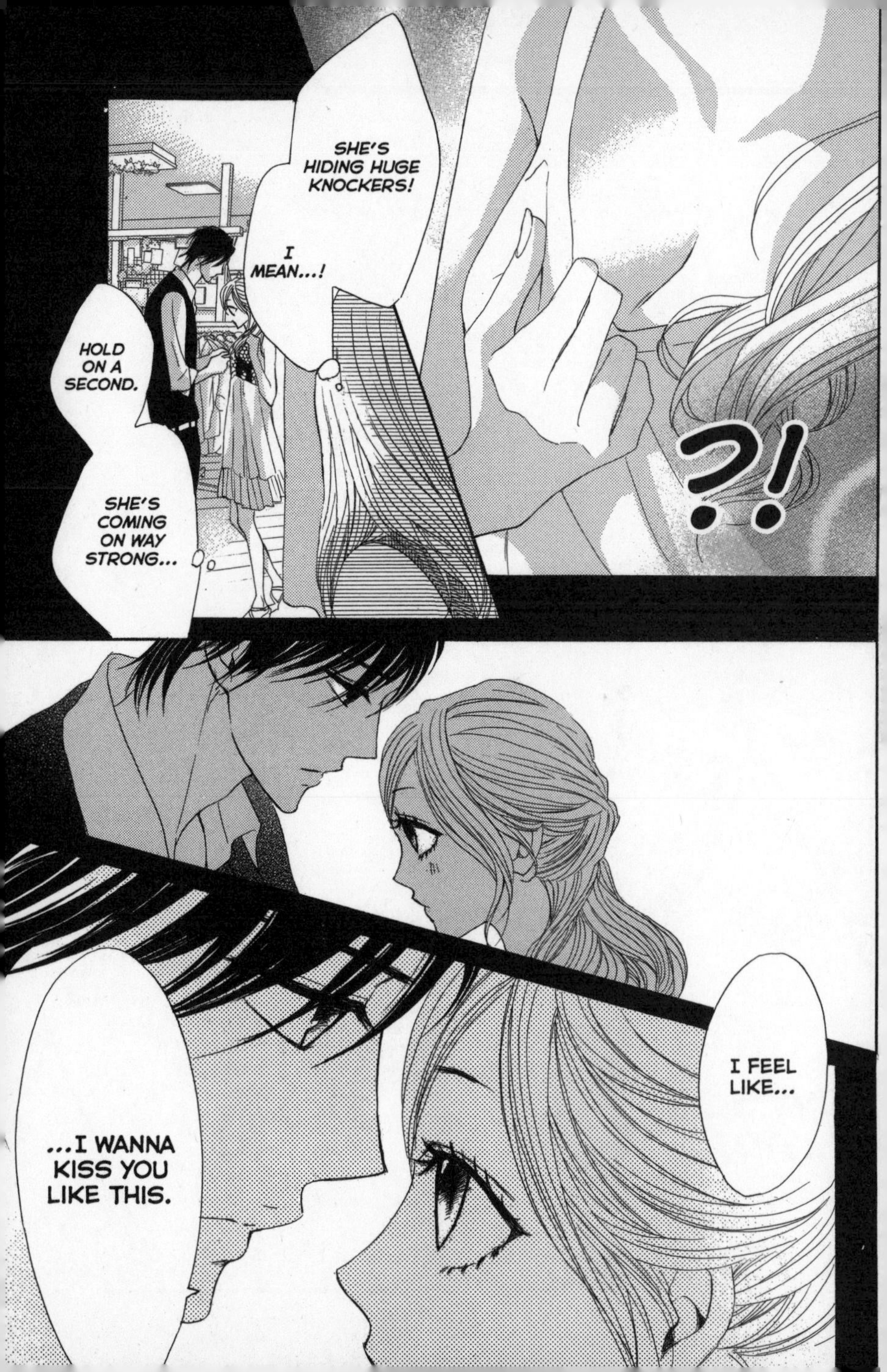
?!
SHE'S HIDING HUGE KNOCKERS!
I MEAN...!
HOLD ON A SECOND.
SHE'S COMING ON WAY STRONG...
I FEEL LIKE...
...I WANNA KISS YOU LIKE THIS.

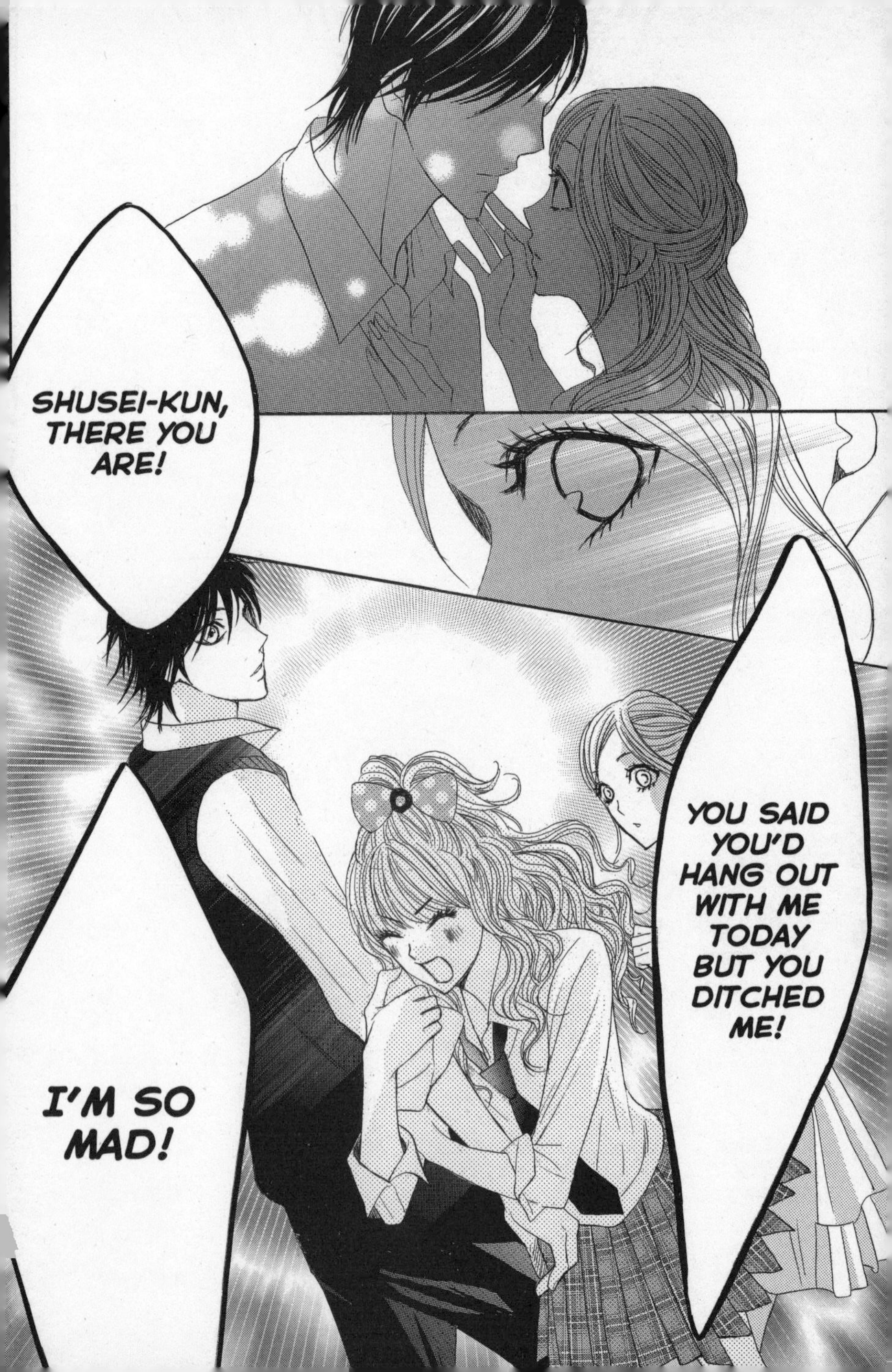
SHUSEI-KUN, THERE YOU ARE!
YOU SAID YOU'D HANG OUT WITH ME TODAY BUT YOU DITCHED ME!
I'M SO MAD!

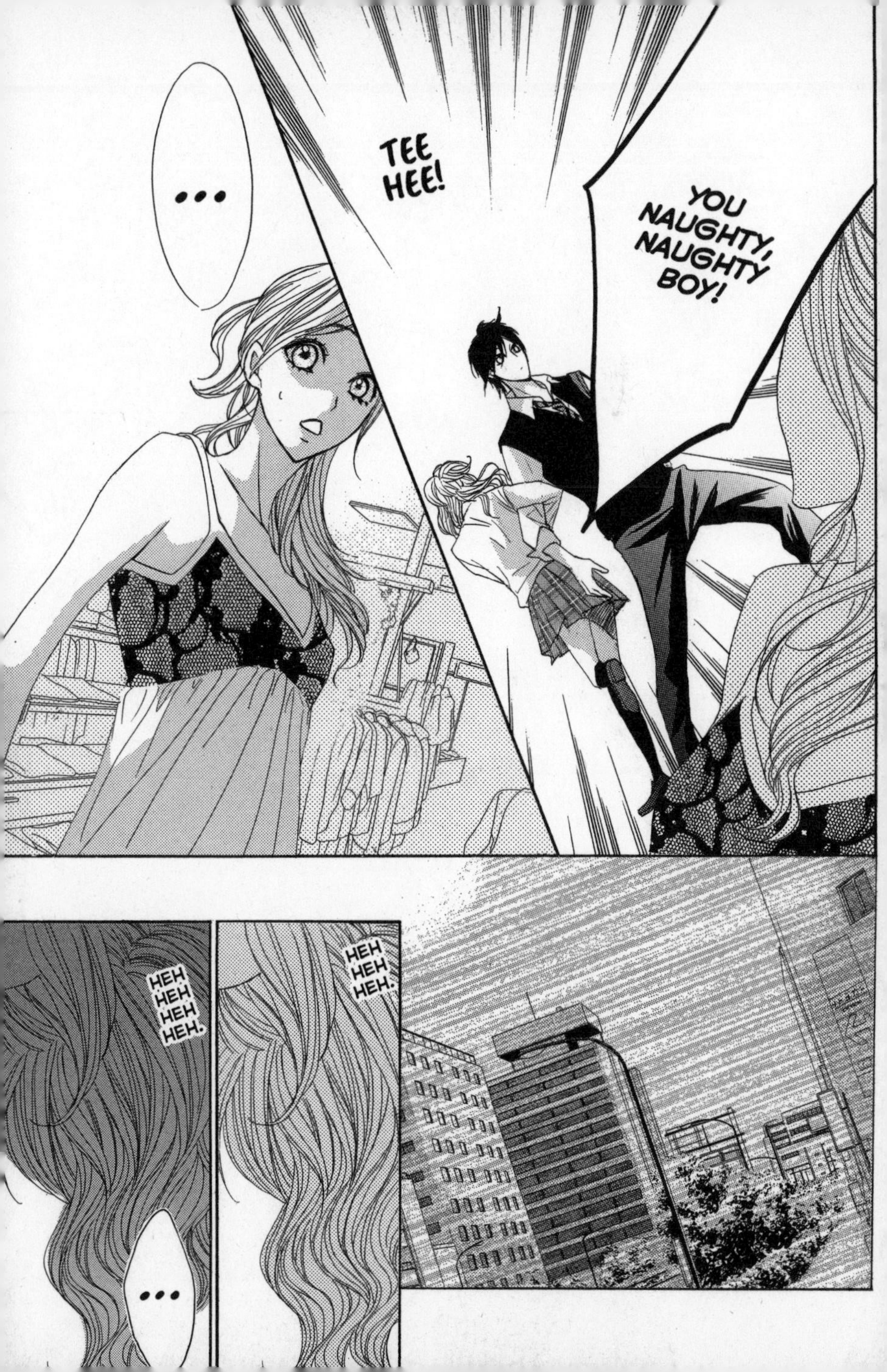
YOU NAUGHTY, NAUGHTY BOY!
TEE HEE!
...
HEH HEH HEH.
HEH HEH HEH HEH.
...

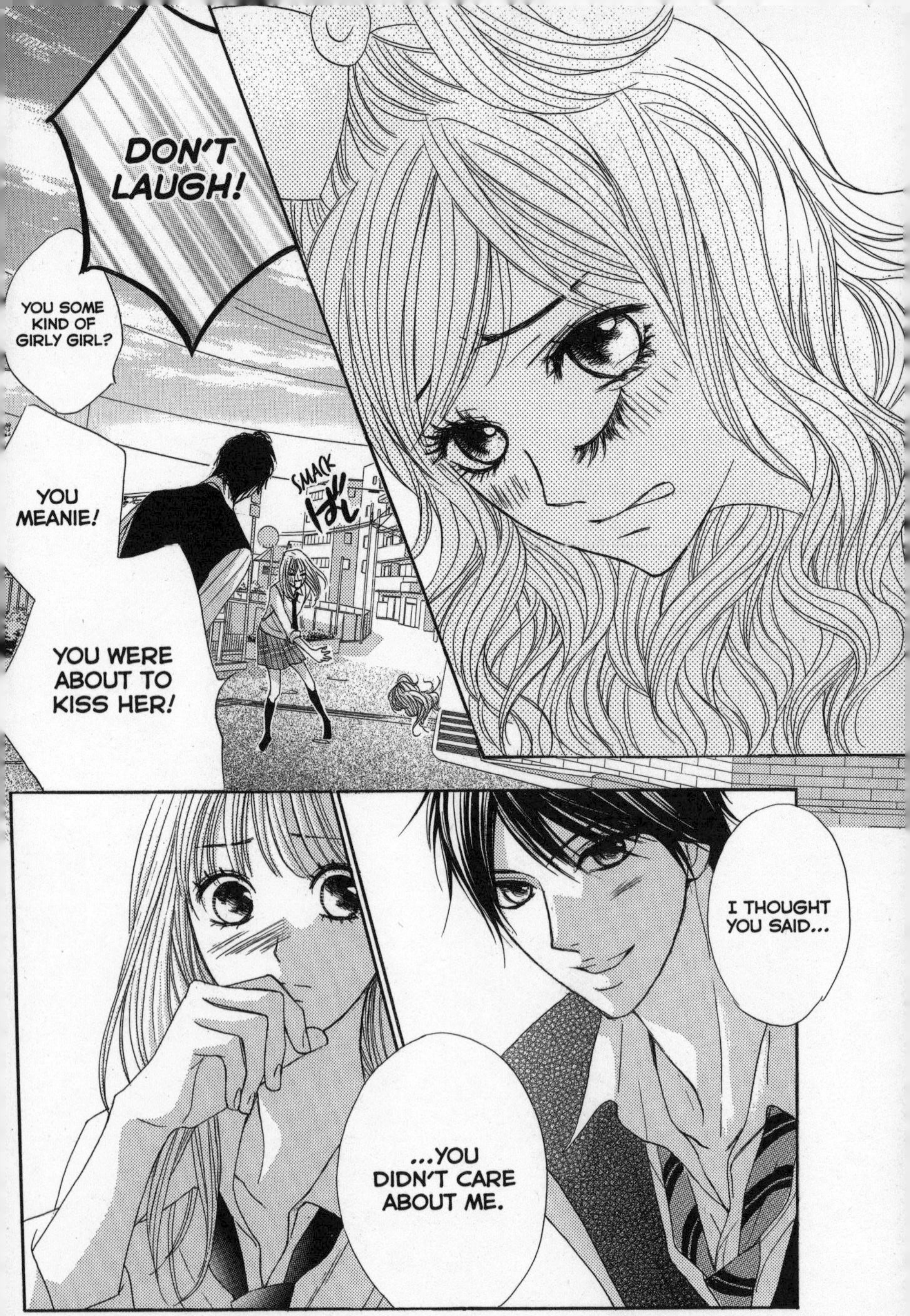
DON'T LAUGH!
YOU SOME KIND OF GIRLY GIRL?
YOU MEANIE!
SMACK
YOU WERE ABOUT TO KISS HER!
I THOUGHT YOU SAID...
...YOU DIDN'T CARE ABOUT ME.

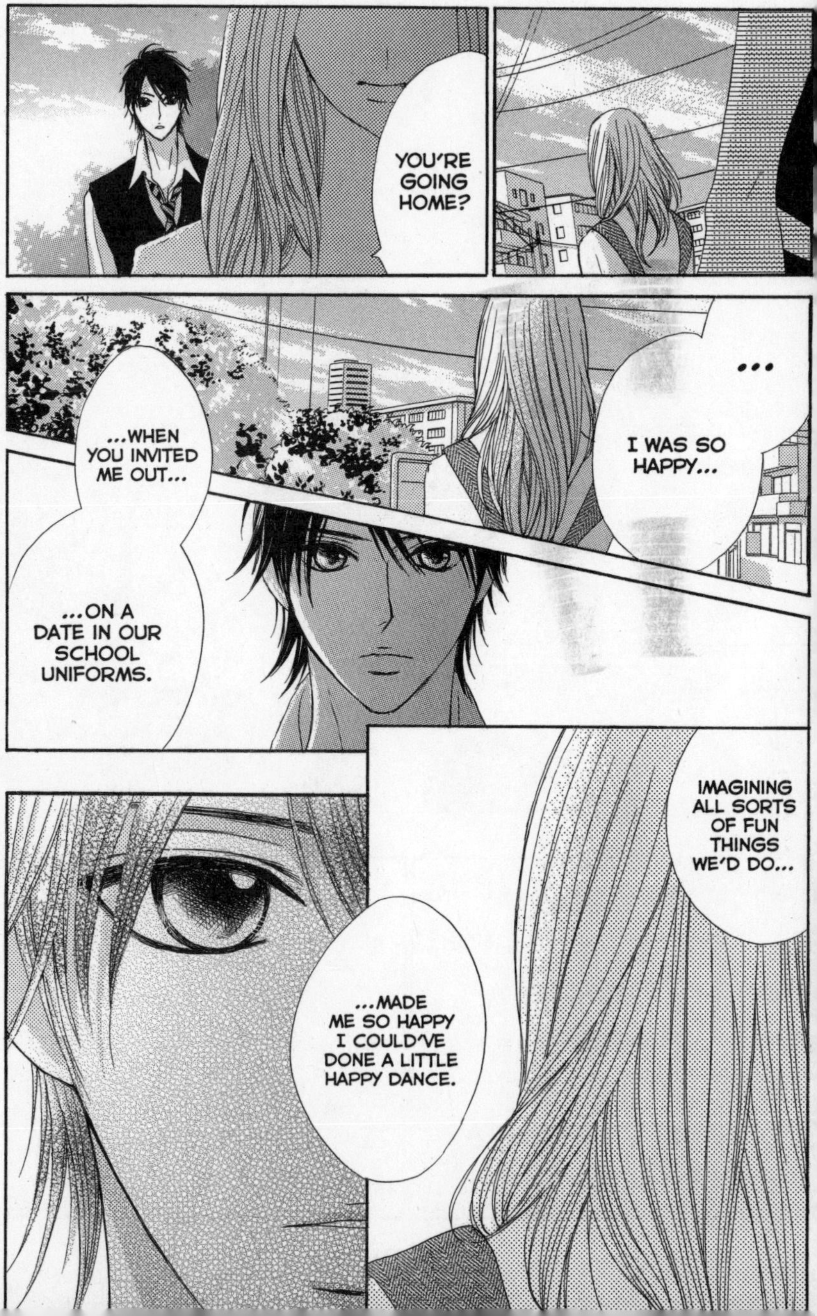
YOU'RE GOING HOME?
...
I WAS SO HAPPY...
...WHEN YOU INVITED ME OUT...
...ON A DATE IN OUR SCHOOL UNIFORMS.
IMAGINING ALL SORTS OF FUN THINGS WE'D DO...
...MADE ME SO HAPPY I COULD'VE DONE A LITTLE HAPPY DANCE.

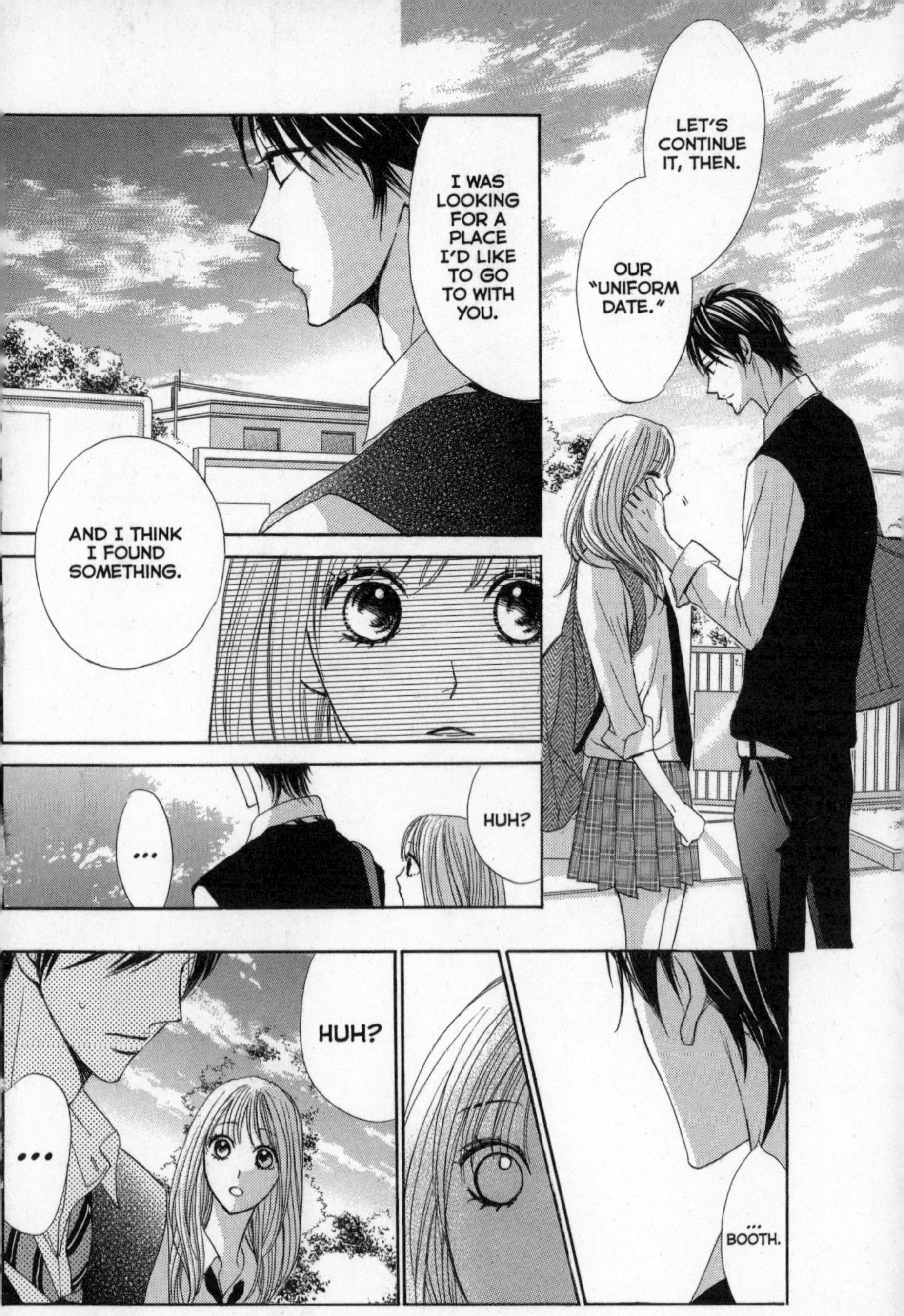
LET'S CONTINUE IT, THEN.
OUR "UNIFORM DATE."
I WAS LOOKING FOR A PLACE I'D LIKE TO GO TO WITH YOU.
AND I THINK I FOUND SOMETHING.
HUH?
...
... BOOTH.
HUH?
...

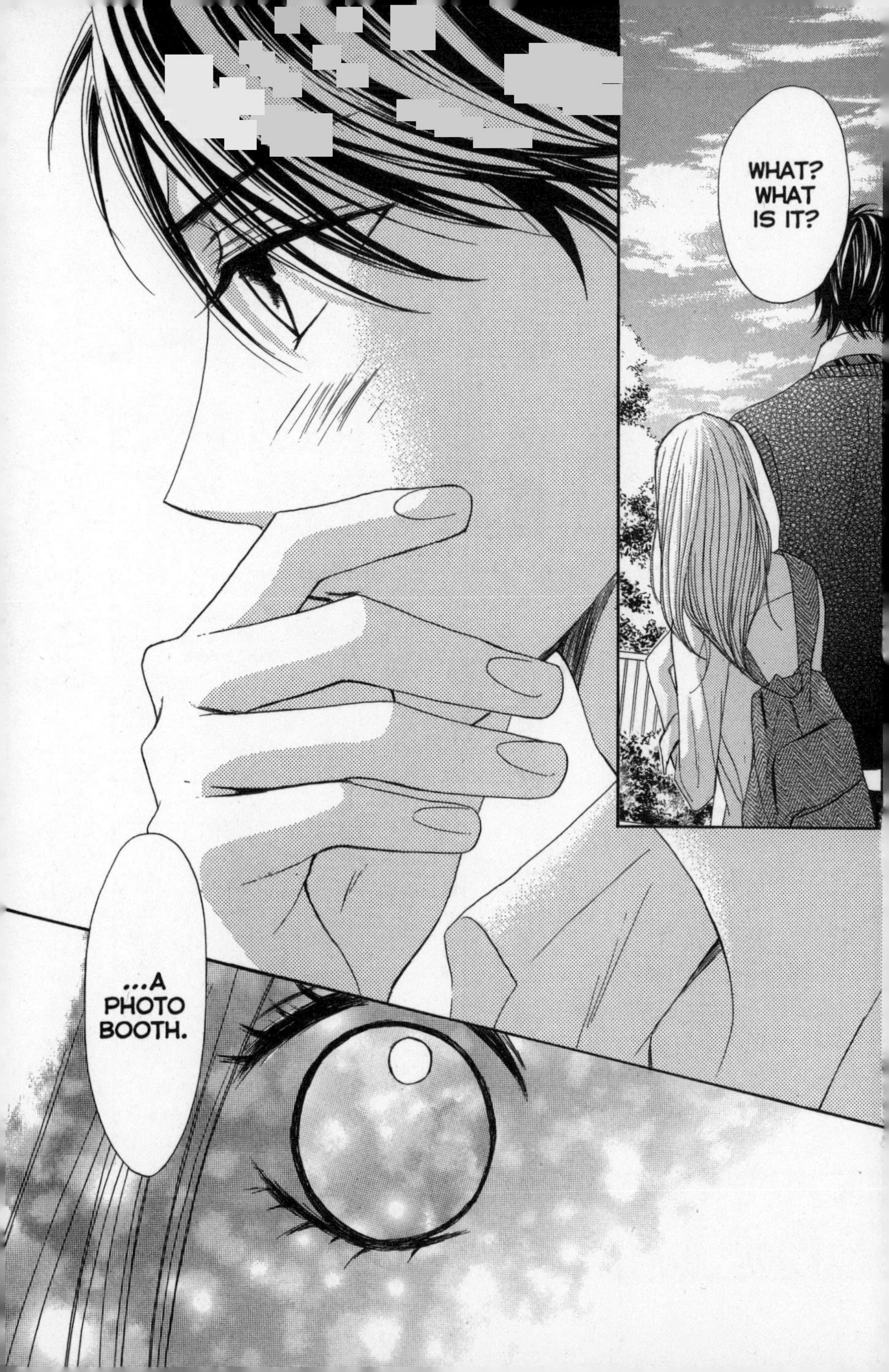
WHAT? WHAT IS IT?
...A PHOTO BOOTH.

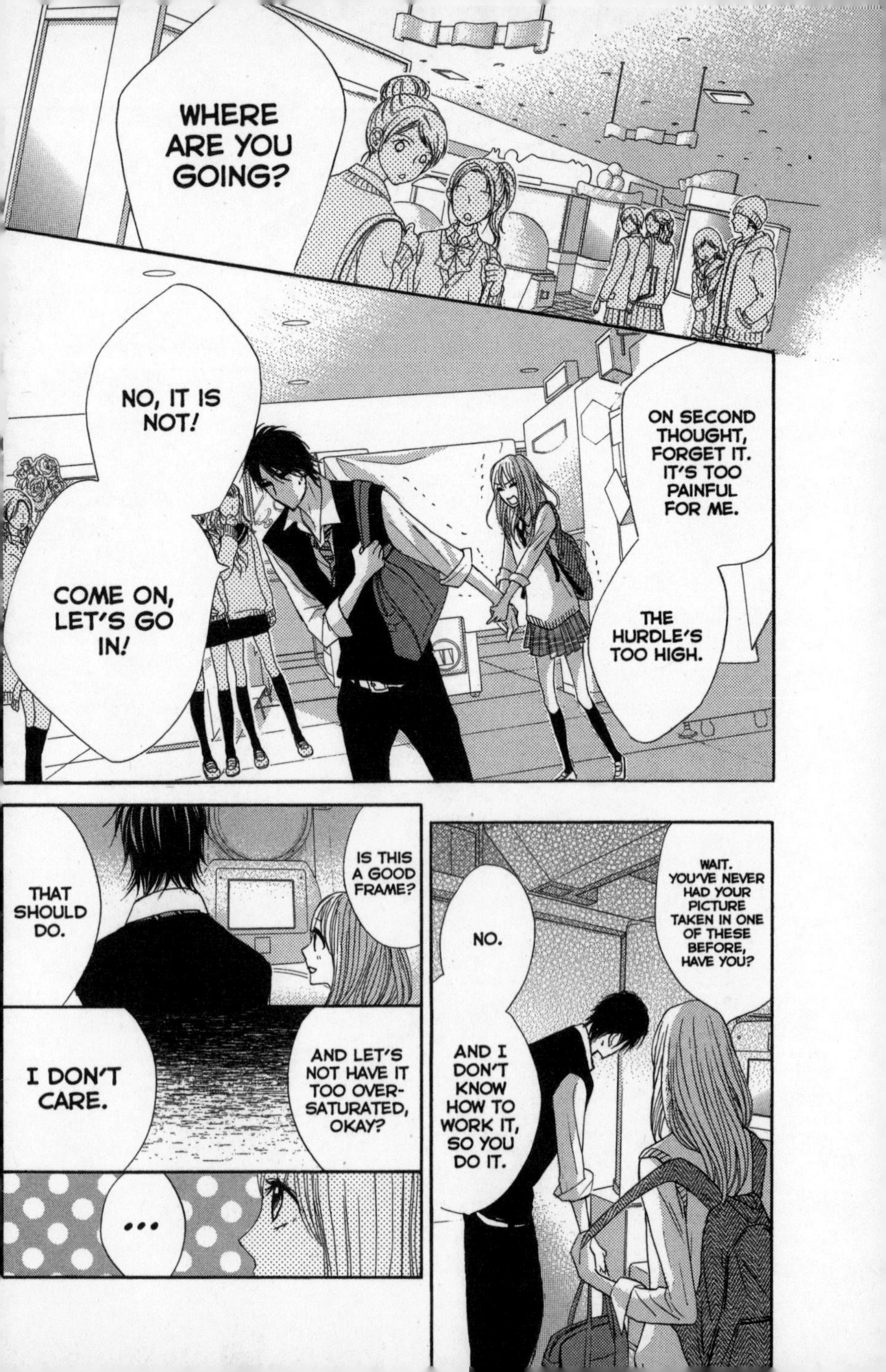
WHERE ARE YOU GOING?
ON SECOND THOUGHT, FORGET IT. IT'S TOO PAINFUL FOR ME.
THE HURDLE'S TOO HIGH.
NO, IT IS NOT!
COME ON, LET'S GO IN!
WAIT. YOU'VE NEVER HAD YOUR PICTURE TAKEN IN ONE OF THESE BEFORE, HAVE YOU?
NO.
AND I DON'T KNOW HOW TO WORK IT, SO YOU DO IT.
IS THIS A GOOD FRAME?
THAT SHOULD DO.
AND LET'S NOT HAVE IT TOO OVER-SATURATED, OKAY?
I DON'T CARE.
...

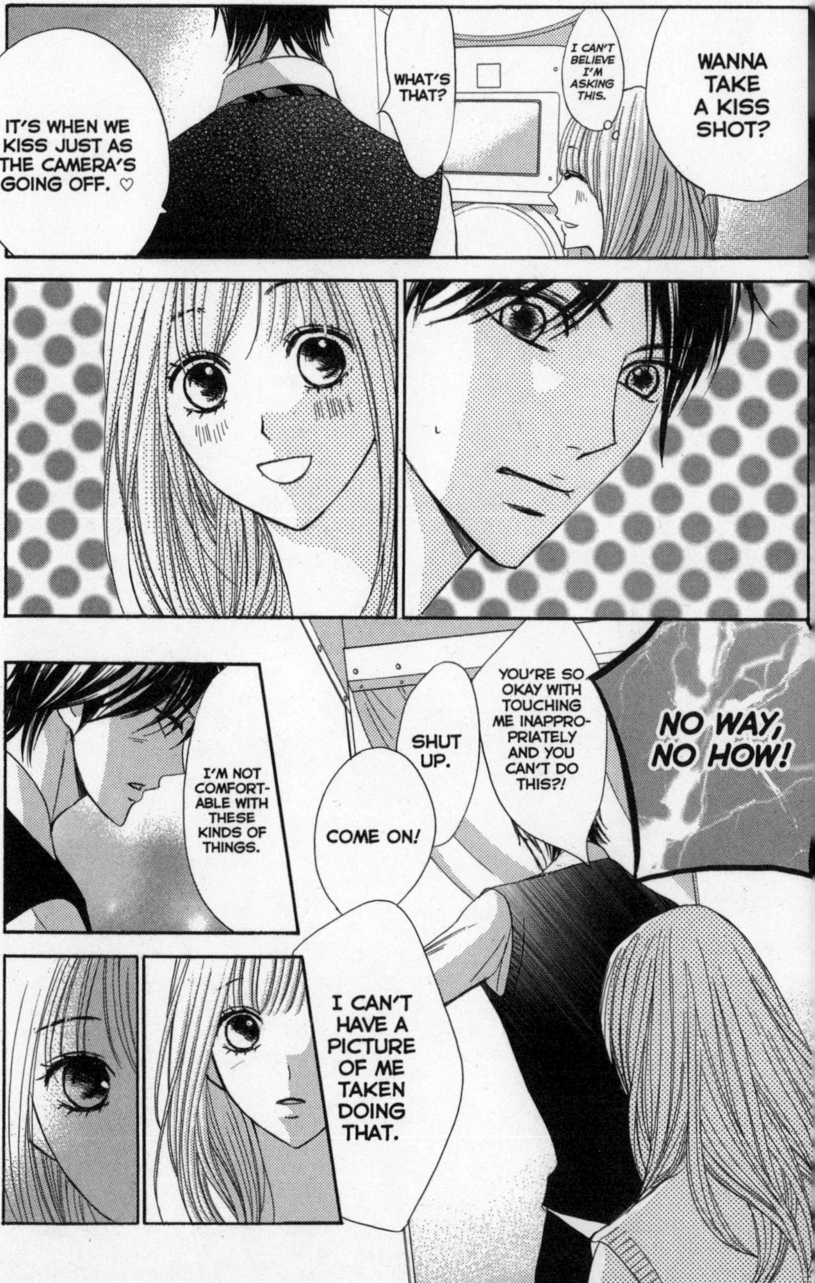
WANNA TAKE A KISS SHOT?
I CAN'T BELIEVE I'M ASKING THIS.
WHAT'S THAT?
IT'S WHEN WE KISS JUST AS THE CAMERA'S GOING OFF. ♡
NO WAY, NO HOW!
YOU'RE SO OKAY WITH TOUCHING ME INAPPROPRIATELY AND YOU CAN'T DO THIS?!
SHUT UP.
COME ON!
I'M NOT COMFORTABLE WITH THESE KINDS OF THINGS.
I CAN'T HAVE A PICTURE OF ME TAKEN DOING THAT.

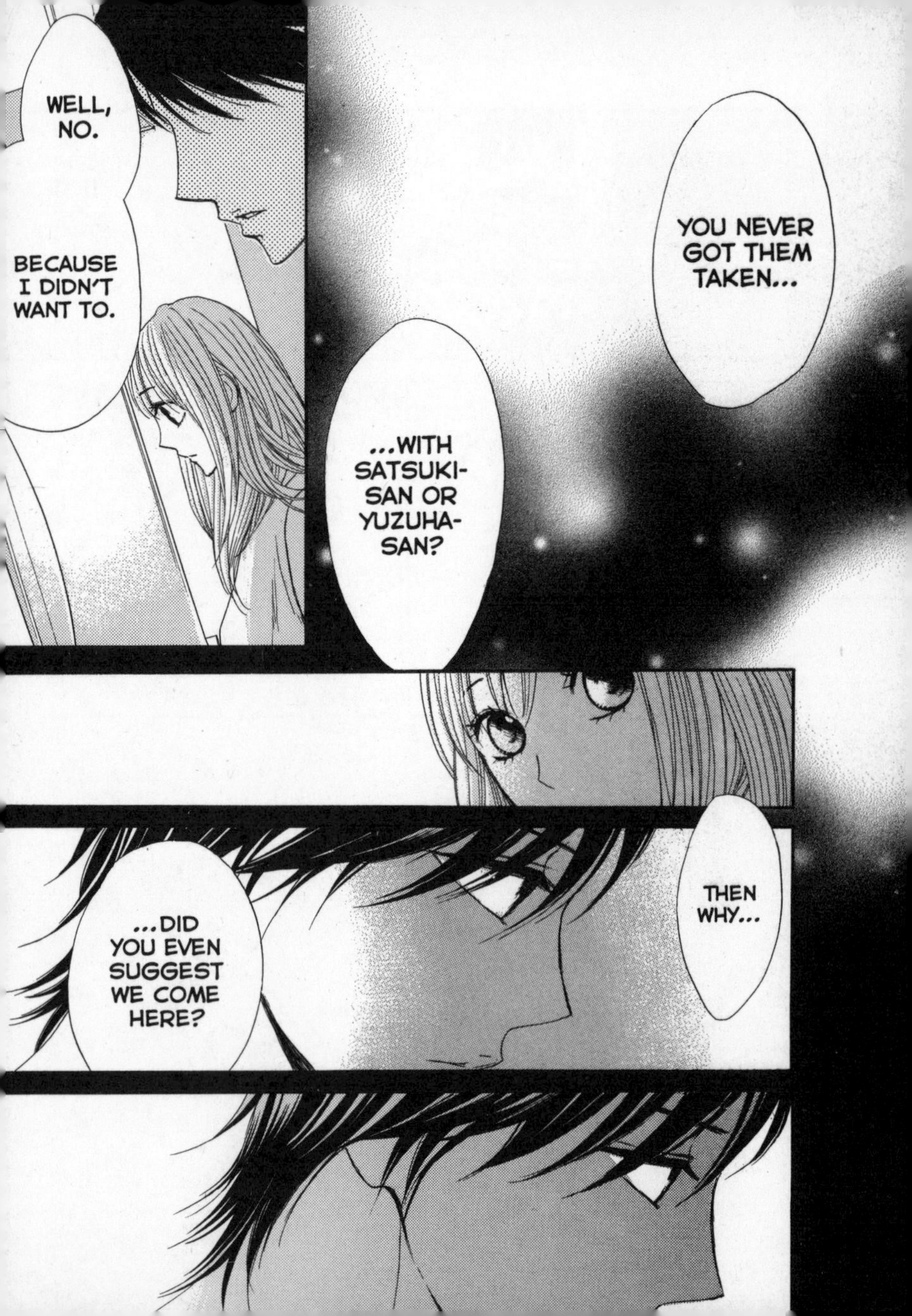
YOU NEVER GOT THEM TAKEN...
...WITH SATSUKI-SAN OR YUZUHA-SAN?
WELL, NO.
BECAUSE I DIDN'T WANT TO.
THEN WHY...
...DID YOU EVEN SUGGEST WE COME HERE?

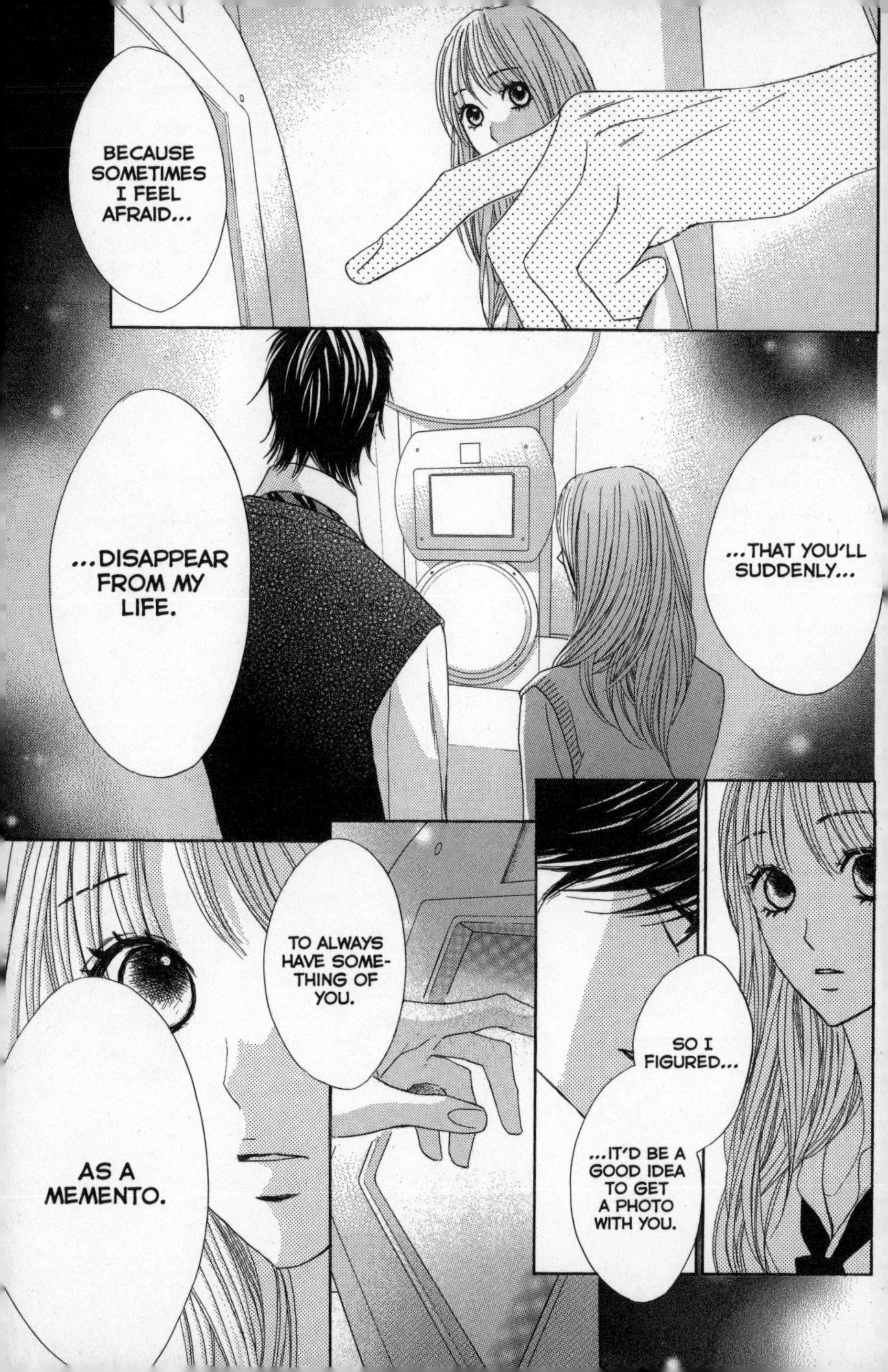
BECAUSE SOMETIMES I FEEL AFRAID...
...THAT YOU'LL SUDDENLY...
...DISAPPEAR FROM MY LIFE.
SO I FIGURED...
...IT'D BE A GOOD IDEA TO GET A PHOTO WITH YOU.
TO ALWAYS HAVE SOME-THING OF YOU.
AS A MEMENTO.

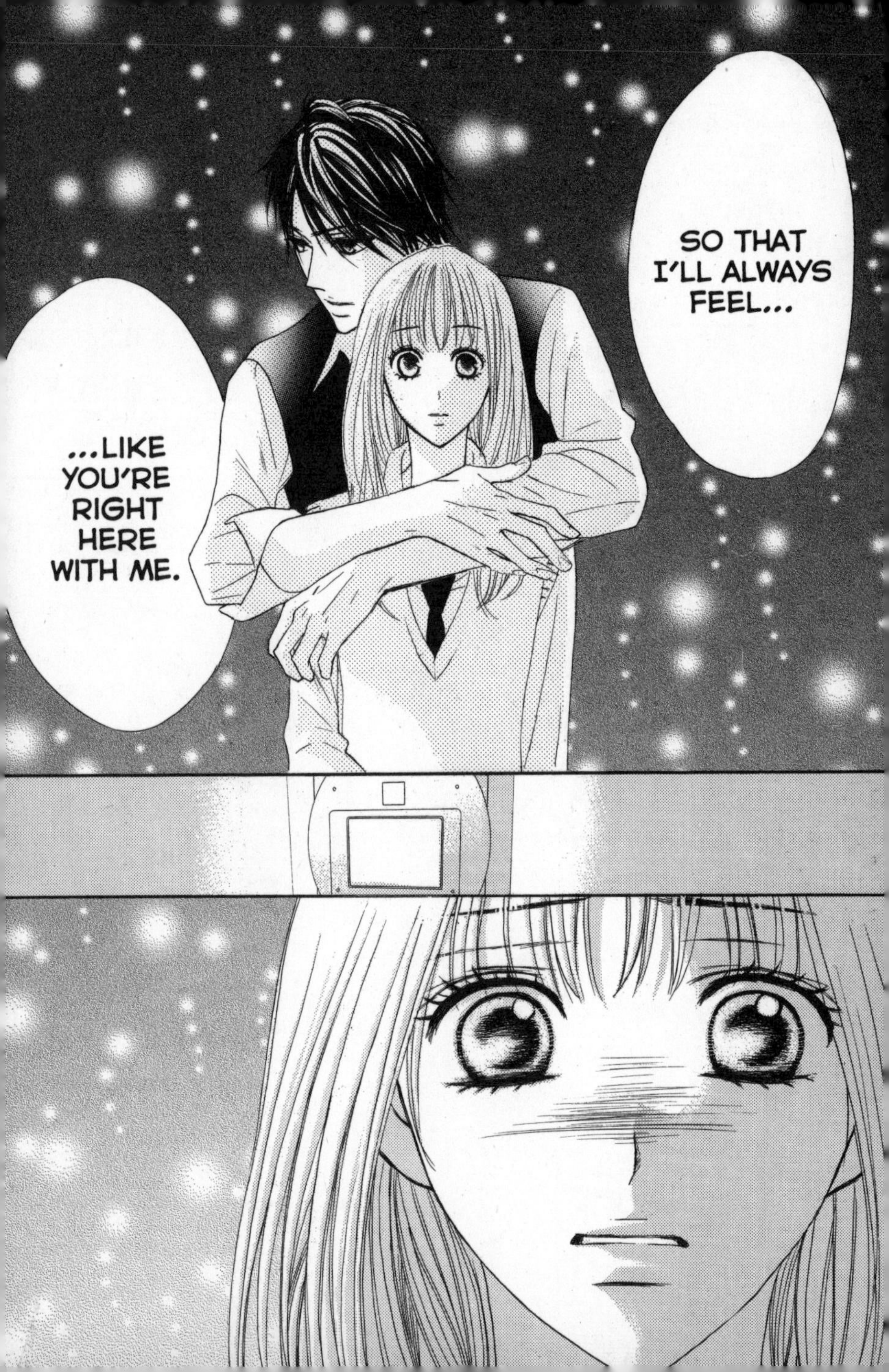
SO THAT I'LL ALWAYS FEEL...
...LIKE YOU'RE RIGHT HERE WITH ME.

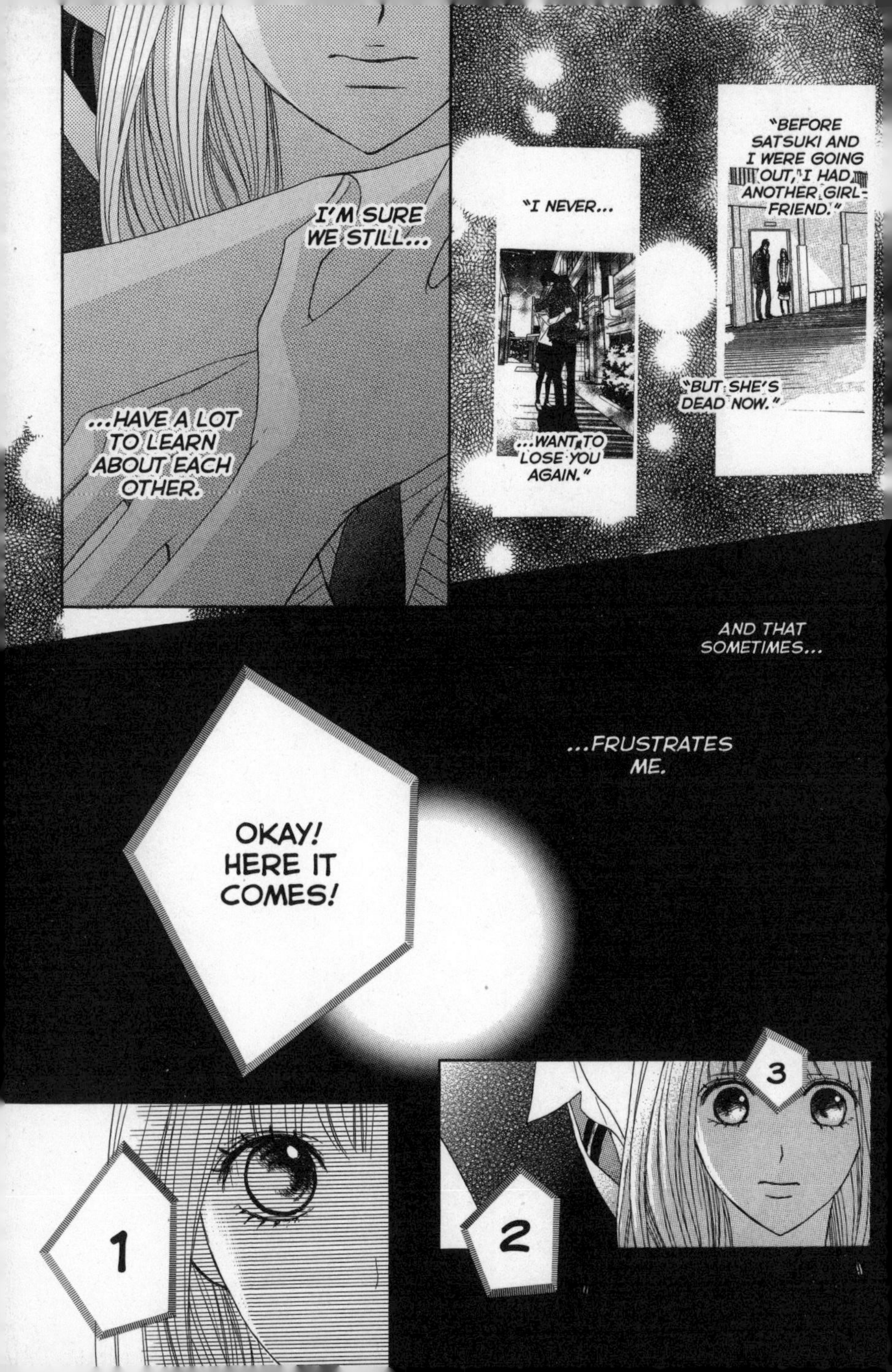
"BEFORE SATSUKI AND I WERE GOING OUT, I HAD ANOTHER GIRL-FRIEND."
"BUT SHE'S DEAD NOW."
"I NEVER...
...WANT TO LOSE YOU AGAIN."
I'M SURE WE STILL...
...HAVE A LOT TO LEARN ABOUT EACH OTHER.
AND THAT SOMETIMES...
...FRUSTRATES ME.
OKAY! HERE IT COMES!
3
2
1

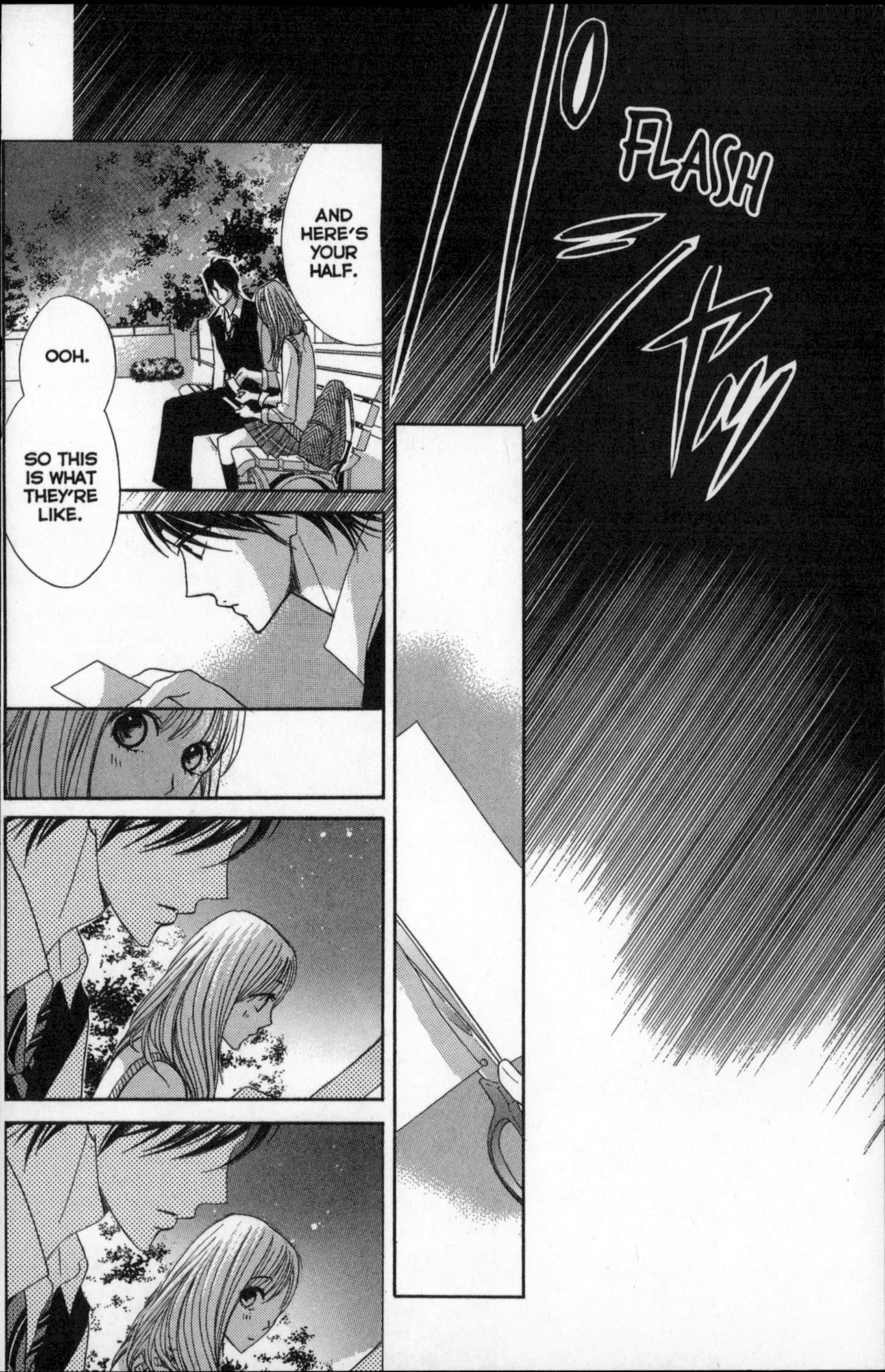
FLASH
AND HERE'S YOUR HALF.
OOH.
SO THIS IS WHAT THEY'RE LIKE.

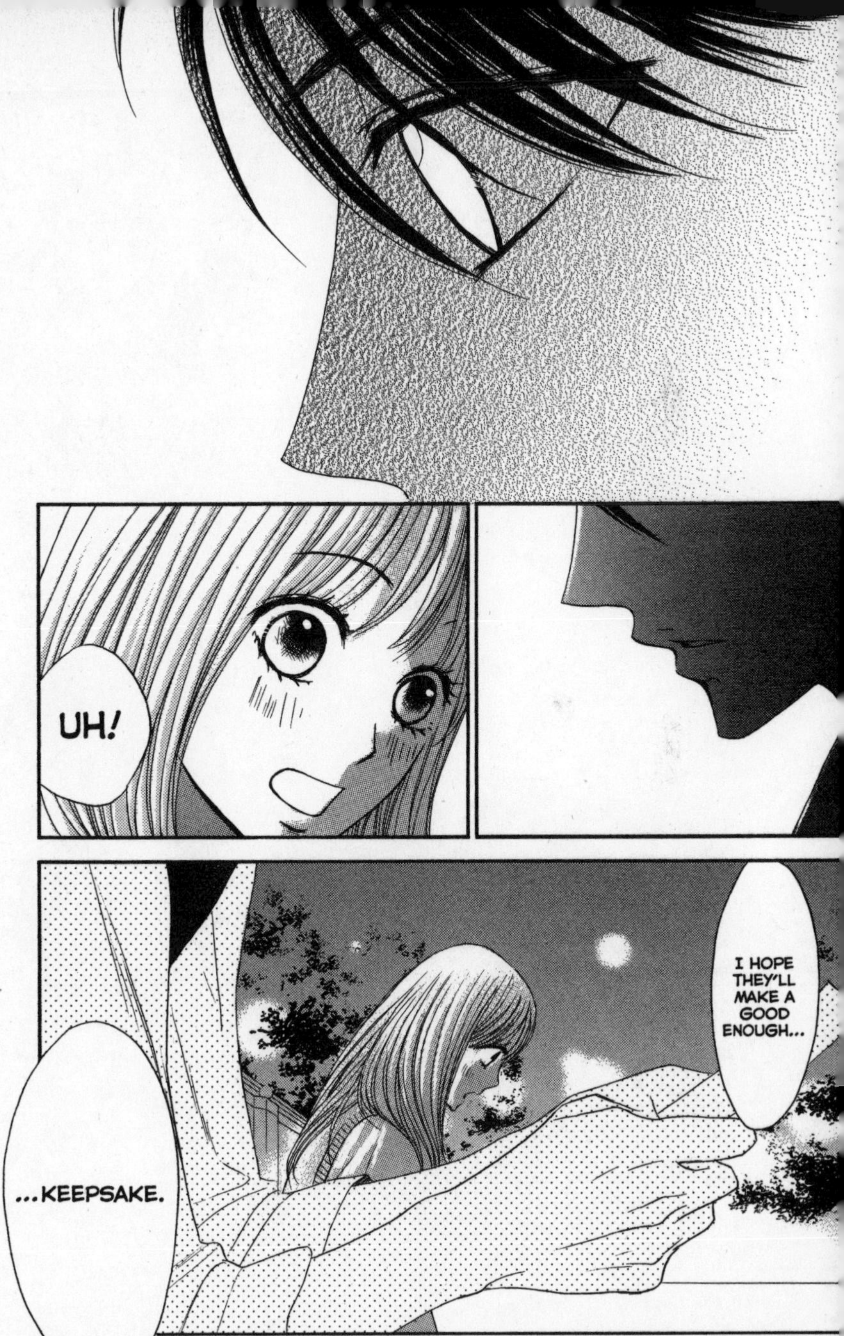
UH!
I HOPE THEY'LL MAKE A GOOD ENOUGH...
...KEEPSAKE.

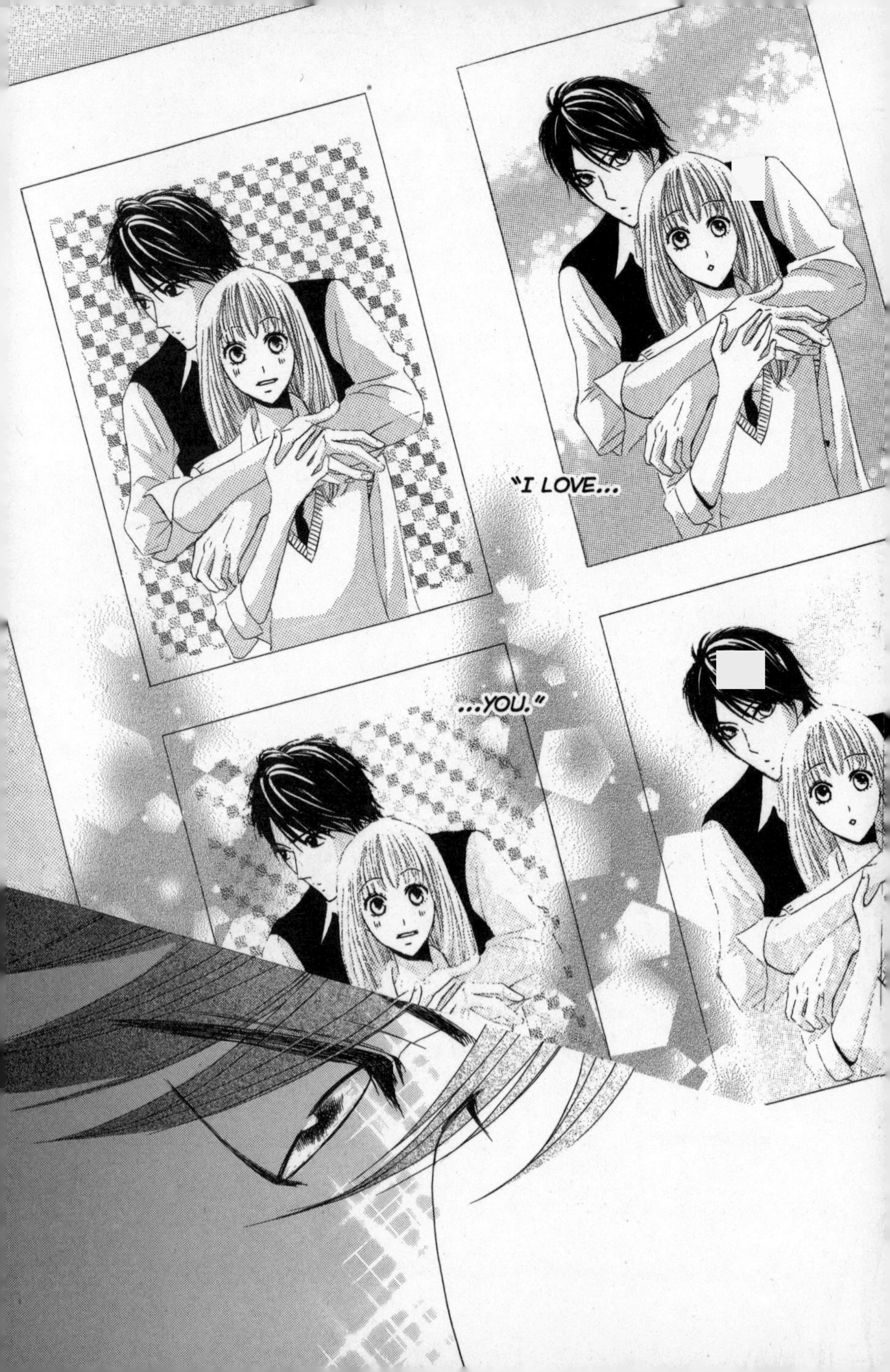
"I LOVE...
...YOU."

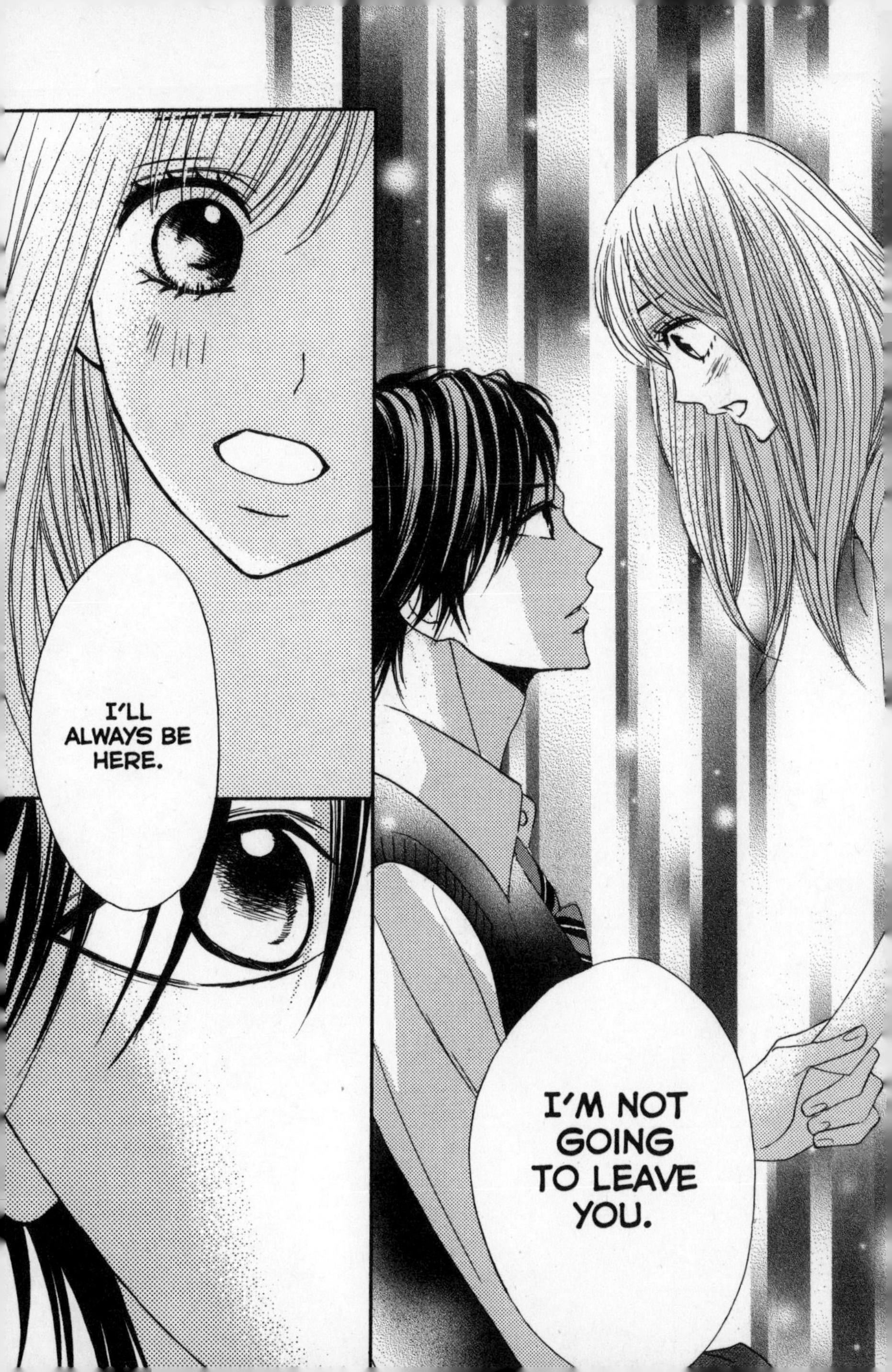
I'M NOT GOING TO LEAVE YOU.
I'LL ALWAYS BE HERE.

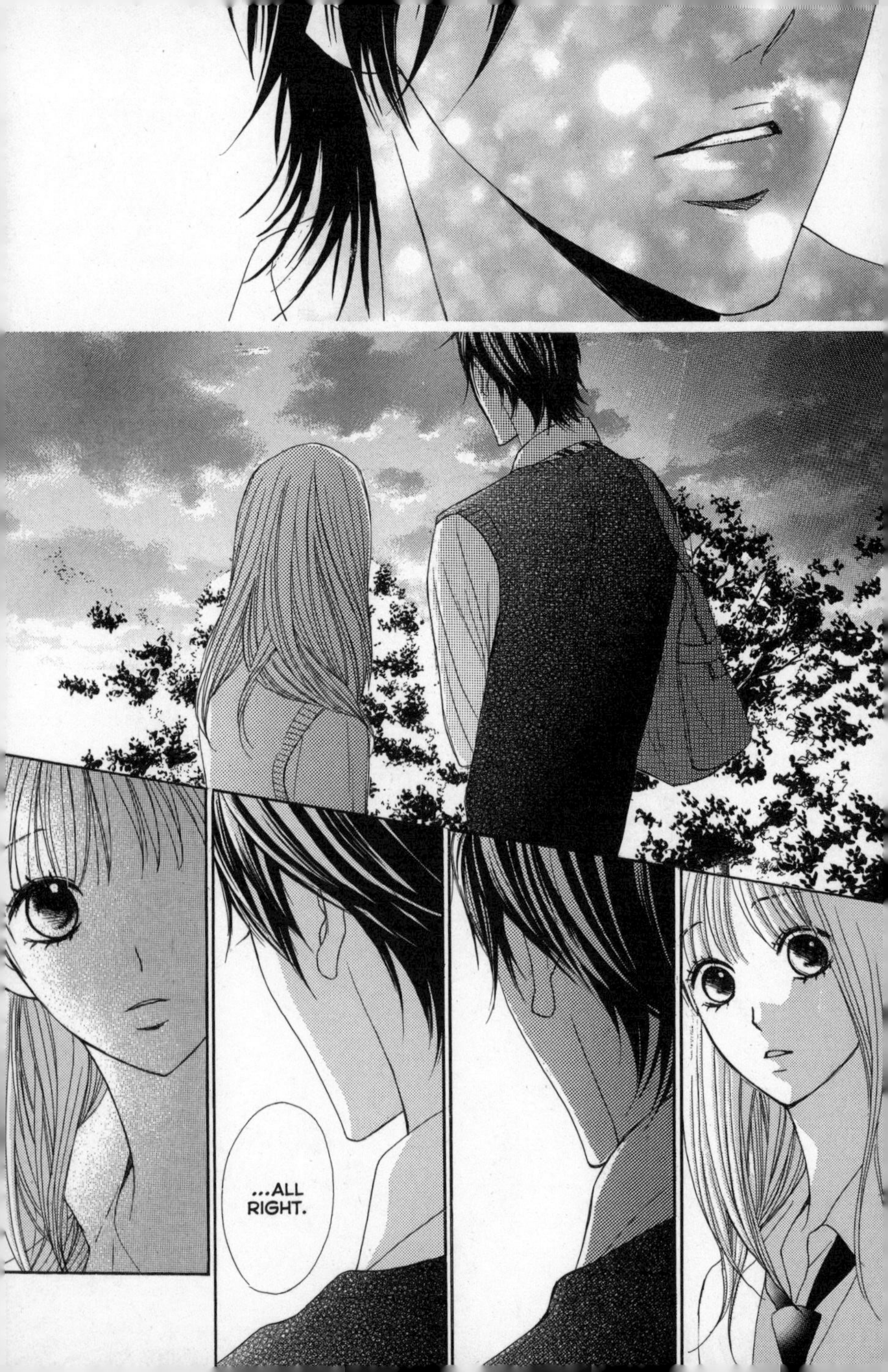
...ALL RIGHT.

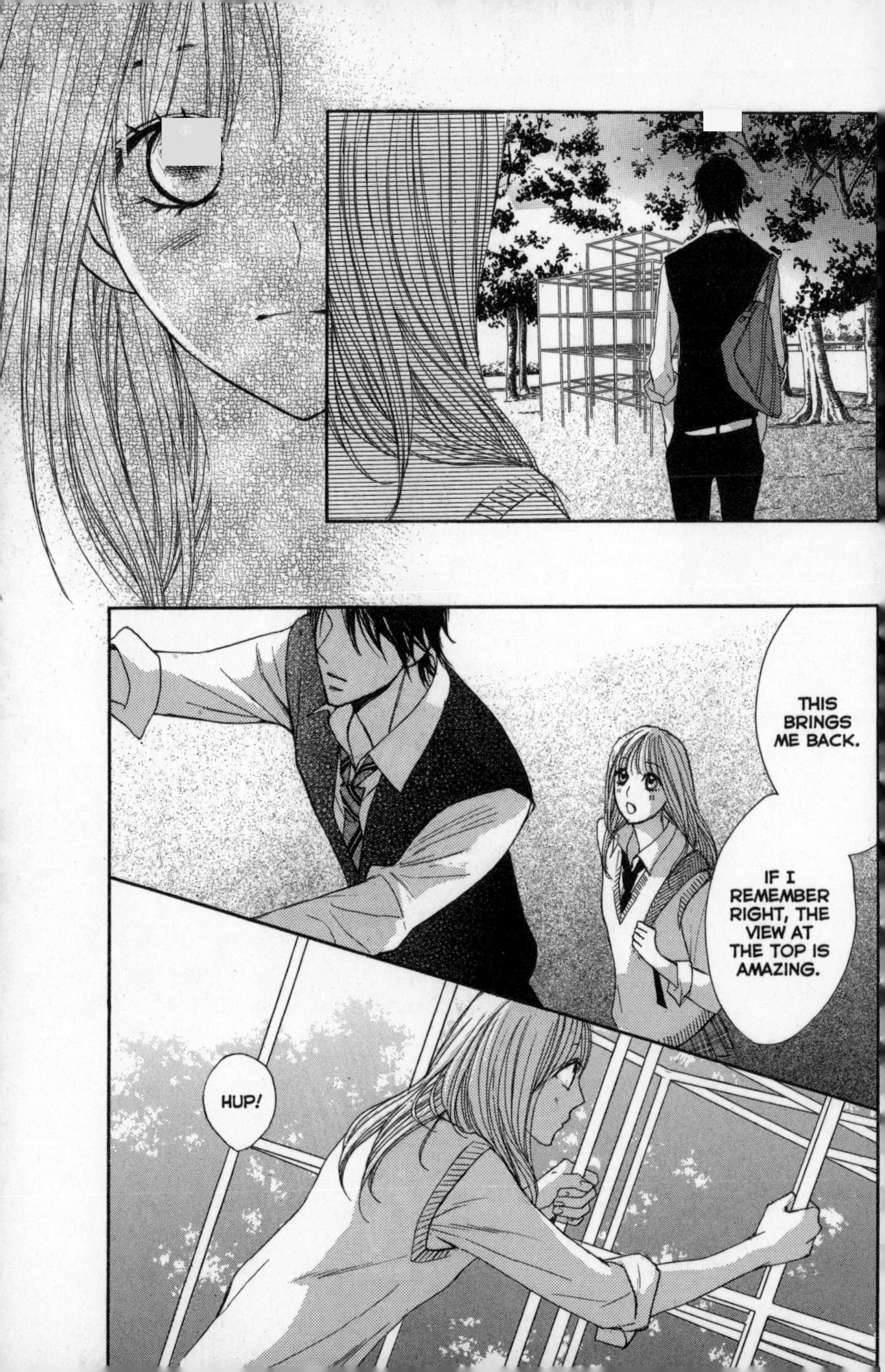
THIS BRINGS ME BACK.
IF I REMEMBER RIGHT, THE VIEW AT THE TOP IS AMAZING.
HUP!

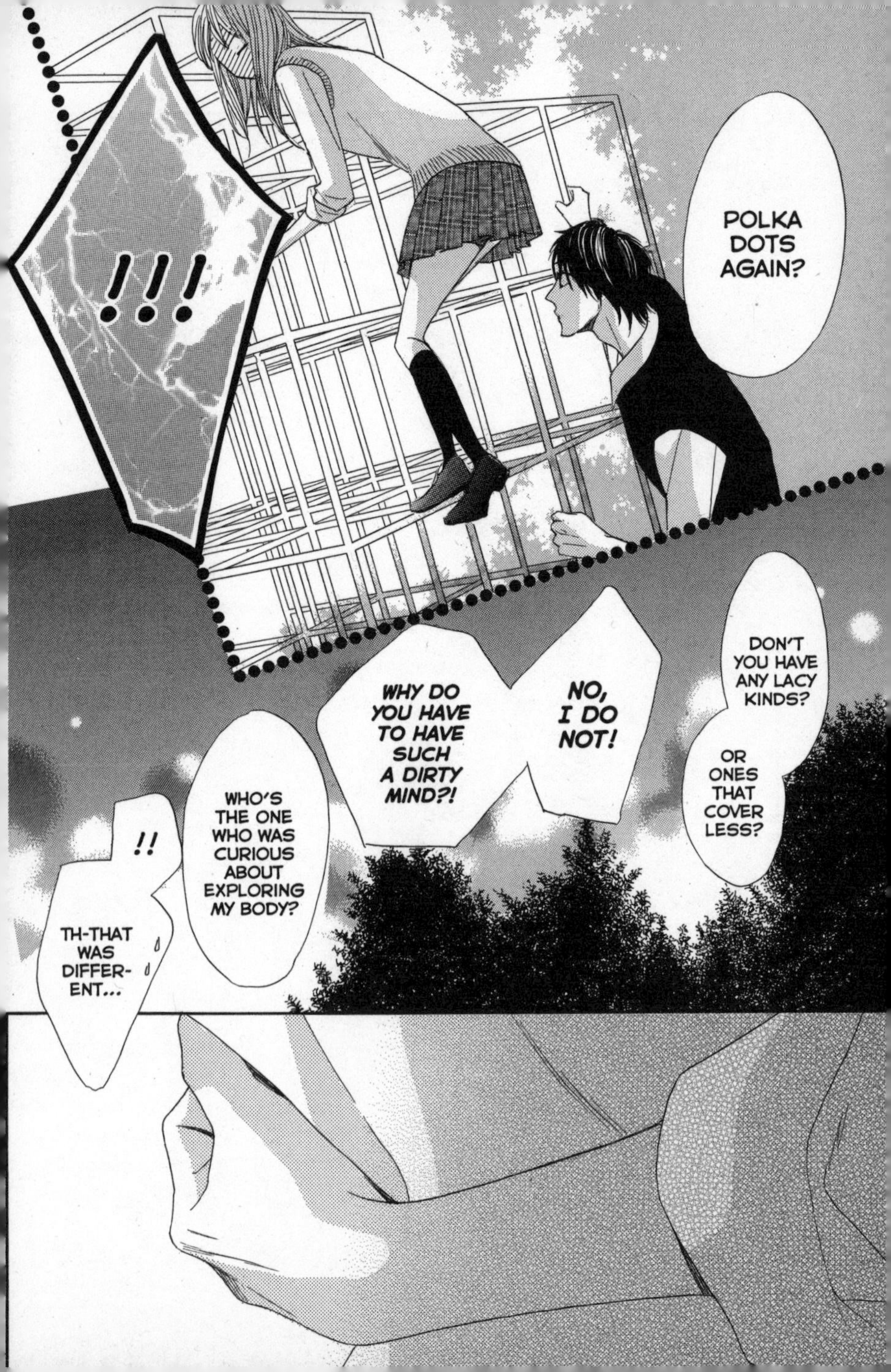
POLKA DOTS AGAIN?
!!!
DON'T YOU HAVE ANY LACY KINDS?
OR ONES THAT COVER LESS?
NO, I DO NOT!
WHY DO YOU HAVE TO HAVE SUCH A DIRTY MIND?!
WHO'S THE ONE WHO WAS CURIOUS ABOUT EXPLORING MY BODY?
!!
TH-THAT WAS DIFFER-ENT...

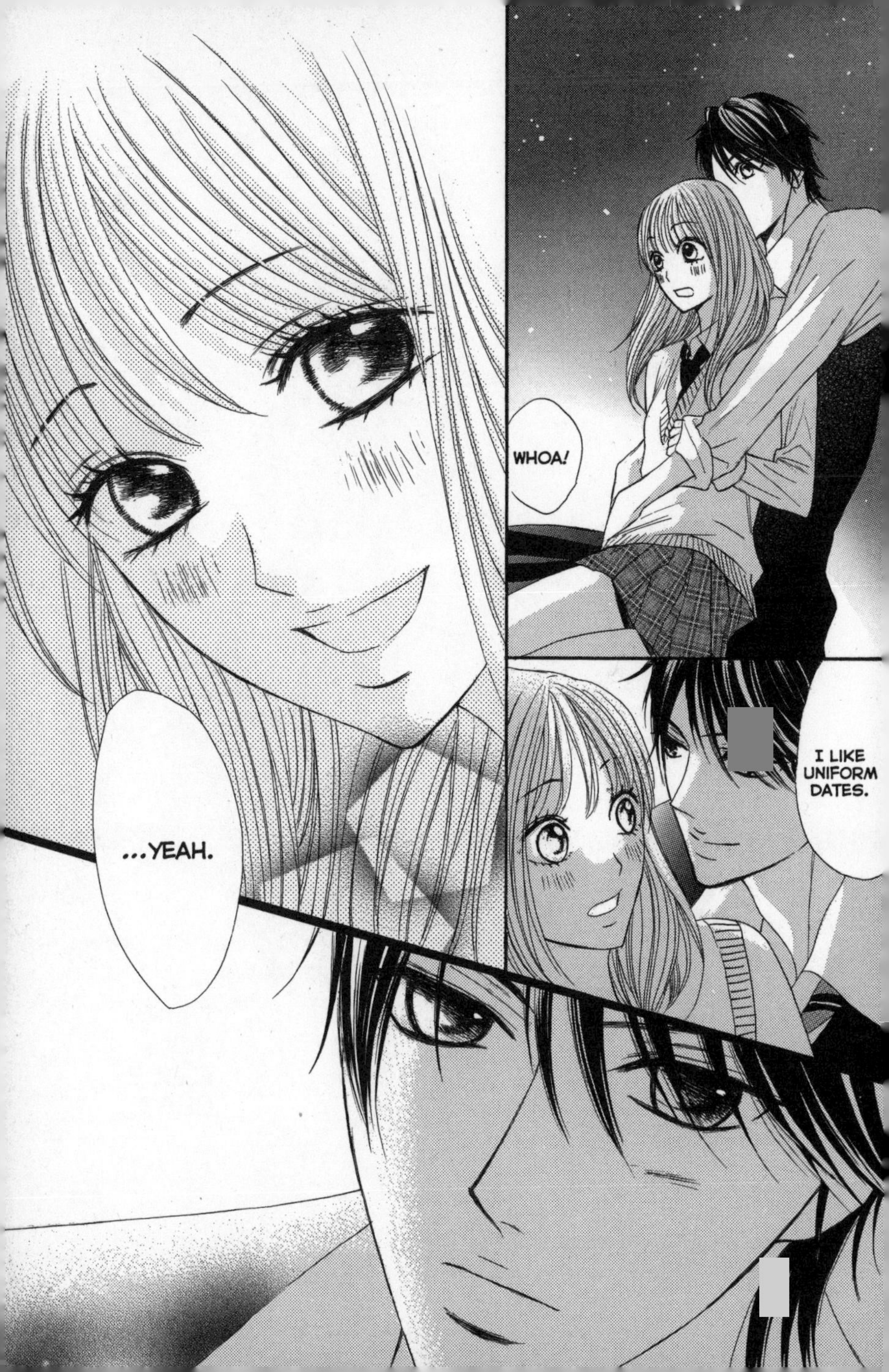
WHOA!
I LIKE UNIFORM DATES.
...YEAH.

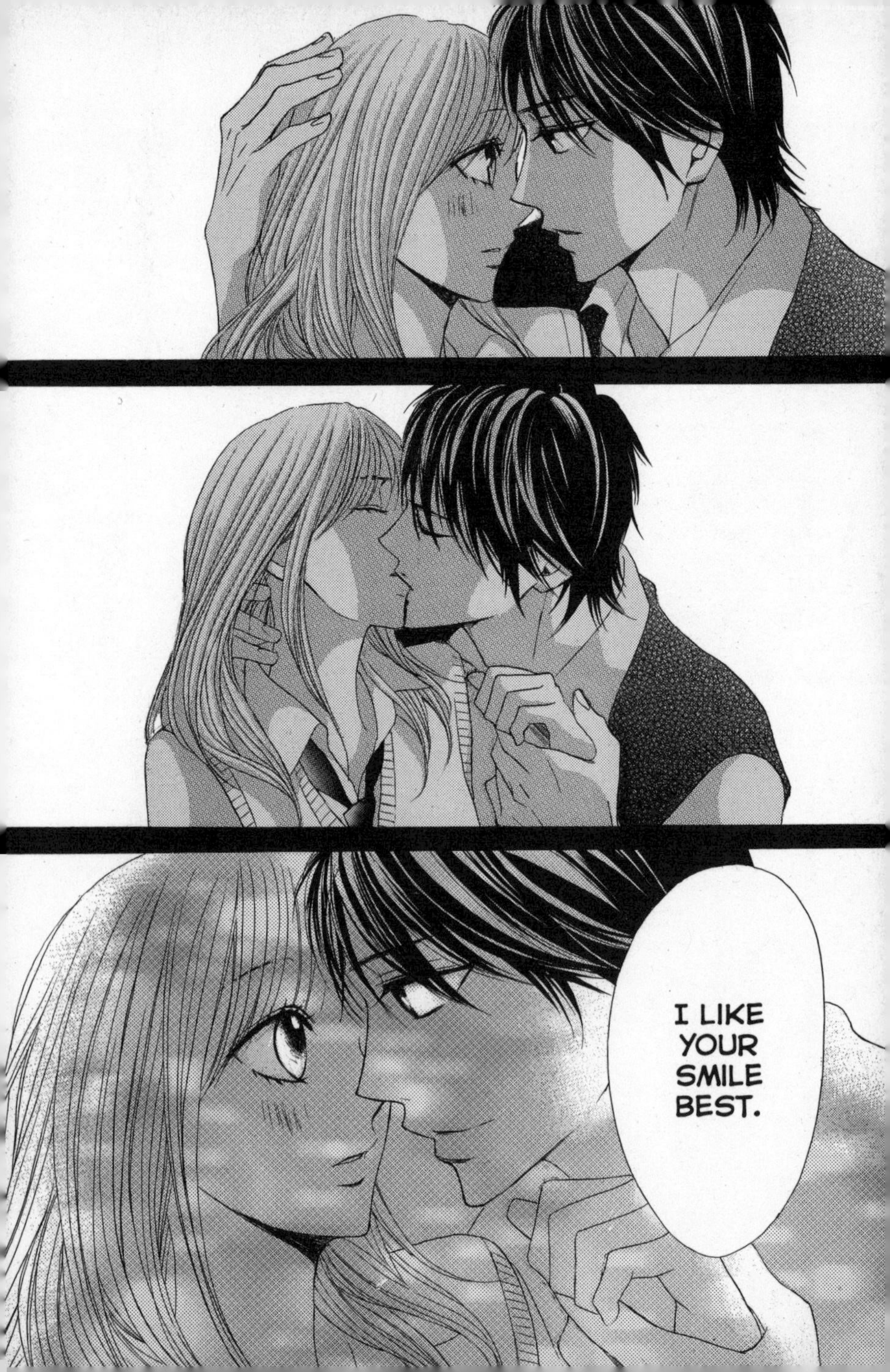
I LIKE YOUR SMILE BEST.

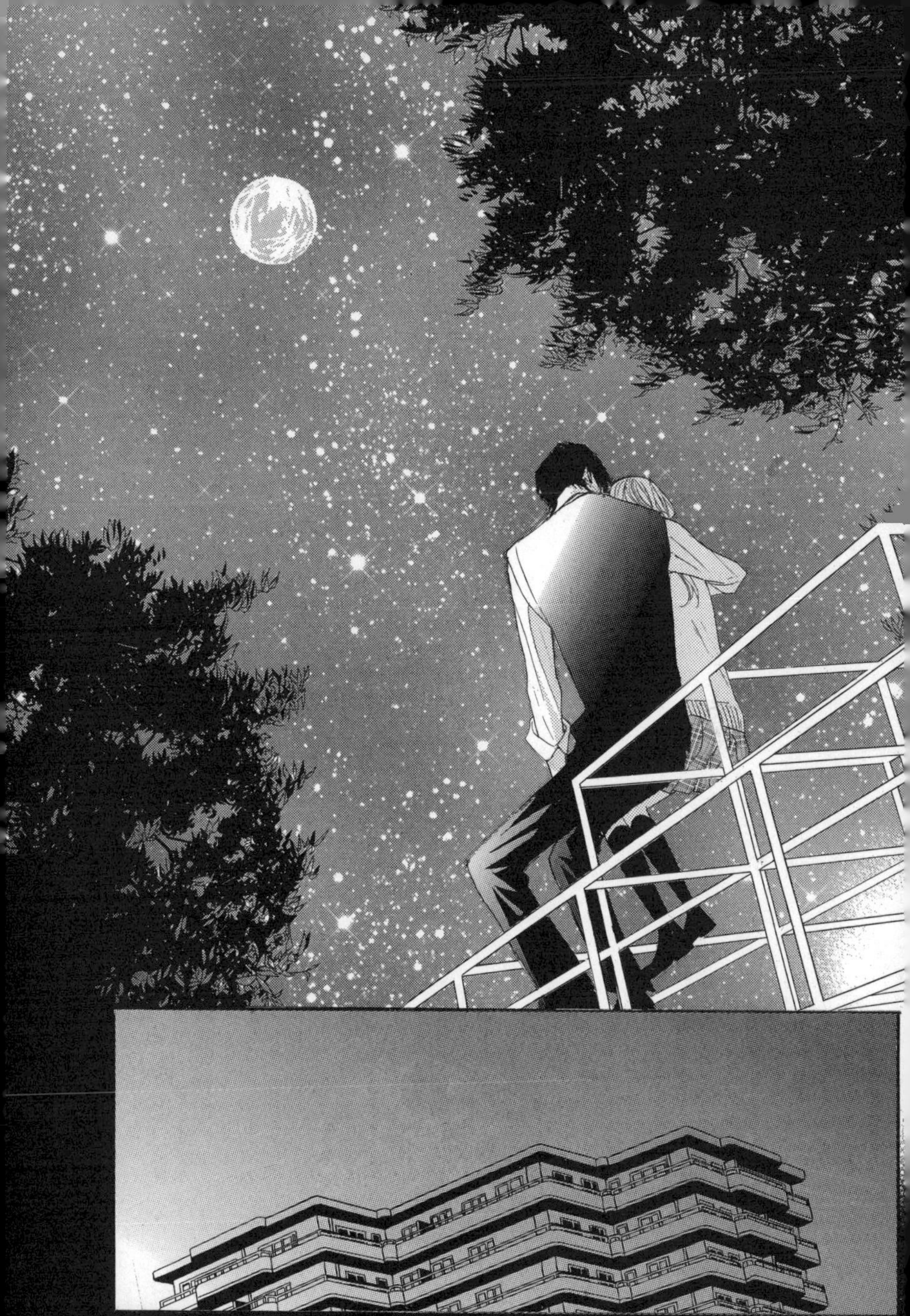

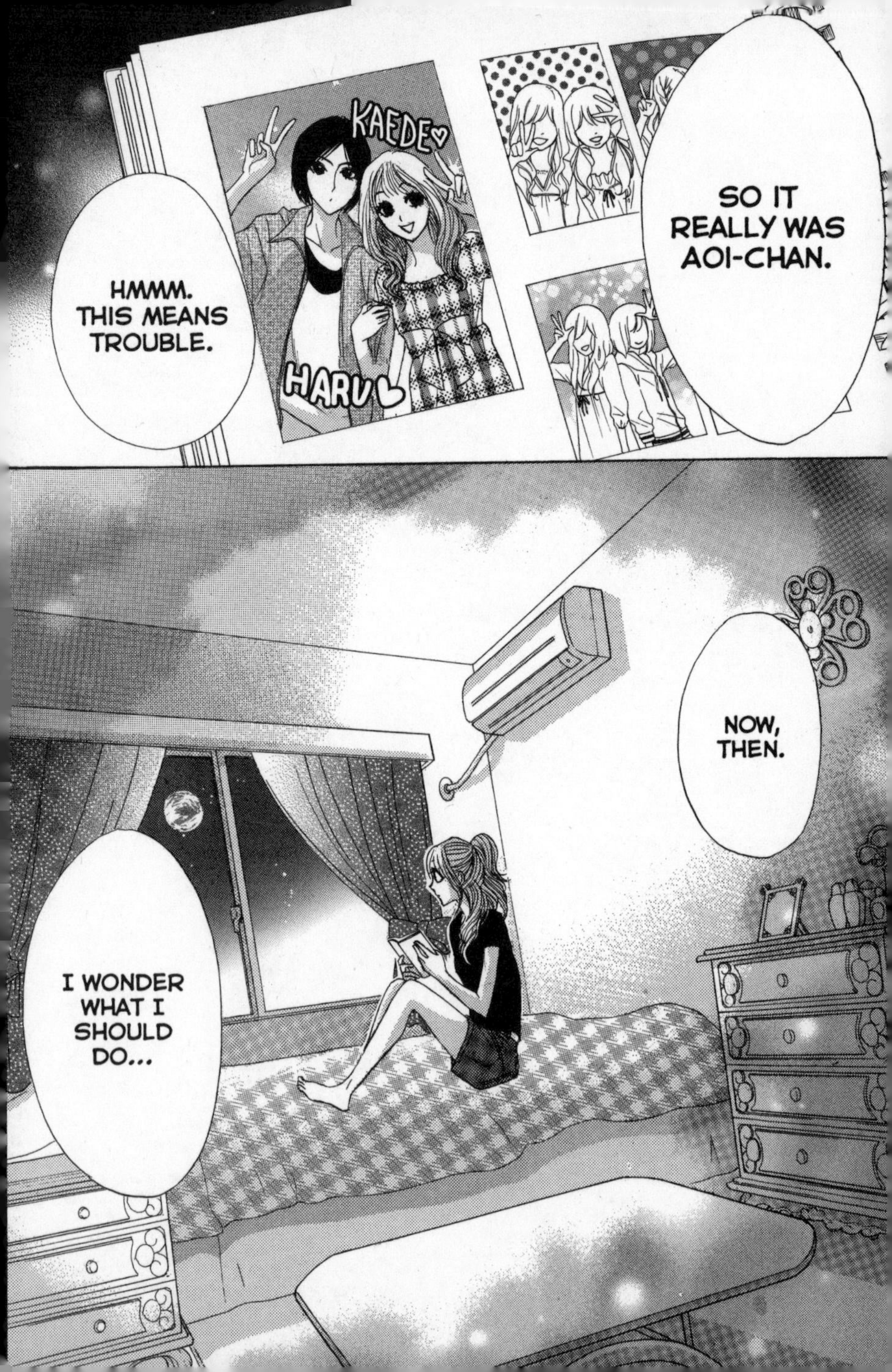
SO IT REALLY WAS AOI-CHAN.
KAEDE♥
HARU♥
HMMM. THIS MEANS TROUBLE.
NOW, THEN.
I WONDER WHAT I SHOULD DO...

L♥DK

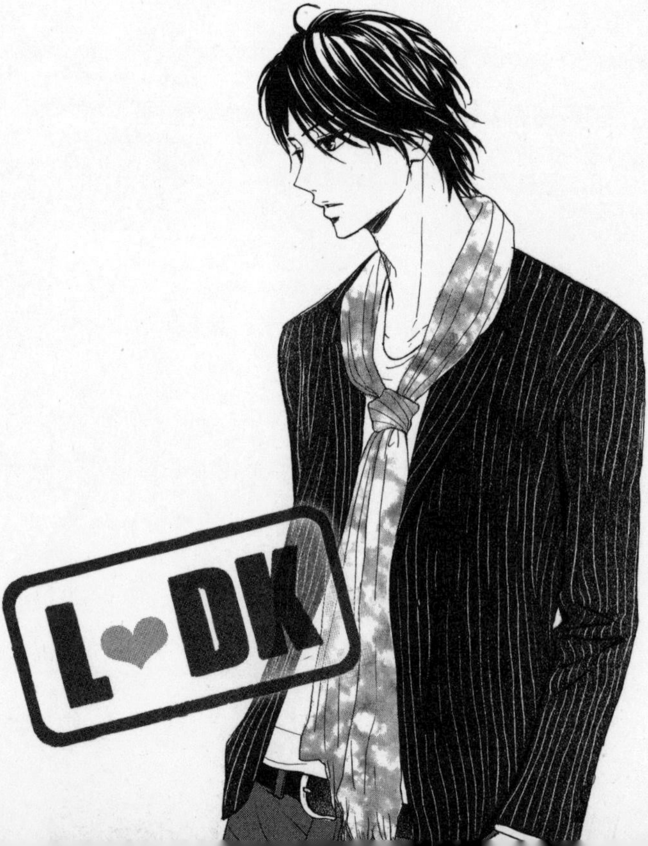
L♥DK

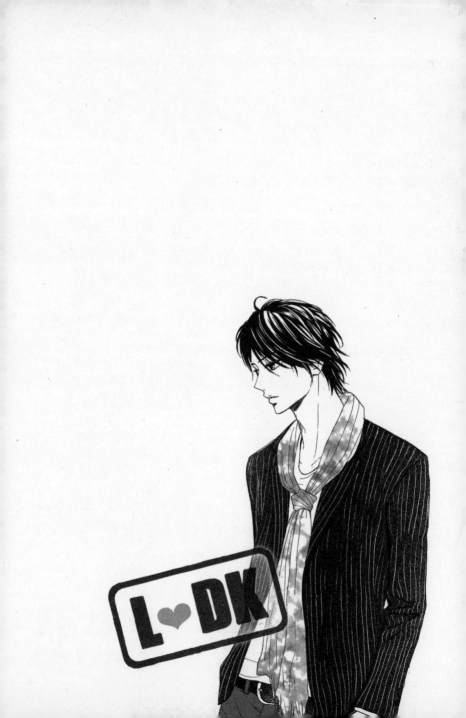

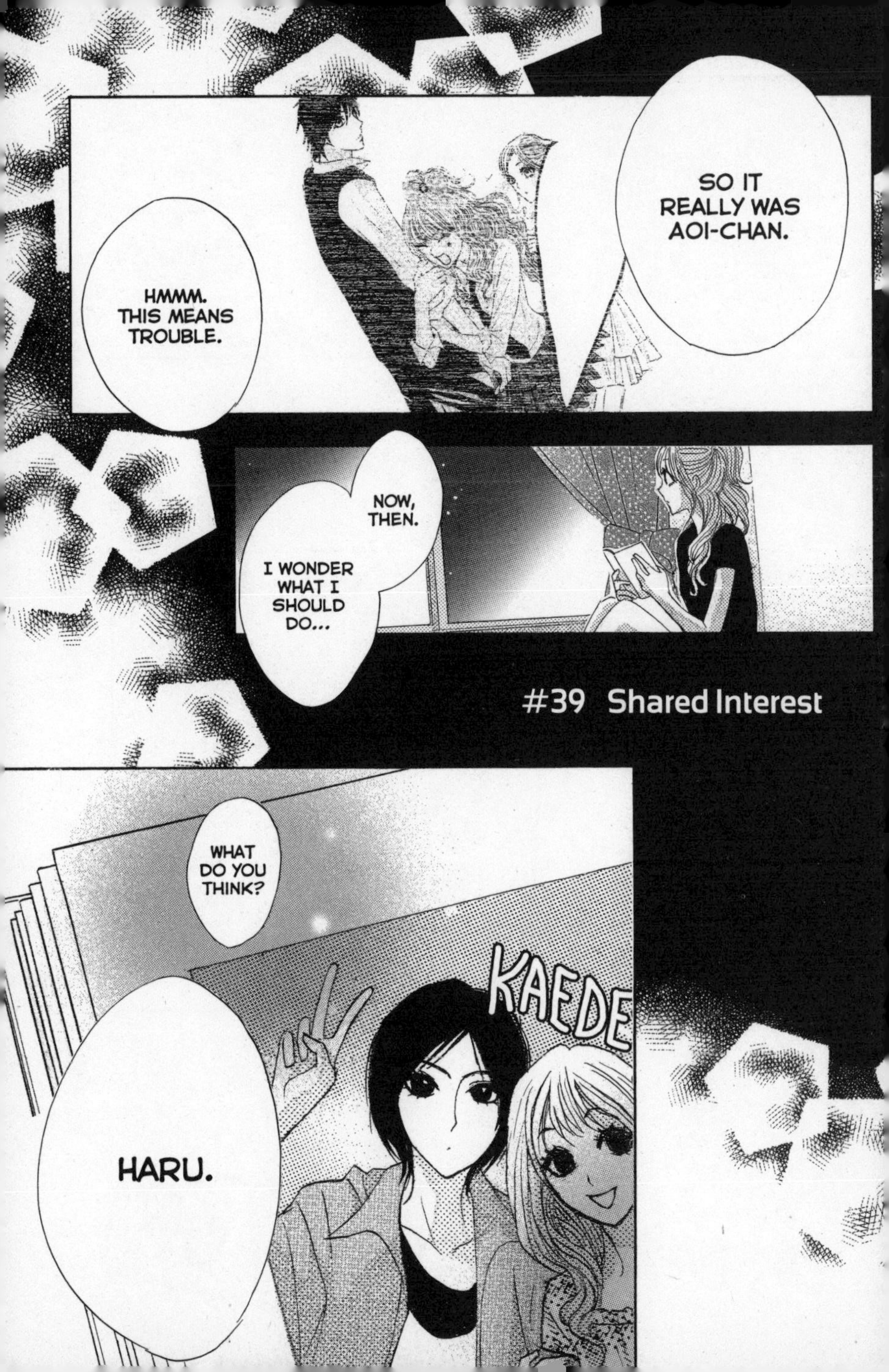
SO IT REALLY WAS AOI-CHAN.
HMMM. THIS MEANS TROUBLE.
NOW, THEN.
I WONDER WHAT I SHOULD DO...
#39 Shared Interest
WHAT DO YOU THINK?
KAEDE
HARU.

HM HM HM HMMMM. ♪
HM...
YOU SOUND HAPPY.
WHAT'RE YOUR PLANS TODAY?
I'M GOING TO HARU'S HOUSE!
WITH KAEDE-CHAN.
HA!
APPARENTLY HARU'S ALSO A REALLY GOOD COOK.
SHE ALSO HAS A LITTLE BROTHER.

L♥DK

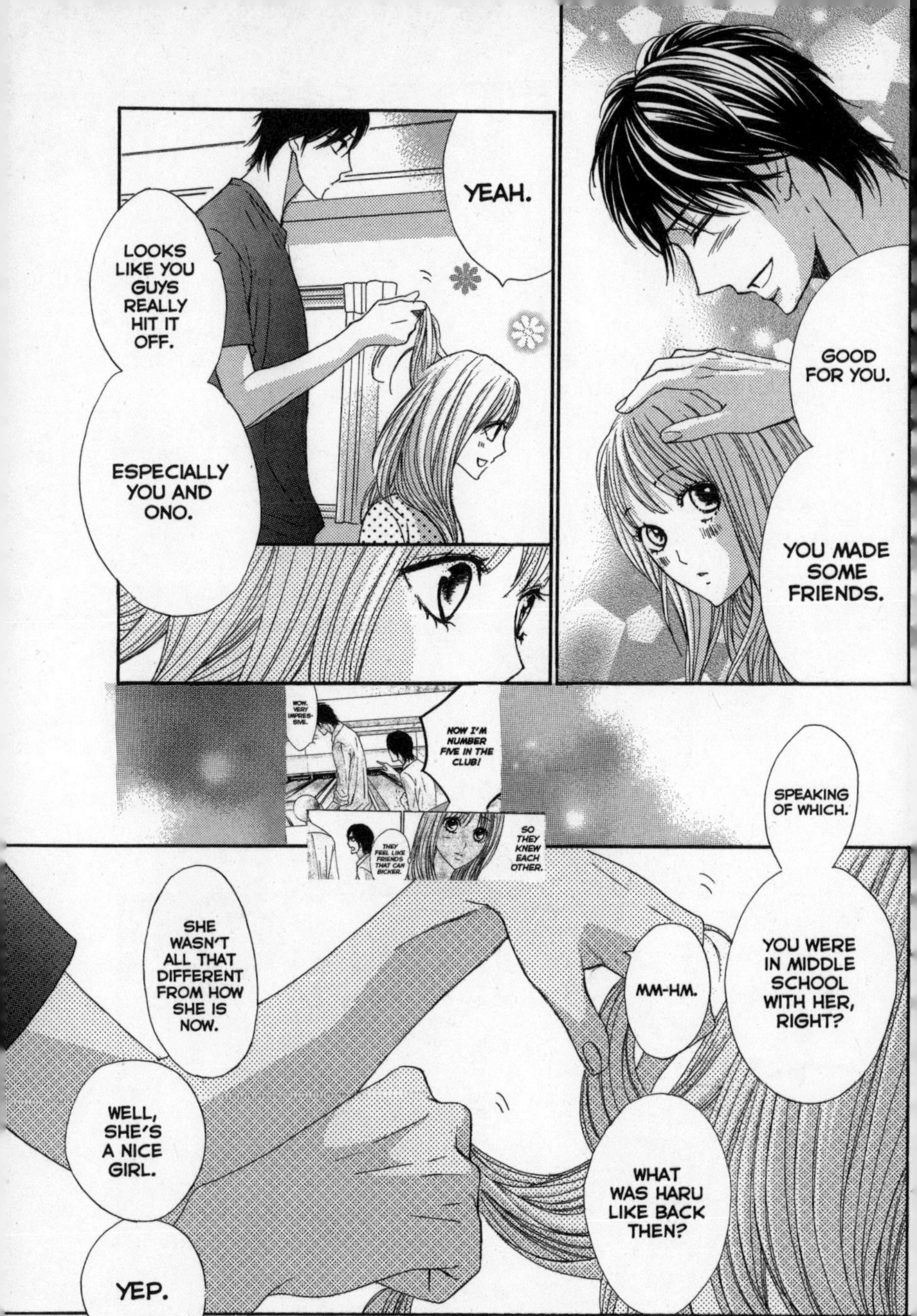
GOOD FOR YOU.
YOU MADE SOME FRIENDS.
YEAH.
LOOKS LIKE YOU GUYS REALLY HIT IT OFF.
ESPECIALLY YOU AND ONO.
NOW I'M NUMBER FIVE IN THE CLUB!
WOW. VERY IMPRESSIVE.
SO THEY KNEW EACH OTHER.
THEY FEEL LIKE FRIENDS THAT CAN BICKER.
SPEAKING OF WHICH.
YOU WERE IN MIDDLE SCHOOL WITH HER, RIGHT?
MM-HM.
WHAT WAS HARU LIKE BACK THEN?
SHE WASN'T ALL THAT DIFFERENT FROM HOW SHE IS NOW.
WELL, SHE'S A NICE GIRL.
YEP.

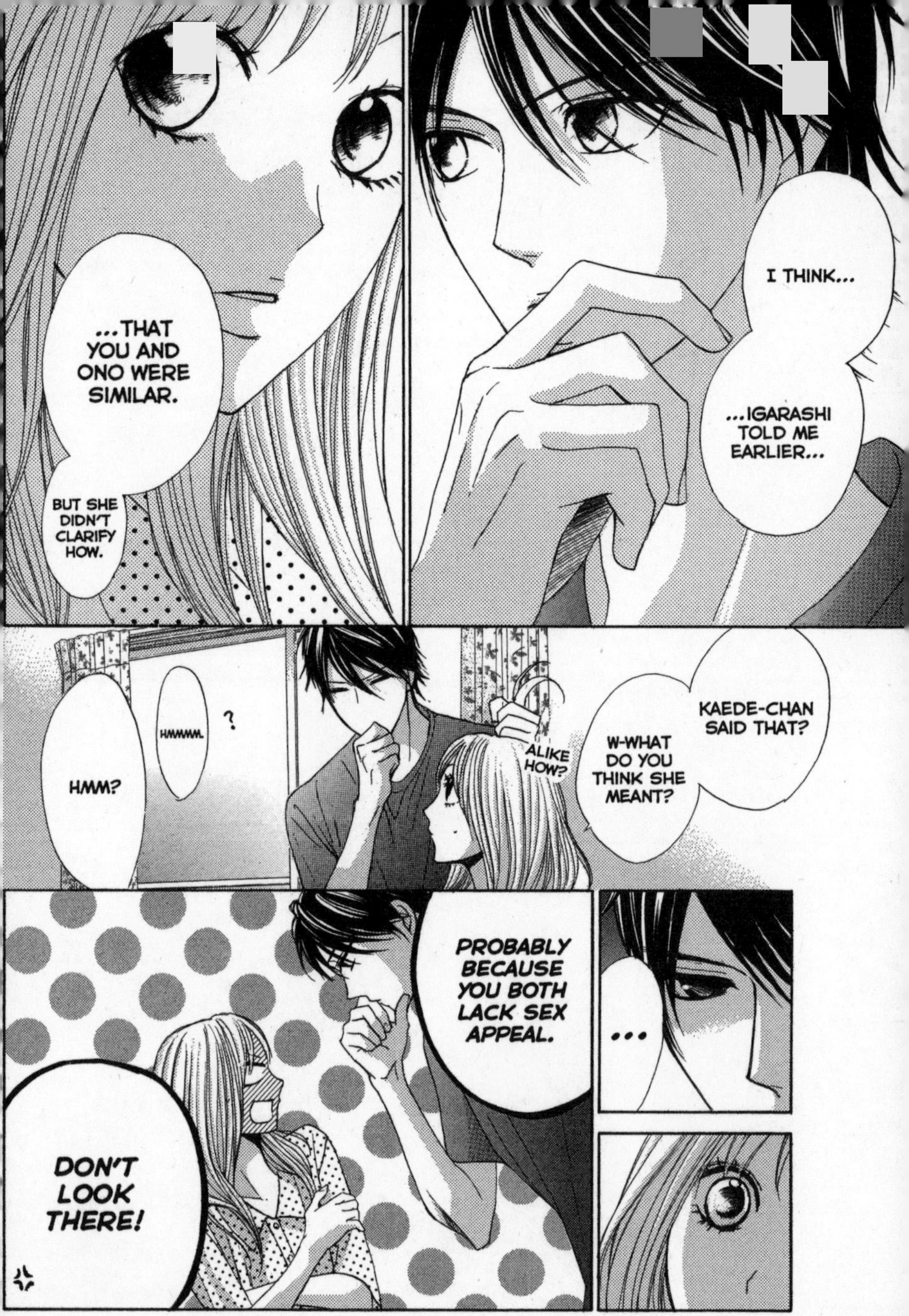
I THINK...
...IGARASHI TOLD ME EARLIER...
...THAT YOU AND ONO WERE SIMILAR.
BUT SHE DIDN'T CLARIFY HOW.
KAEDE-CHAN SAID THAT?
W-WHAT DO YOU THINK SHE MEANT?
ALIKE HOW?
?
HMMMM.
HMM?
...
PROBABLY BECAUSE YOU BOTH LACK SEX APPEAL.
DON'T LOOK THERE!

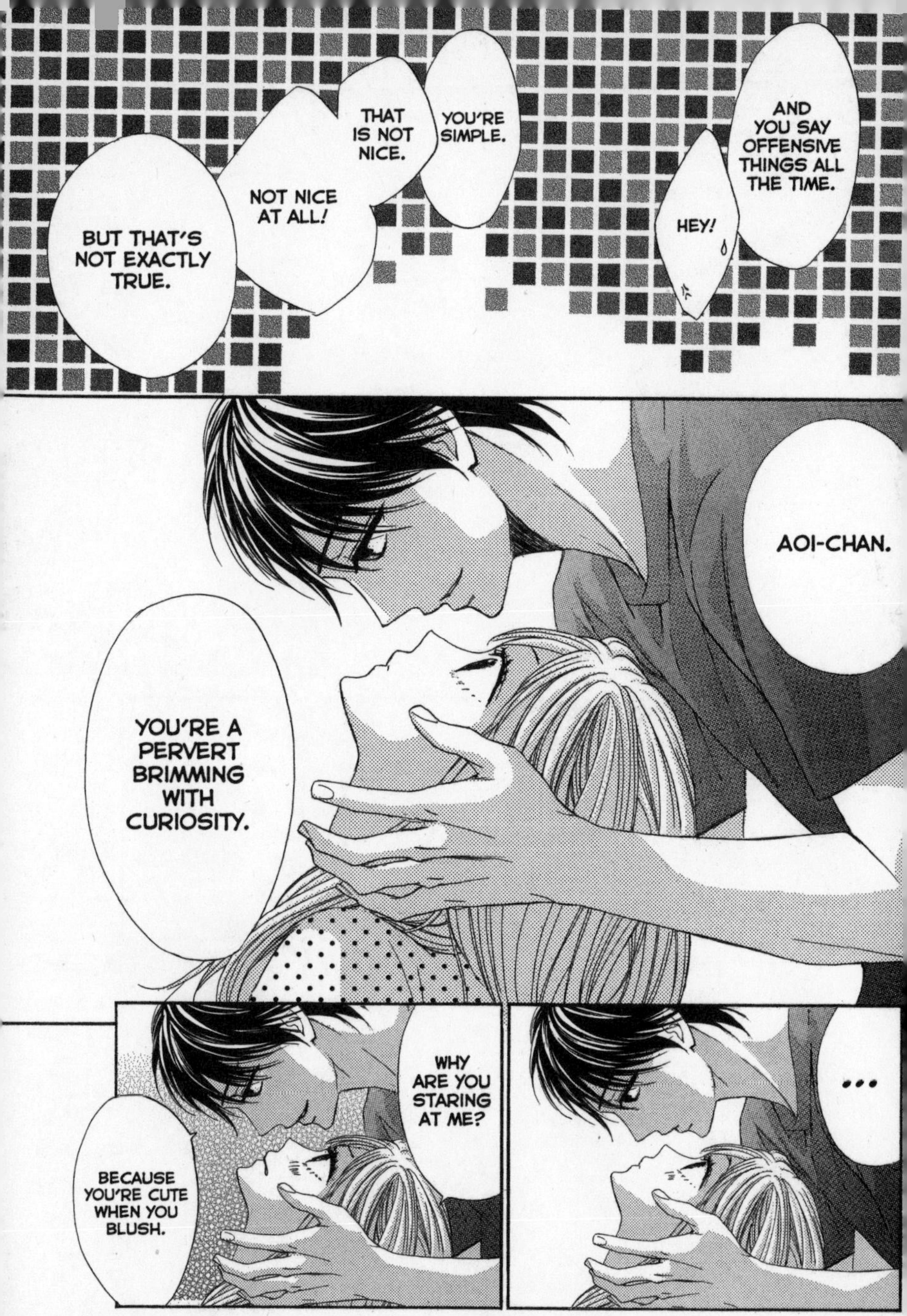
AND YOU SAY OFFENSIVE THINGS ALL THE TIME.
HEY!
YOU'RE SIMPLE.
THAT IS NOT NICE.
NOT NICE AT ALL!
BUT THAT'S NOT EXACTLY TRUE.
AOI-CHAN.
YOU'RE A PERVERT BRIMMING WITH CURIOSITY.
...
WHY ARE YOU STARING AT ME?
BECAUSE YOU'RE CUTE WHEN YOU BLUSH.

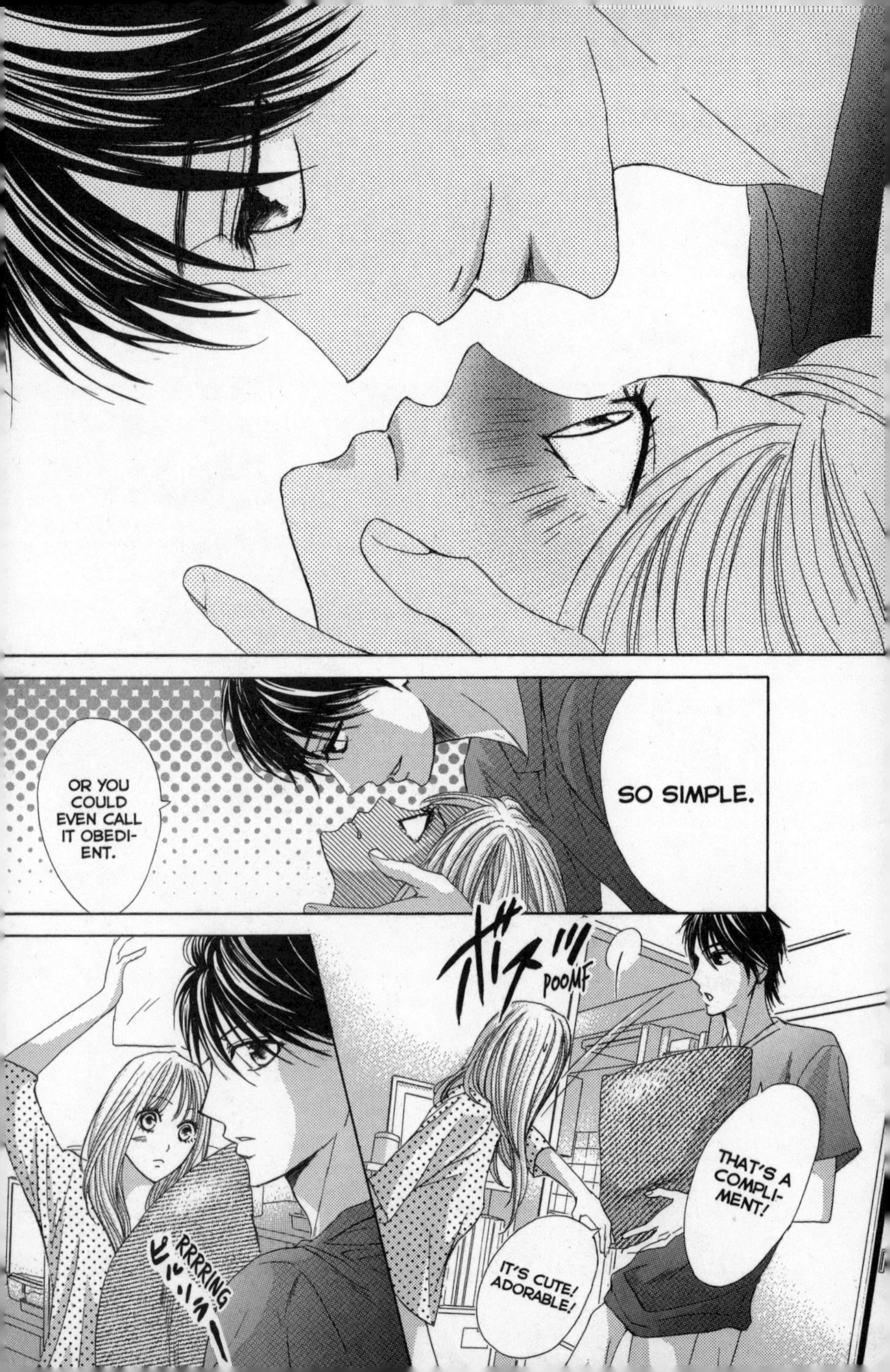
SO SIMPLE.
OR YOU COULD EVEN CALL IT OBEDI-ENT.
POOMF
THAT'S A COMPLI-MENT!
IT'S CUTE! ADORABLE!
RRRRING

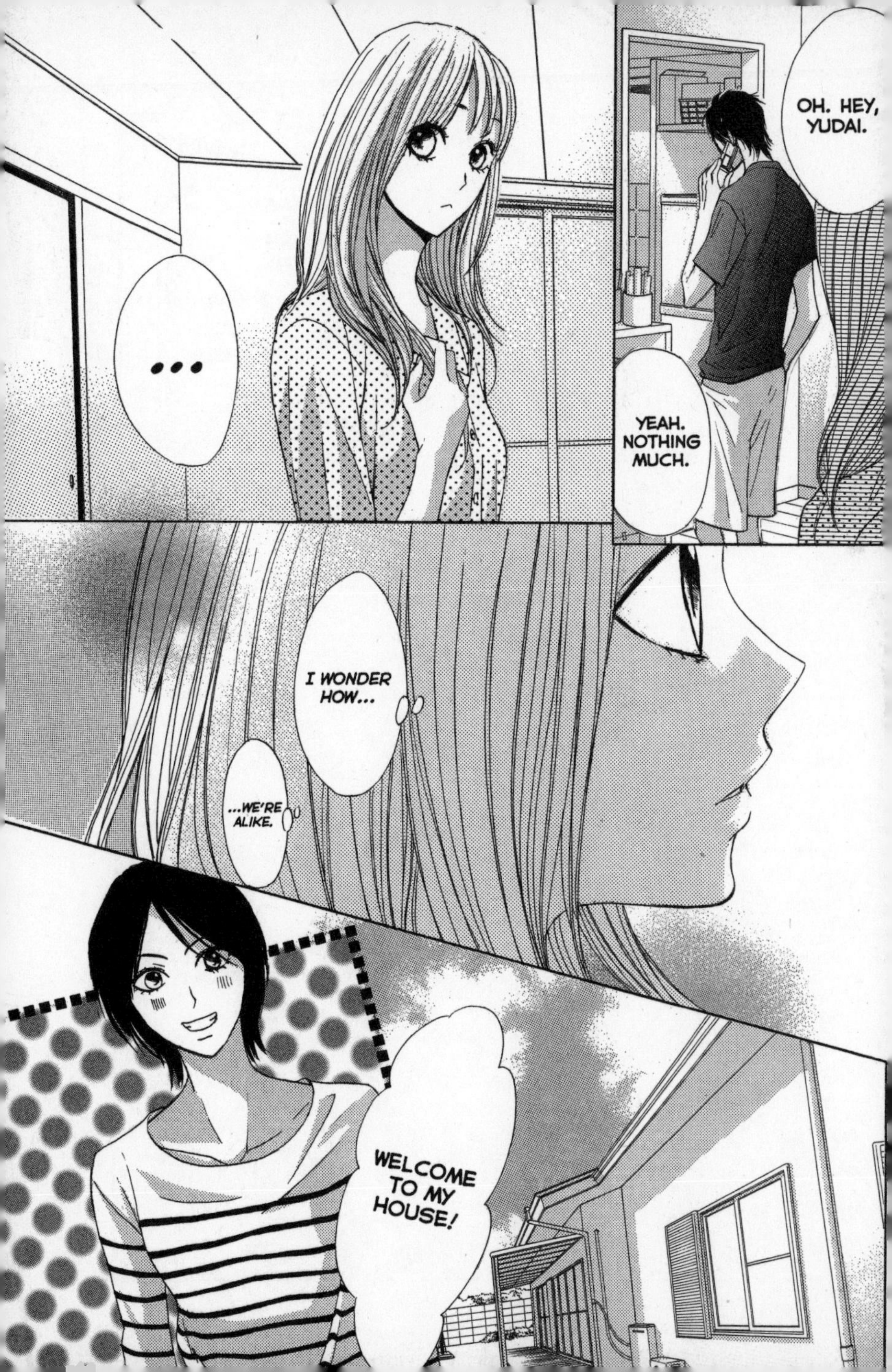
OH. HEY, YUDAI.
YEAH. NOTHING MUCH.
...
I WONDER HOW...
...WE'RE ALIKE.
WELCOME TO MY HOUSE!

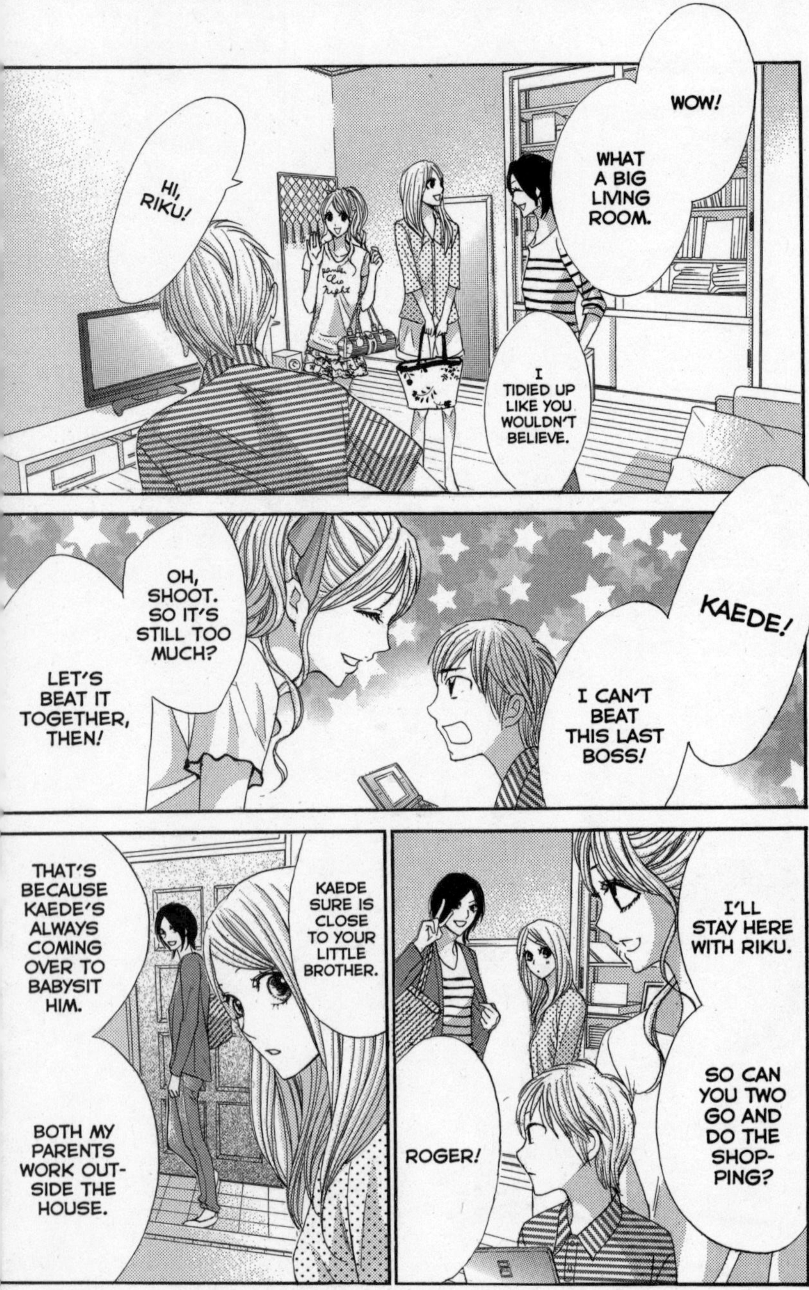
WOW!
WHAT A BIG LIVING ROOM.
HI, RIKU!
I TIDIED UP LIKE YOU WOULDN'T BELIEVE.
KAEDE!
I CAN'T BEAT THIS LAST BOSS!
OH, SHOOT. SO IT'S STILL TOO MUCH?
LET'S BEAT IT TOGETHER, THEN!
I'LL STAY HERE WITH RIKU.
SO CAN YOU TWO GO AND DO THE SHOP-PING?
ROGER!
KAEDE SURE IS CLOSE TO YOUR LITTLE BROTHER.
THAT'S BECAUSE KAEDE'S ALWAYS COMING OVER TO BABYSIT HIM.
BOTH MY PARENTS WORK OUT-SIDE THE HOUSE.

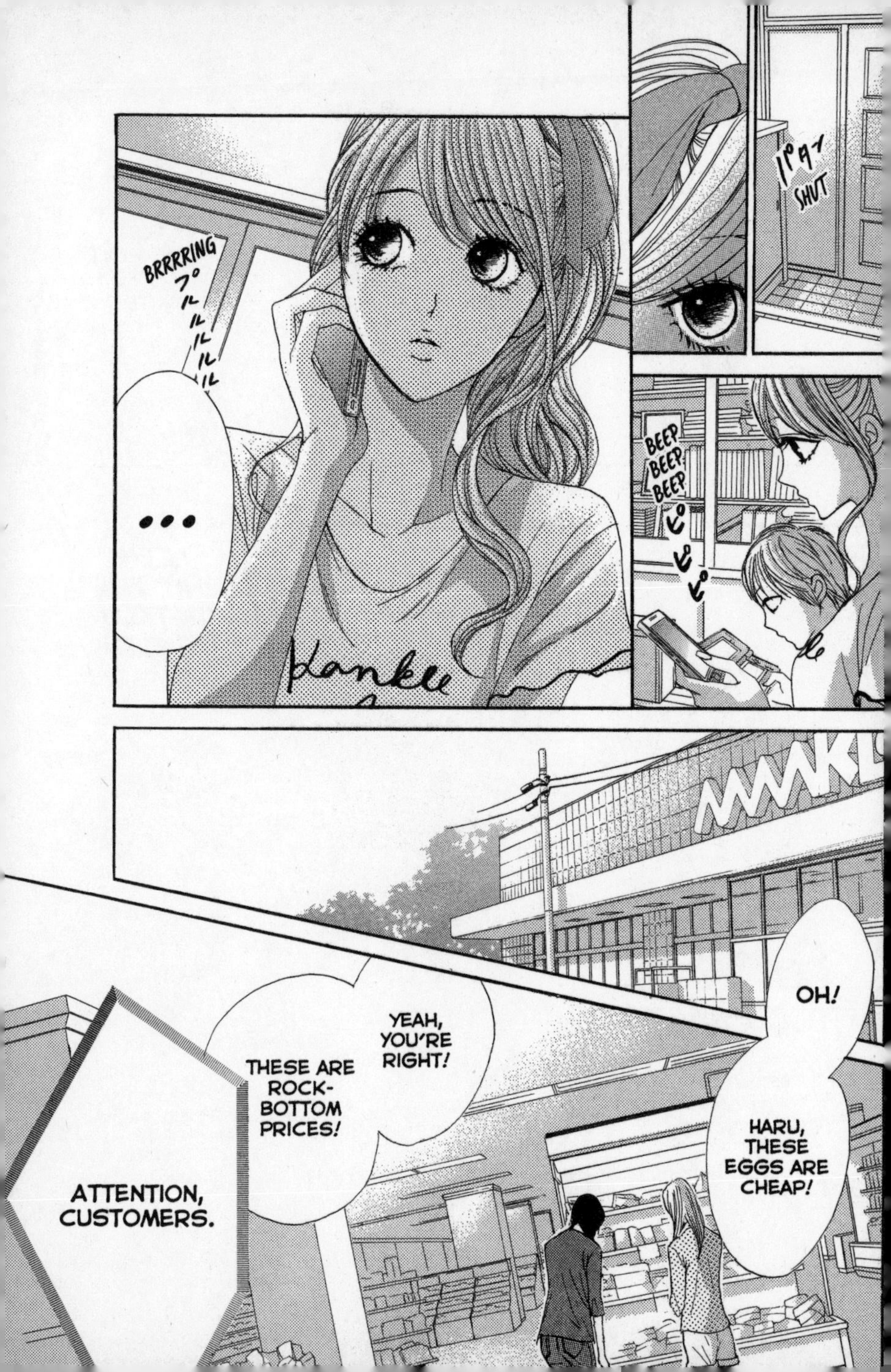
パタン
SHUT
BEEP BEEP BEEP
ピピピ
BRRRRING
プルルルル
...
OH!
HARU, THESE EGGS ARE CHEAP!
YEAH, YOU'RE RIGHT!
THESE ARE ROCK-BOTTOM PRICES!
ATTENTION, CUSTOMERS.

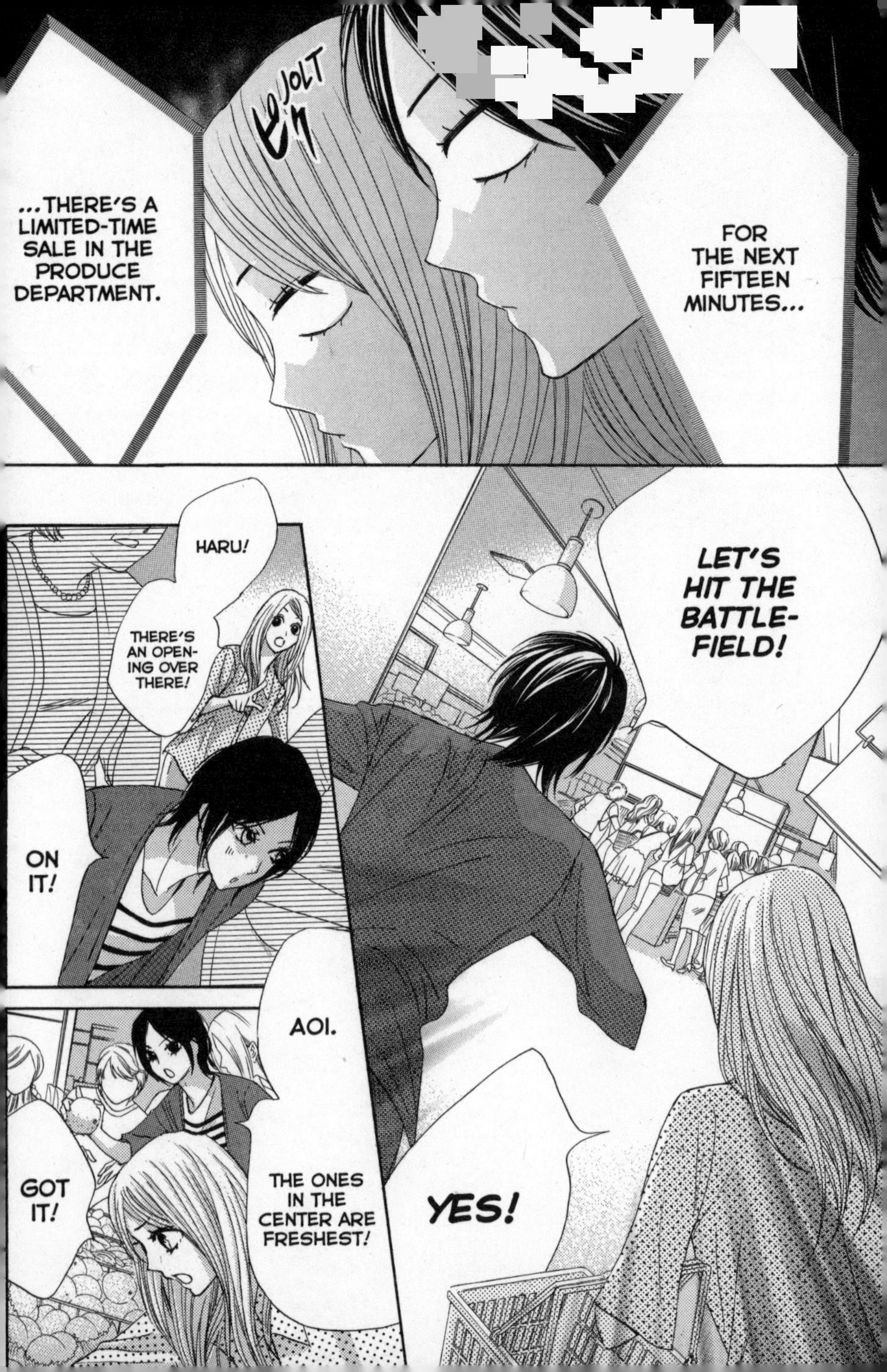
JOLT
FOR THE NEXT FIFTEEN MINUTES...
...THERE'S A LIMITED-TIME SALE IN THE PRODUCE DEPARTMENT.
LET'S HIT THE BATTLE-FIELD!
YES!
HARU!
THERE'S AN OPEN-ING OVER THERE!
ON IT!
AOI.
THE ONES IN THE CENTER ARE FRESHEST!
GOT IT!

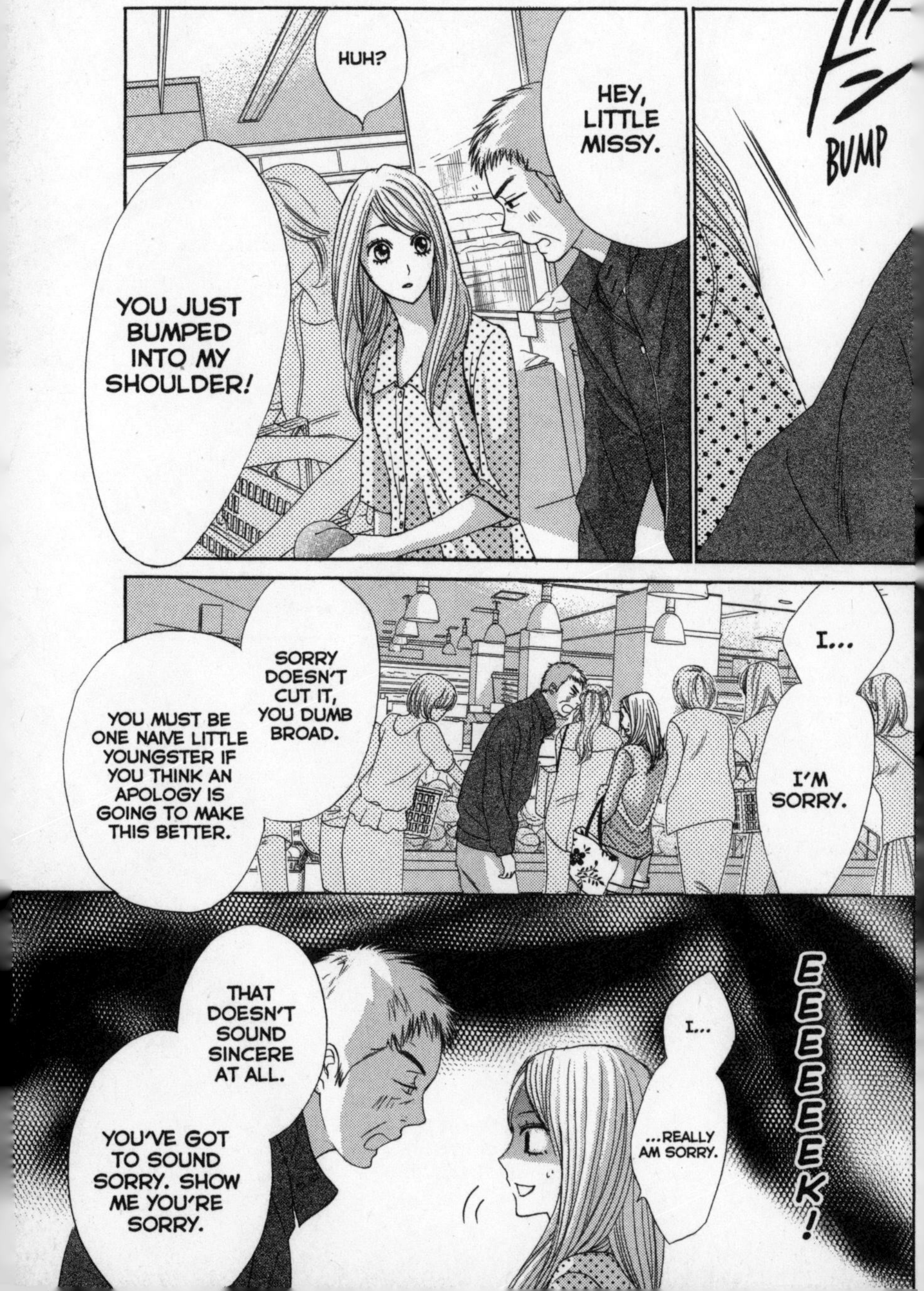
BUMP
HEY, LITTLE MISSY.
HUH?
YOU JUST BUMPED INTO MY SHOULDER!
I...
I'M SORRY.
SORRY DOESN'T CUT IT, YOU DUMB BROAD.
YOU MUST BE ONE NAIVE LITTLE YOUNGSTER IF YOU THINK AN APOLOGY IS GOING TO MAKE THIS BETTER.
EEEEEEK!
I...
...REALLY AM SORRY.
THAT DOESN'T SOUND SINCERE AT ALL.
YOU'VE GOT TO SOUND SORRY. SHOW ME YOU'RE SORRY.

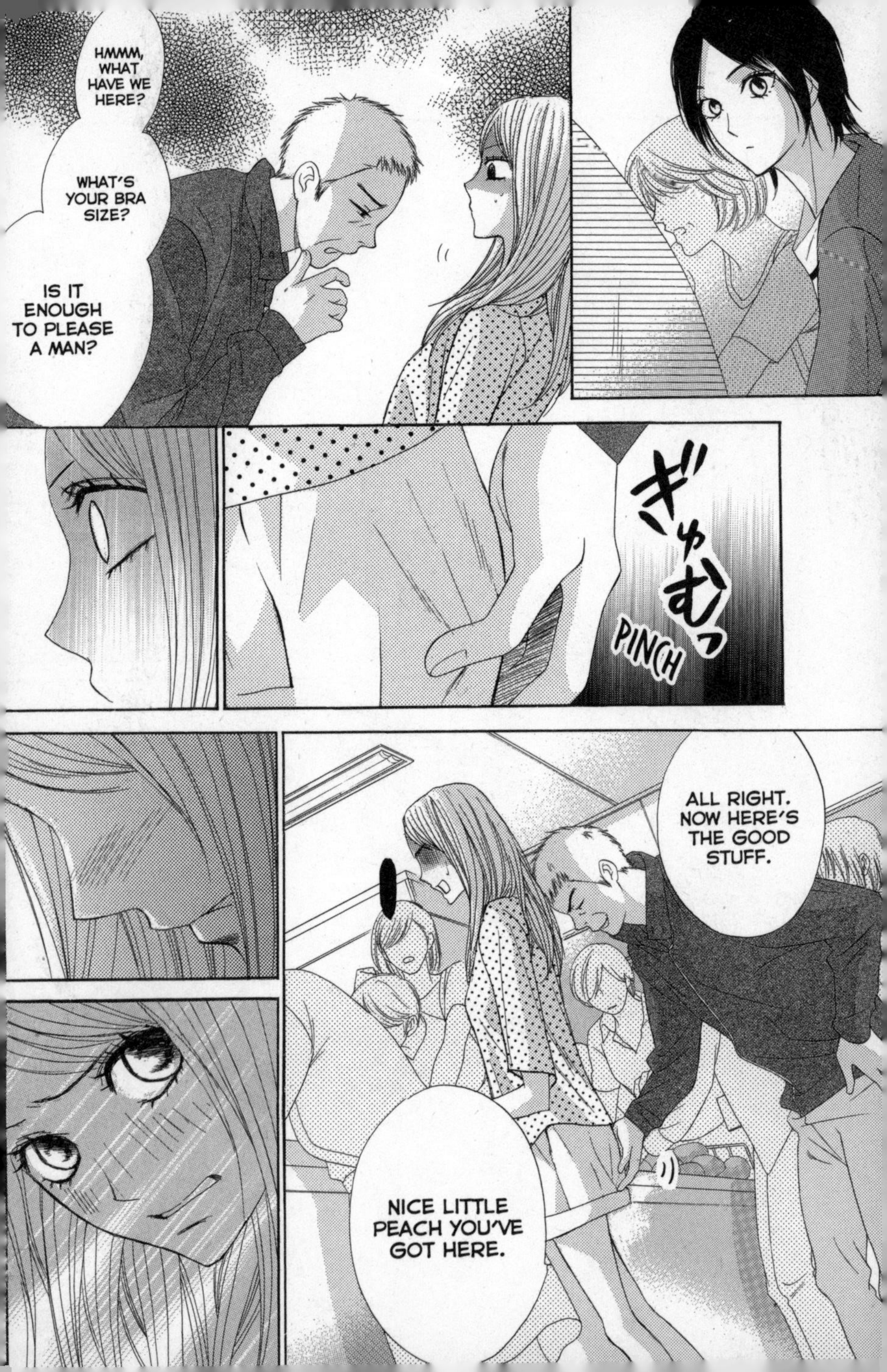
HMMM, WHAT HAVE WE HERE?
WHAT'S YOUR BRA SIZE?
IS IT ENOUGH TO PLEASE A MAN?
ぎゅむっ
PINCH
ALL RIGHT. NOW HERE'S THE GOOD STUFF.
NICE LITTLE PEACH YOU'VE GOT HERE.

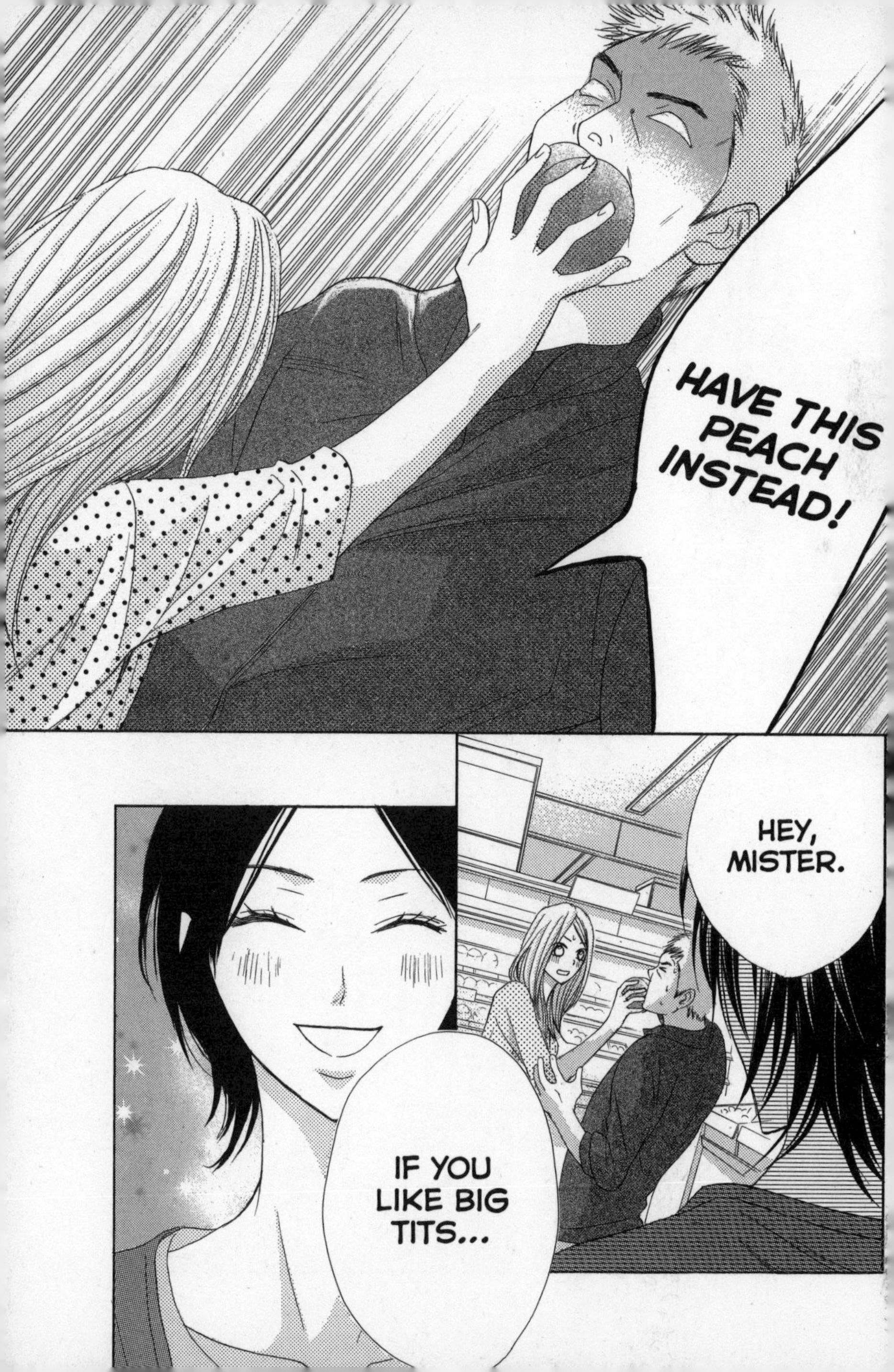
HAVE THIS PEACH INSTEAD!
HEY, MISTER.
IF YOU LIKE BIG TITS...

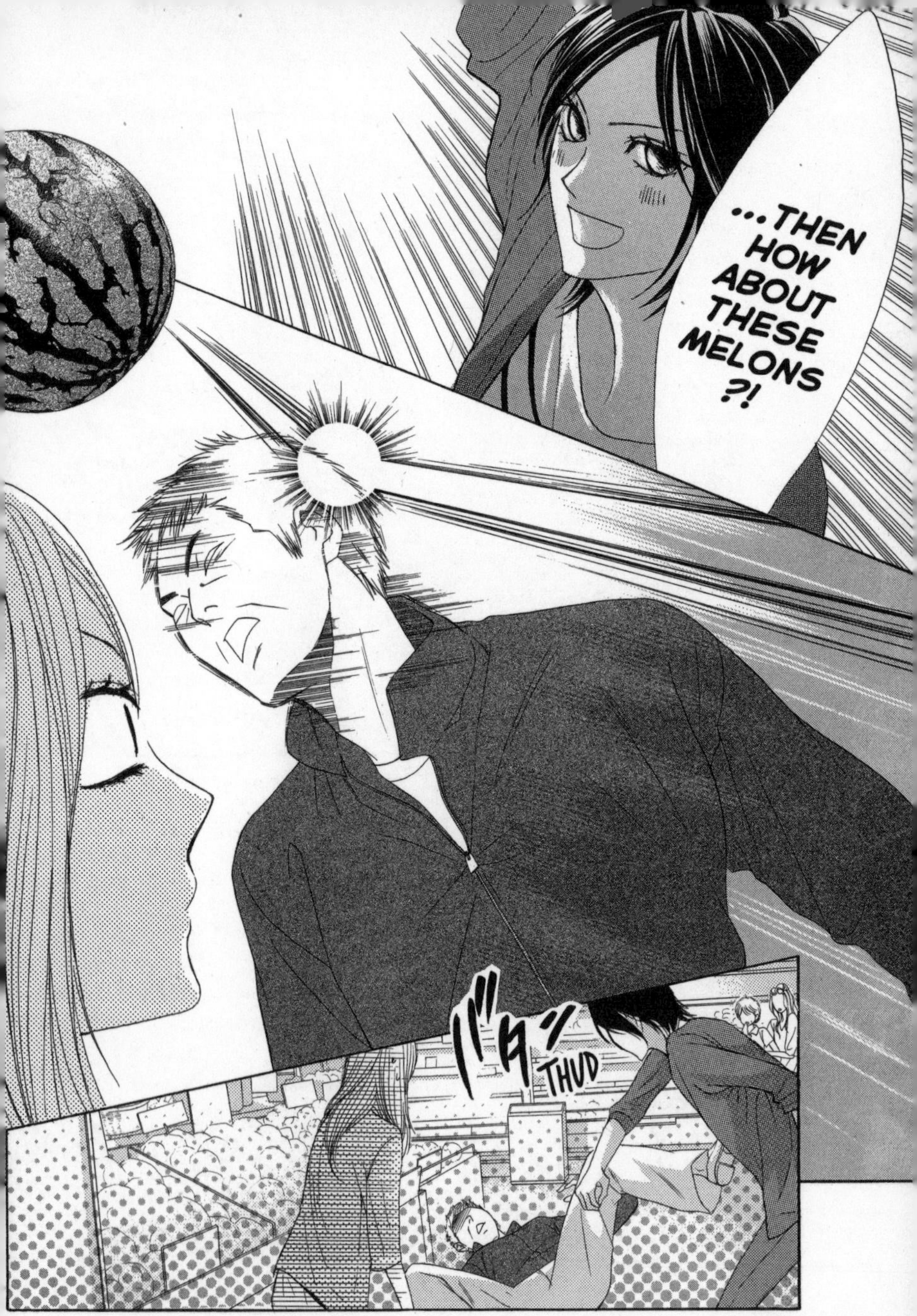
...THEN HOW ABOUT THESE MELONS ?!
バタン
THUD

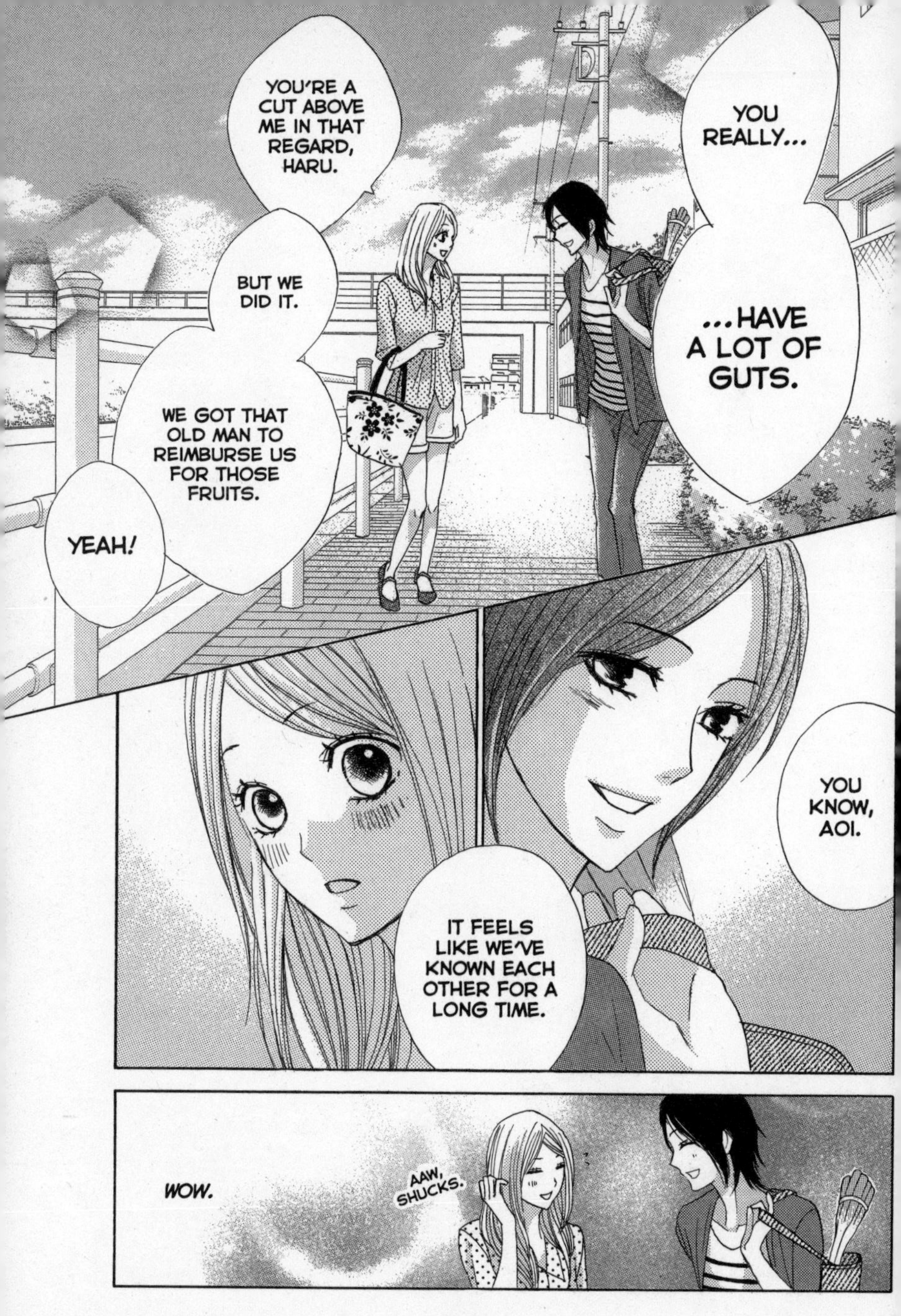
YOU REALLY...
...HAVE A LOT OF GUTS.
YOU'RE A CUT ABOVE ME IN THAT REGARD, HARU.
BUT WE DID IT.
WE GOT THAT OLD MAN TO REIMBURSE US FOR THOSE FRUITS.
YEAH!
YOU KNOW, AOI.
IT FEELS LIKE WE'VE KNOWN EACH OTHER FOR A LONG TIME.
AAW, SHUCKS.
WOW.

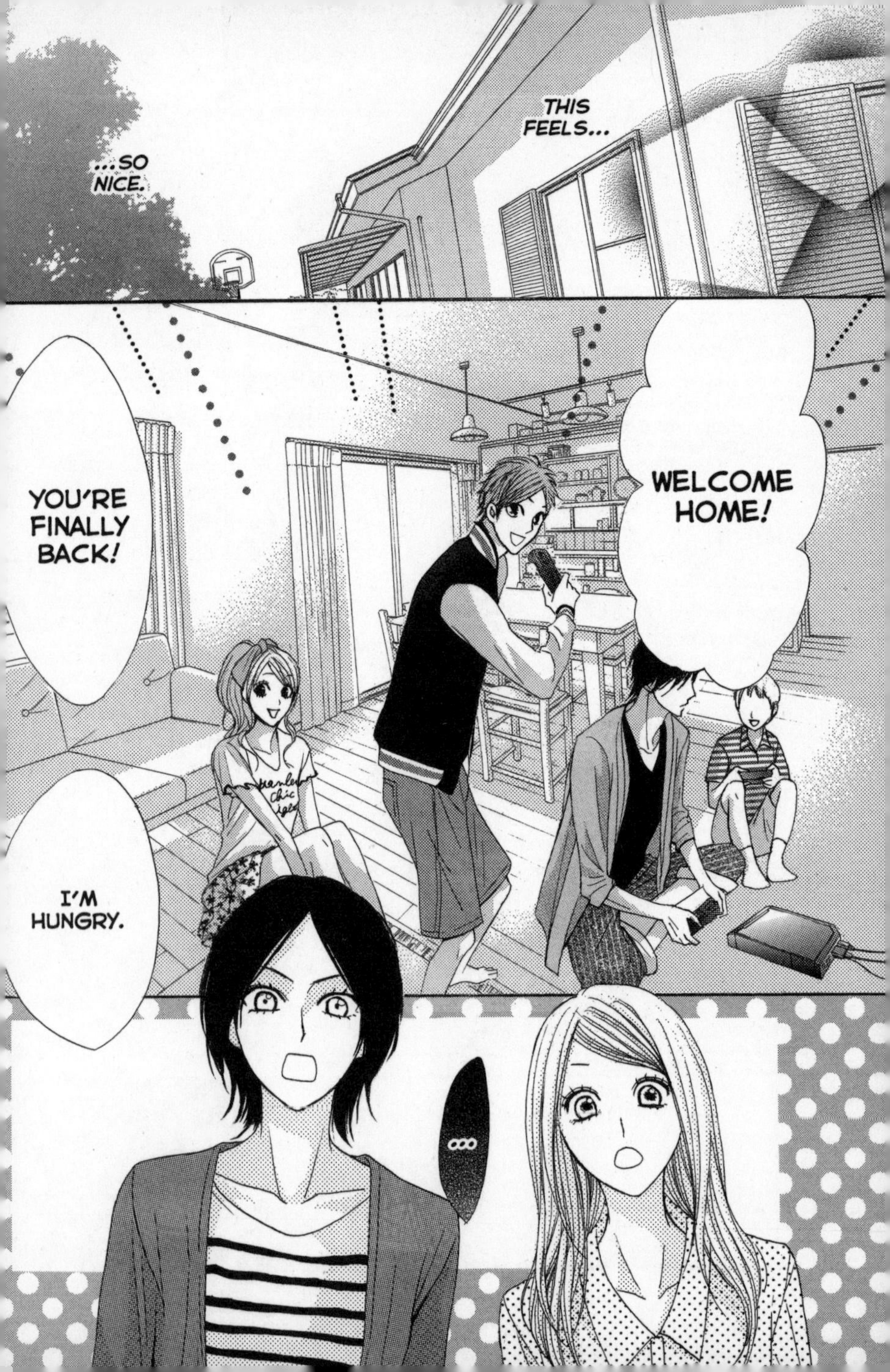
THIS FEELS...
...SO NICE.
WELCOME HOME!
YOU'RE FINALLY BACK!
I'M HUNGRY.
...

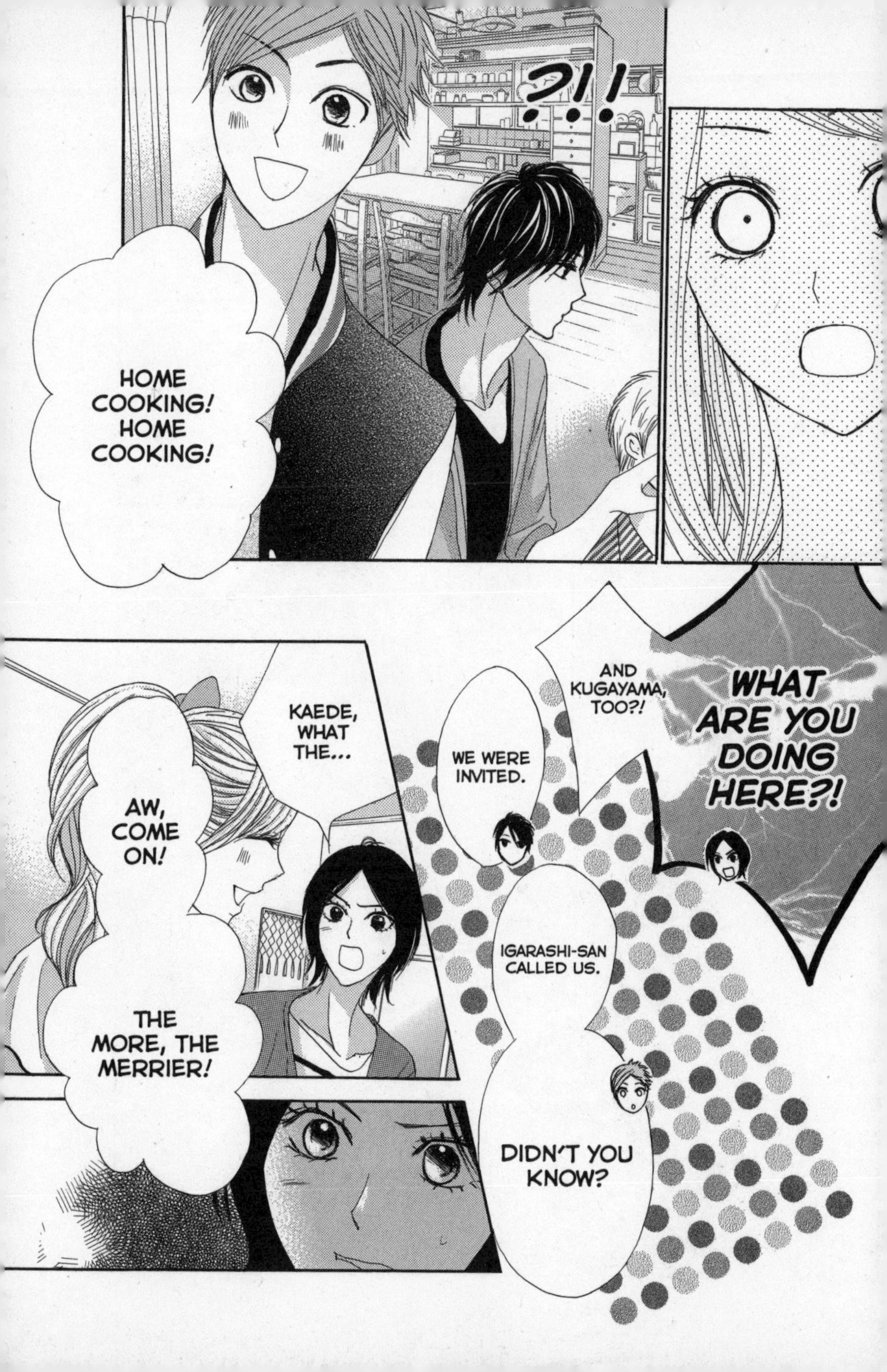
?!!
HOME COOKING! HOME COOKING!
WHAT ARE YOU DOING HERE?!
AND KUGAYAMA, TOO?!
WE WERE INVITED.
IGARASHI-SAN CALLED US.
DIDN'T YOU KNOW?
KAEDE, WHAT THE...
AW, COME ON!
THE MORE, THE MERRIER!

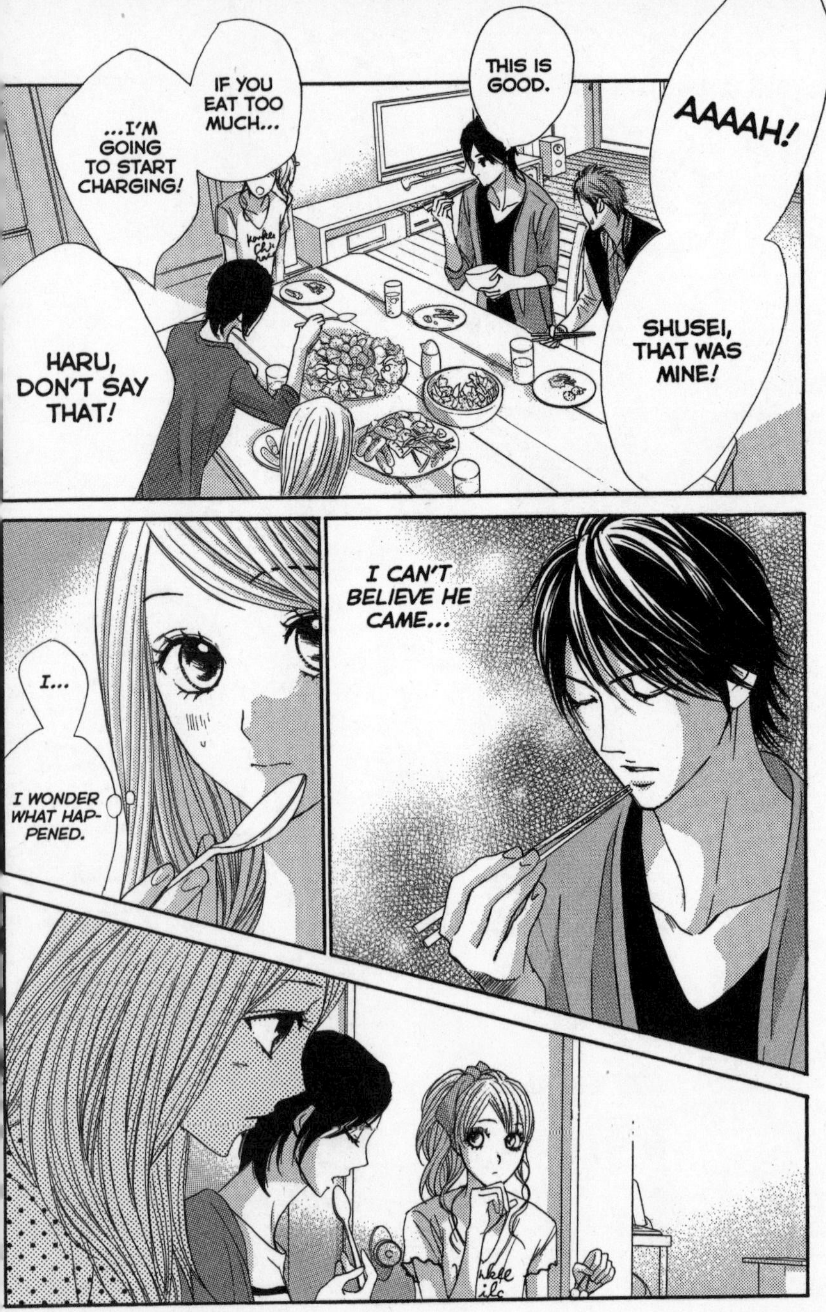
AAAAH!
SHUSEI, THAT WAS MINE!
THIS IS GOOD.
IF YOU EAT TOO MUCH...
...I'M GOING TO START CHARGING!
HARU, DON'T SAY THAT!
I CAN'T BELIEVE HE CAME...
I...
I WONDER WHAT HAPPENED.

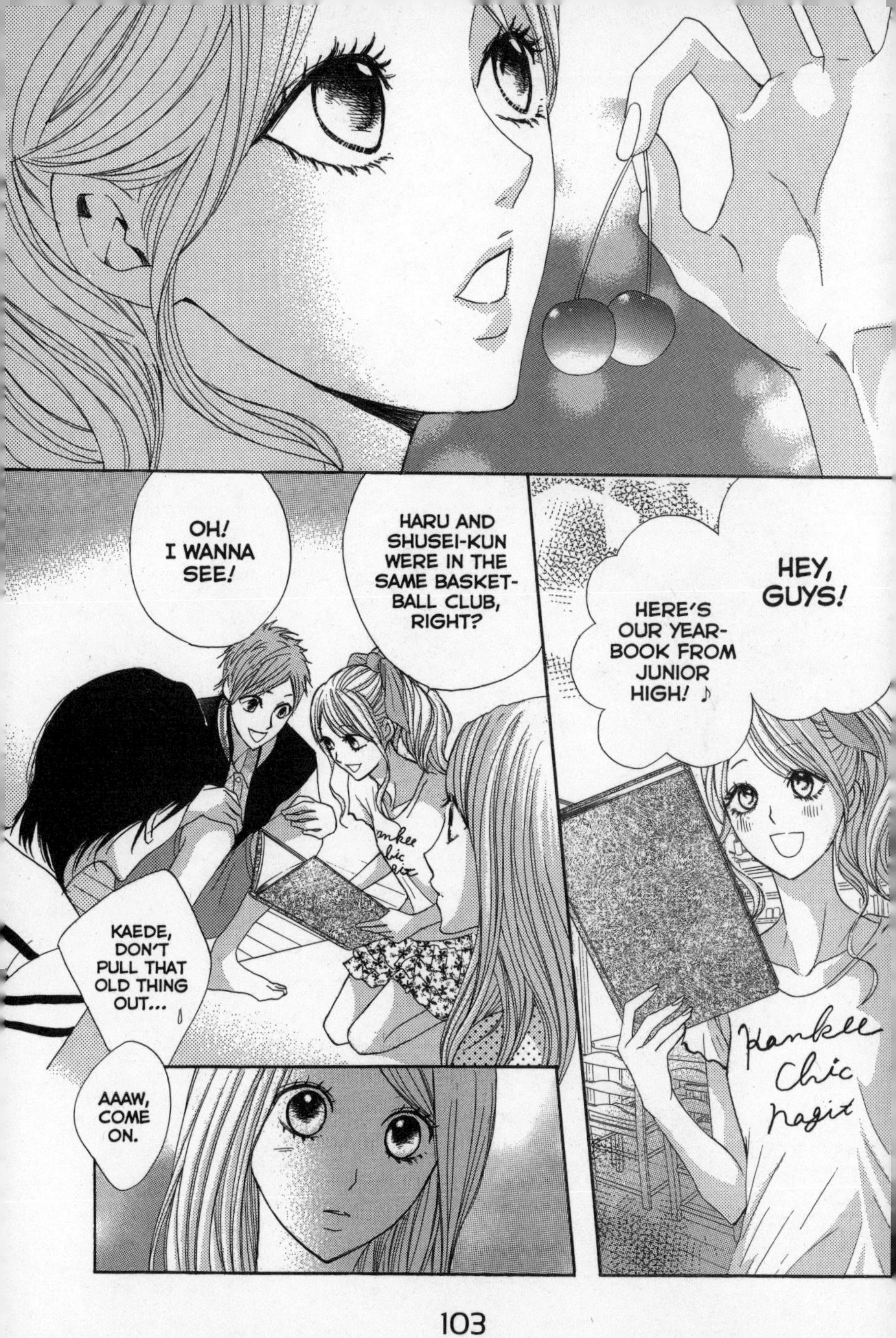
HEY, GUYS!
HERE'S OUR YEAR-BOOK FROM JUNIOR HIGH! ♪
HARU AND SHUSEI-KUN WERE IN THE SAME BASKET-BALL CLUB, RIGHT?
OH! I WANNA SEE!
KAEDE, DON'T PULL THAT OLD THING OUT...
AAAW, COME ON.
Hankee Chic nagit

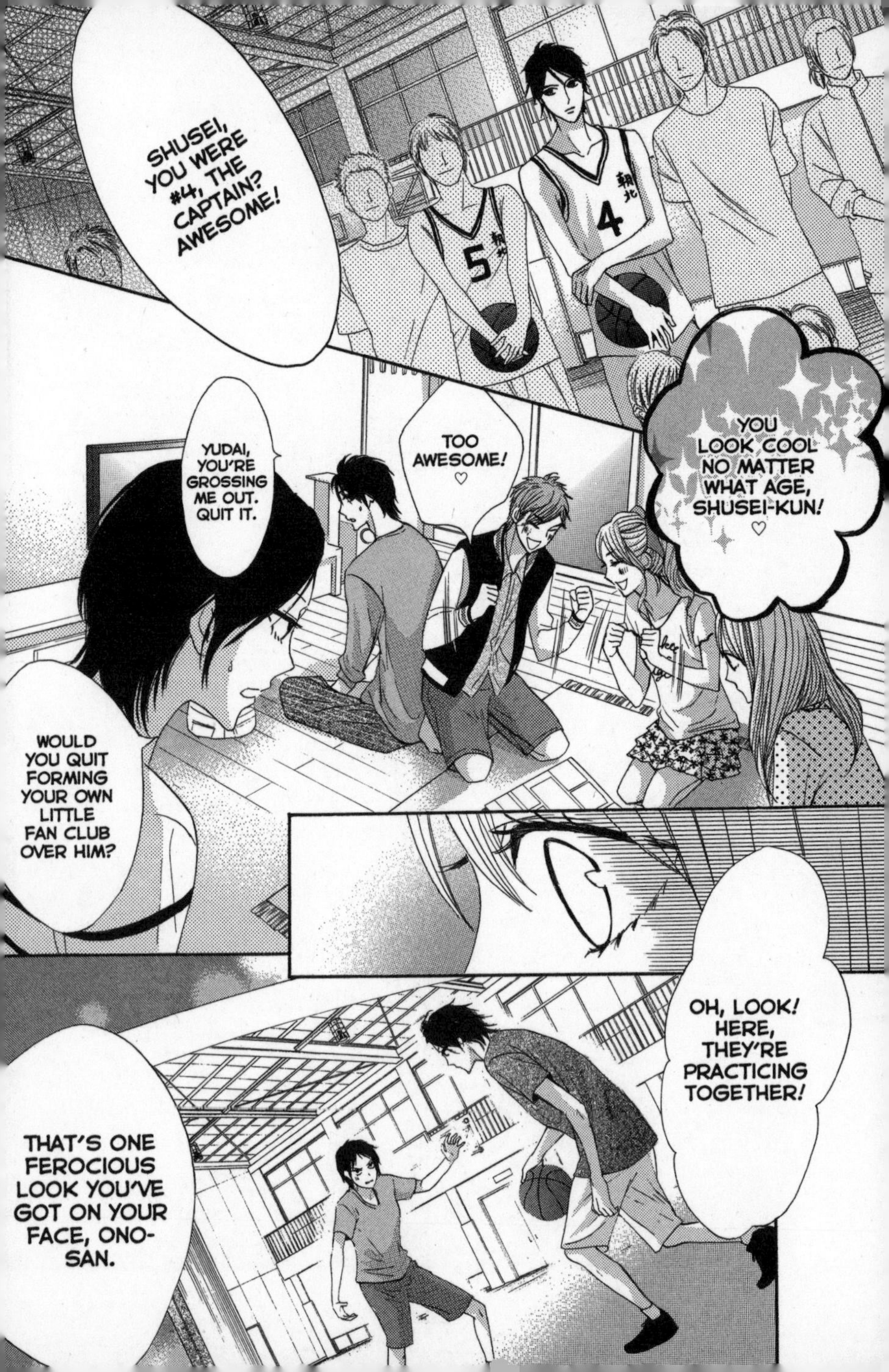
SHUSEI, YOU WERE #4, THE CAPTAIN? AWESOME!
YOU LOOK COOL NO MATTER WHAT AGE, SHUSEI-KUN! ♡
TOO AWESOME! ♡
YUDAI, YOU'RE GROSSING ME OUT. QUIT IT.
WOULD YOU QUIT FORMING YOUR OWN LITTLE FAN CLUB OVER HIM?
OH, LOOK! HERE, THEY'RE PRACTICING TOGETHER!
THAT'S ONE FEROCIOUS LOOK YOU'VE GOT ON YOUR FACE, ONO-SAN.

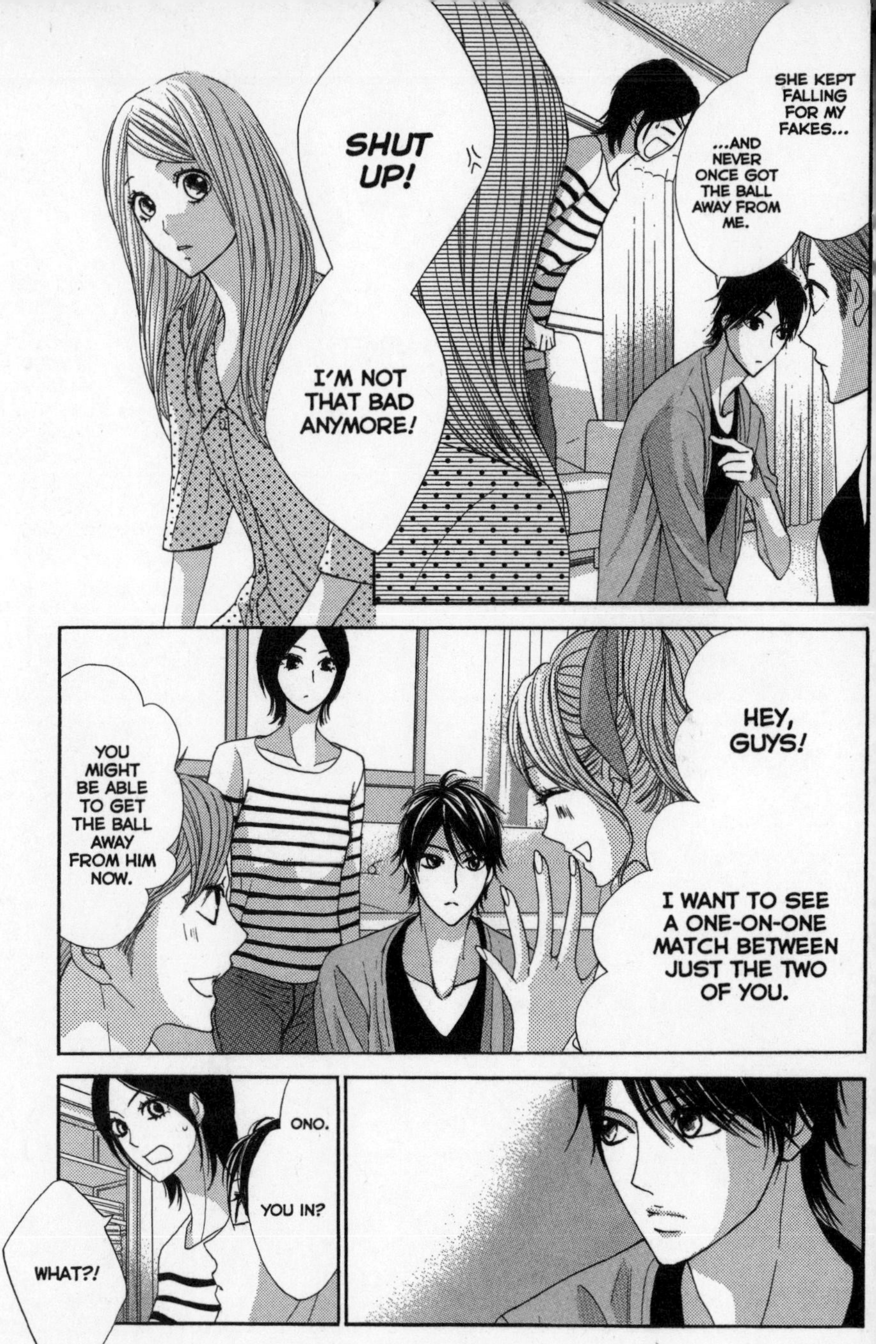
SHE KEPT FALLING FOR MY FAKES...
...AND NEVER ONCE GOT THE BALL AWAY FROM ME.
SHUT UP!
I'M NOT THAT BAD ANYMORE!
HEY, GUYS!
I WANT TO SEE A ONE-ON-ONE MATCH BETWEEN JUST THE TWO OF YOU.
YOU MIGHT BE ABLE TO GET THE BALL AWAY FROM HIM NOW.
ONO.
YOU IN?
WHAT?!

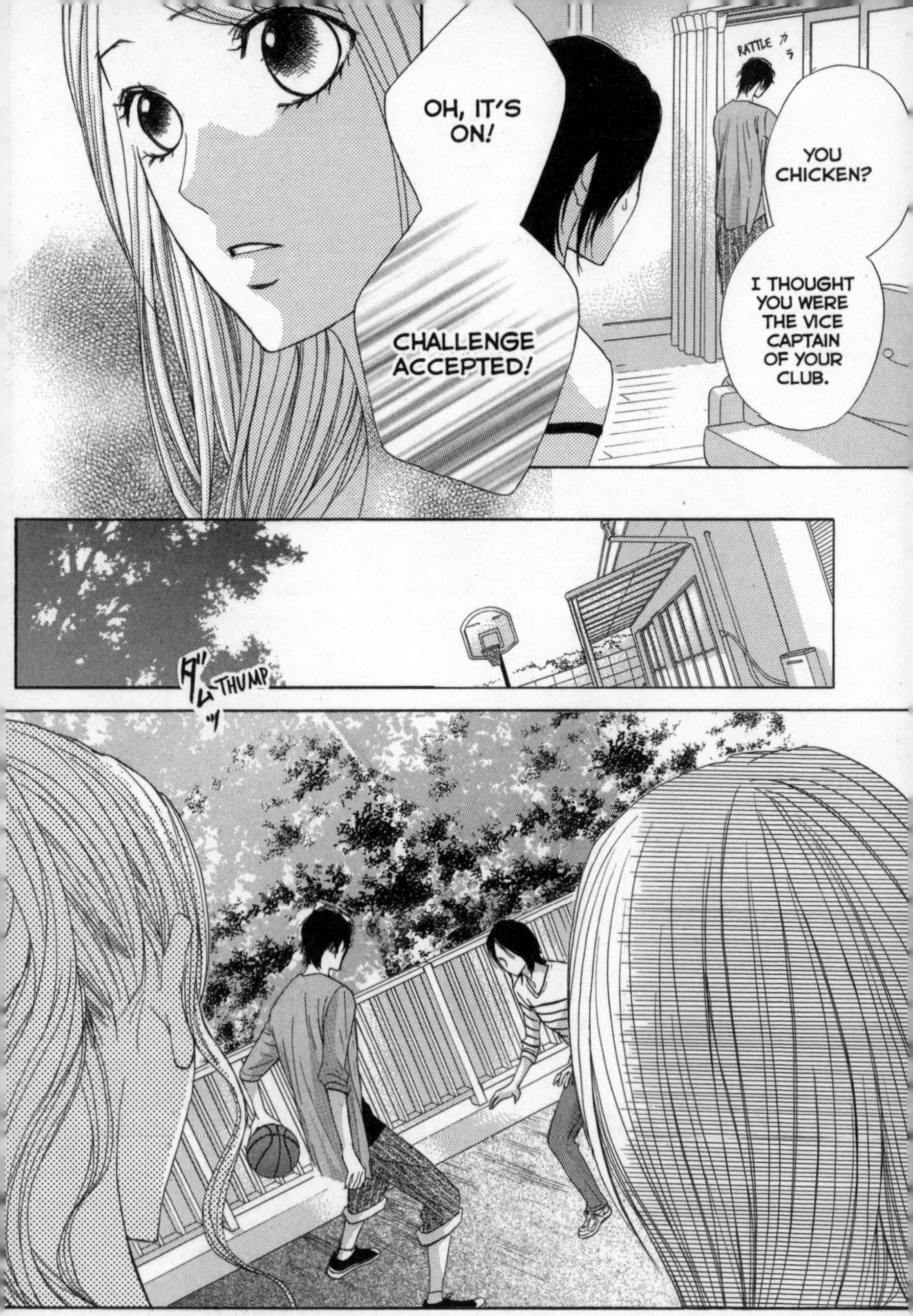
RATTLE カラ
YOU CHICKEN?
I THOUGHT YOU WERE THE VICE CAPTAIN OF YOUR CLUB.
OH, IT'S ON!
CHALLENGE ACCEPTED!
ダムッ THUMP

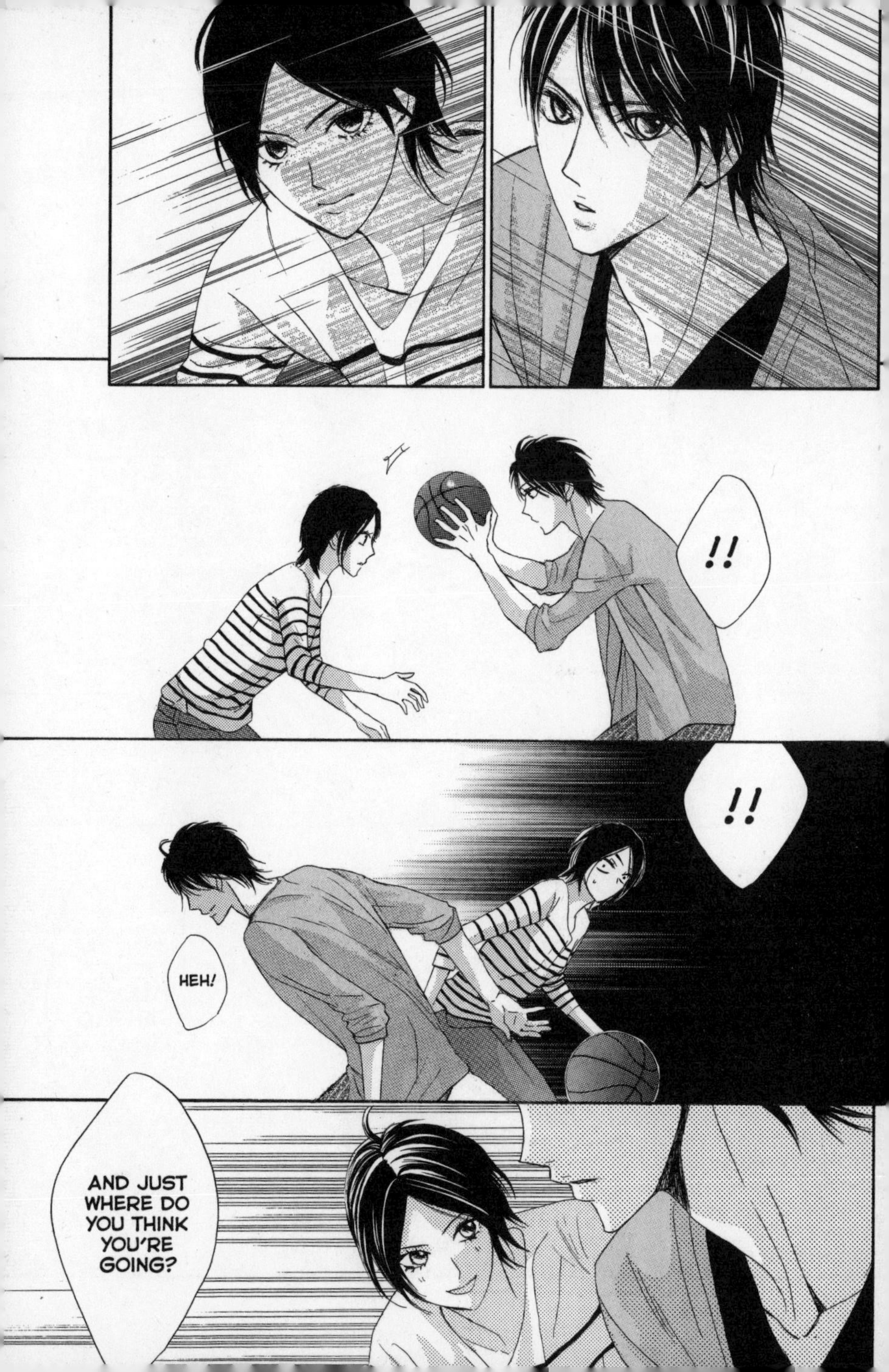
!!
!!
HEH!
AND JUST WHERE DO YOU THINK YOU'RE GOING?

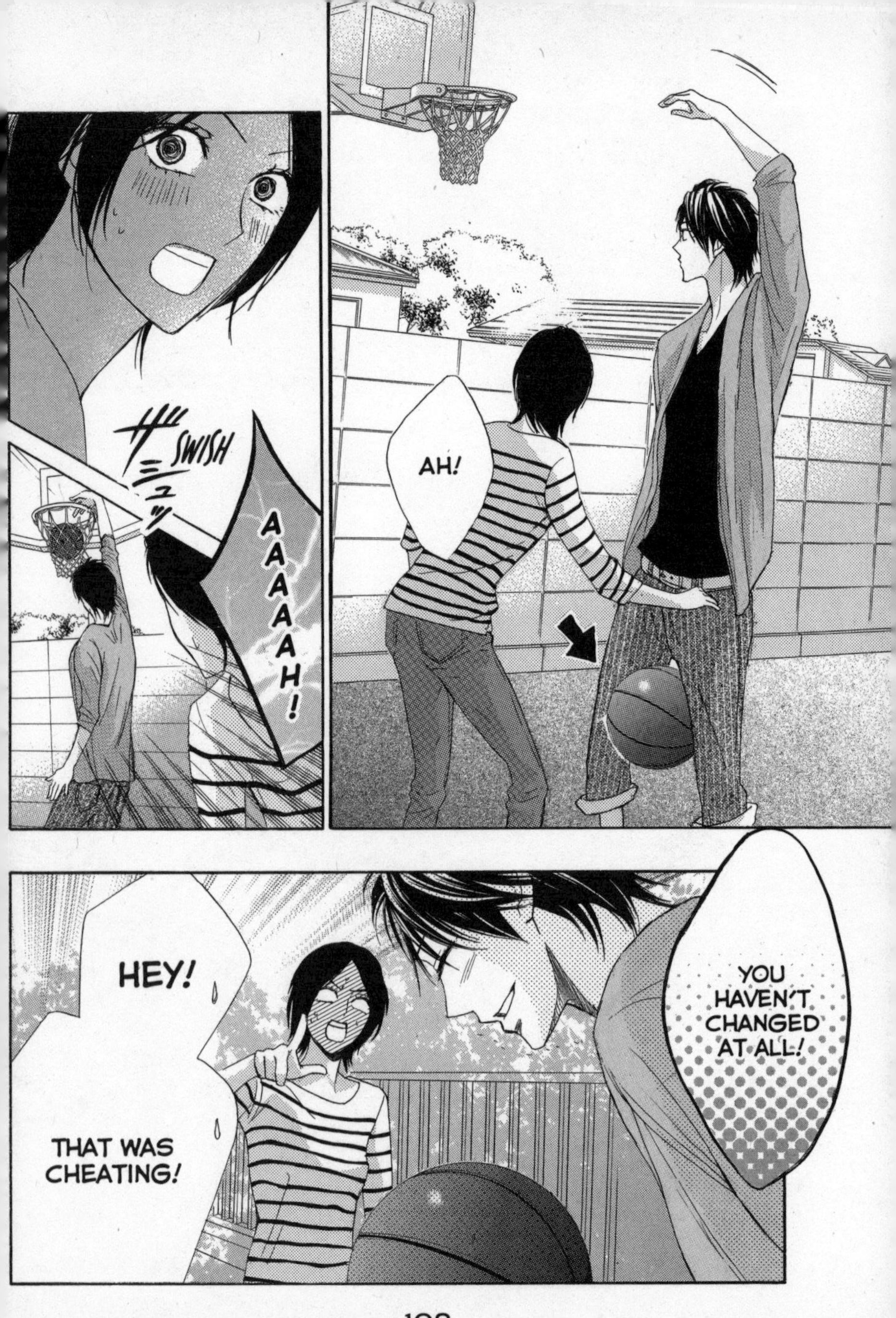
AH!
ザシュッ
SWISH
AAAAAAH!
YOU HAVEN'T CHANGED AT ALL!
HEY!
THAT WAS CHEATING!

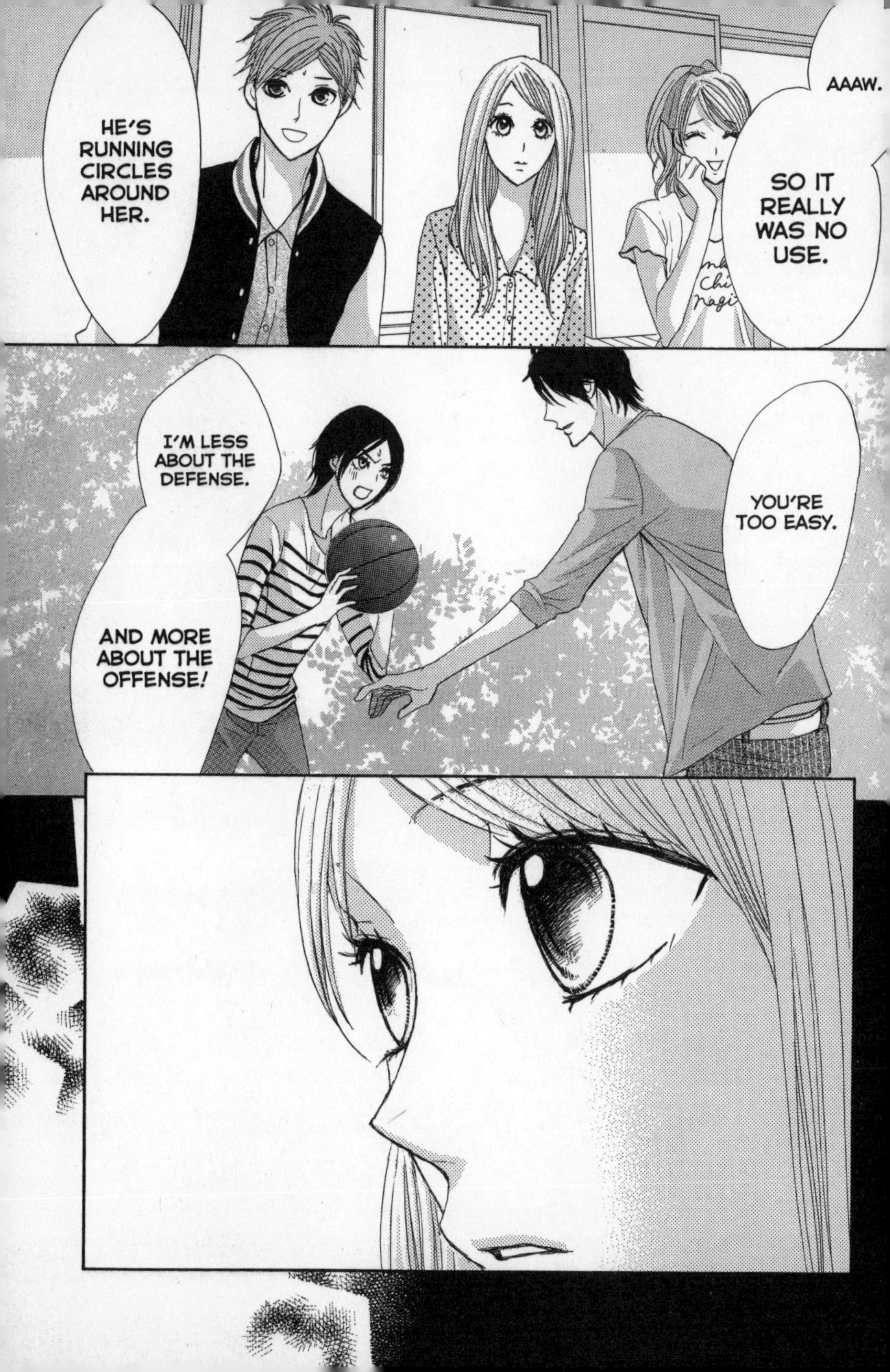
AAAW.
SO IT REALLY WAS NO USE.
HE'S RUNNING CIRCLES AROUND HER.
YOU'RE TOO EASY.
I'M LESS ABOUT THE DEFENSE.
AND MORE ABOUT THE OFFENSE!

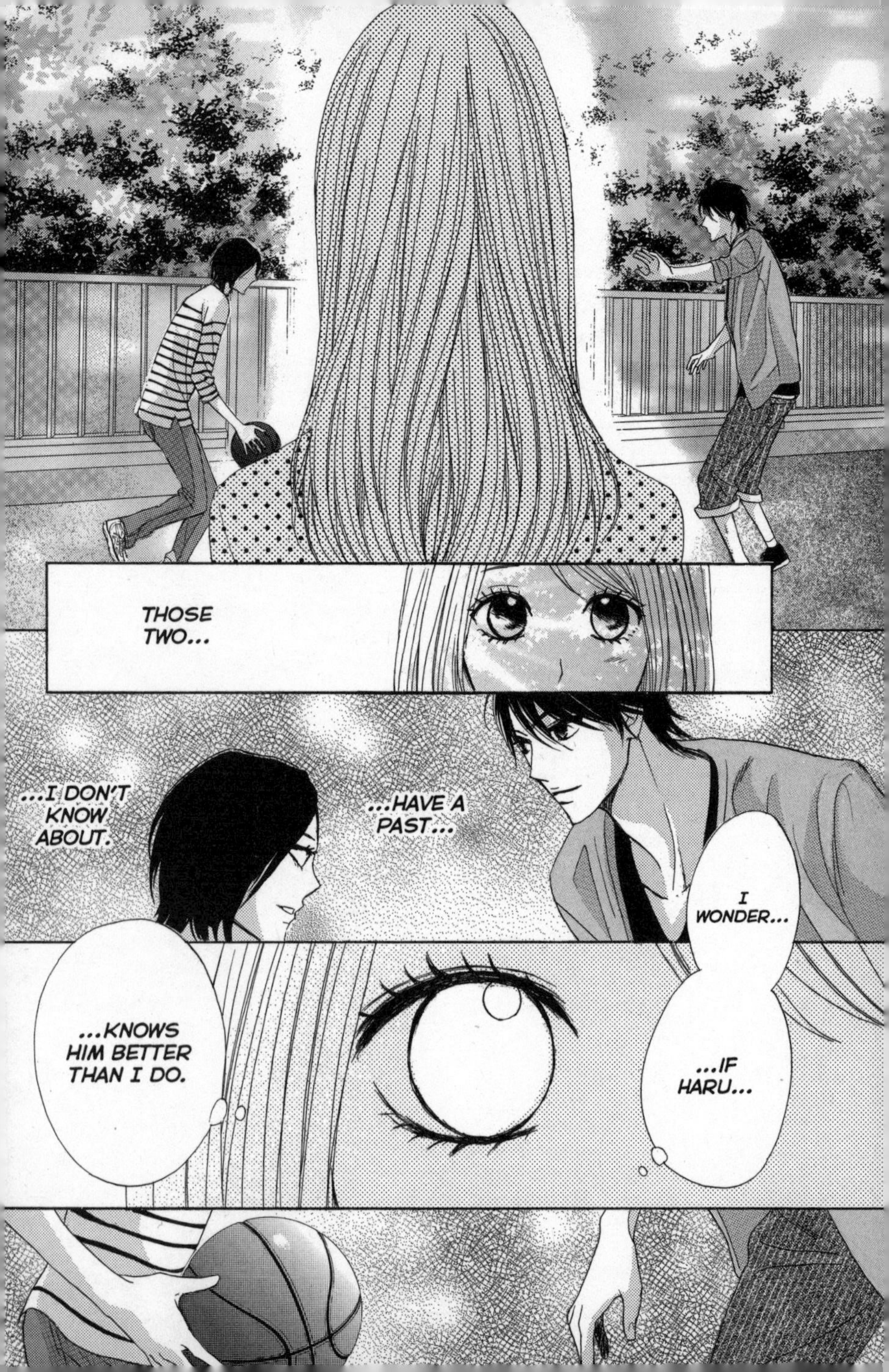
THOSE TWO...
...HAVE A PAST...
...I DON'T KNOW ABOUT.
I WONDER...
...IF HARU...
...KNOWS HIM BETTER THAN I DO.

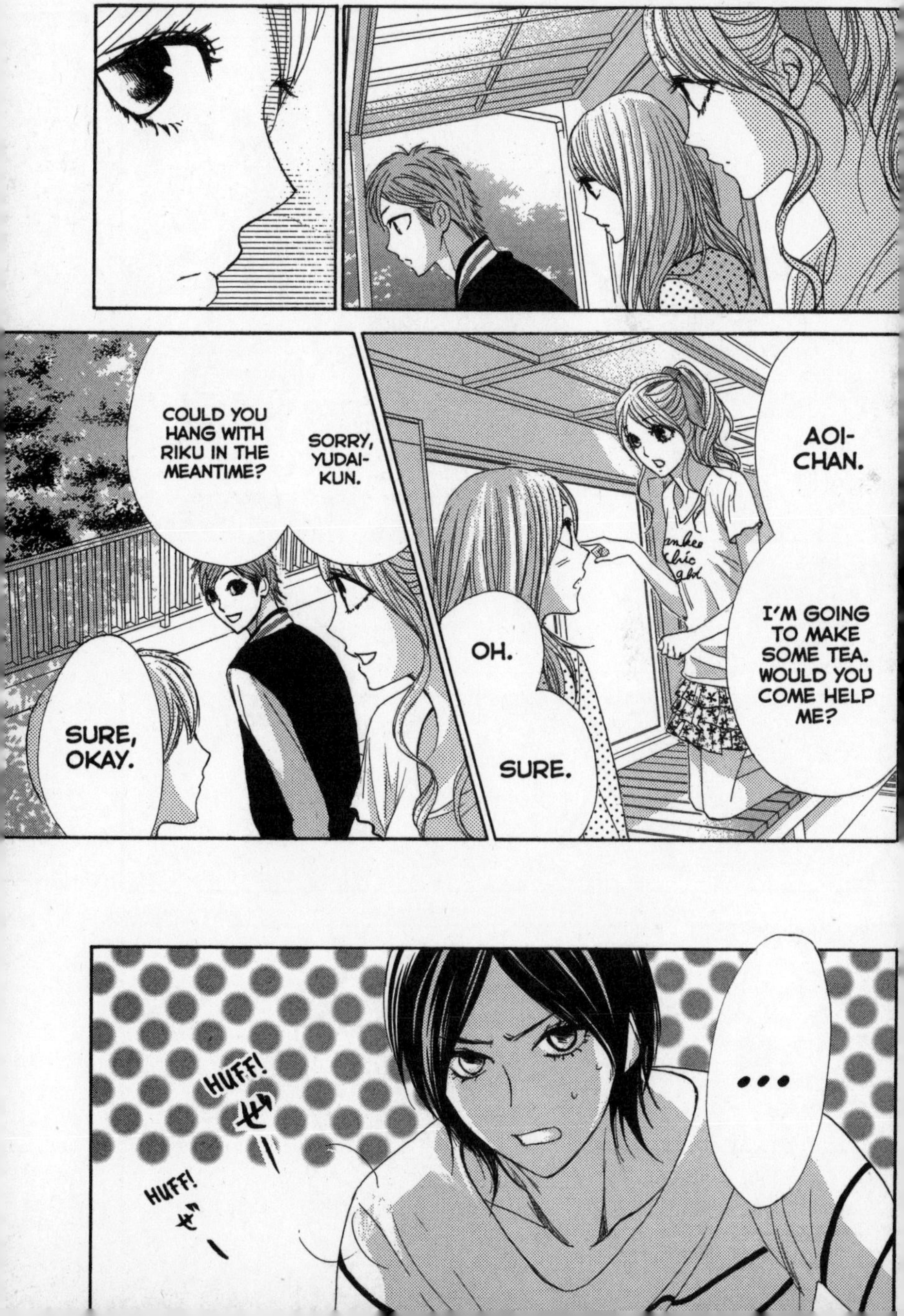
AOI-CHAN.
I'M GOING TO MAKE SOME TEA. WOULD YOU COME HELP ME?
OH.
SURE.
SORRY, YUDAI-KUN.
COULD YOU HANG WITH RIKU IN THE MEANTIME?
SURE, OKAY.
...
HUFF! ぜー
HUFF! ぜー

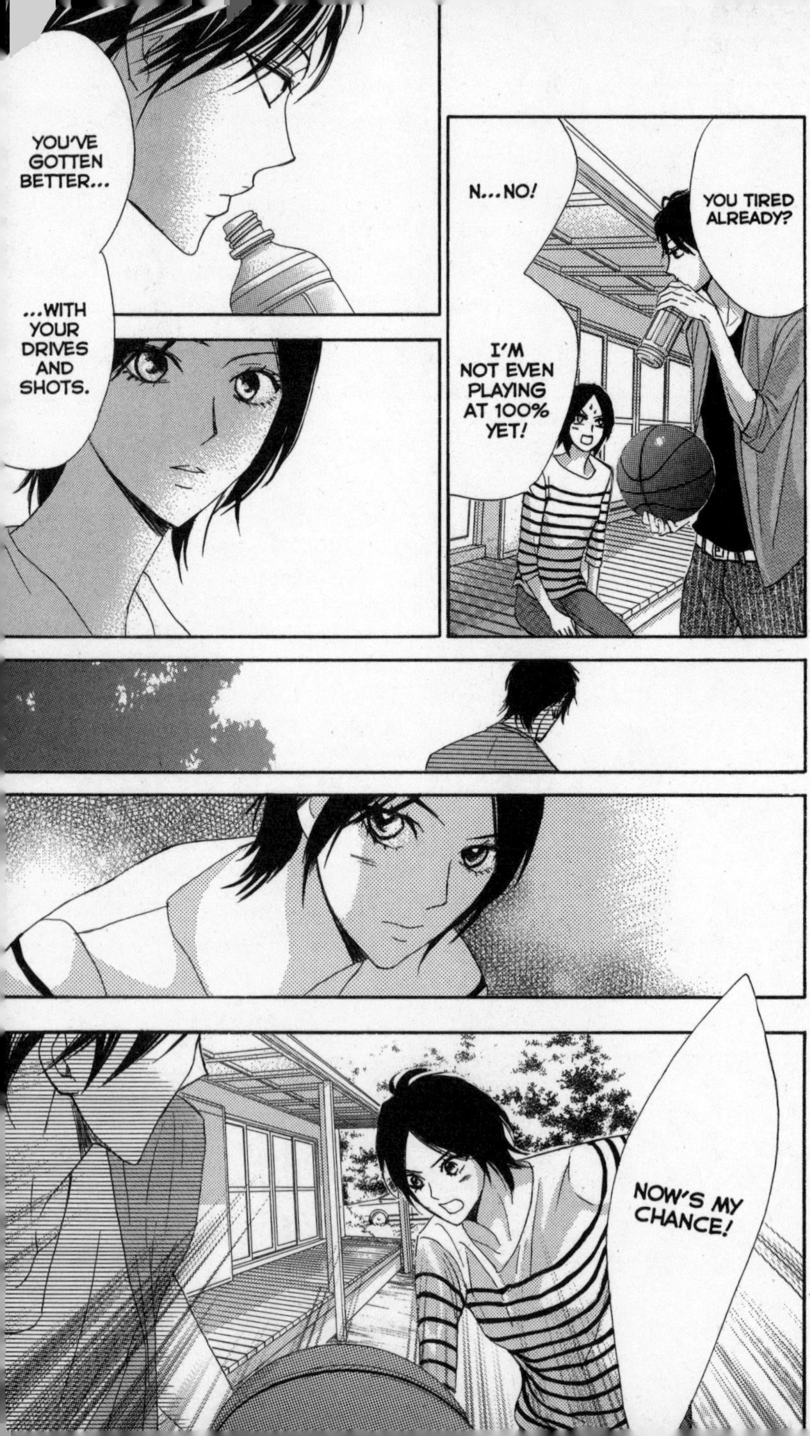
YOU TIRED ALREADY?
N...NO!
I'M NOT EVEN PLAYING AT 100% YET!
YOU'VE GOTTEN BETTER...
...WITH YOUR DRIVES AND SHOTS.
NOW'S MY CHANCE!

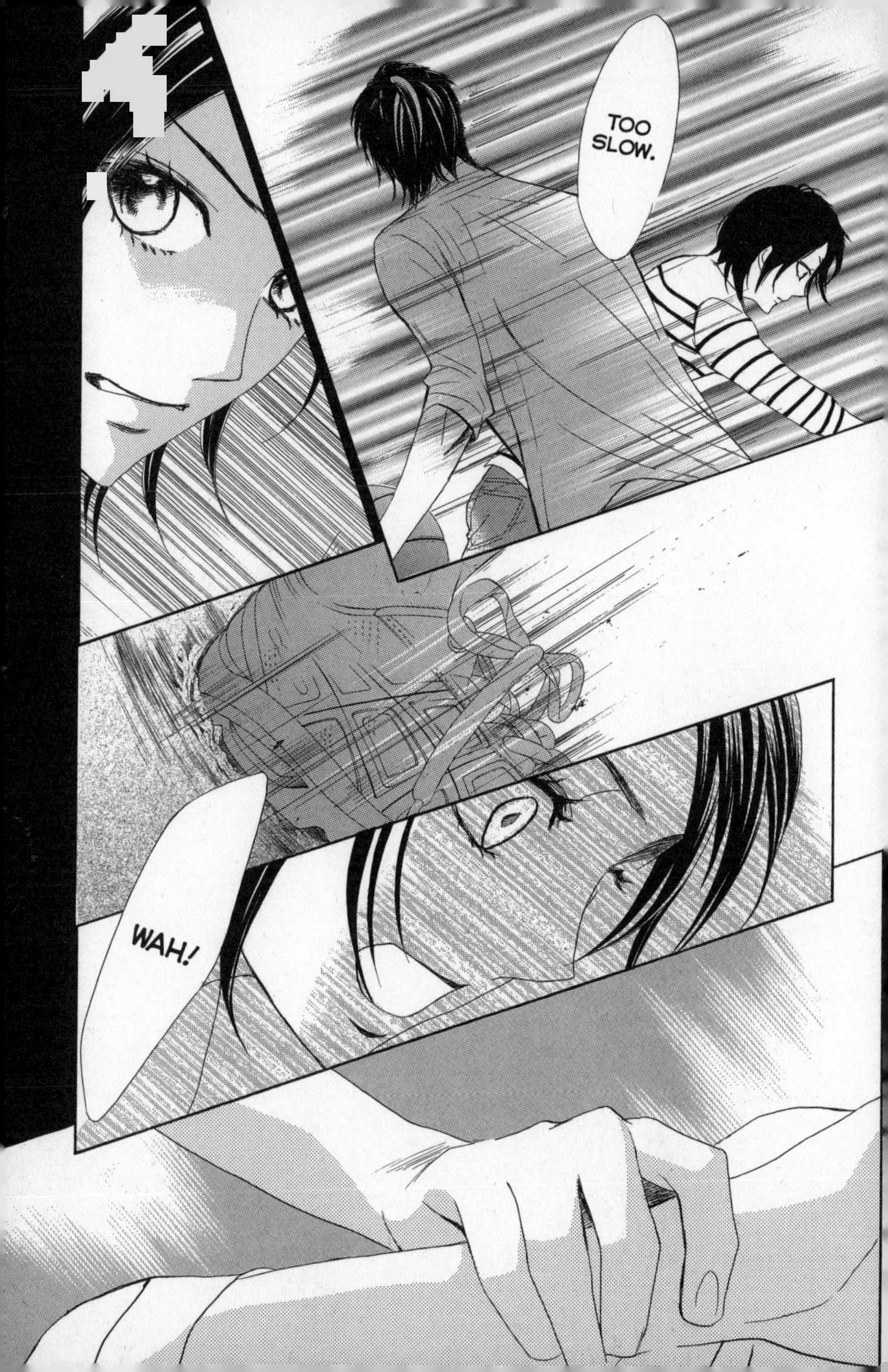
TOO SLOW.
WAH!

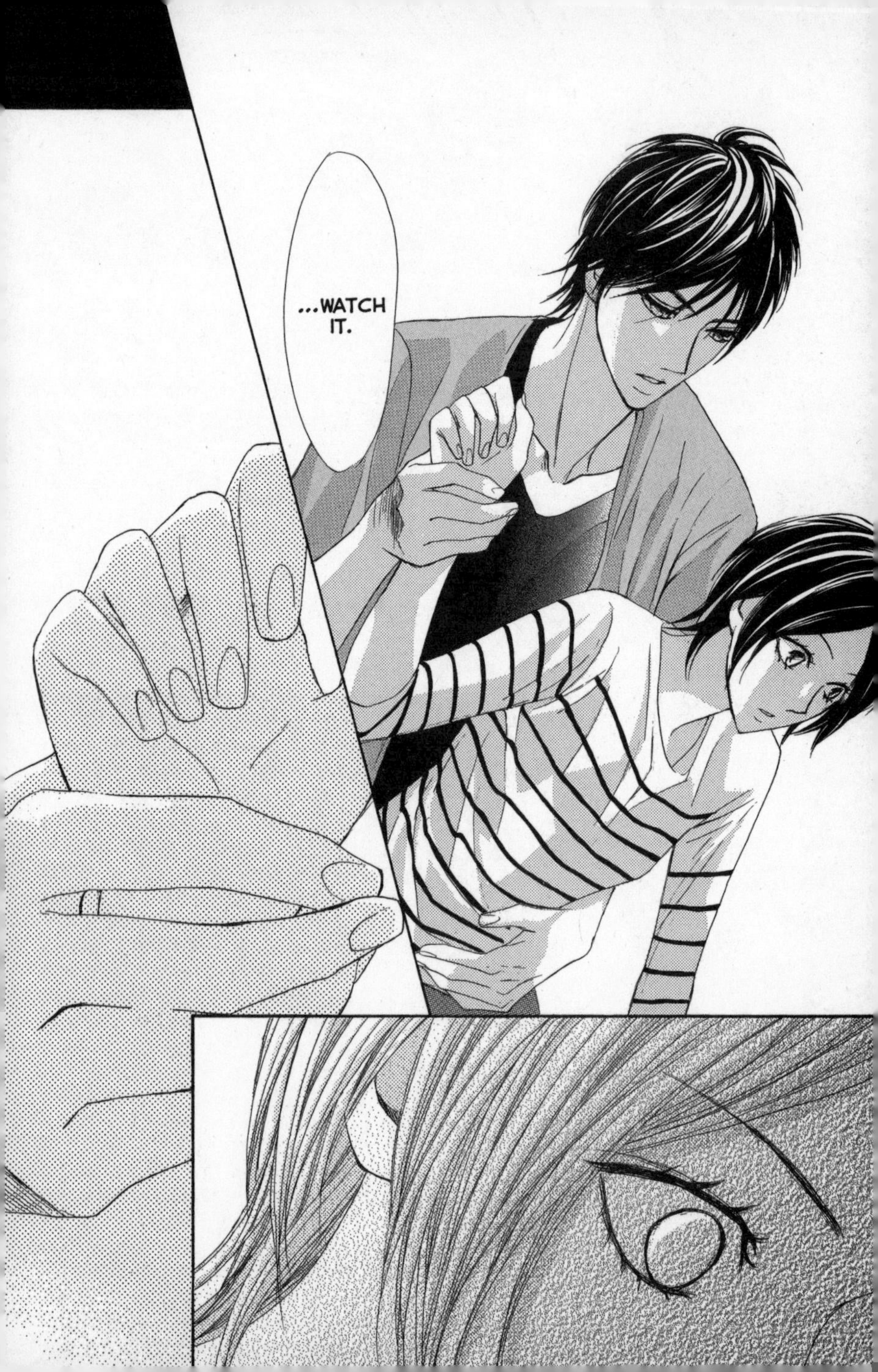
...WATCH IT.

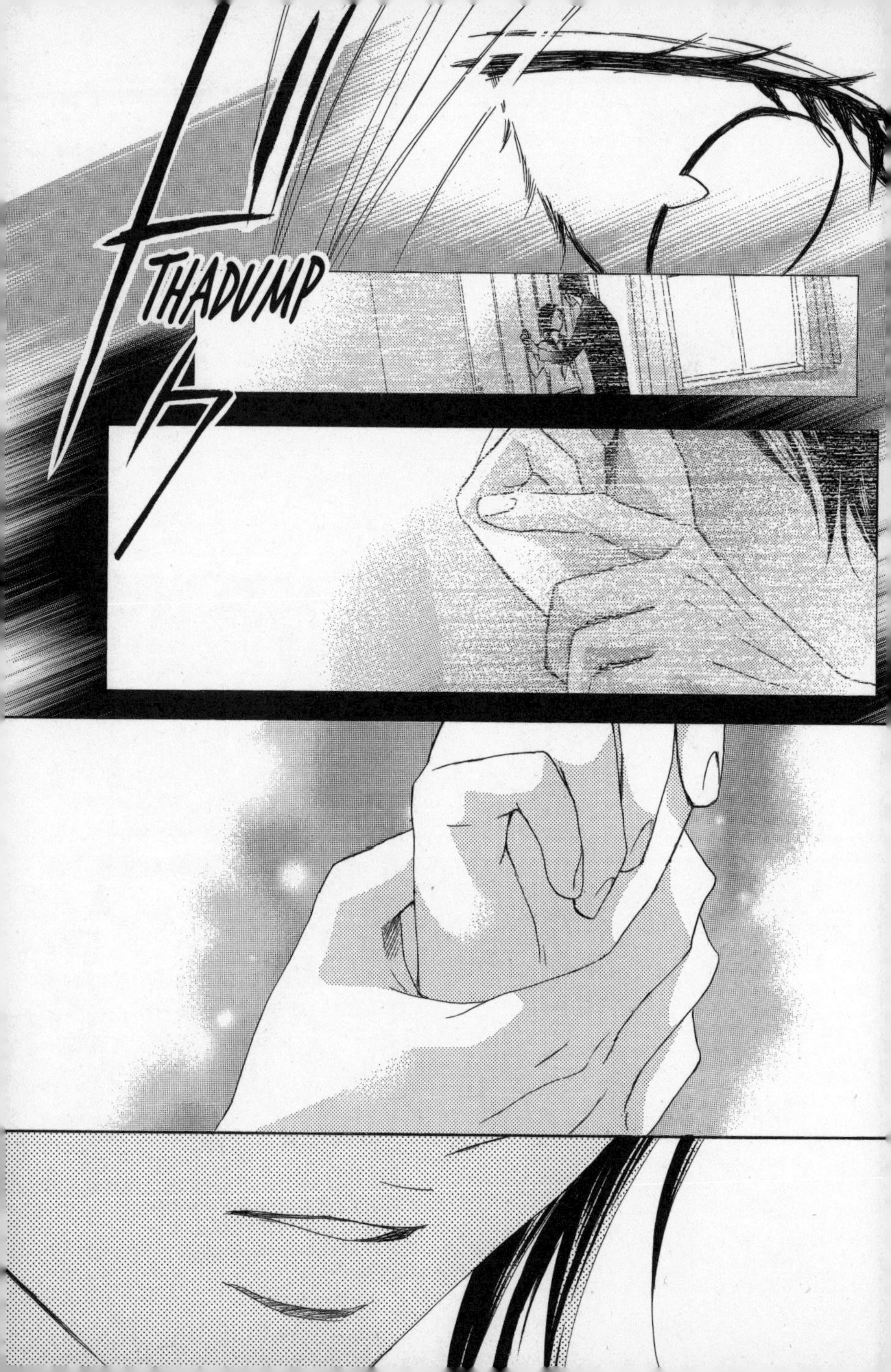
THADUMP

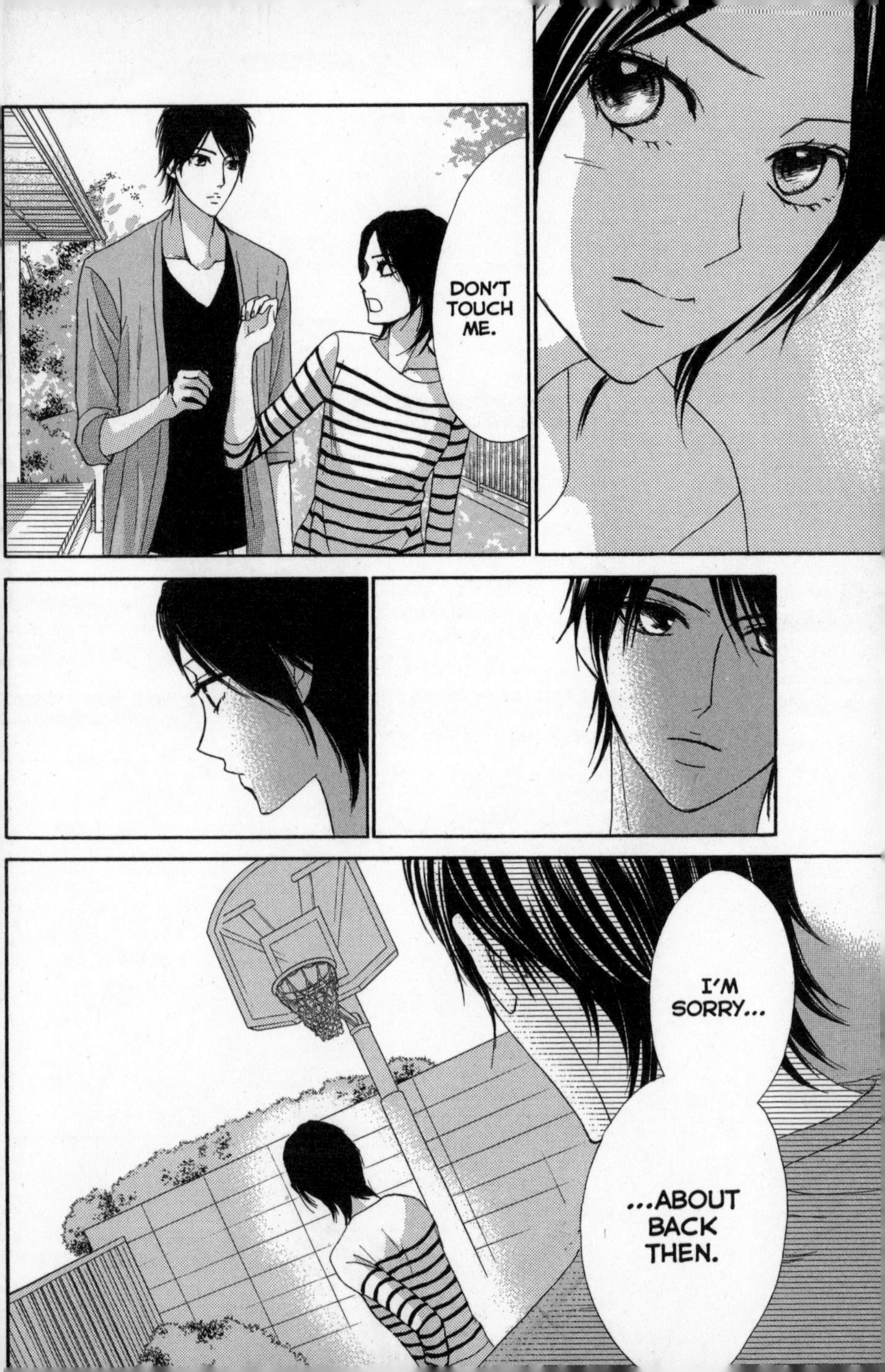
DON'T TOUCH ME.
I'M SORRY...
...ABOUT BACK THEN.

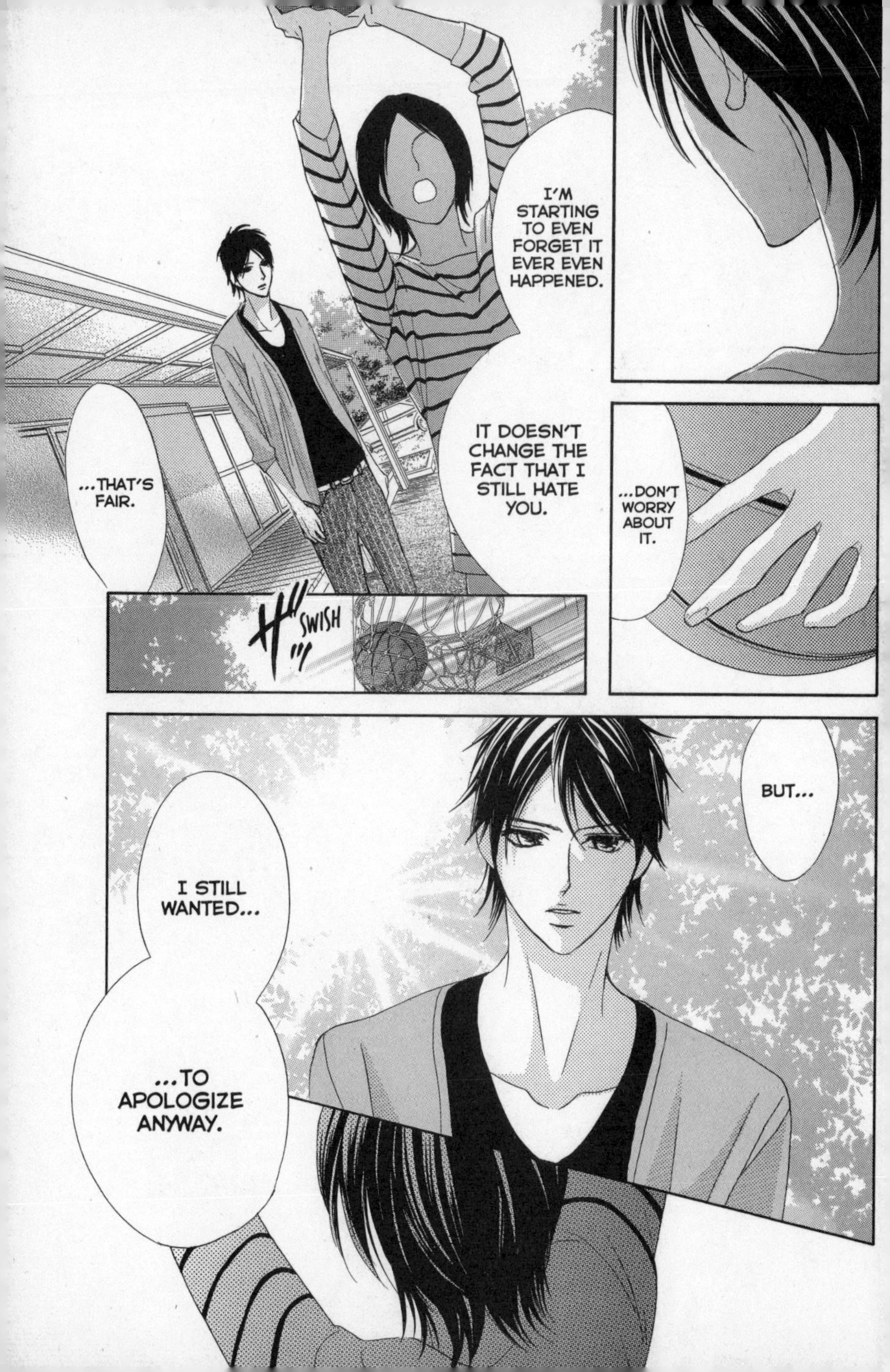
...DON'T WORRY ABOUT IT.
I'M STARTING TO EVEN FORGET IT EVER EVEN HAPPENED.
IT DOESN'T CHANGE THE FACT THAT I STILL HATE YOU.
...THAT'S FAIR.
SWISH
BUT...
I STILL WANTED...
...TO APOLOGIZE ANYWAY.

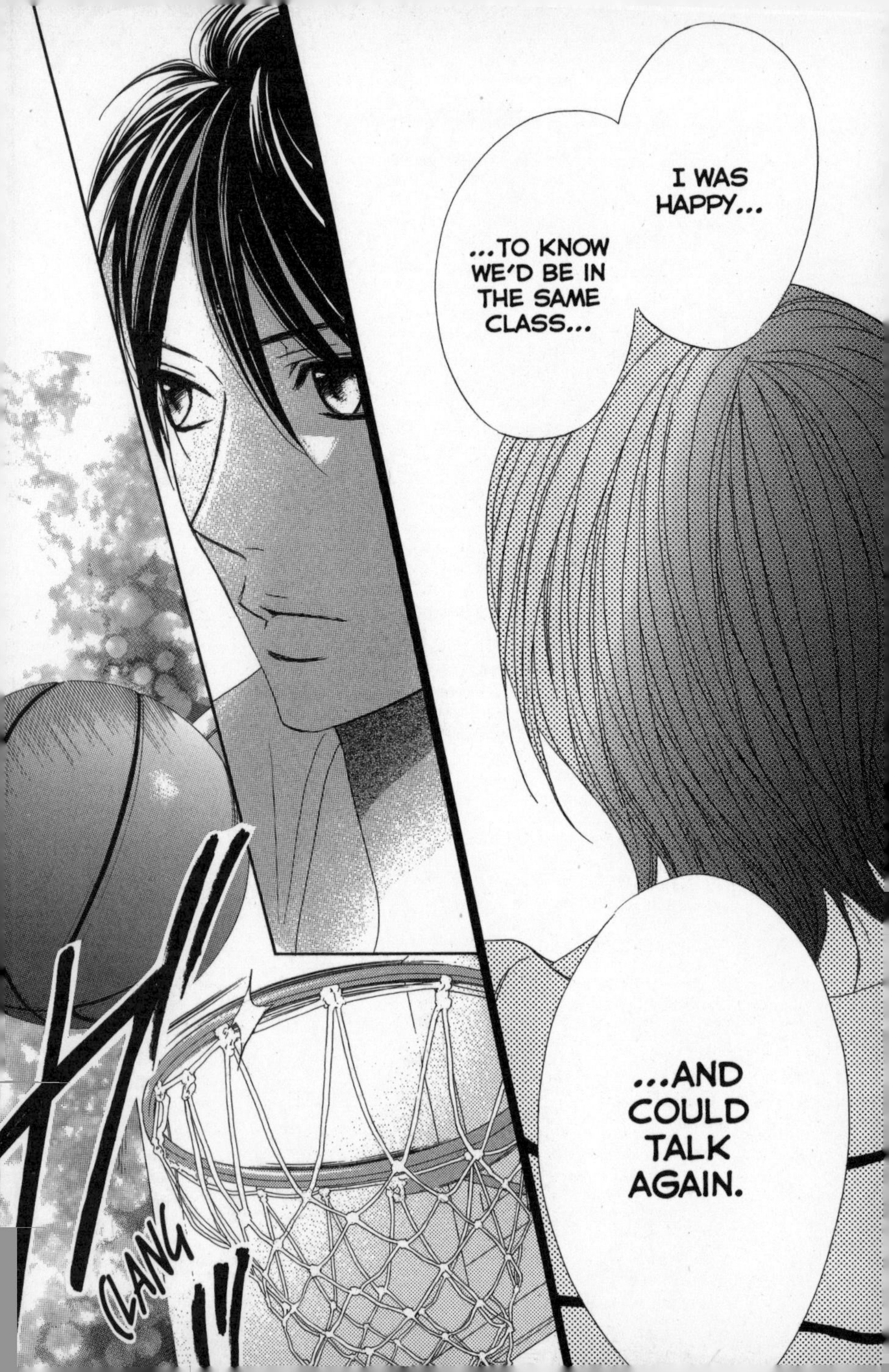
I WAS HAPPY...
...TO KNOW WE'D BE IN THE SAME CLASS...
...AND COULD TALK AGAIN.
CLANG!!

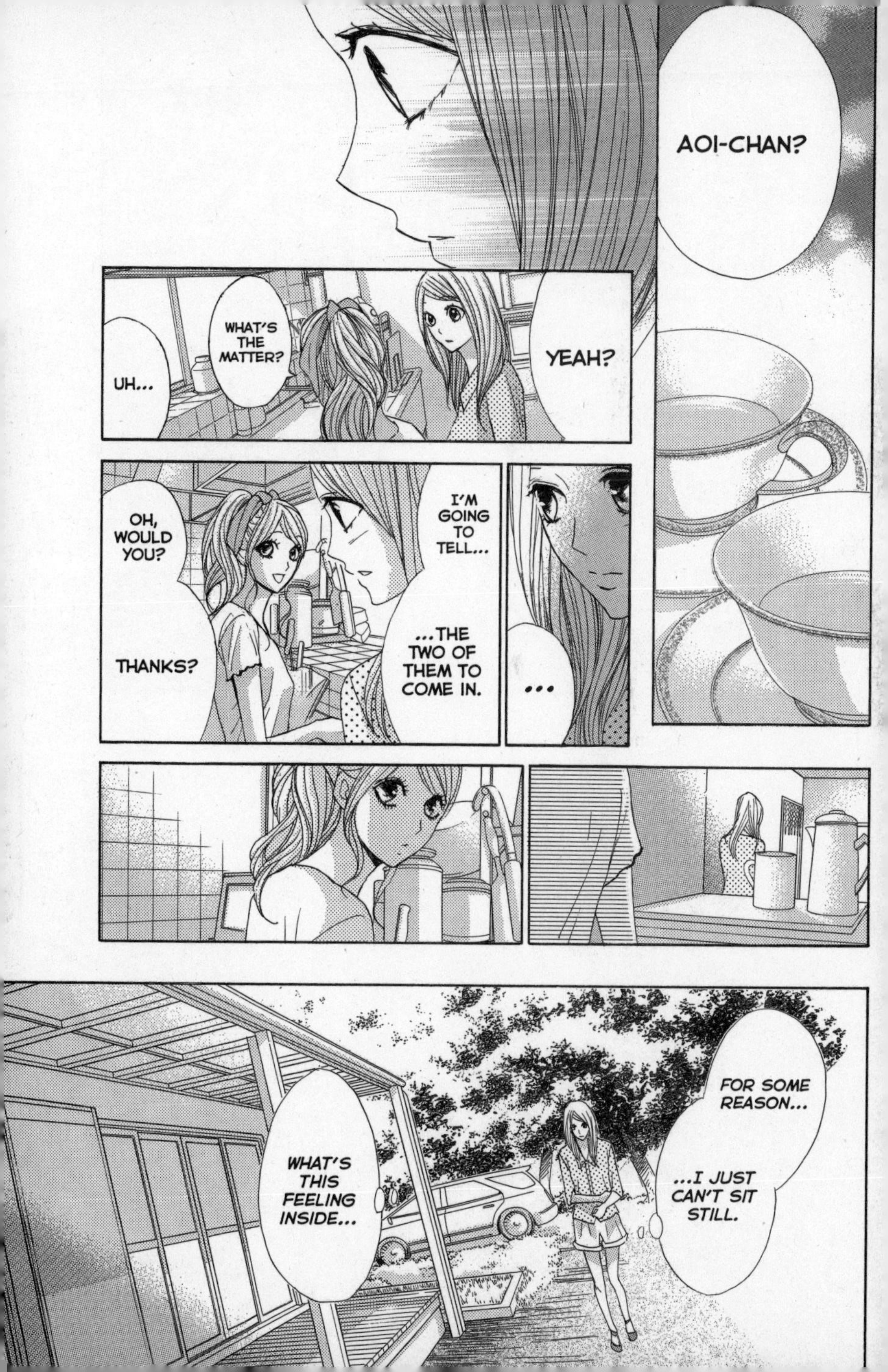
AOI-CHAN?
YEAH?
WHAT'S THE MATTER?
UH...
...
I'M GOING TO TELL...
...THE TWO OF THEM TO COME IN.
OH, WOULD YOU?
THANKS?
FOR SOME REASON...
...I JUST CAN'T SIT STILL.
WHAT'S THIS FEELING INSIDE...

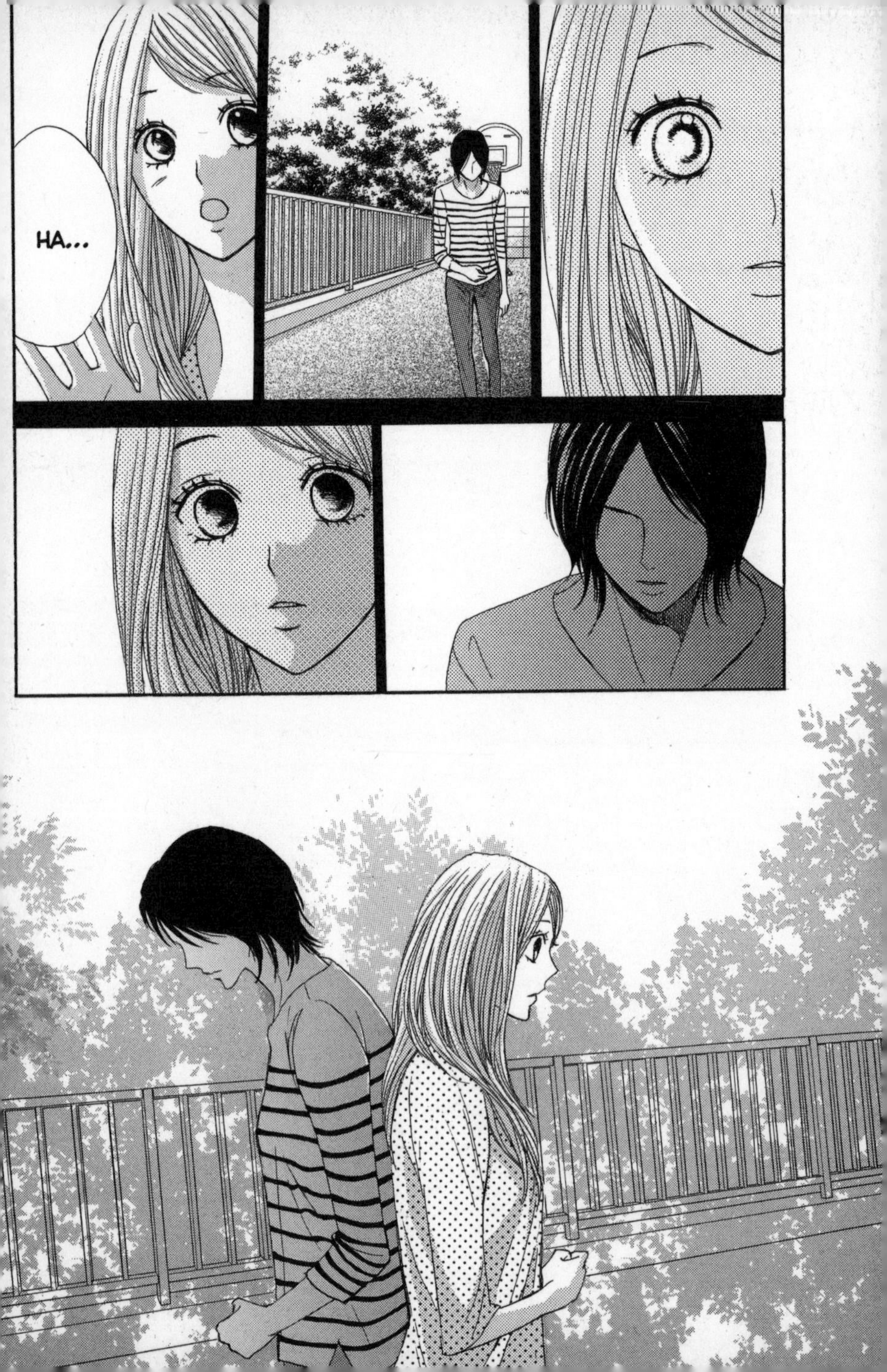
HA...

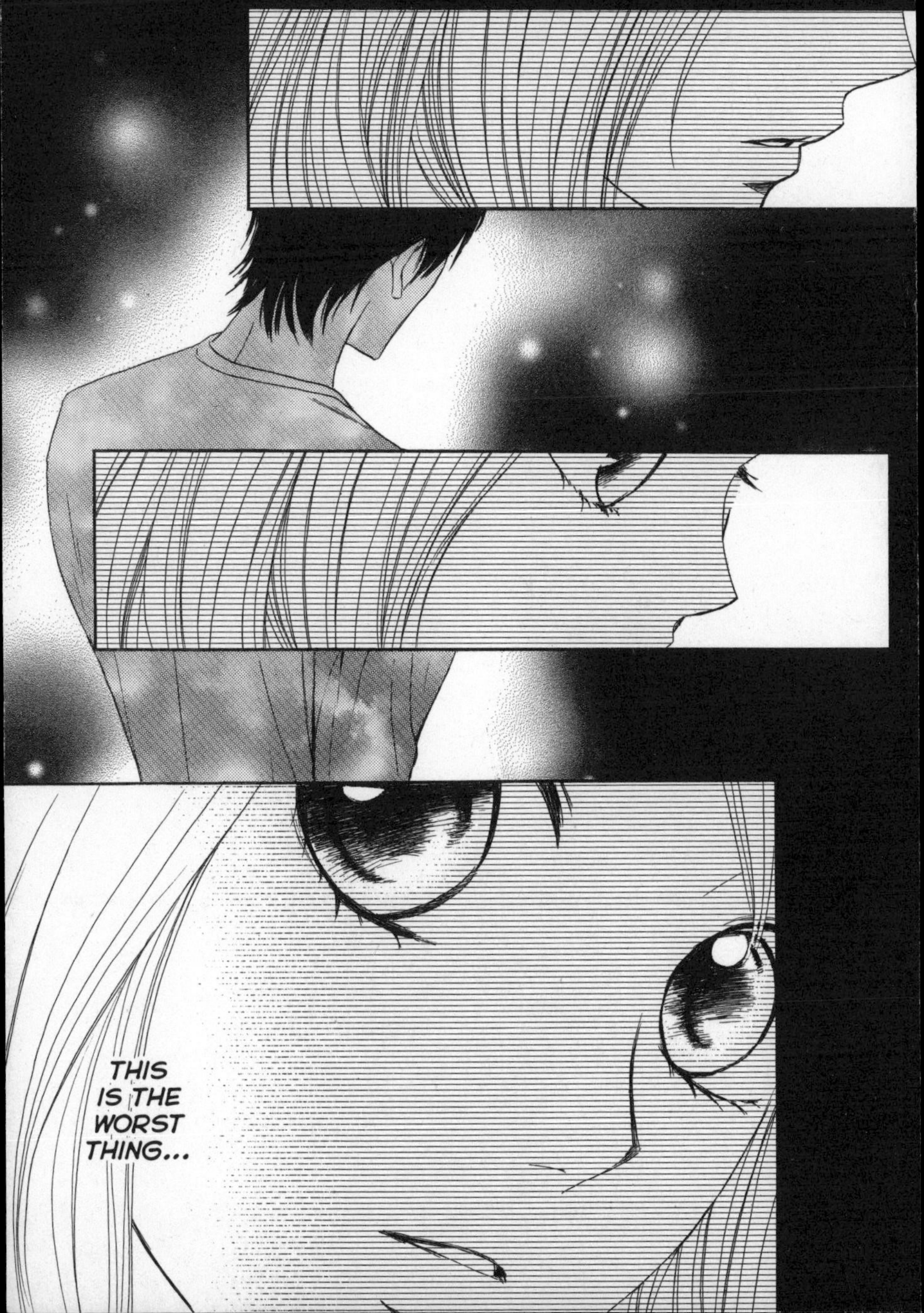
THIS IS THE WORST THING...

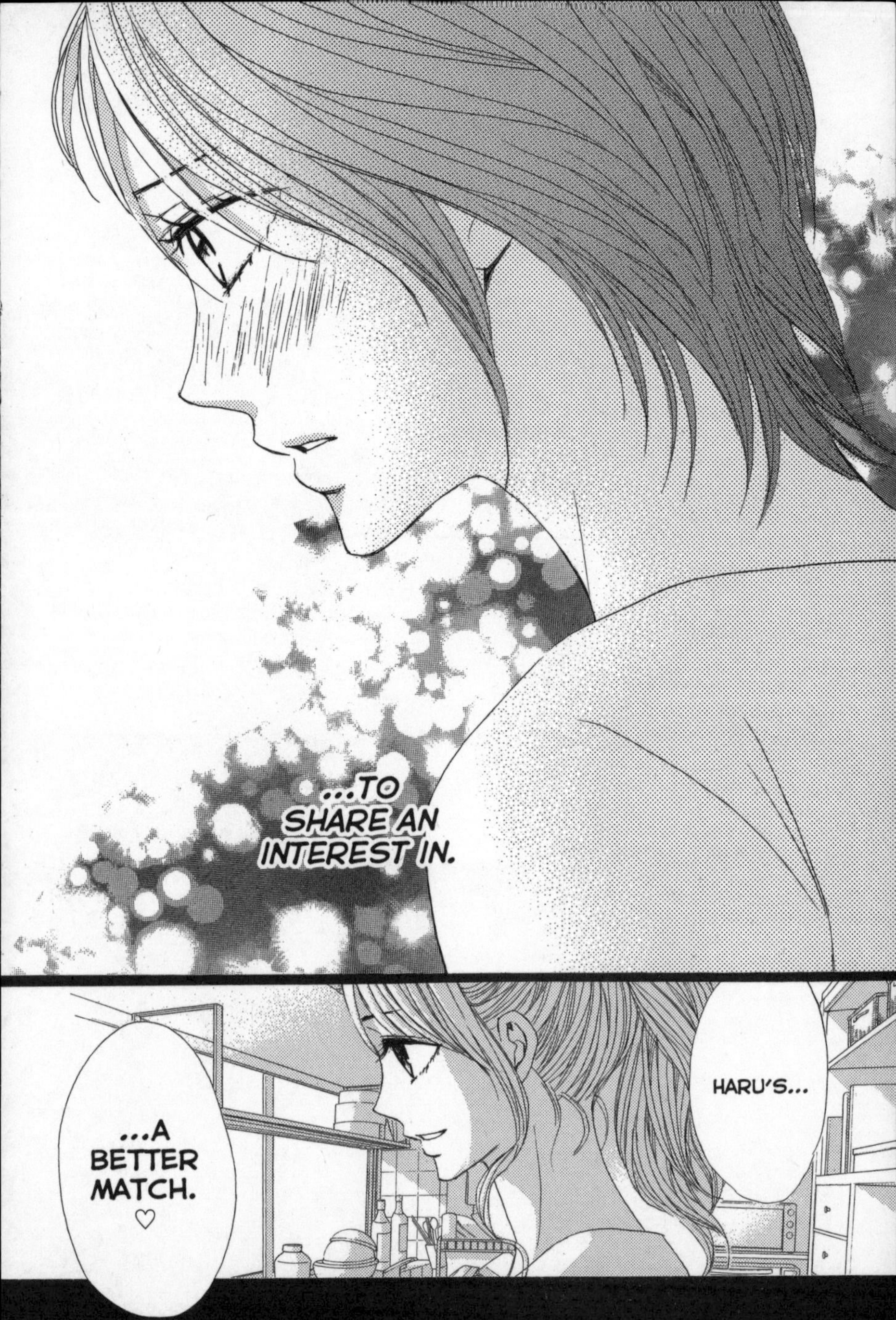
...TO SHARE AN INTEREST IN.
HARU'S...
...A BETTER MATCH. ♡

L♥DK

#40 Surprise

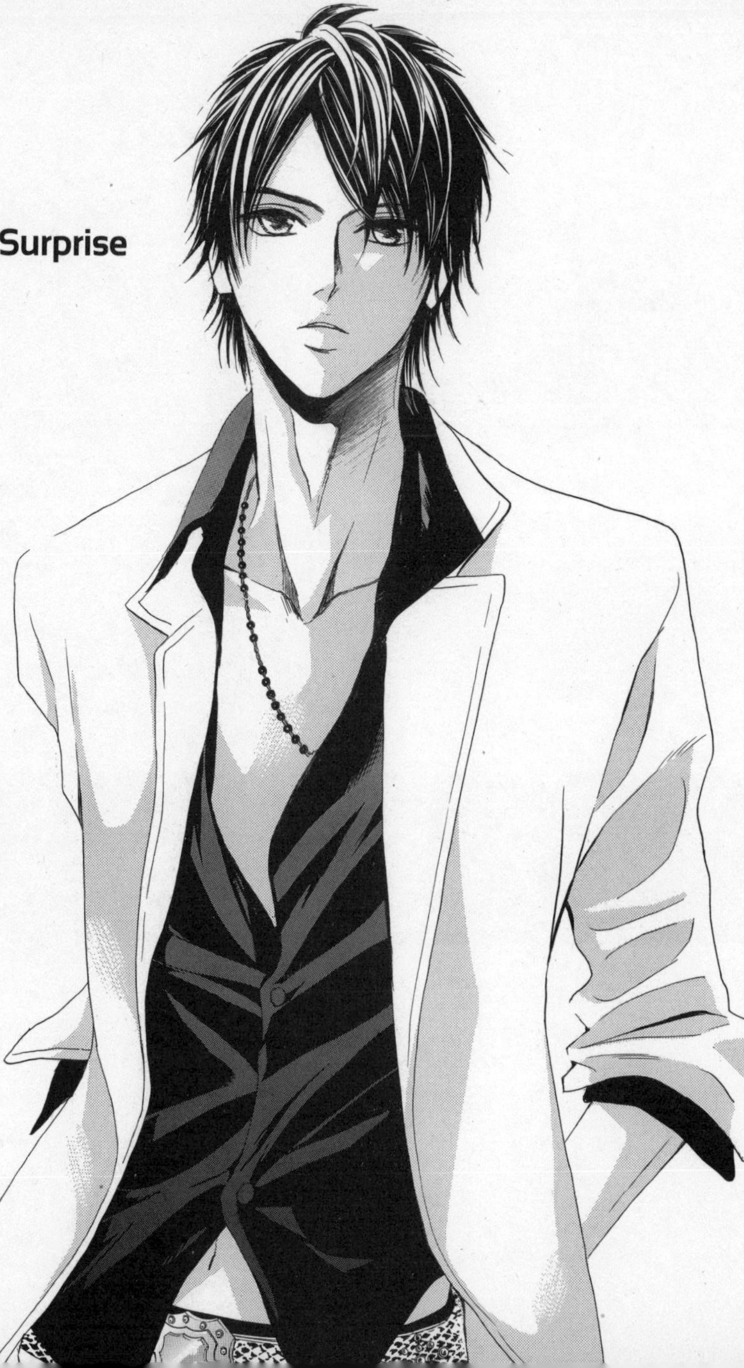

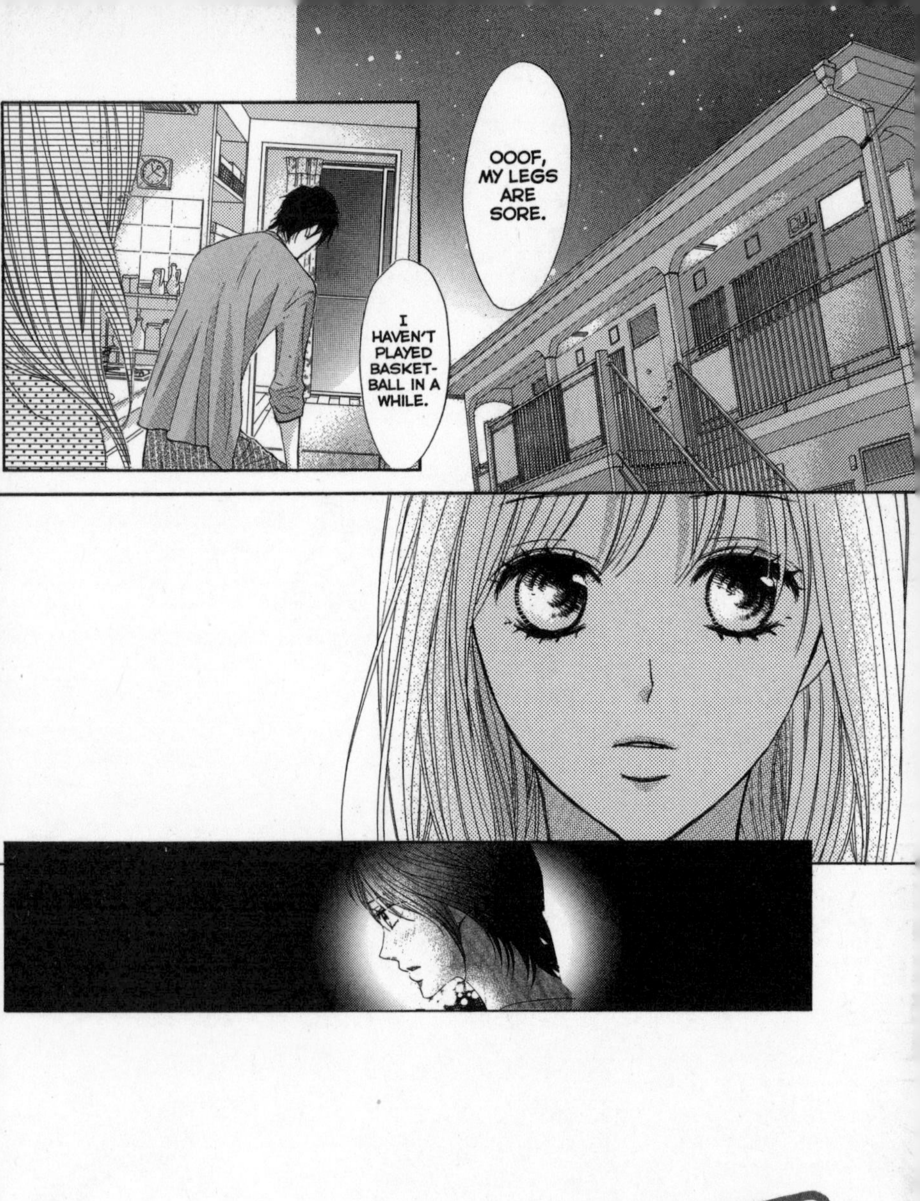
OOOF, MY LEGS ARE SORE.
I HAVEN'T PLAYED BASKET-BALL IN A WHILE.

L♥DK

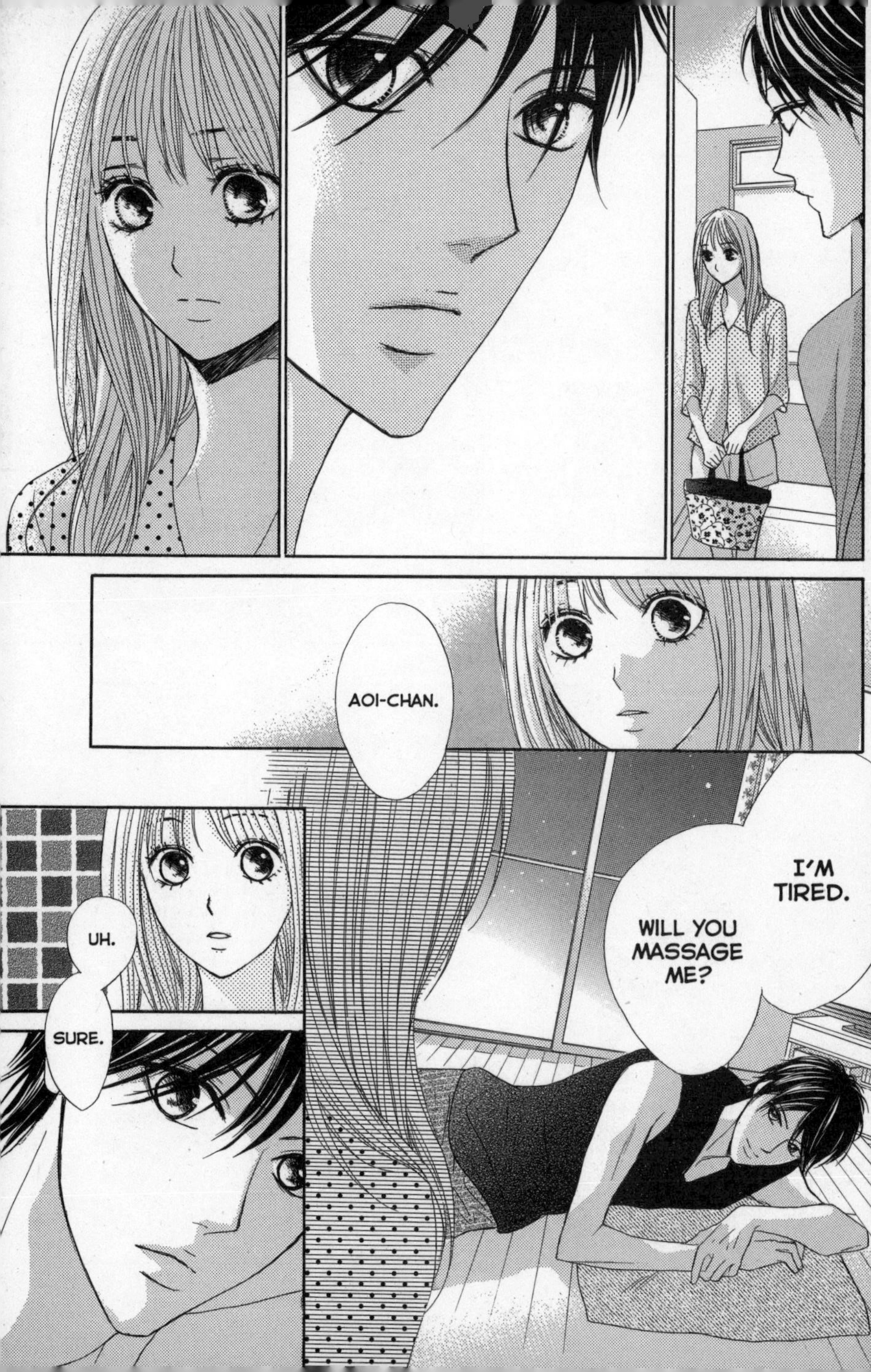
AOI-CHAN.
I'M TIRED.
WILL YOU MASSAGE ME?
UH.
SURE.

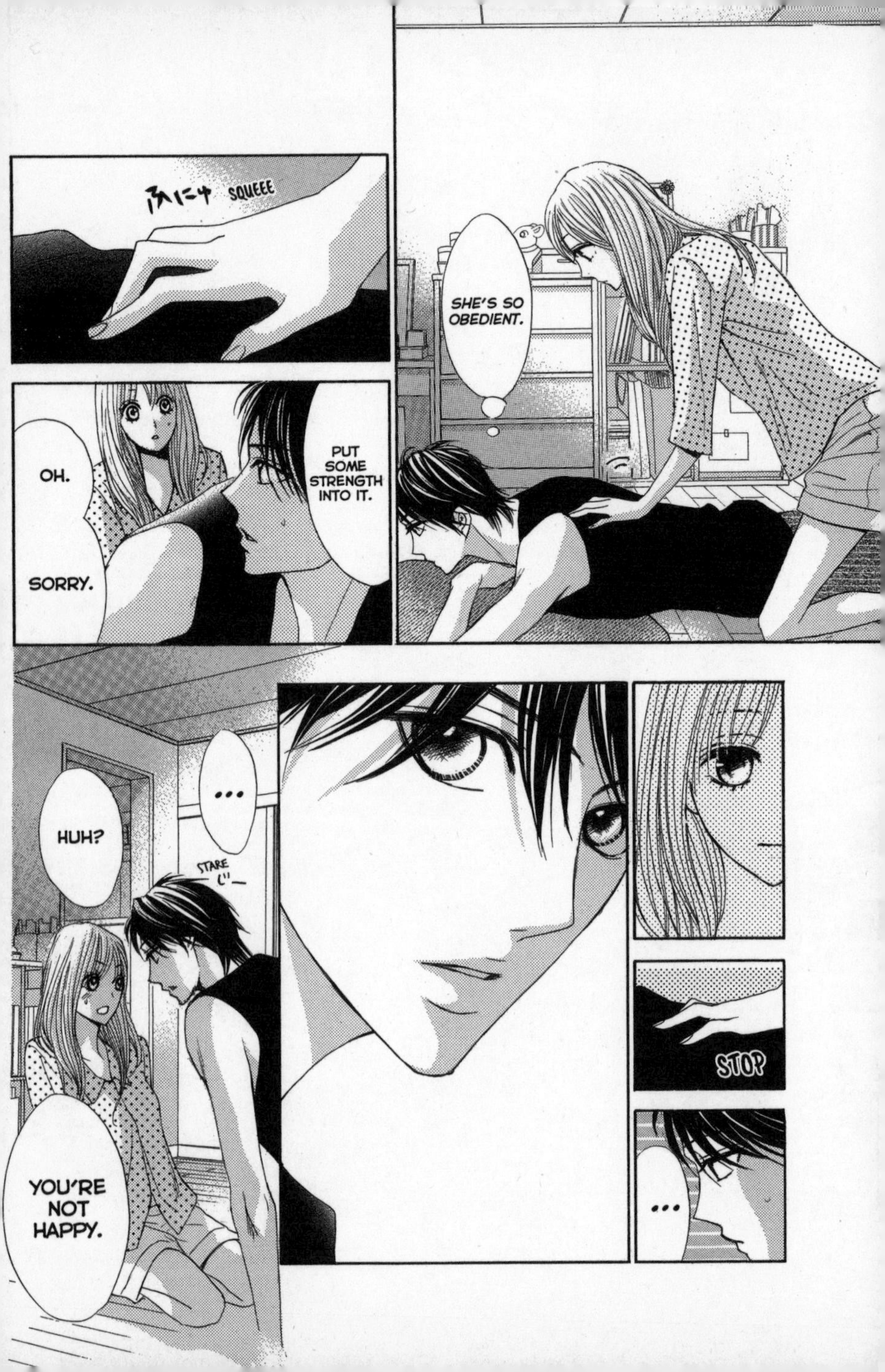

SHE'S SO OBEDIENT.
SQUEEE
PUT SOME STRENGTH INTO IT.
OH.
SORRY.
STOP
...
...
HUH?
STARE
YOU'RE NOT HAPPY.

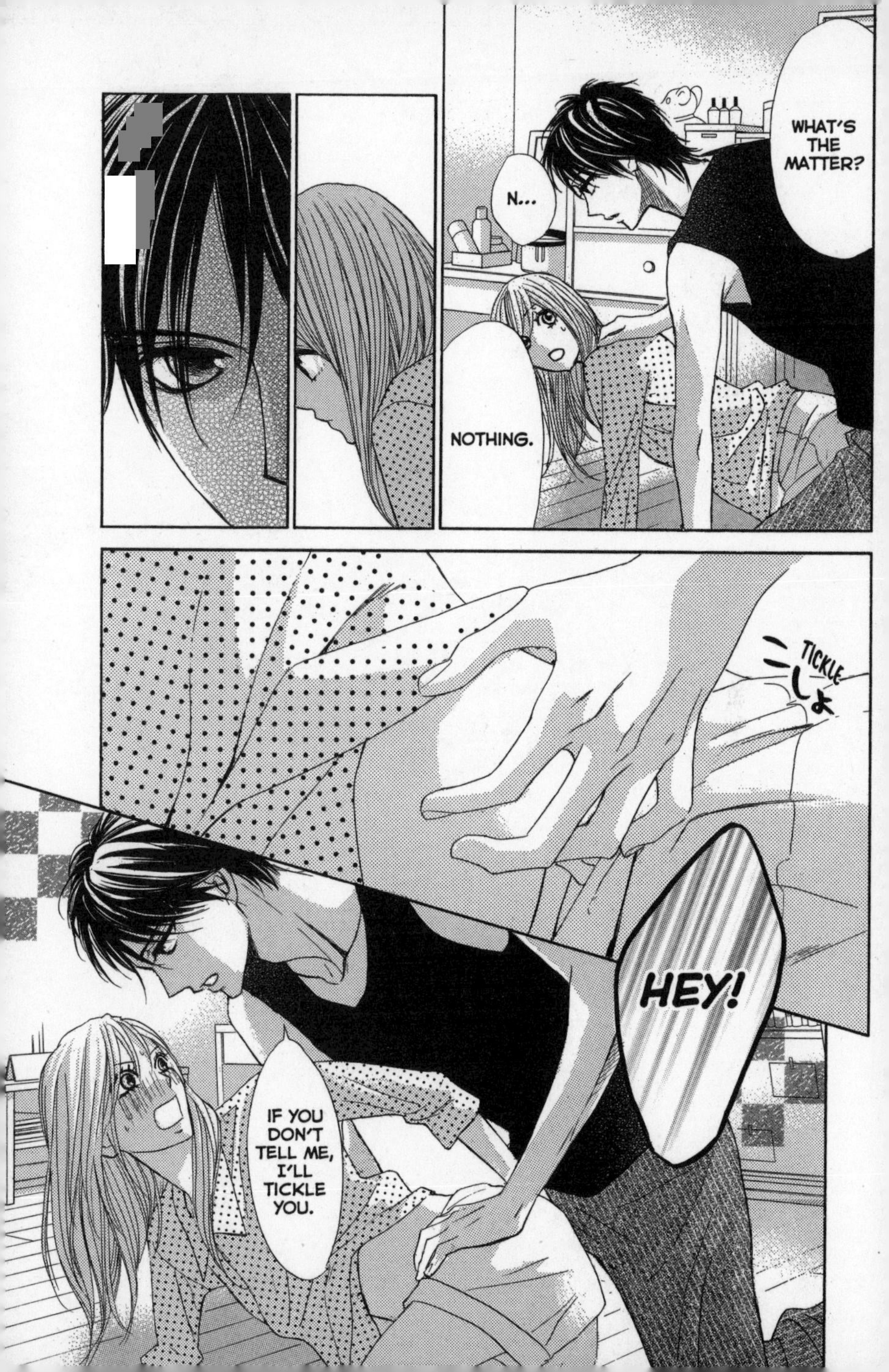
WHAT'S THE MATTER?
N...
NOTHING.
TICKLE
HEY!
IF YOU DON'T TELL ME, I'LL TICKLE YOU.

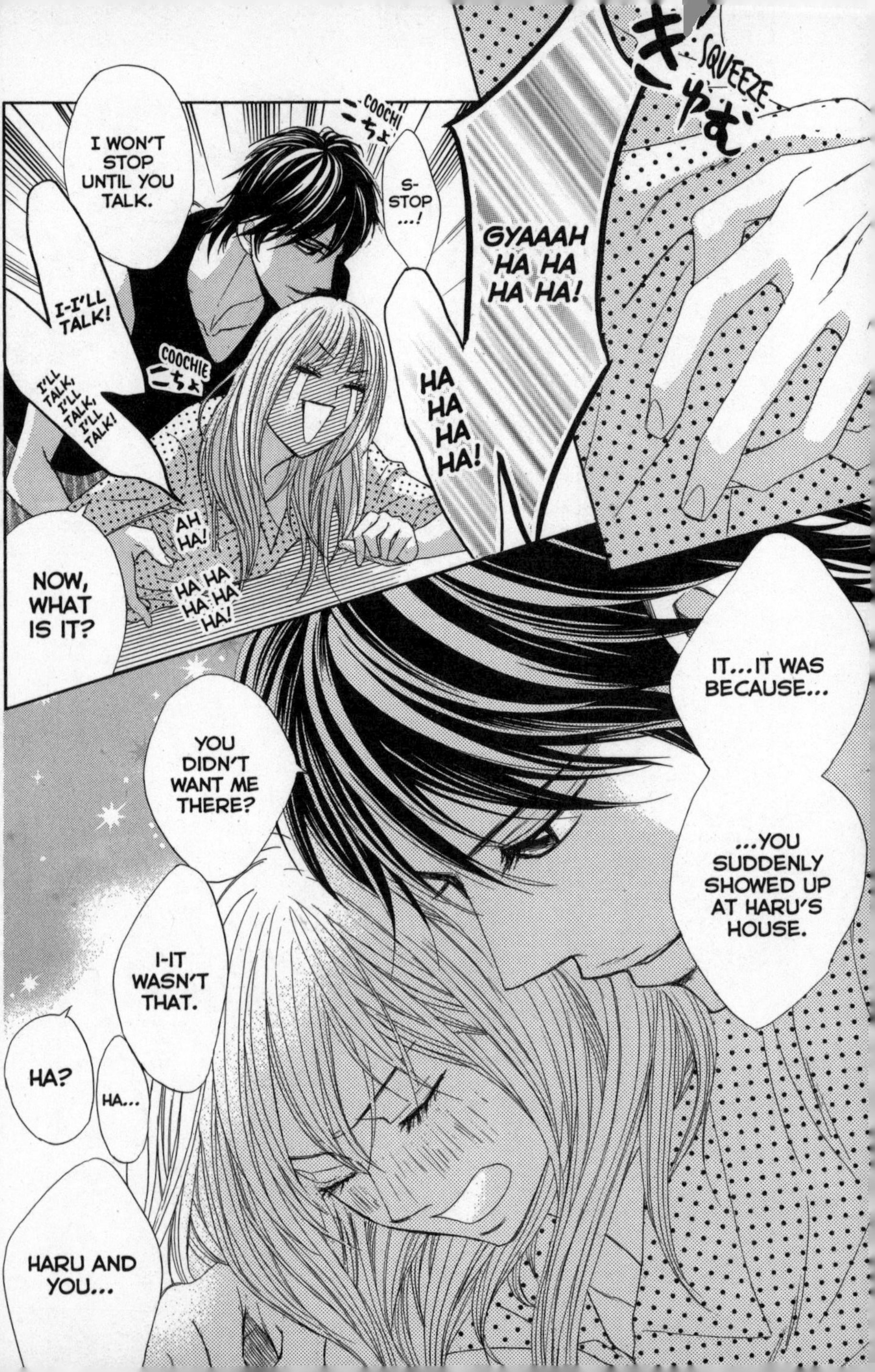
きゅむ
SQUEEZE
GYAAAH HA HA HA HA!
HA HA HA HA!
こちょ
COOCHI
S-STOP...!
I WON'T STOP UNTIL YOU TALK.
I-I'LL TALK!
こちょ
COOCHIE
I'LL TALK, I'LL TALK, I'LL TALK!
AH HA!
HA HA HA HA HA!
NOW, WHAT IS IT?
IT...IT WAS BECAUSE...
...YOU SUDDENLY SHOWED UP AT HARU'S HOUSE.
YOU DIDN'T WANT ME THERE?
I-IT WASN'T THAT.
HA?
HA...
HARU AND YOU...

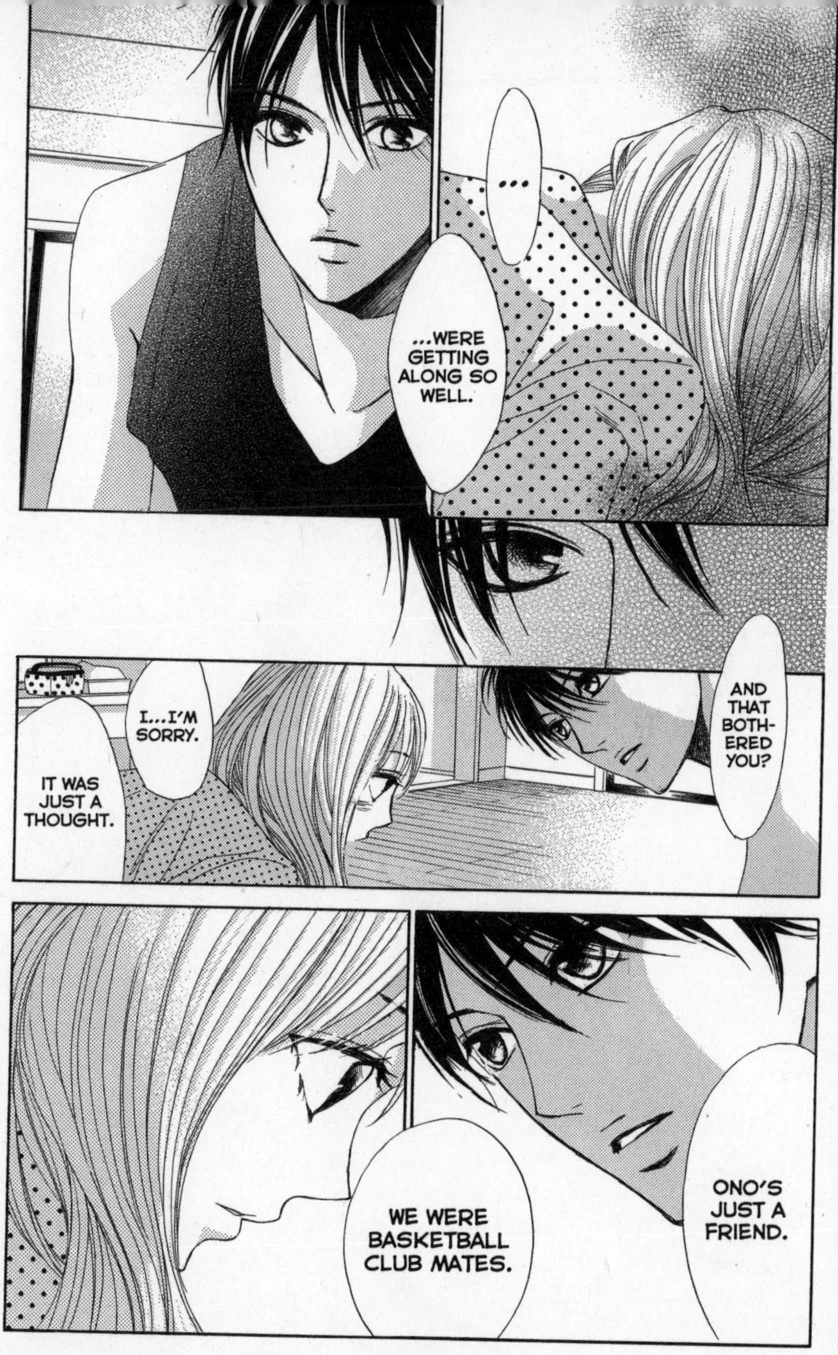
...
...WERE GETTING ALONG SO WELL.
AND THAT BOTHERED YOU?
I...I'M SORRY.
IT WAS JUST A THOUGHT.
ONO'S JUST A FRIEND.
WE WERE BASKETBALL CLUB MATES.

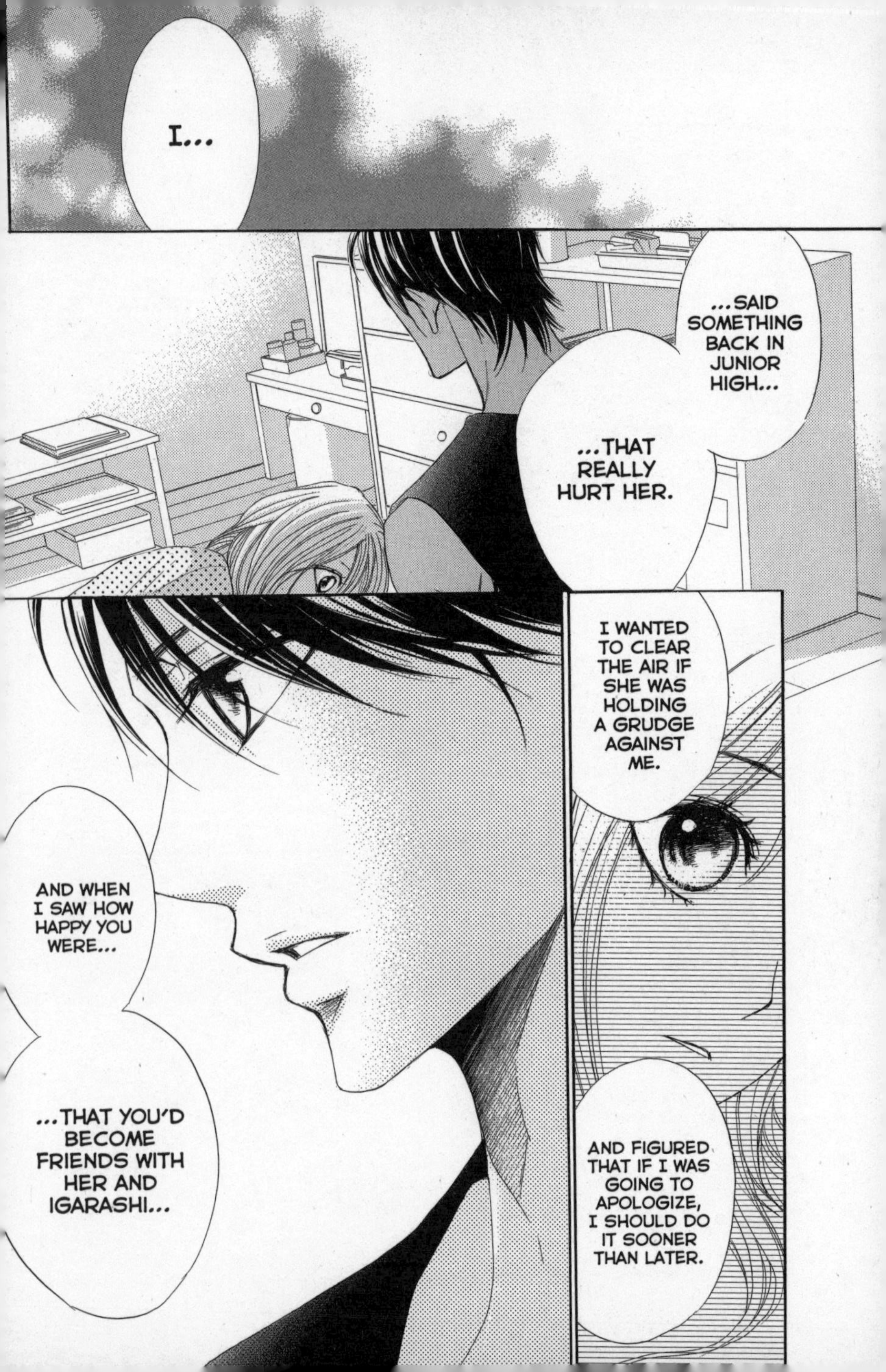
I...
...SAID SOMETHING BACK IN JUNIOR HIGH...
...THAT REALLY HURT HER.
I WANTED TO CLEAR THE AIR IF SHE WAS HOLDING A GRUDGE AGAINST ME.
AND FIGURED THAT IF I WAS GOING TO APOLOGIZE, I SHOULD DO IT SOONER THAN LATER.
AND WHEN I SAW HOW HAPPY YOU WERE...
...THAT YOU'D BECOME FRIENDS WITH HER AND IGARASHI...

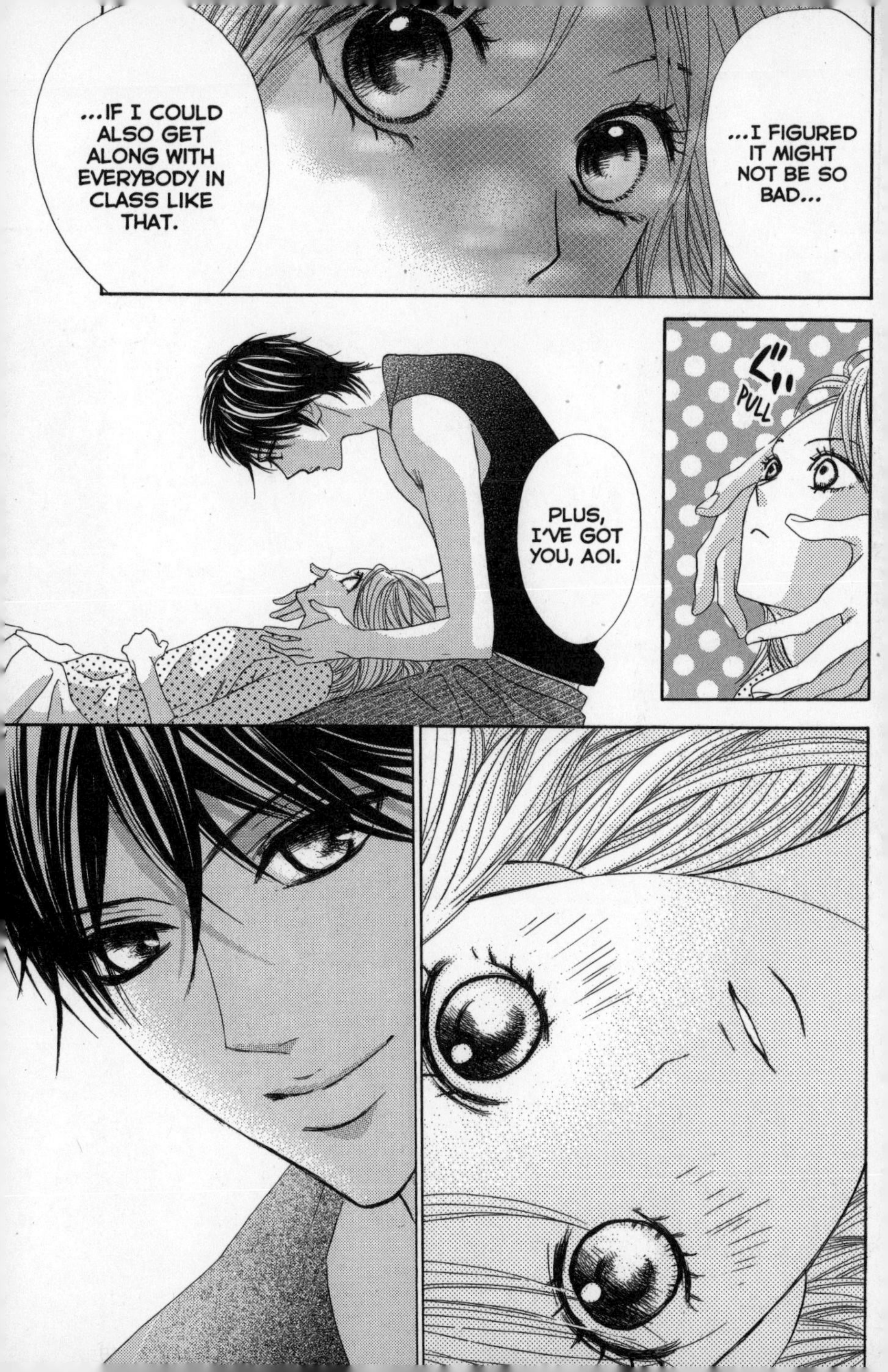
...I FIGURED IT MIGHT NOT BE SO BAD...
...IF I COULD ALSO GET ALONG WITH EVERYBODY IN CLASS LIKE THAT.
ぐい
PULL
PLUS, I'VE GOT YOU, AOI.

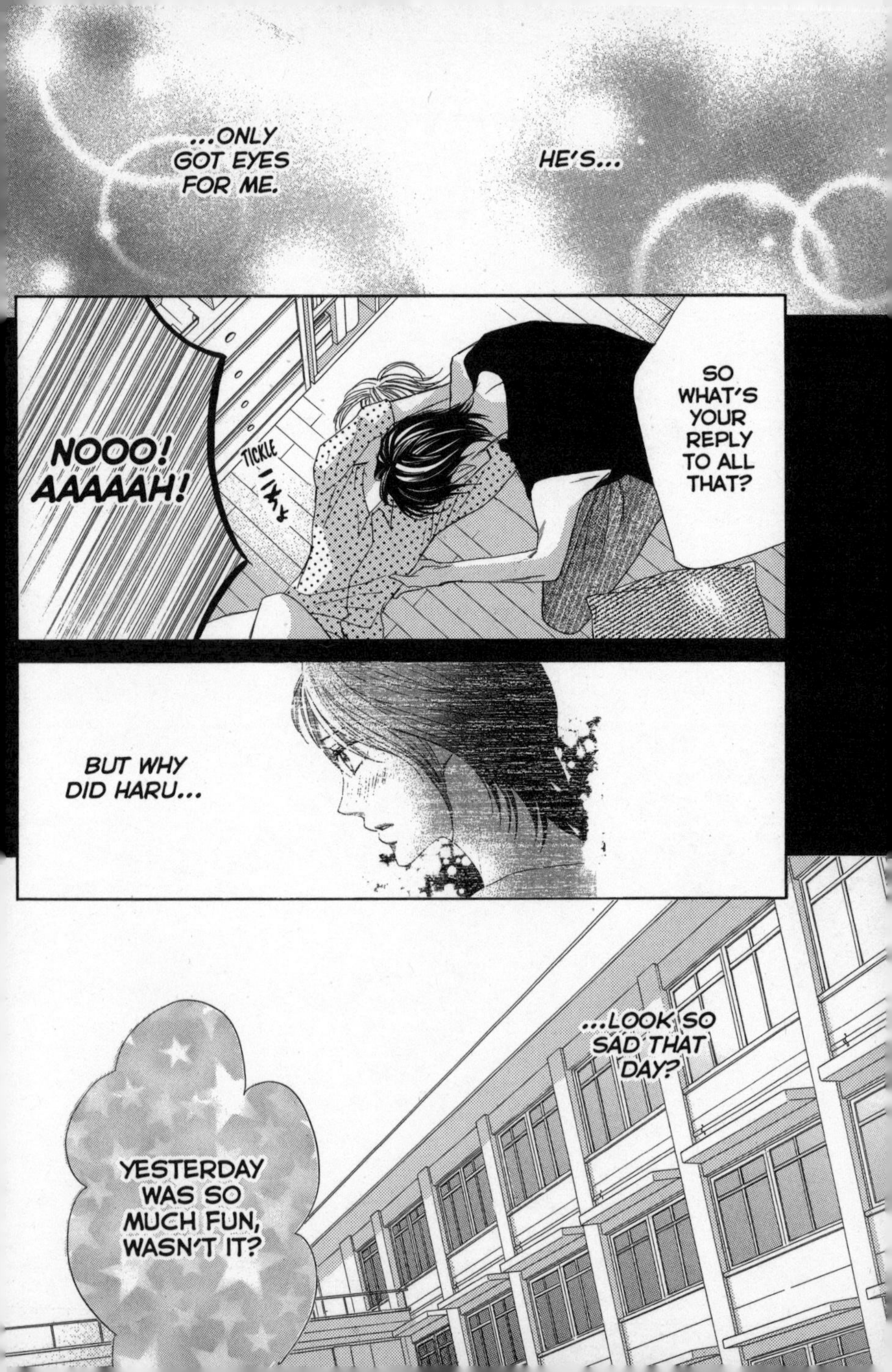
HE'S...
...ONLY GOT EYES FOR ME.
SO WHAT'S YOUR REPLY TO ALL THAT?
TICKLE
NOOO! AAAAAH!
BUT WHY DID HARU...
...LOOK SO SAD THAT DAY?
YESTERDAY WAS SO MUCH FUN, WASN'T IT?

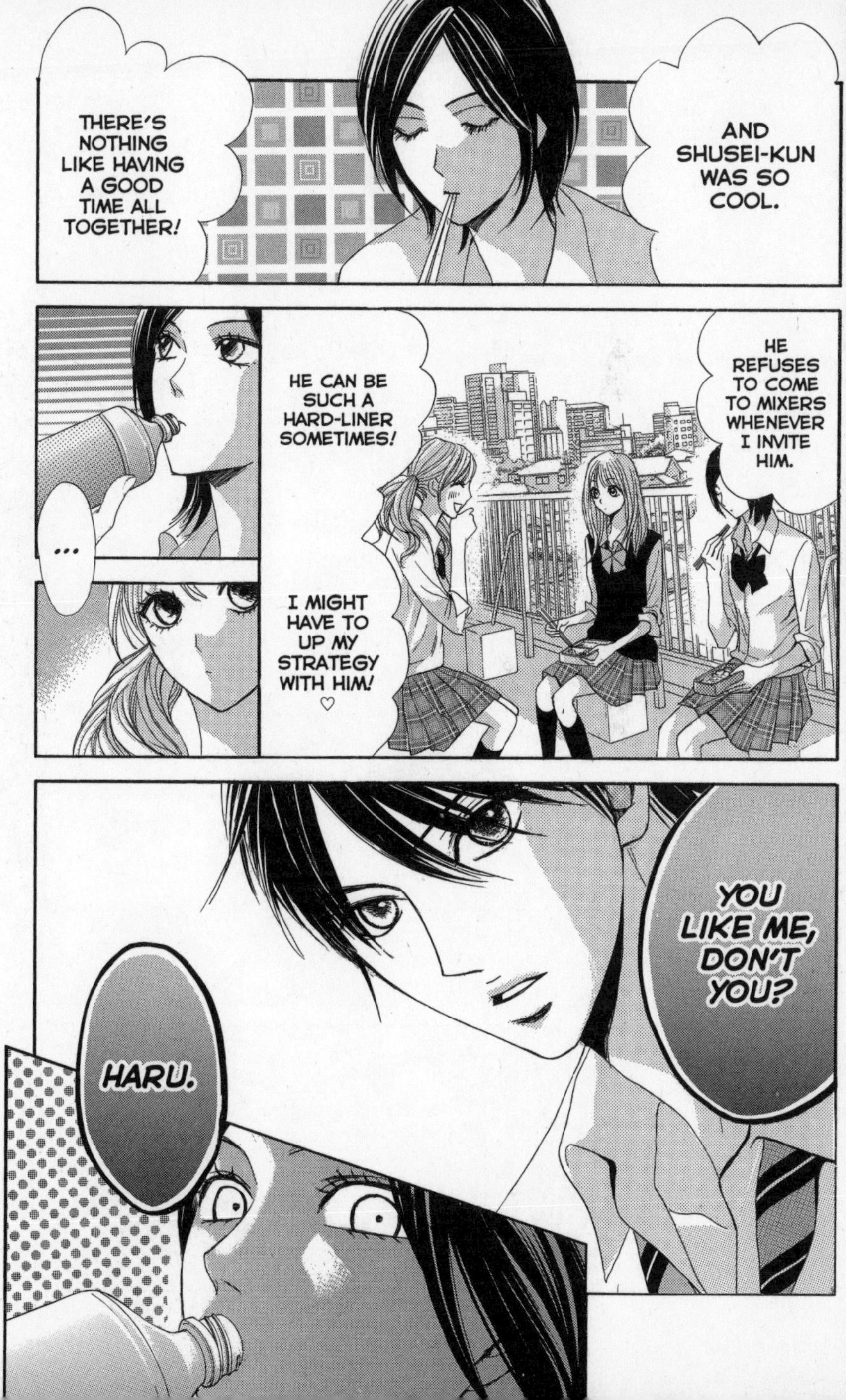
AND SHUSEI-KUN WAS SO COOL.
THERE'S NOTHING LIKE HAVING A GOOD TIME ALL TOGETHER!
HE REFUSES TO COME TO MIXERS WHENEVER I INVITE HIM.
HE CAN BE SUCH A HARD-LINER SOMETIMES!
I MIGHT HAVE TO UP MY STRATEGY WITH HIM! ♡
...
YOU LIKE ME, DON'T YOU?
HARU.

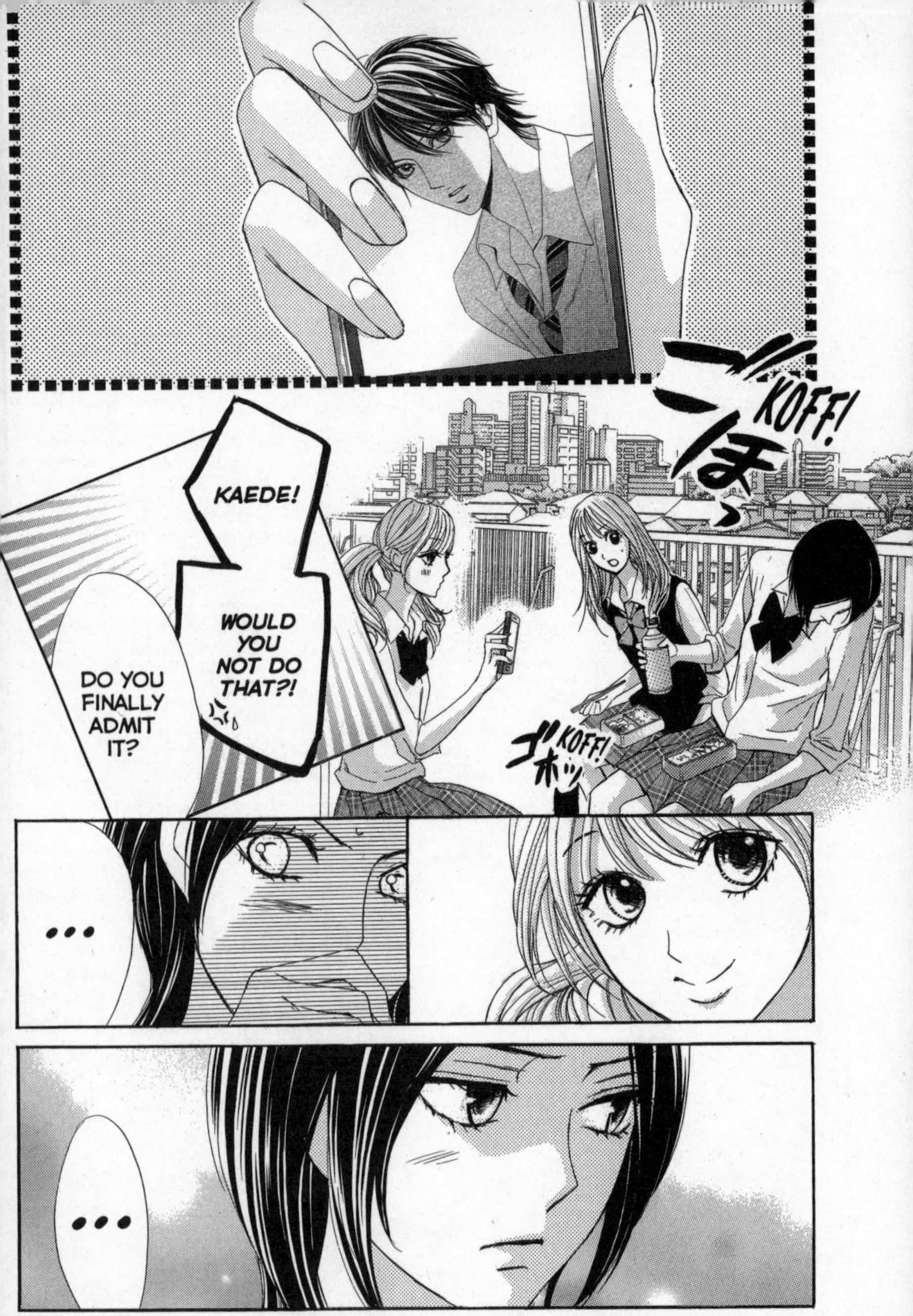
ごほっ
KOFF!
ゴホッ
KOFF!
KAEDE!
WOULD YOU NOT DO THAT?!
DO YOU FINALLY ADMIT IT?
...
...

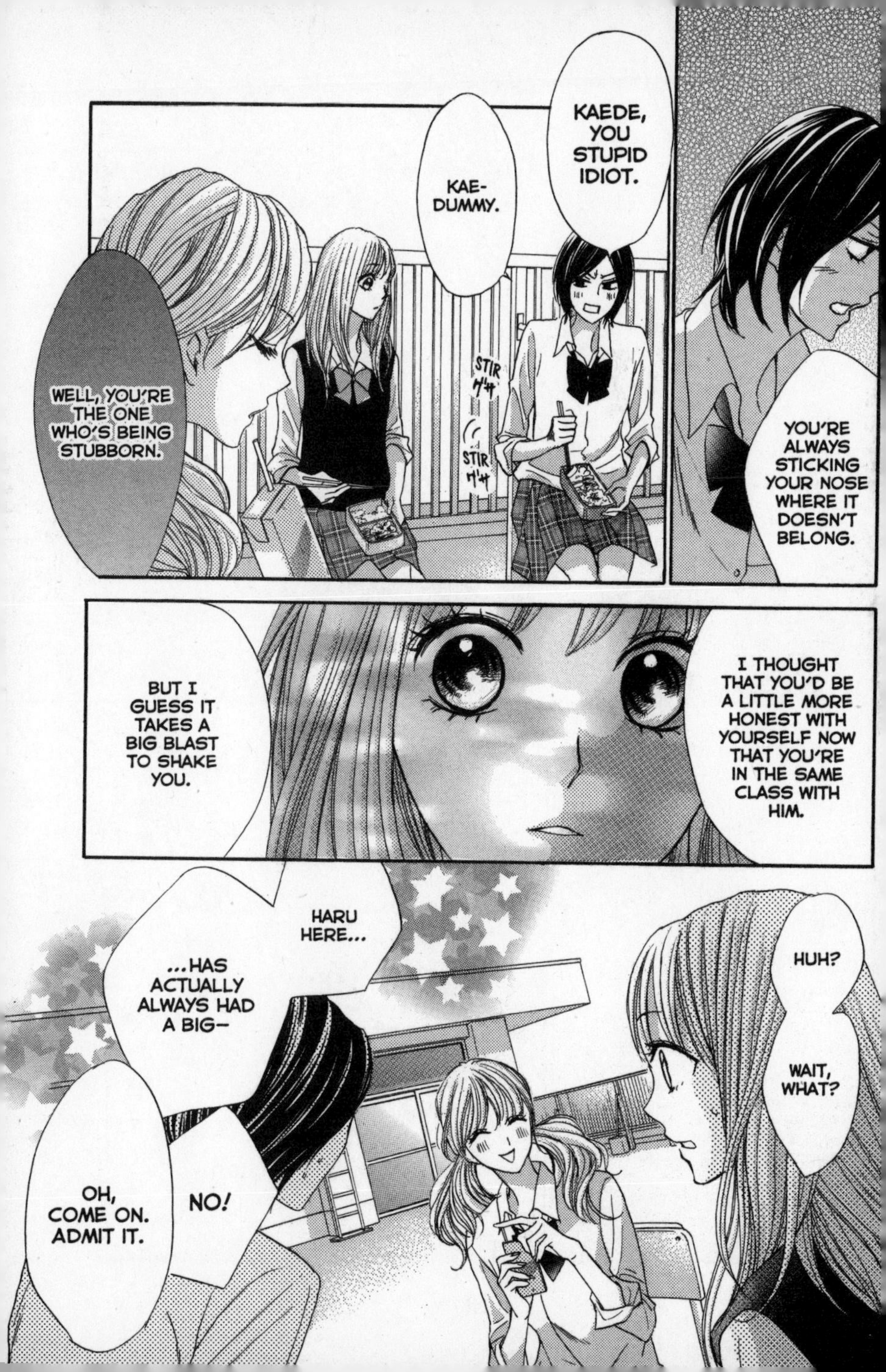
YOU'RE ALWAYS STICKING YOUR NOSE WHERE IT DOESN'T BELONG.
KAEDE, YOU STUPID IDIOT.
KAE-DUMMY.
STIR
STIR
WELL, YOU'RE THE ONE WHO'S BEING STUBBORN.
I THOUGHT THAT YOU'D BE A LITTLE MORE HONEST WITH YOURSELF NOW THAT YOU'RE IN THE SAME CLASS WITH HIM.
BUT I GUESS IT TAKES A BIG BLAST TO SHAKE YOU.
HARU HERE...
...HAS ACTUALLY ALWAYS HAD A BIG—
HUH?
WAIT, WHAT?
NO!
OH, COME ON. ADMIT IT.

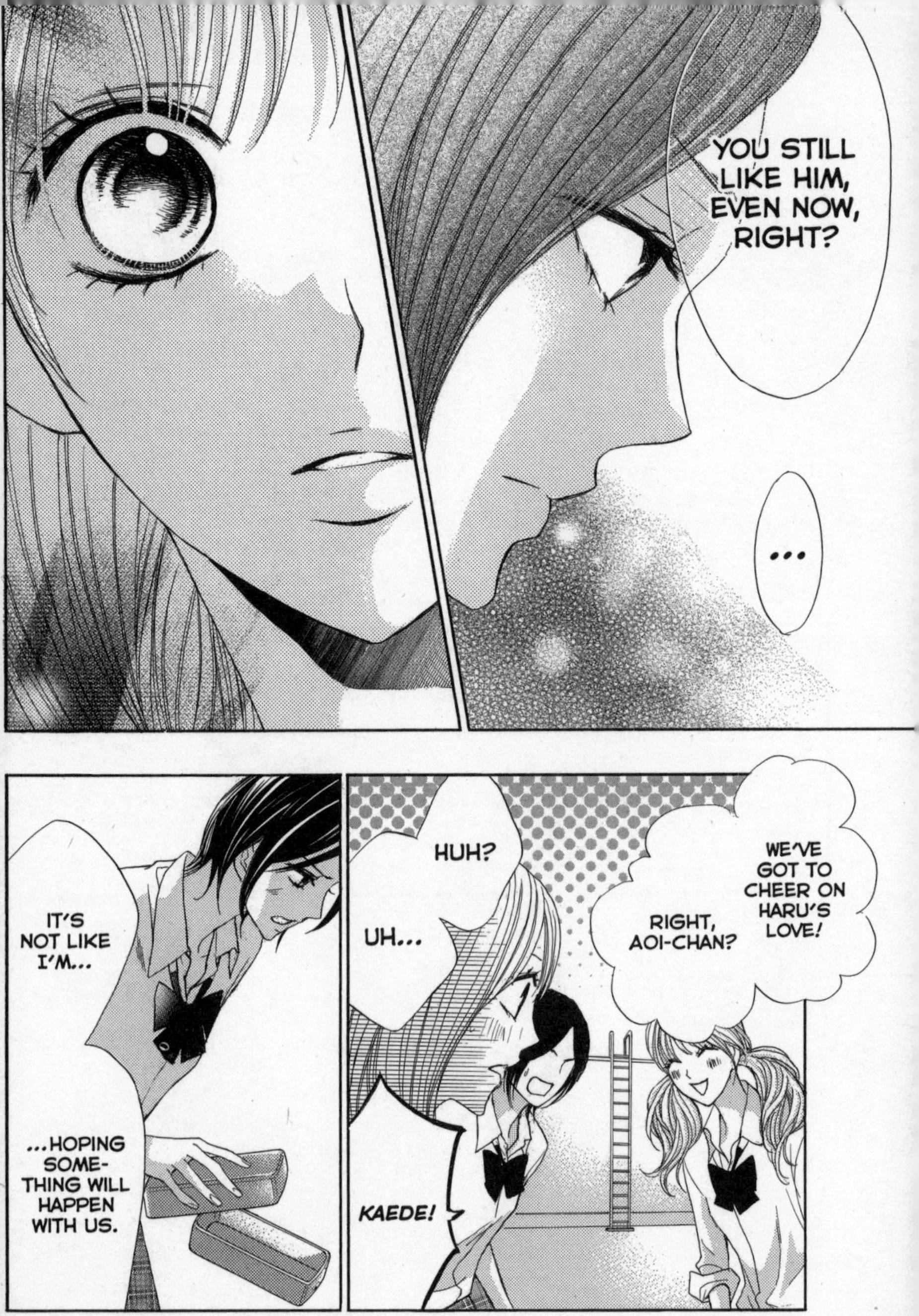
YOU STILL LIKE HIM, EVEN NOW, RIGHT?
...
WE'VE GOT TO CHEER ON HARU'S LOVE!
RIGHT, AOI-CHAN?
HUH?
UH...
KAEDE!
IT'S NOT LIKE I'M...
...HOPING SOME-THING WILL HAPPEN WITH US.

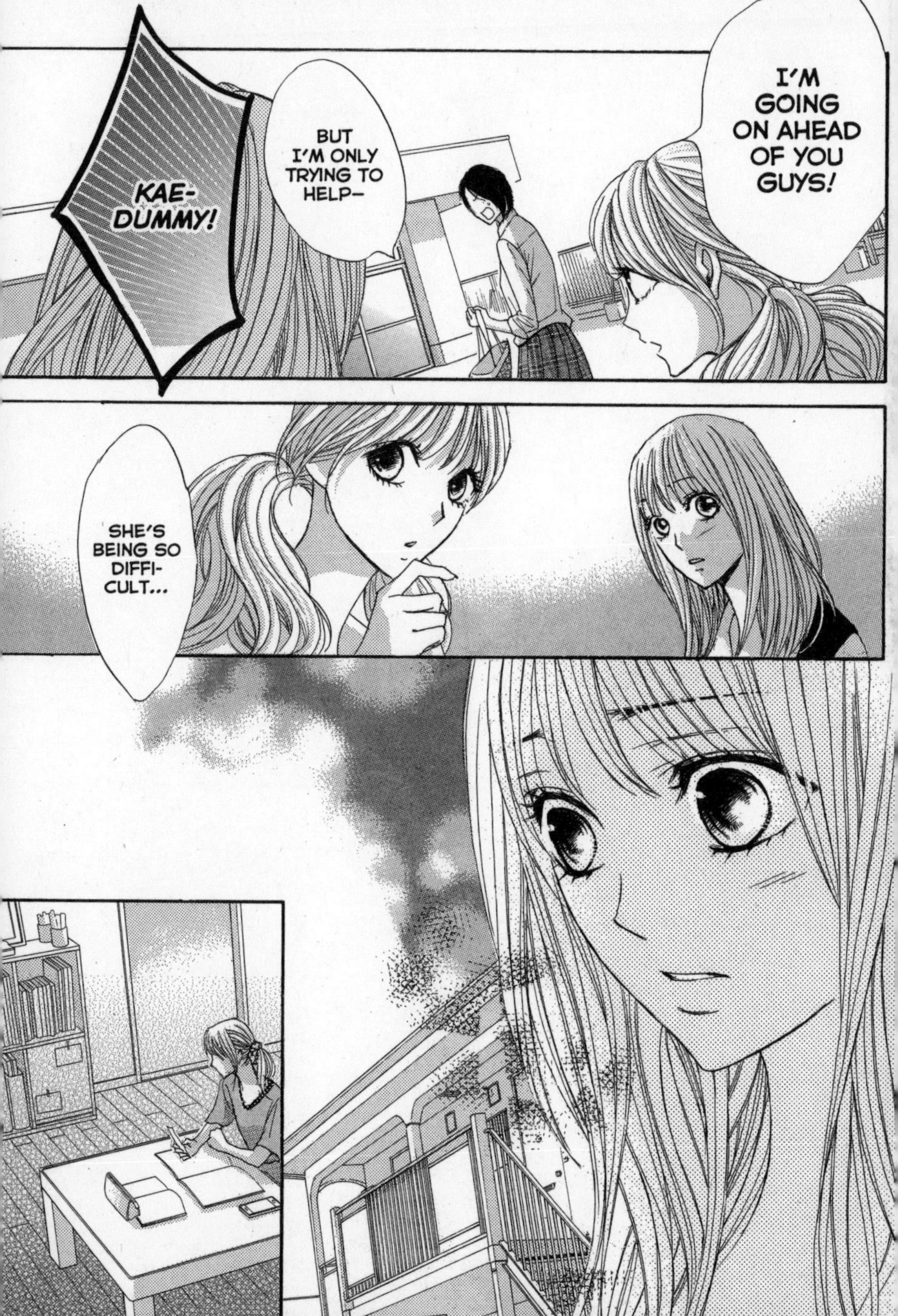
I'M GOING ON AHEAD OF YOU GUYS!
BUT I'M ONLY TRYING TO HELP—
KAE-DUMMY!
SHE'S BEING SO DIFFI-CULT...

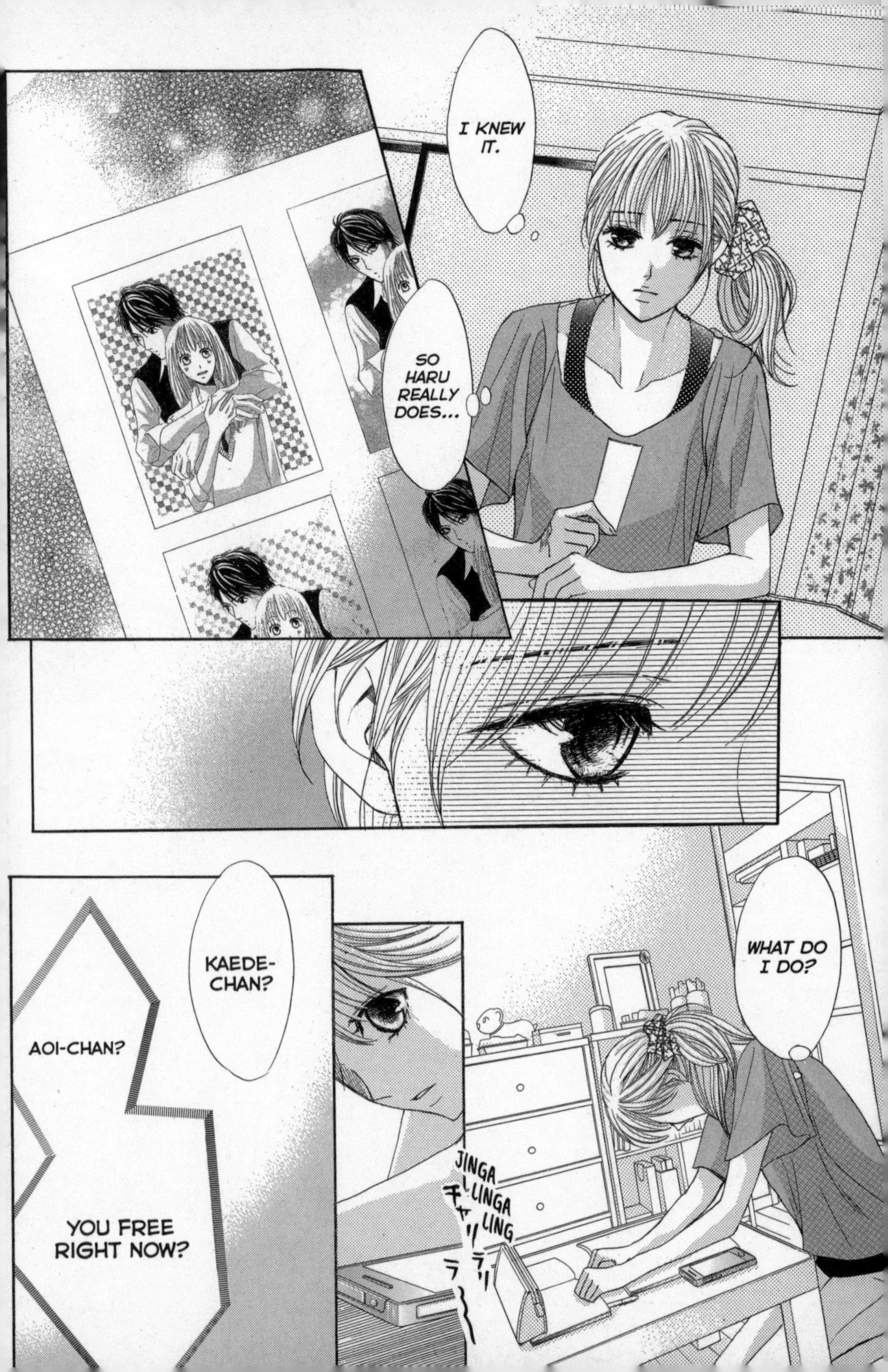
I KNEW IT.
SO HARU REALLY DOES...
WHAT DO I DO?
JINGA LINGA LING
チャリラリラ～
KAEDE-CHAN?
AOI-CHAN?
YOU FREE RIGHT NOW?

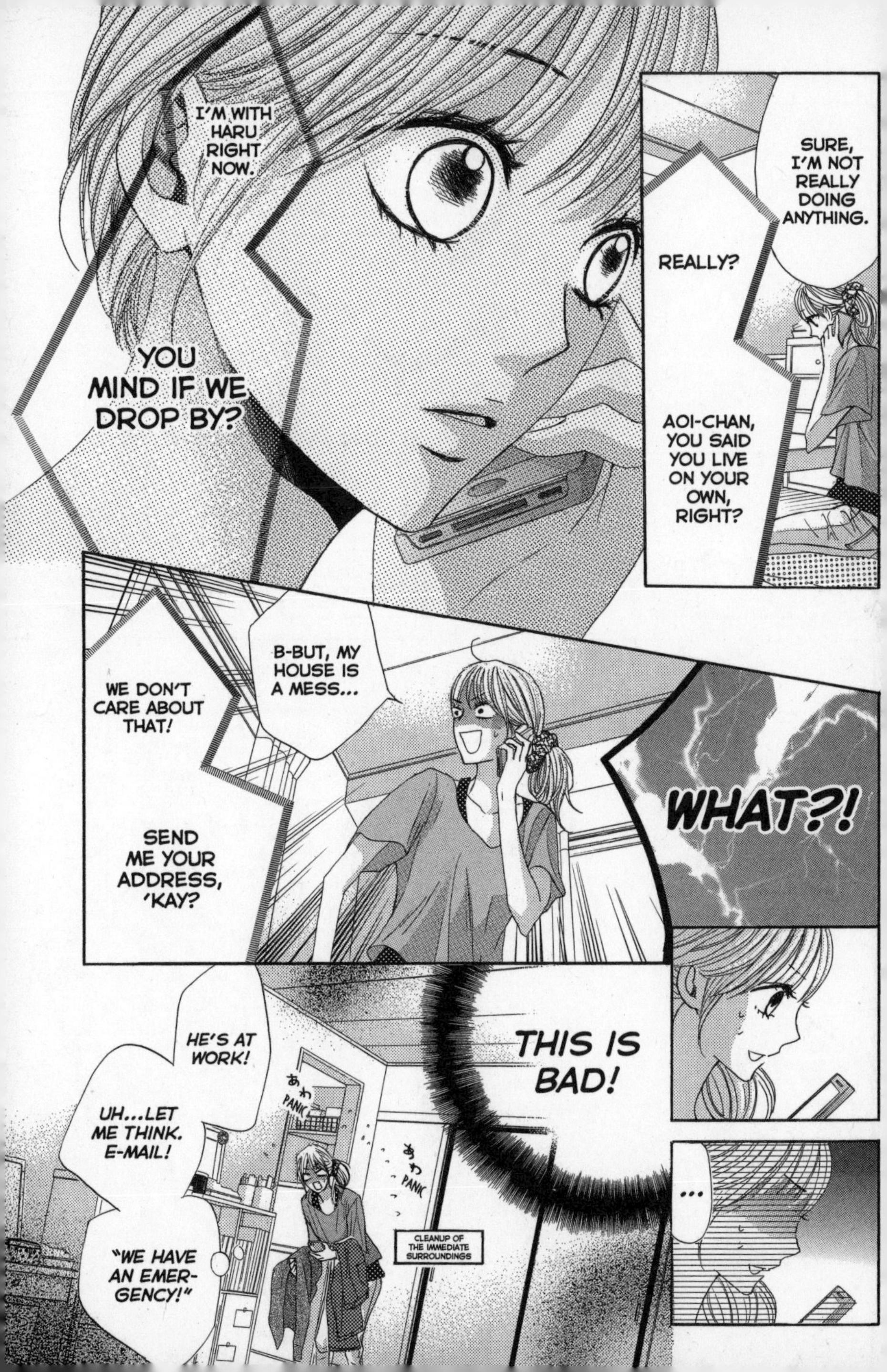
SURE, I'M NOT REALLY DOING ANYTHING.
REALLY?
AOI-CHAN, YOU SAID YOU LIVE ON YOUR OWN, RIGHT?
I'M WITH HARU RIGHT NOW.
YOU MIND IF WE DROP BY?
WHAT?!
B-BUT, MY HOUSE IS A MESS...
WE DON'T CARE ABOUT THAT!
SEND ME YOUR ADDRESS, 'KAY?
...
THIS IS BAD!
HE'S AT WORK!
UH...LET ME THINK. E-MAIL!
"WE HAVE AN EMER-GENCY!"
あわ PANIC
あわ PANIC
CLEANUP OF THE IMMEDIATE SURROUNDINGS

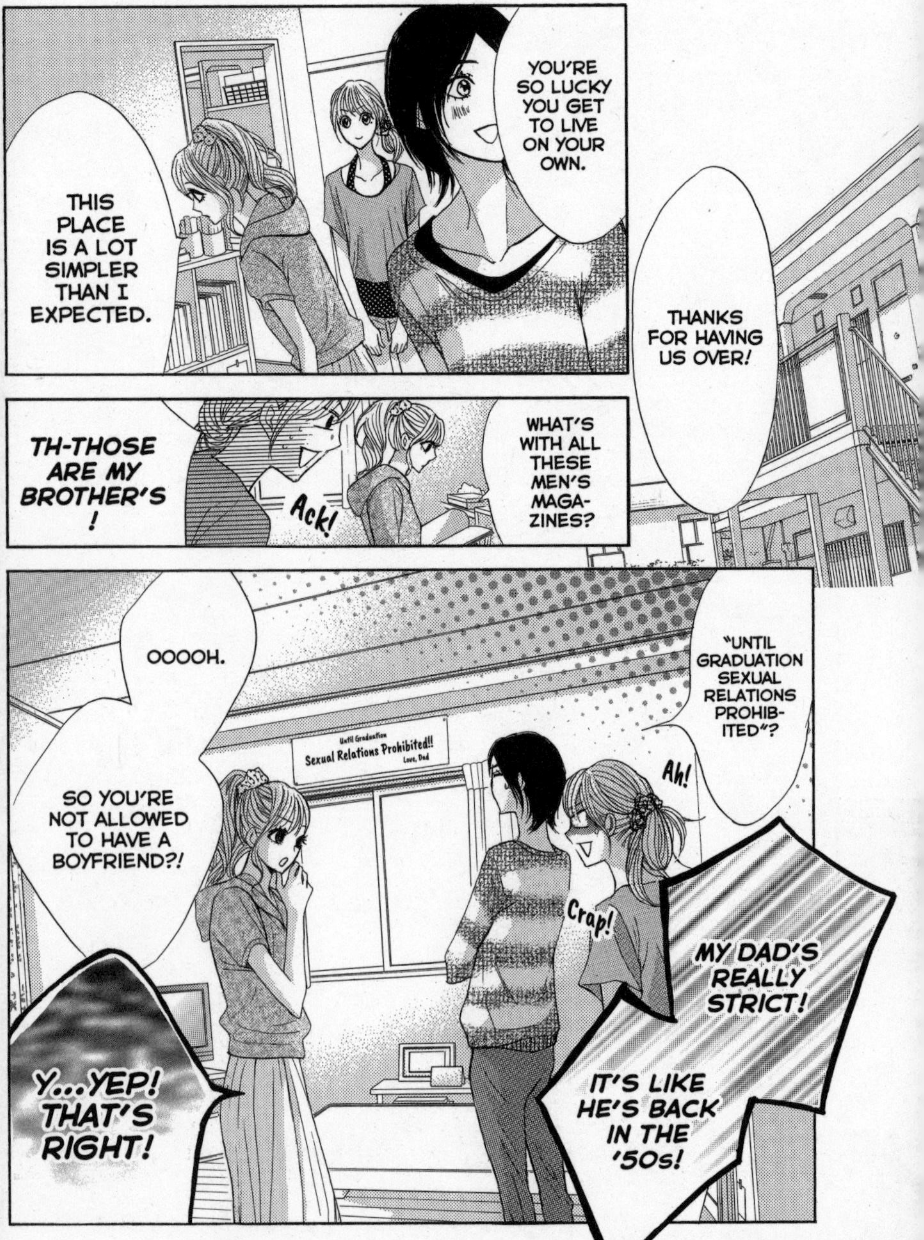
THANKS FOR HAVING US OVER!
YOU'RE SO LUCKY YOU GET TO LIVE ON YOUR OWN.
THIS PLACE IS A LOT SIMPLER THAN I EXPECTED.
WHAT'S WITH ALL THESE MEN'S MAGA-ZINES?
Ack!
TH-THOSE ARE MY BROTHER'S!
"UNTIL GRADUATION SEXUAL RELATIONS PROHIB-ITED"?
Until Graduation Sexual Relations Prohibited!! Love, Dad
Ah!
OOOOH.
SO YOU'RE NOT ALLOWED TO HAVE A BOYFRIEND?!
Crap!
MY DAD'S REALLY STRICT!
IT'S LIKE HE'S BACK IN THE '50s!
Y...YEP! THAT'S RIGHT!

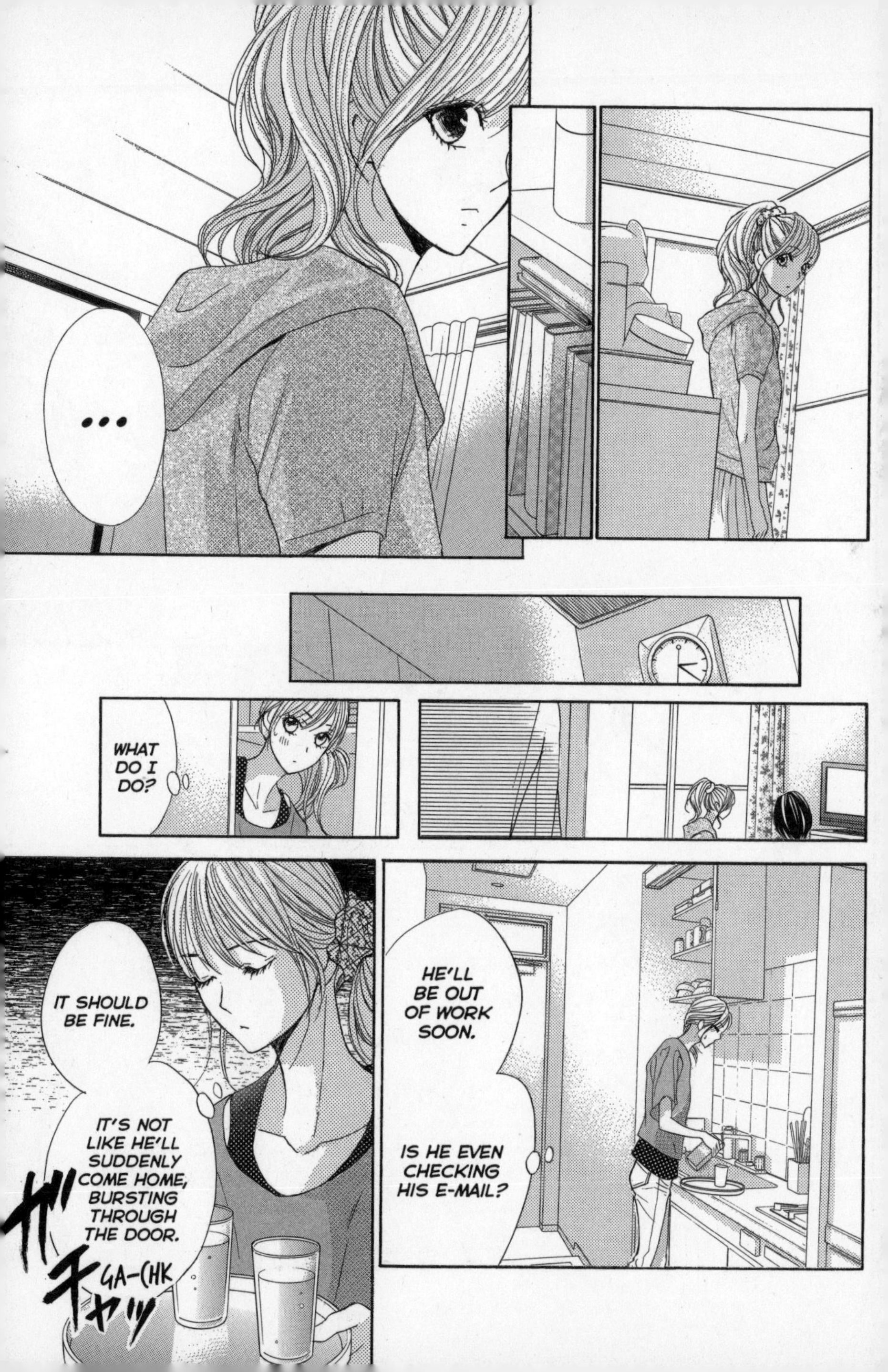
...
WHAT DO I DO?
HE'LL BE OUT OF WORK SOON.
IS HE EVEN CHECKING HIS E-MAIL?
IT SHOULD BE FINE.
IT'S NOT LIKE HE'LL SUDDENLY COME HOME, BURSTING THROUGH THE DOOR.
GA-CHK

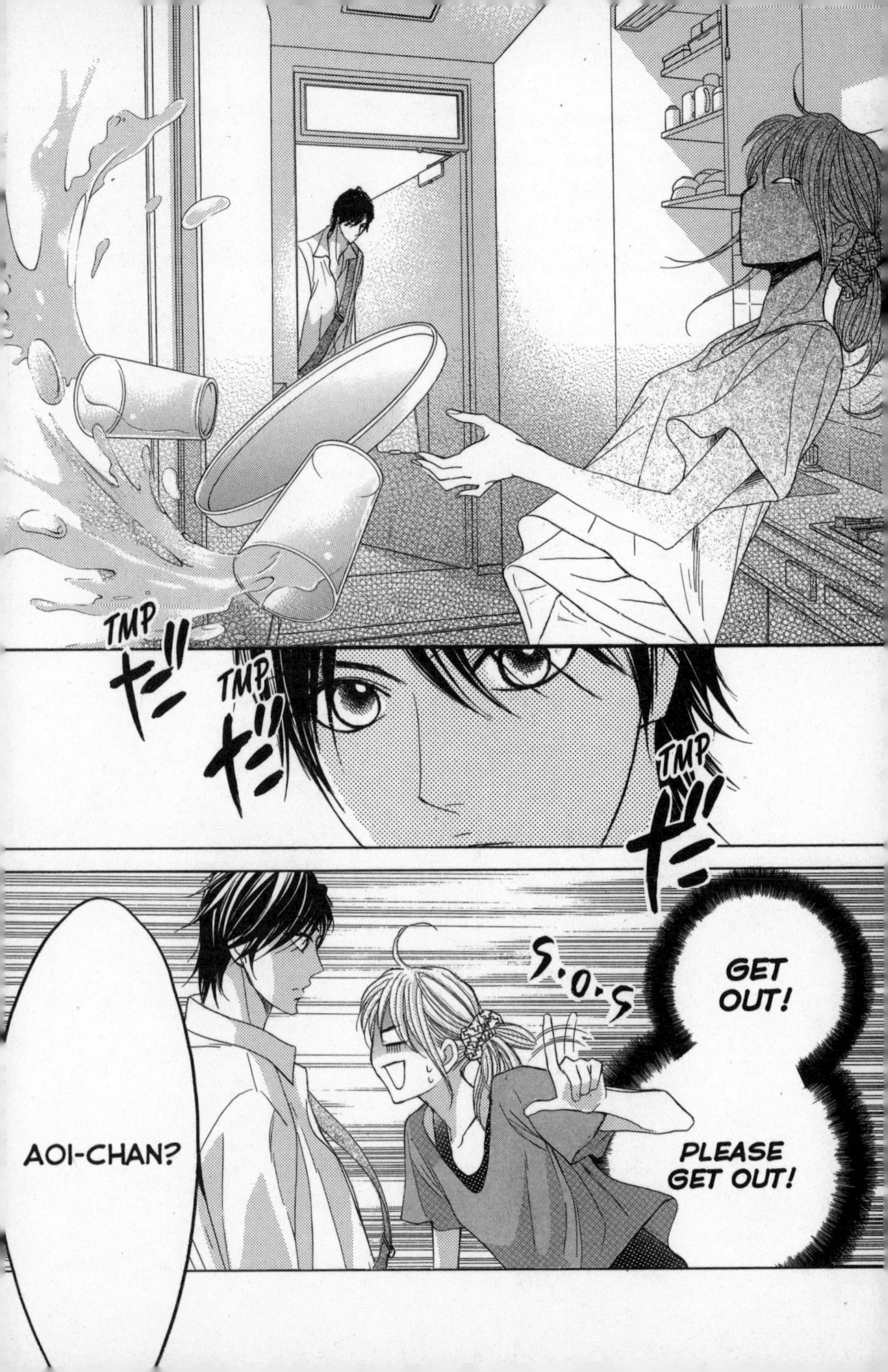
TMP
TMP
TMP
GET OUT!
PLEASE GET OUT!
S.O.S
AOI-CHAN?

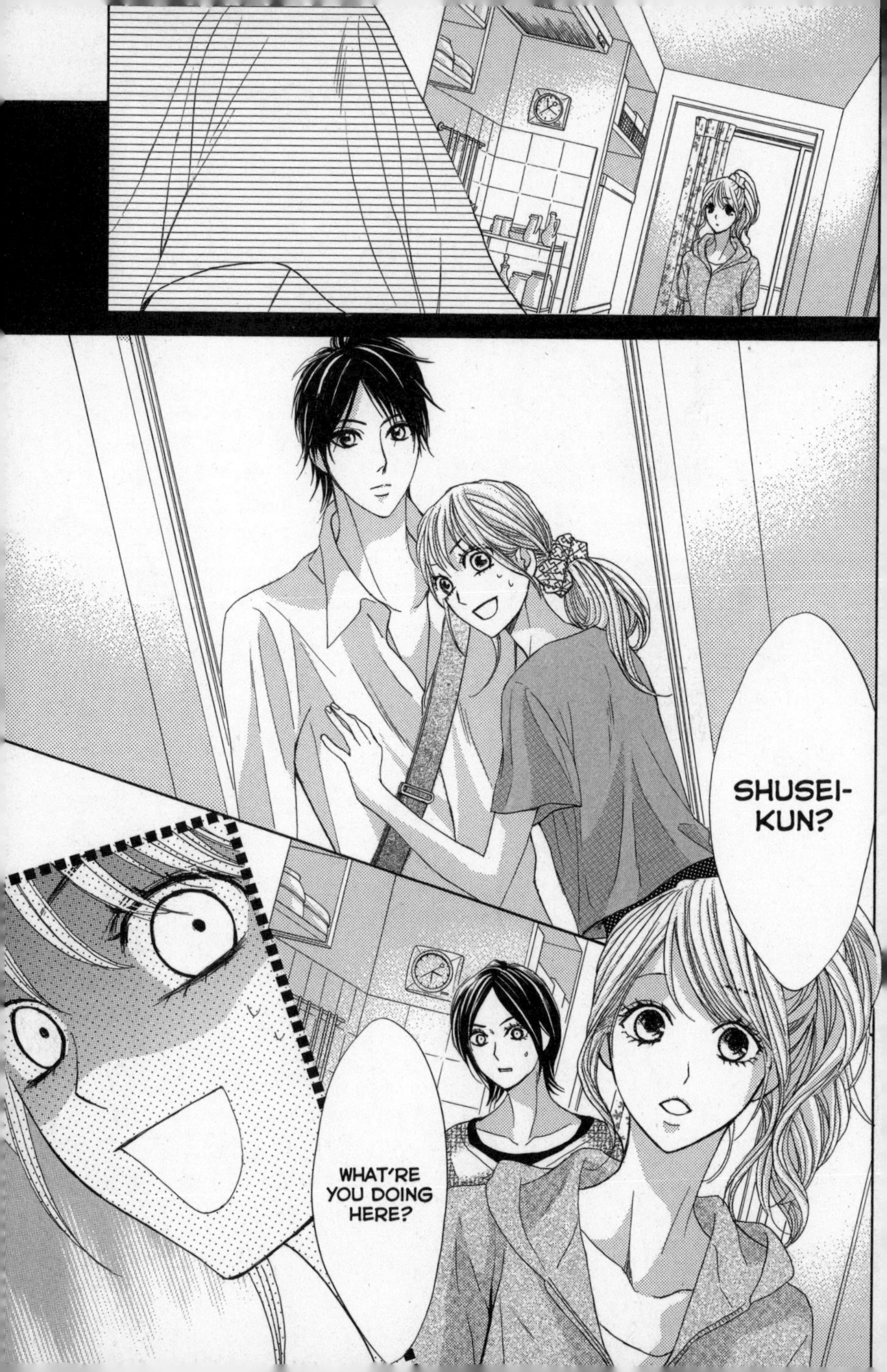
SHUSEI-KUN?
WHAT'RE YOU DOING HERE?

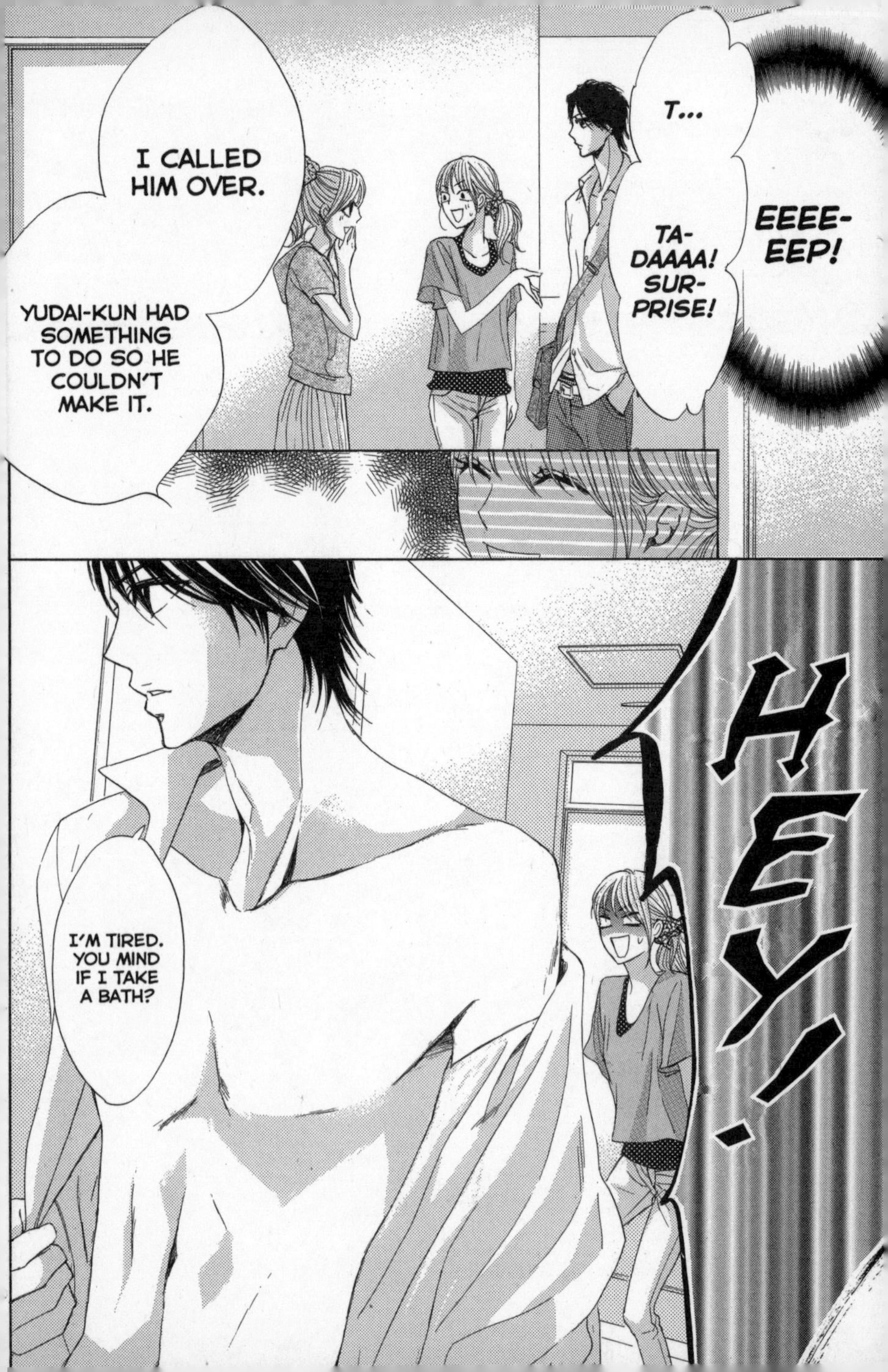
T...
TA-DAAAA! SURPRISE!
EEEE-EEP!
I CALLED HIM OVER.
YUDAI-KUN HAD SOMETHING TO DO SO HE COULDN'T MAKE IT.
HEY!
I'M TIRED. YOU MIND IF I TAKE A BATH?

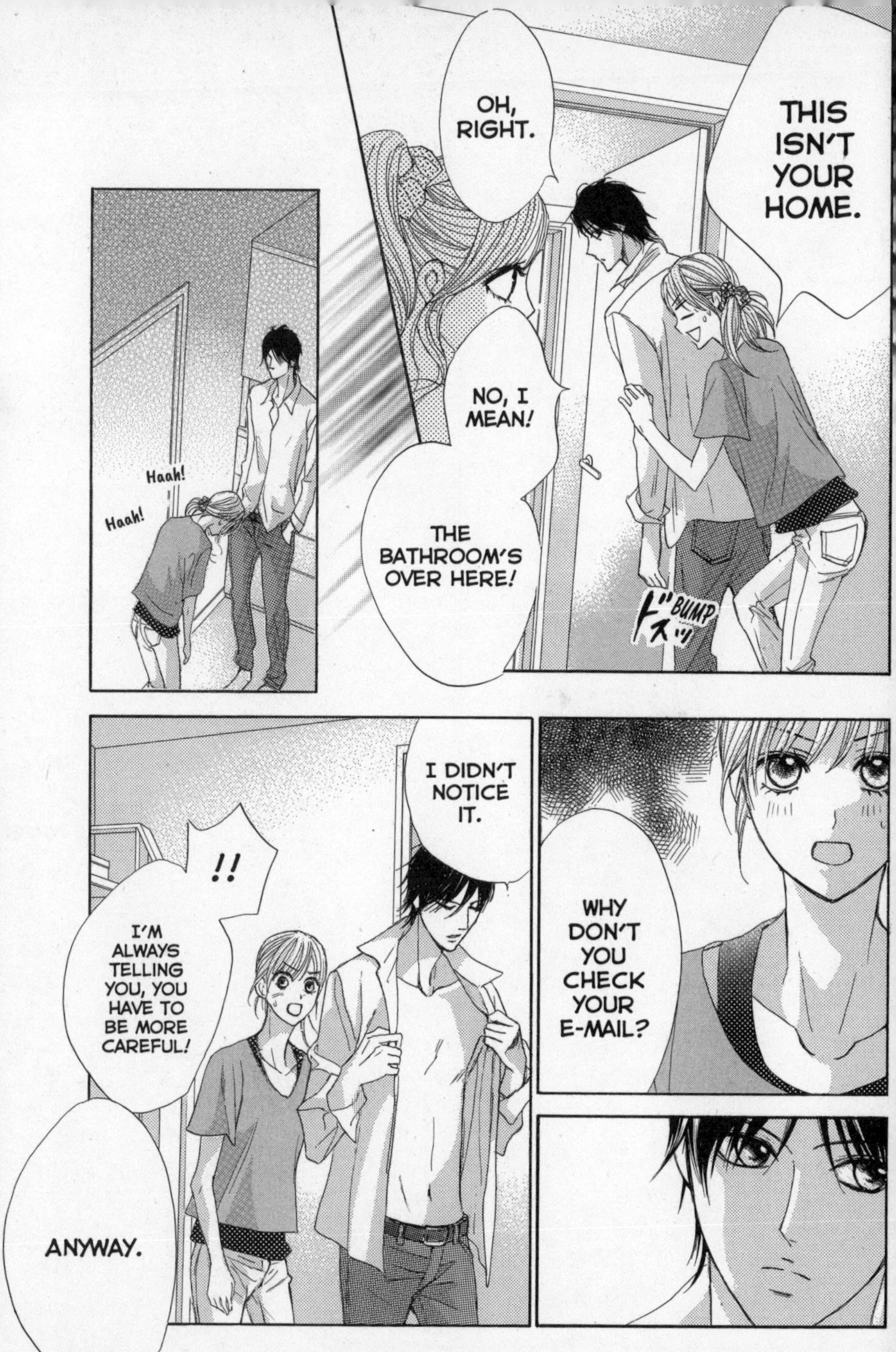
THIS ISN'T YOUR HOME.
OH, RIGHT.
NO, I MEAN!
THE BATHROOM'S OVER HERE!
BUMP
Haah!
Haah!
WHY DON'T YOU CHECK YOUR E-MAIL?
I DIDN'T NOTICE IT.
!!
I'M ALWAYS TELLING YOU, YOU HAVE TO BE MORE CAREFUL!
ANYWAY.

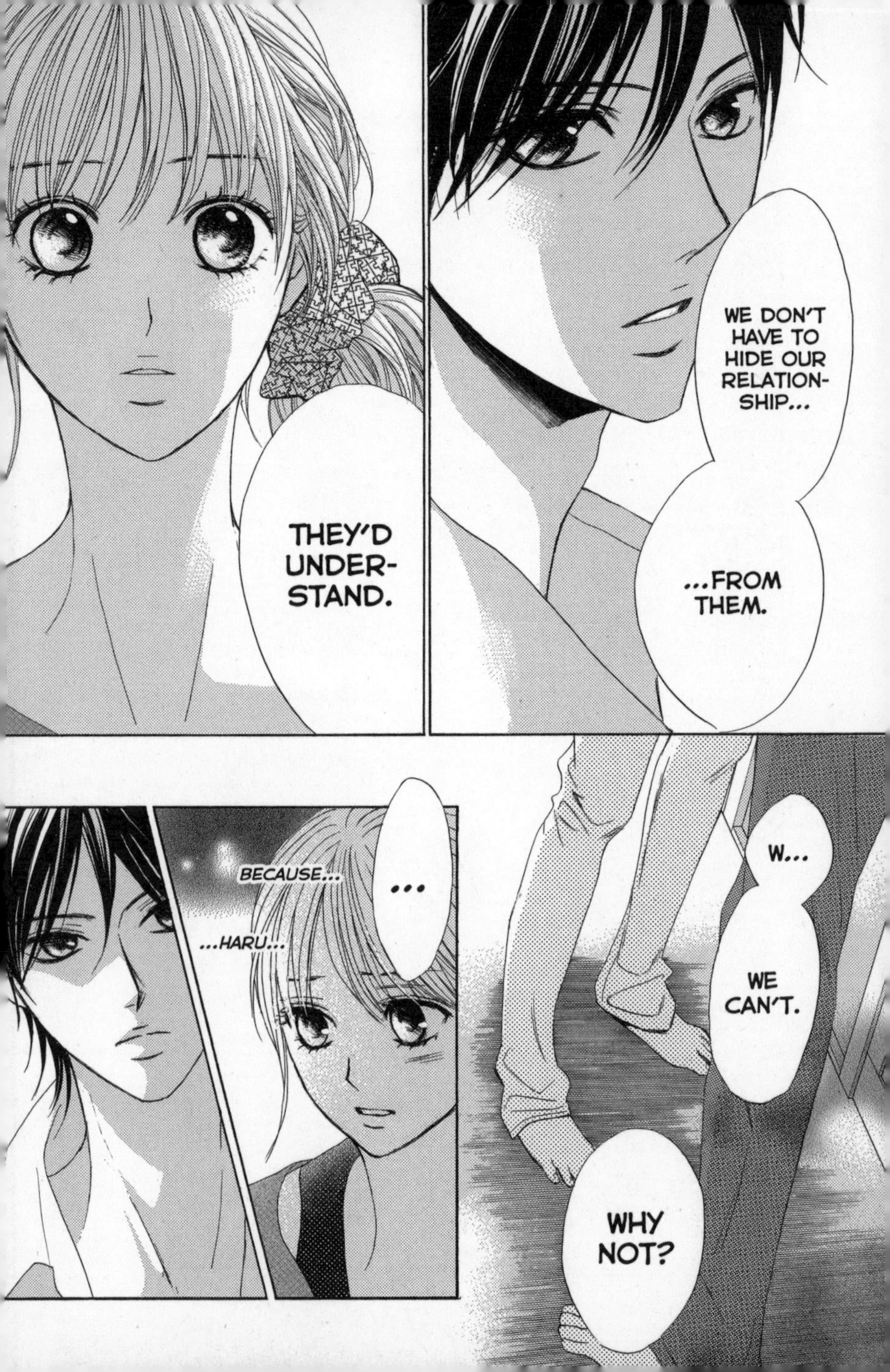

WE DON'T HAVE TO HIDE OUR RELATION-SHIP...
...FROM THEM.
THEY'D UNDER-STAND.
W...
WE CAN'T.
WHY NOT?
...
BECAUSE...
...HARU...

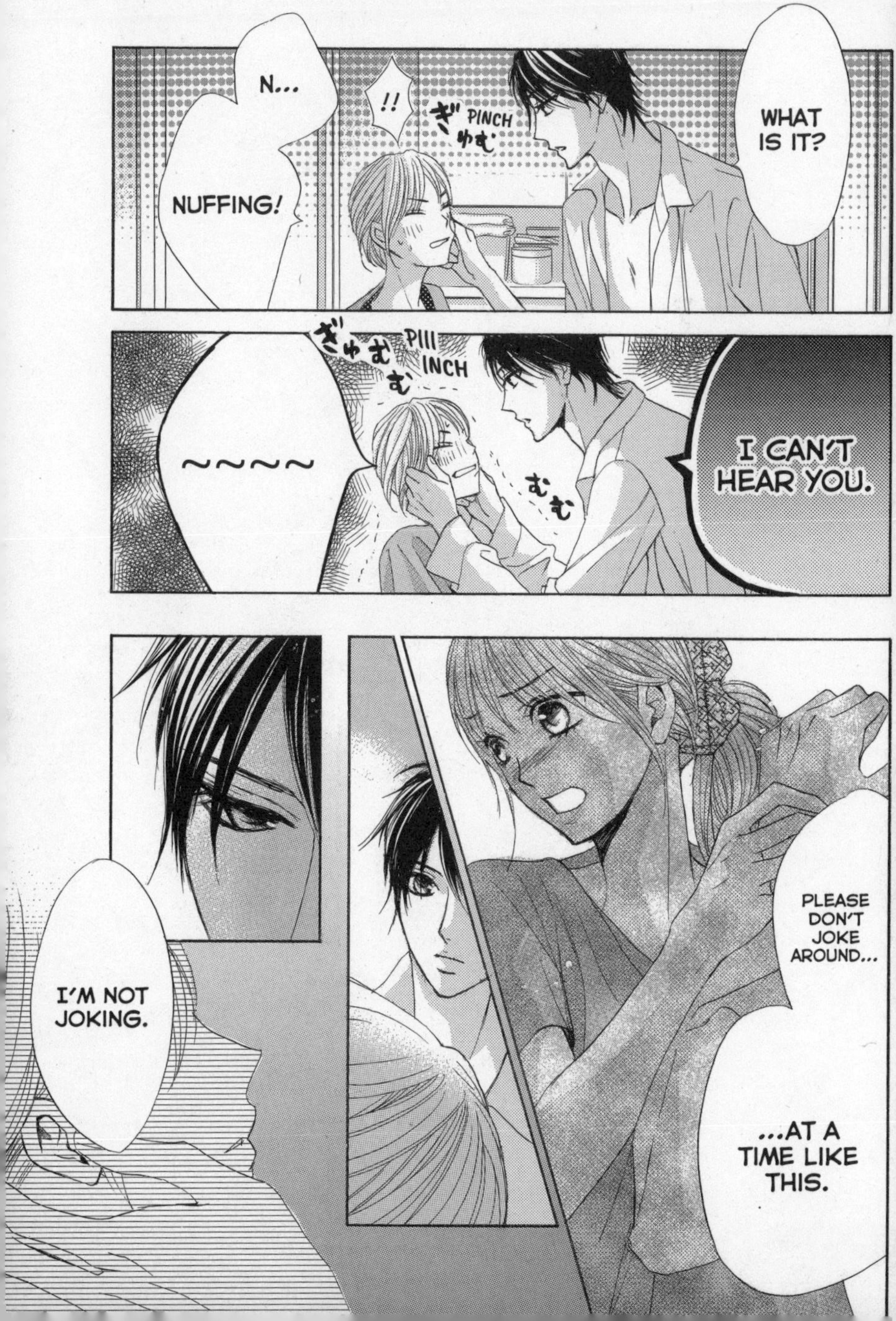
WHAT IS IT?
ぎゅむ
PINCH
!!
N...
NUFFING!
I CAN'T HEAR YOU.
むむ
ぎゅむむ
PIIII INCH
~~~~
PLEASE DON'T JOKE AROUND...
...AT A TIME LIKE THIS.
I'M NOT JOKING.
~~~~

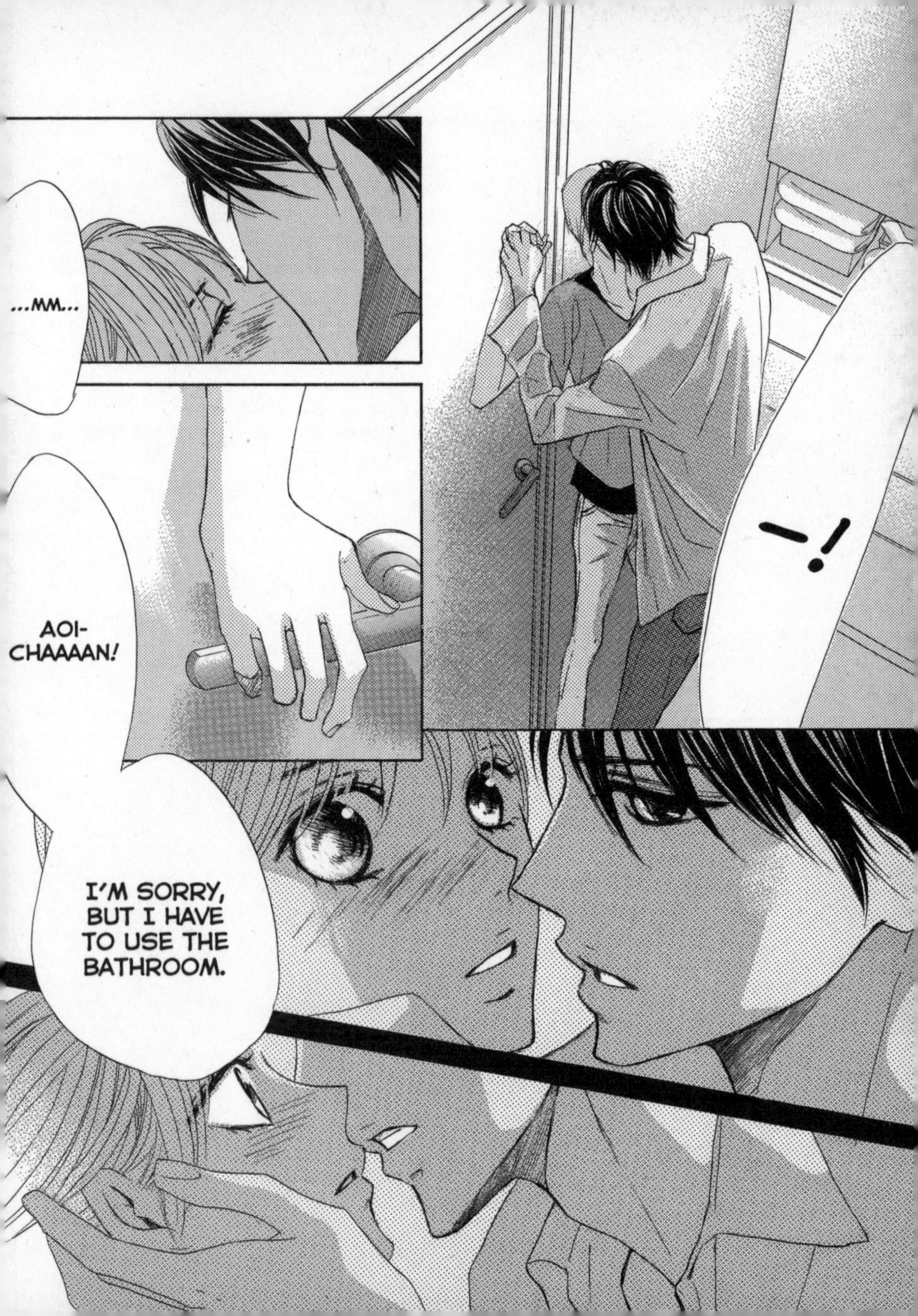
—!
...MM...
AOI-CHAAAAN!
I'M SORRY, BUT I HAVE TO USE THE BATHROOM.

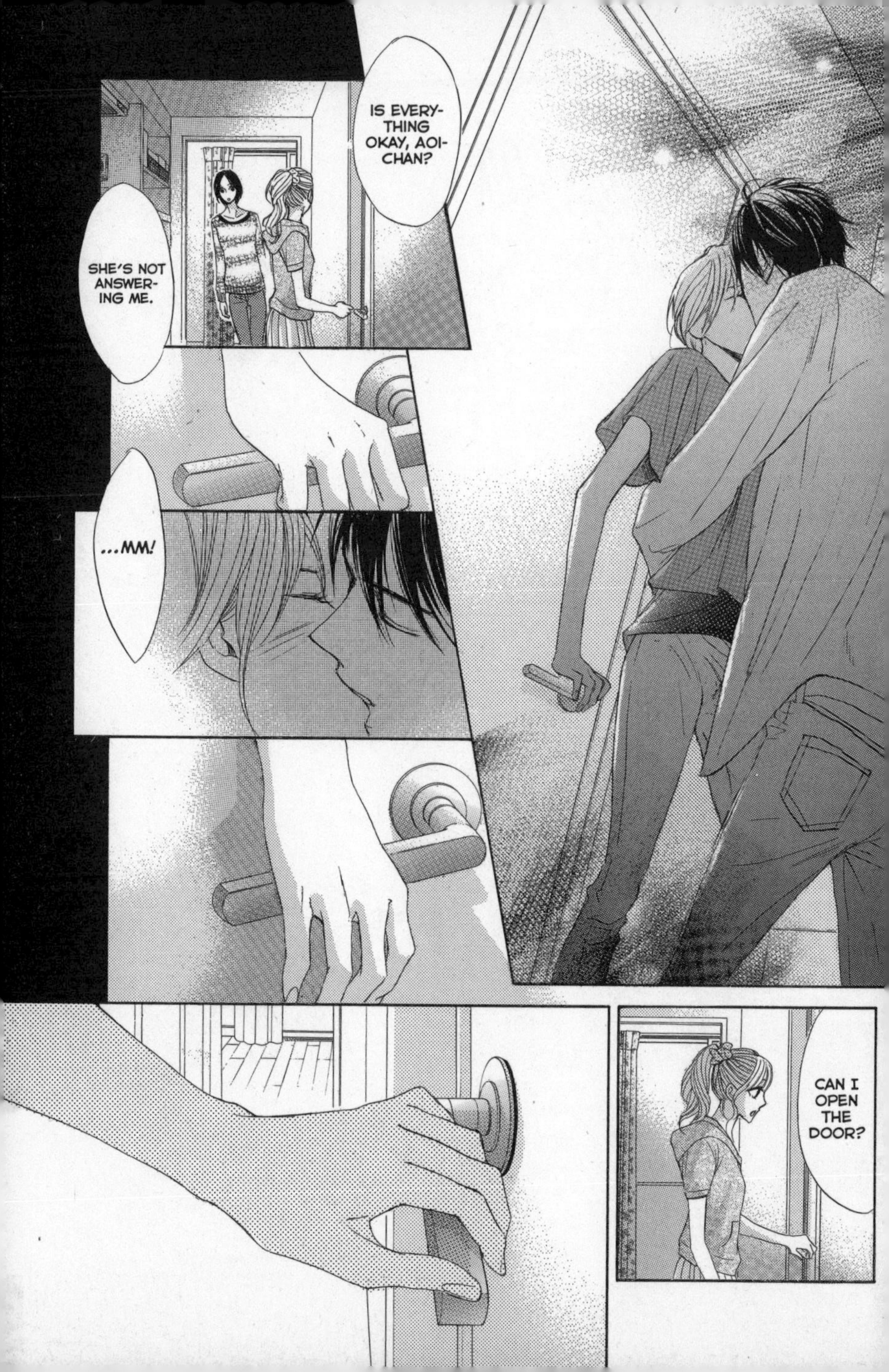
IS EVERY-THING OKAY, AOI-CHAN?
SHE'S NOT ANSWER-ING ME.
...MM!
CAN I OPEN THE DOOR?

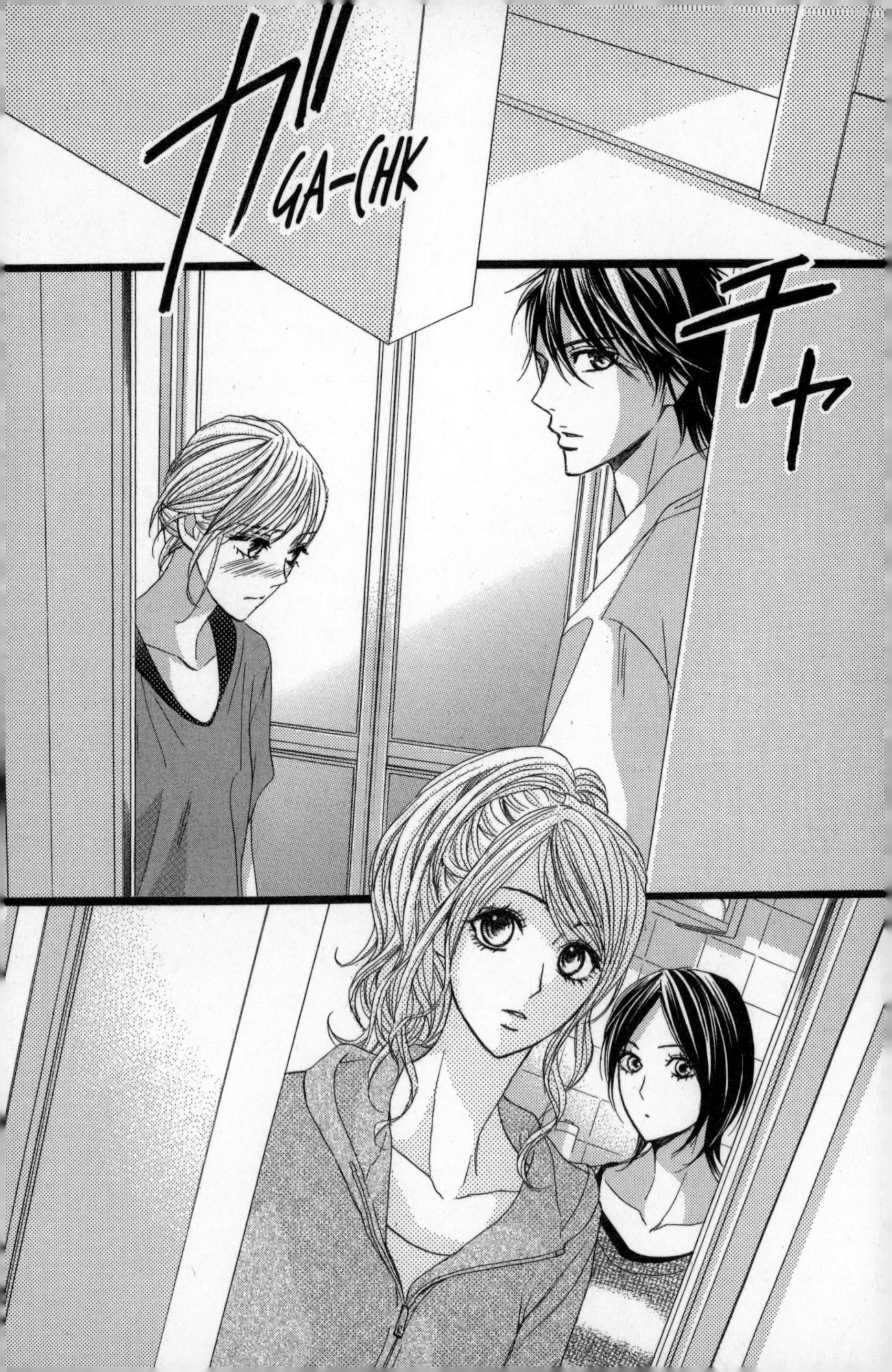
ガ
GA-CHK
チャ

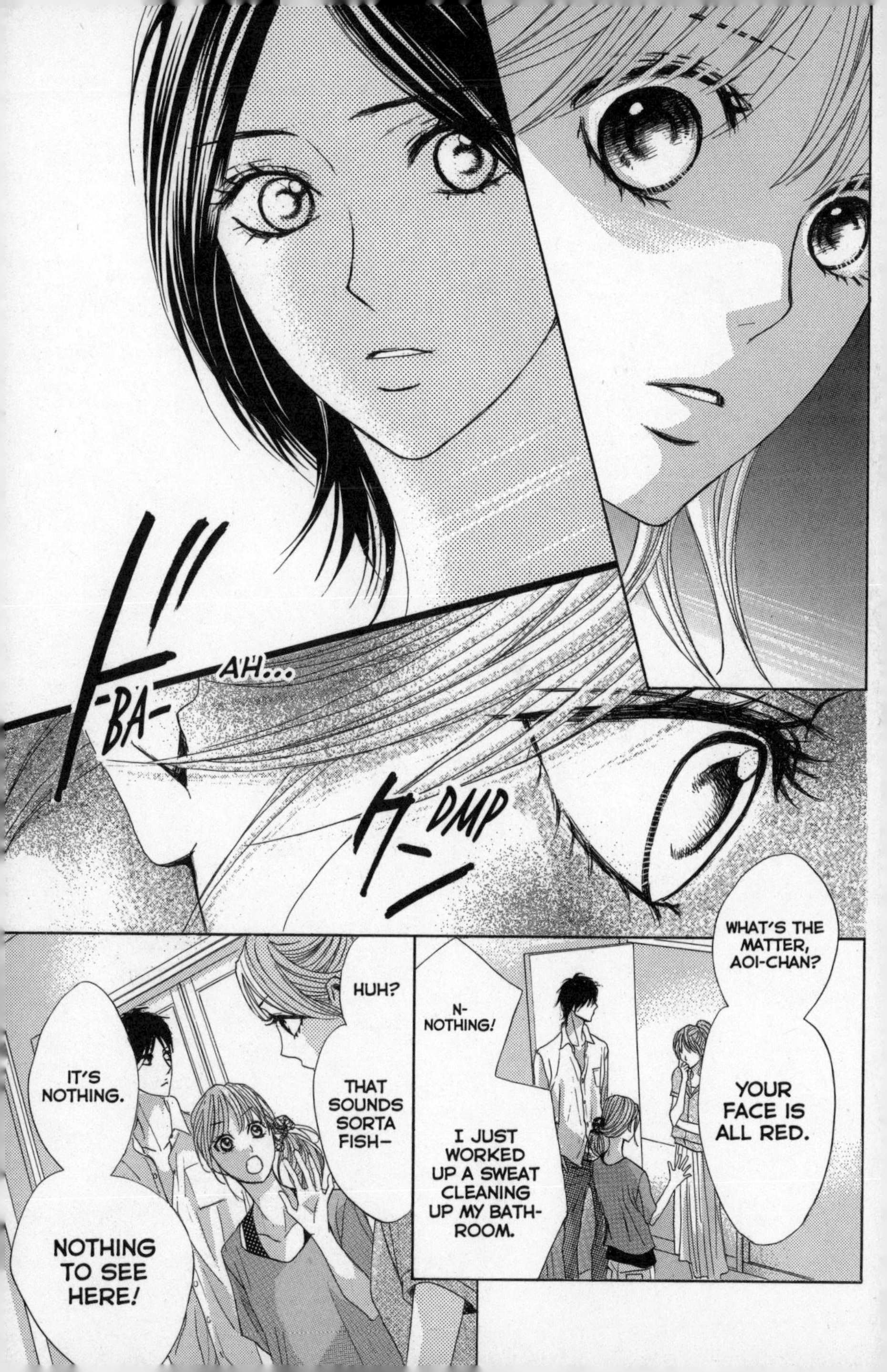
AH...
BA-
DMP
WHAT'S THE MATTER, AOI-CHAN?
YOUR FACE IS ALL RED.
N-NOTHING!
I JUST WORKED UP A SWEAT CLEANING UP MY BATH-ROOM.
HUH?
THAT SOUNDS SORTA FISH-
IT'S NOTHING.
NOTHING TO SEE HERE!

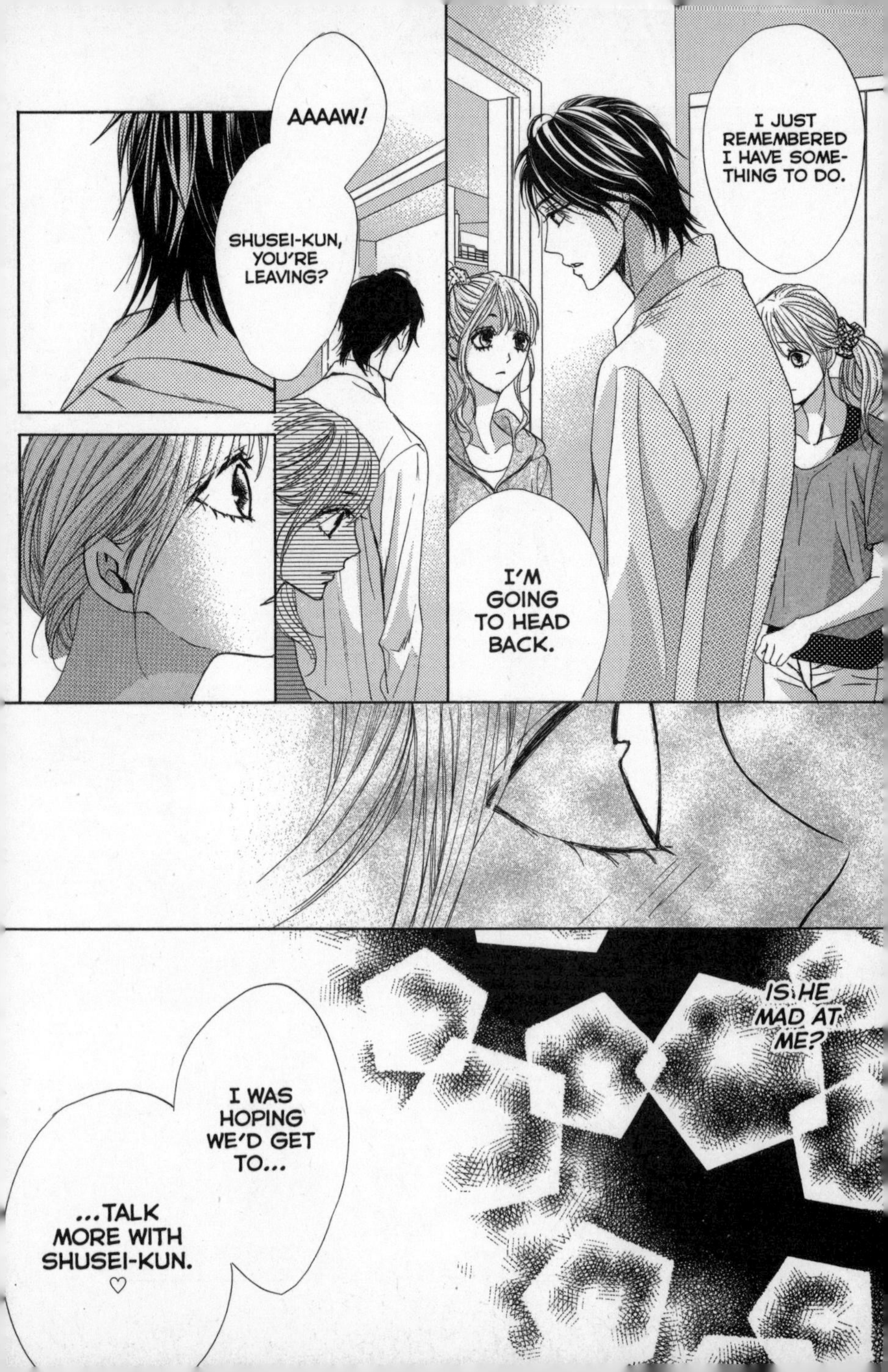
I JUST REMEMBERED I HAVE SOME-THING TO DO.
I'M GOING TO HEAD BACK.
AAAAW!
SHUSEI-KUN, YOU'RE LEAVING?
IS HE MAD AT ME?
I WAS HOPING WE'D GET TO...
...TALK MORE WITH SHUSEI-KUN. ♡

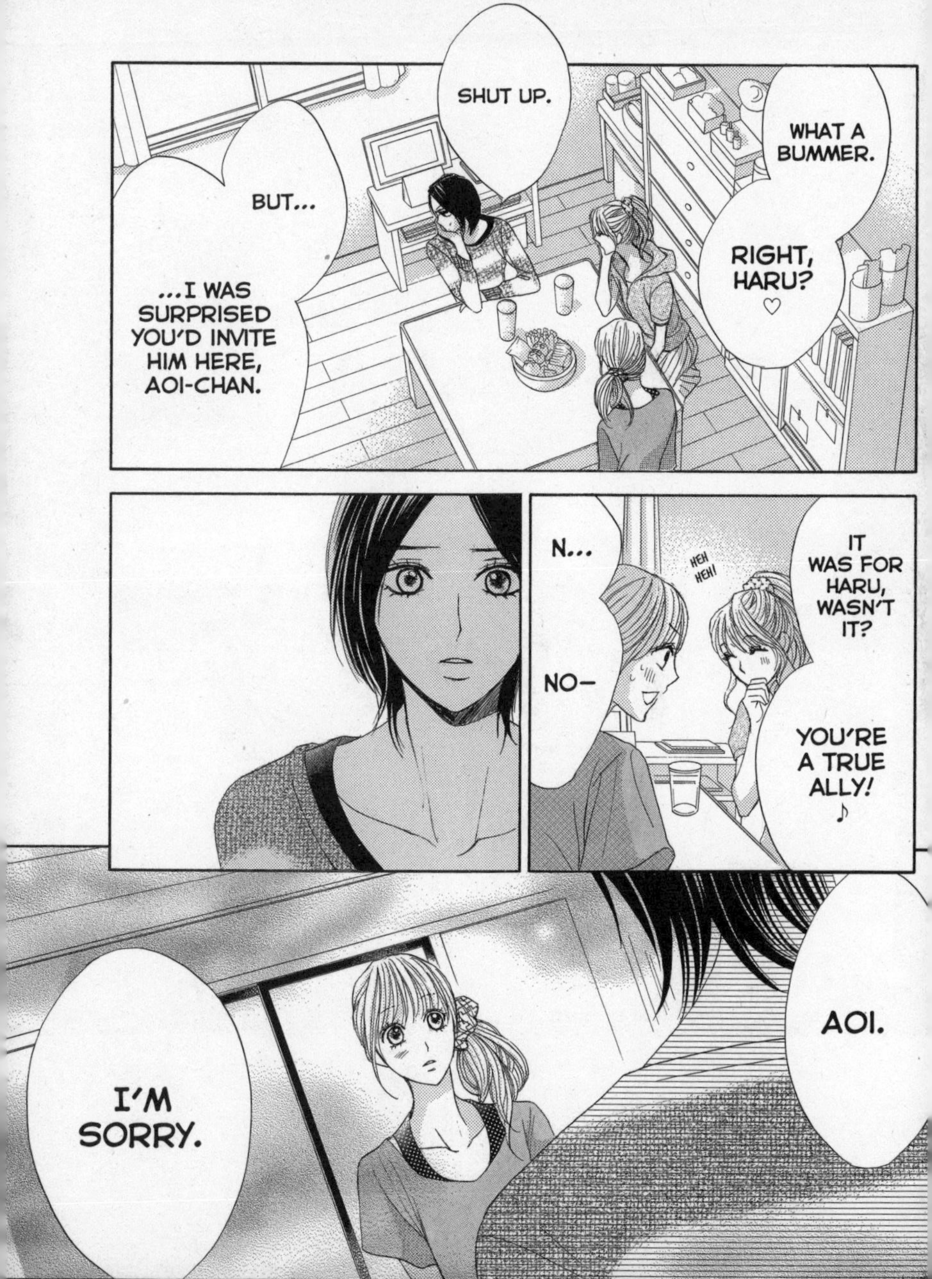
WHAT A BUMMER.
RIGHT, HARU? ♡
SHUT UP.
BUT...
...I WAS SURPRISED YOU'D INVITE HIM HERE, AOI-CHAN.
IT WAS FOR HARU, WASN'T IT?
HEH HEH!
YOU'RE A TRUE ALLY! ♪
N...
NO—
AOI.
I'M SORRY.

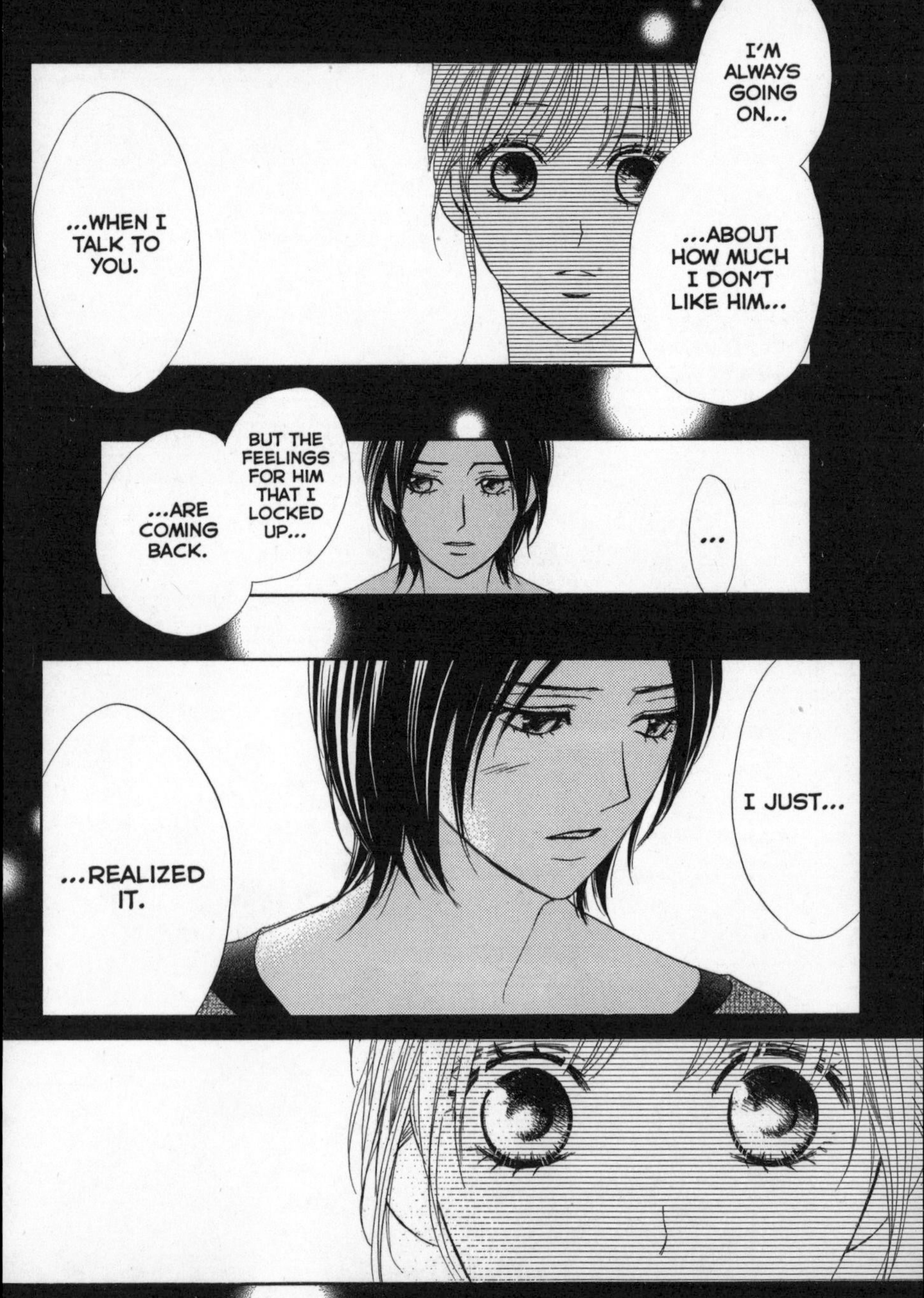
I'M ALWAYS GOING ON...
...ABOUT HOW MUCH I DON'T LIKE HIM...
...WHEN I TALK TO YOU.
...
BUT THE FEELINGS FOR HIM THAT I LOCKED UP...
...ARE COMING BACK.
I JUST...
...REALIZED IT.

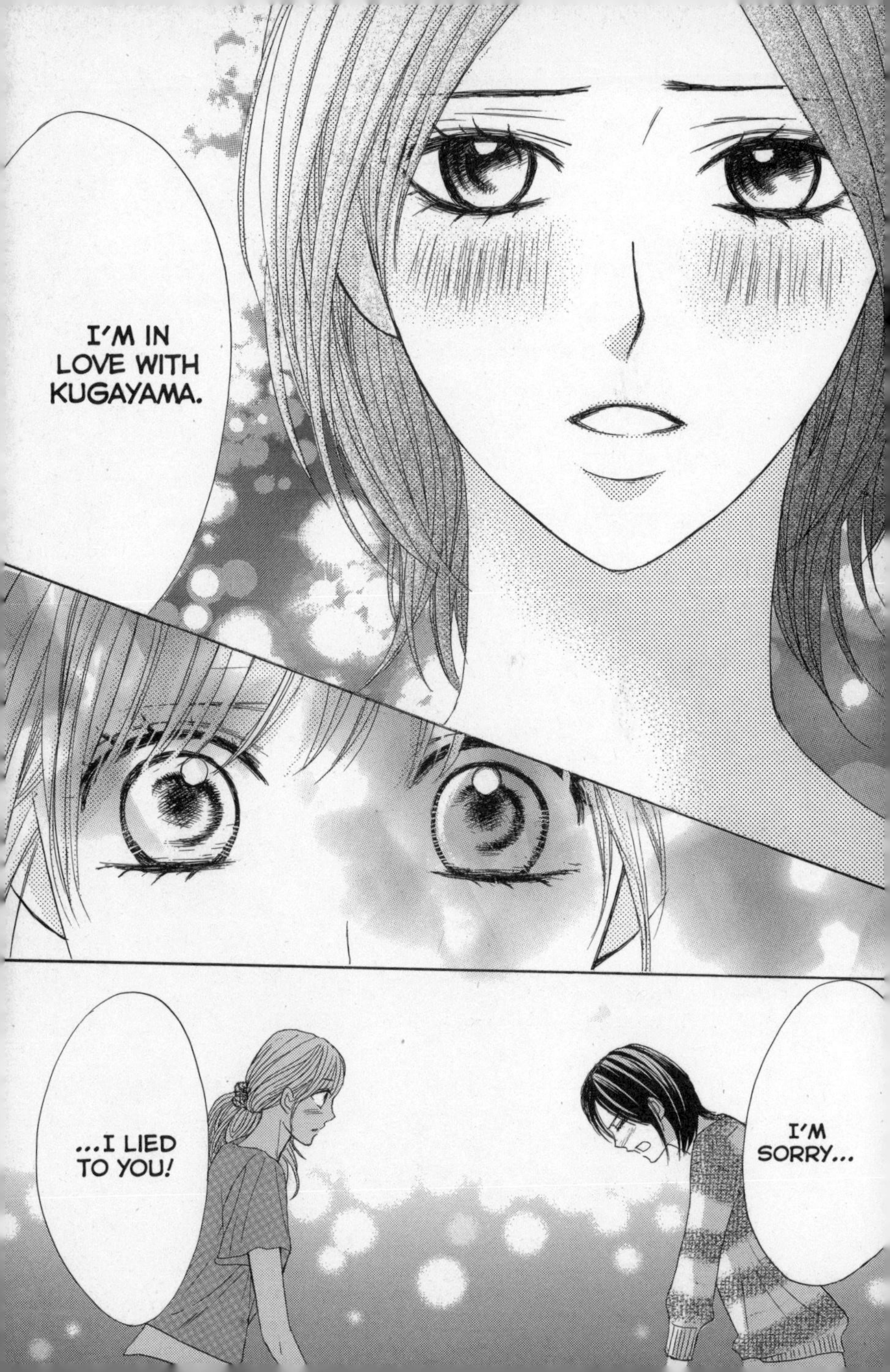
I'M IN LOVE WITH KUGAYAMA.
I'M SORRY...
...I LIED TO YOU!

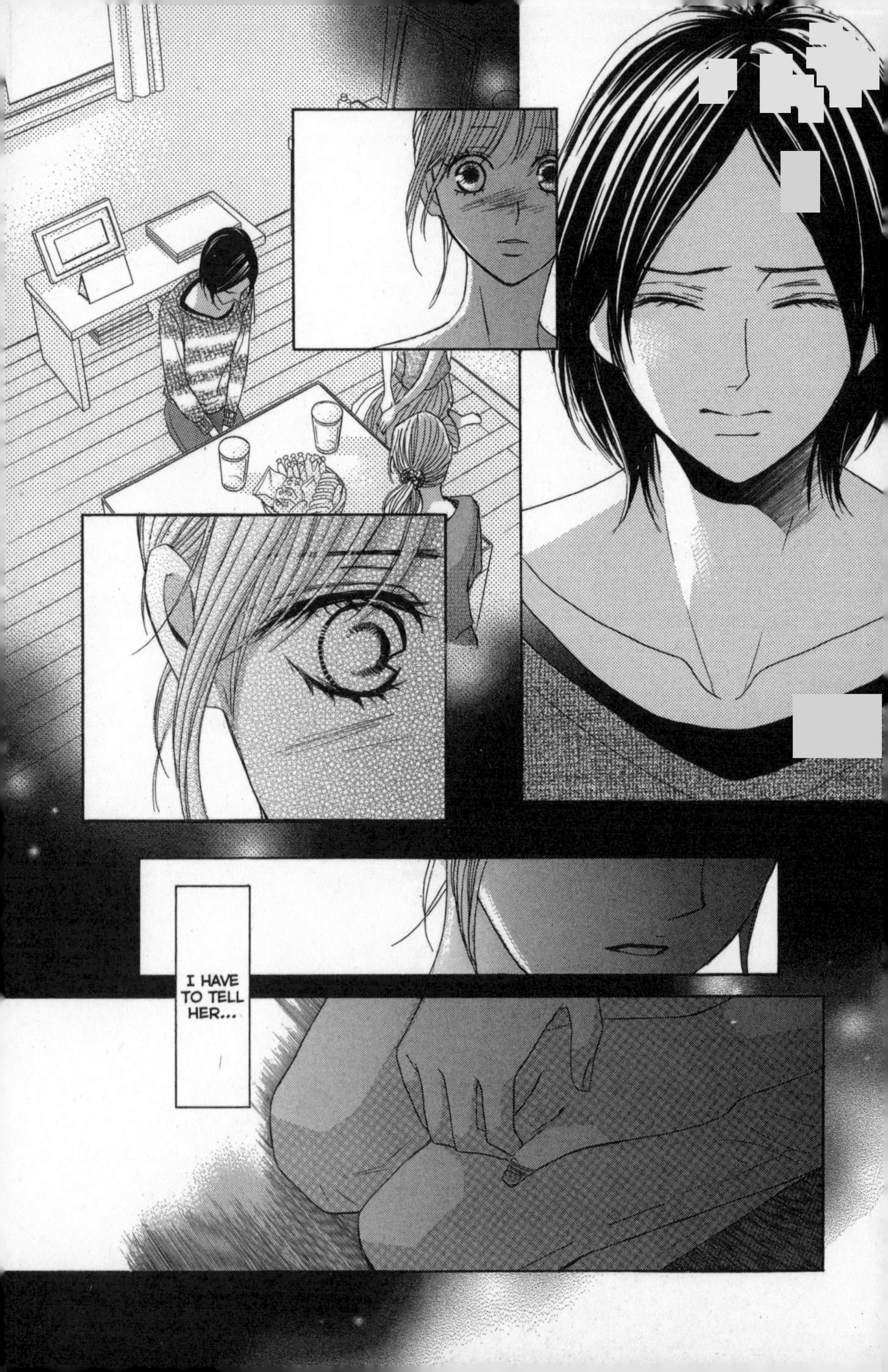
I HAVE TO TELL HER...

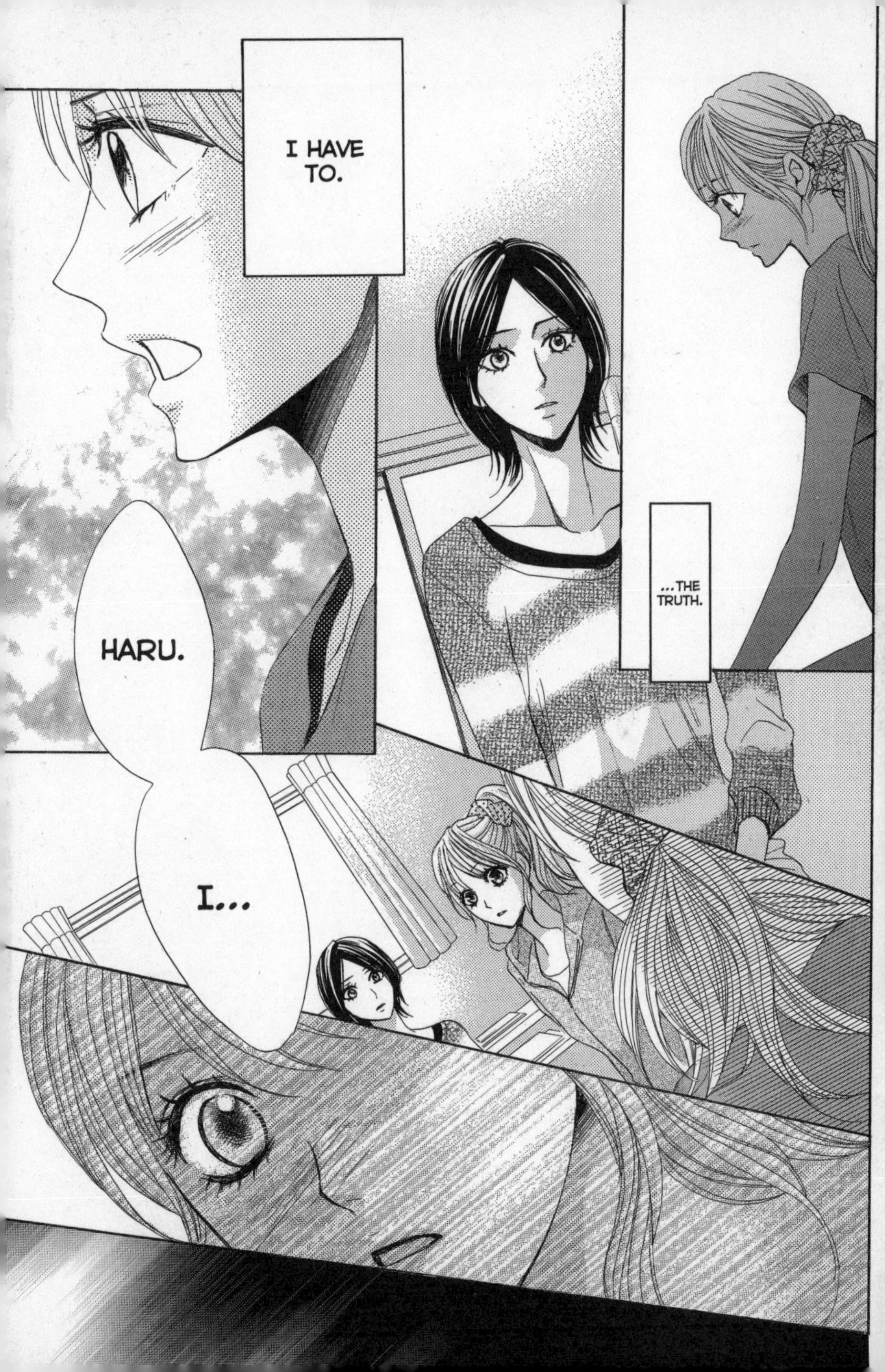
...THE TRUTH.
I HAVE TO.
HARU.
I...

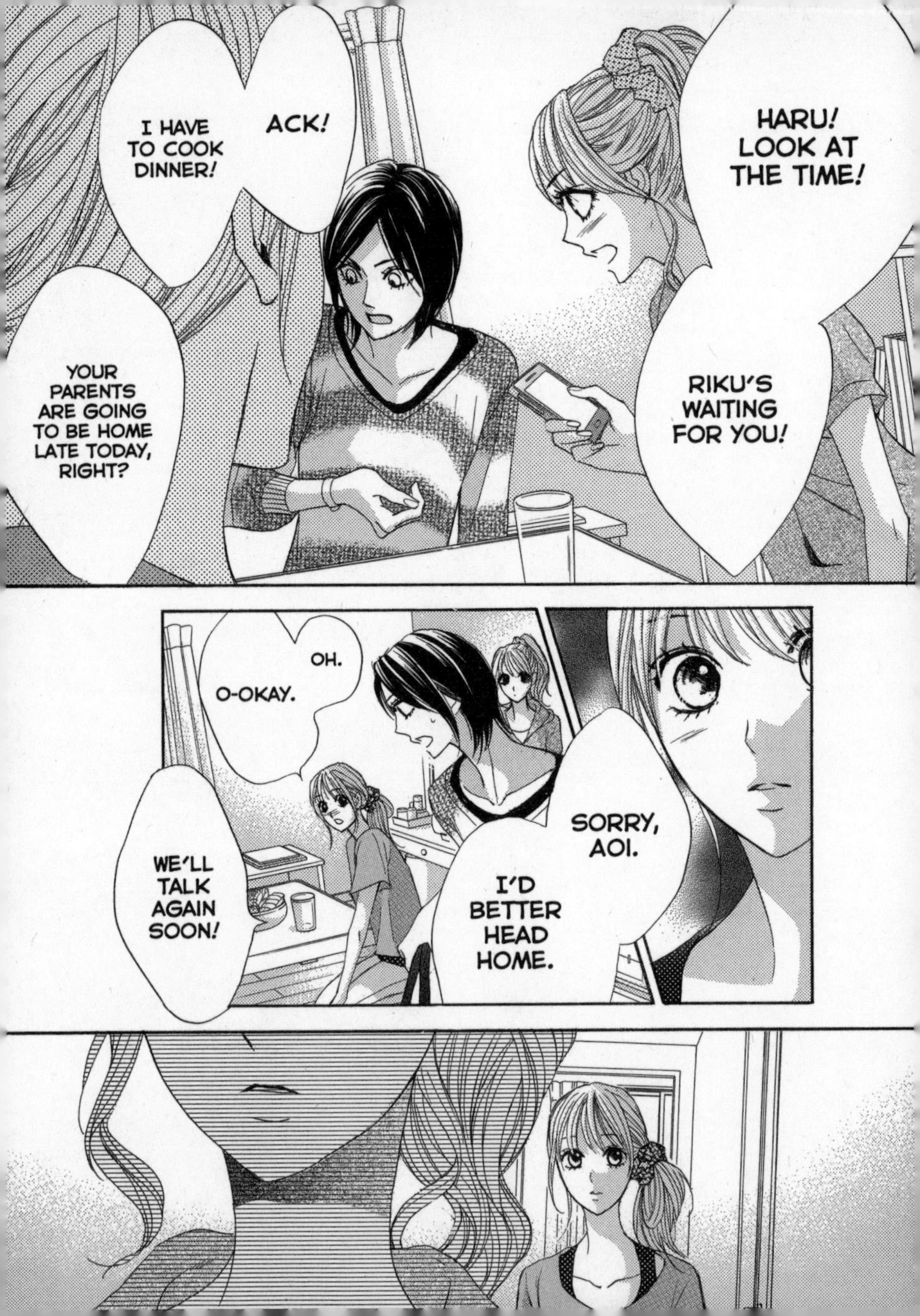
HARU! LOOK AT THE TIME!
ACK!
I HAVE TO COOK DINNER!
RIKU'S WAITING FOR YOU!
YOUR PARENTS ARE GOING TO BE HOME LATE TODAY, RIGHT?
SORRY, AOI.
I'D BETTER HEAD HOME.
OH.
O-OKAY.
WE'LL TALK AGAIN SOON!

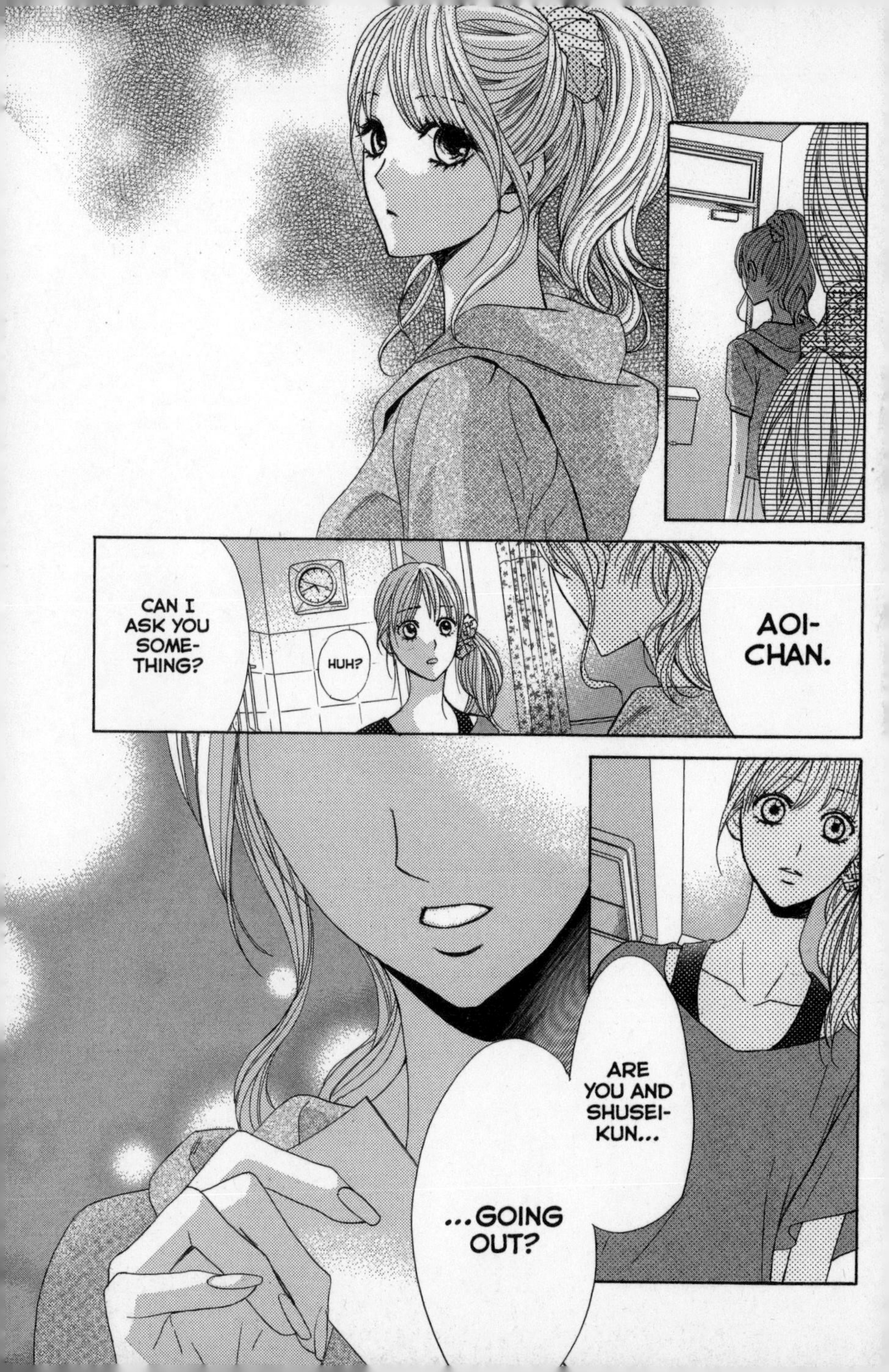
AOI-CHAN.
CAN I ASK YOU SOME-THING?
HUH?
ARE YOU AND SHUSEI-KUN...
...GOING OUT?

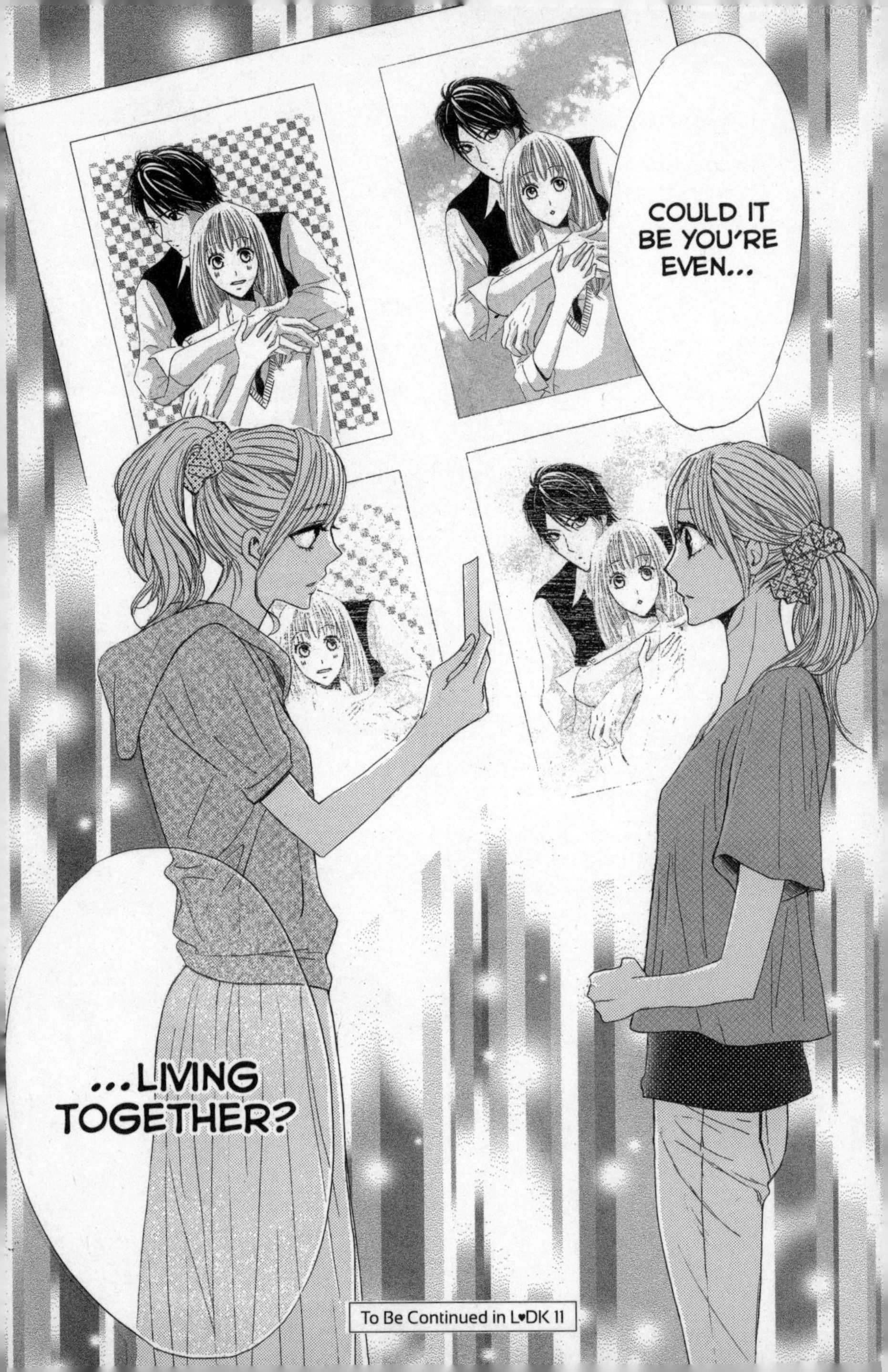
COULD IT BE YOU'RE EVEN...
...LIVING TOGETHER?
To Be Continued in L♥DK 11

L♥DK

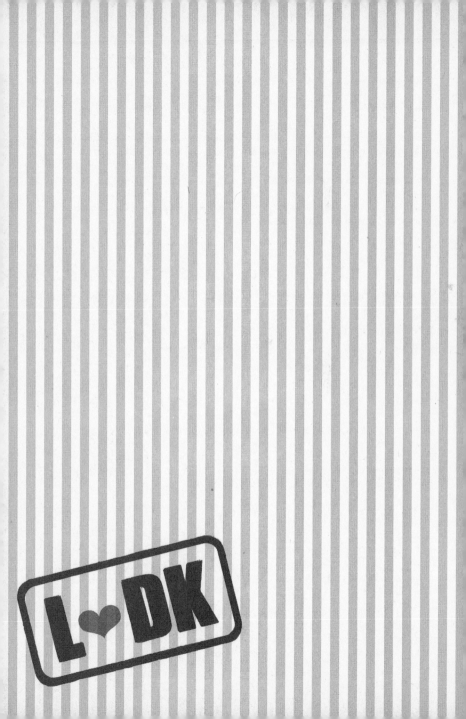

AFTERWORD

Hello, everyone!! Thank you for picking up volume 10 of "L♡DK"! I can't believe we're finally at ten volumes. I've never reached this number before. It's been three and a half years since serialization started in the magazine... That probably explains why my skin isn't as supple as it once was (cry). Thank you, once again, to all of you who have supported me so far!! And to my editor M'da-sama, for all the ***wonderful*** advice you give me on how to depict a "sadistic boy"...

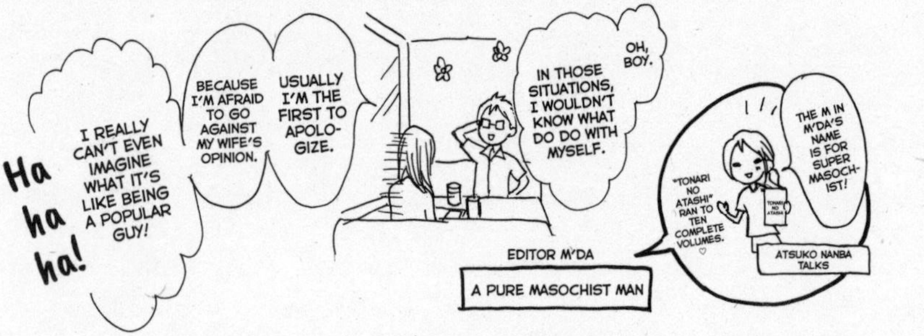
THE M IN M'DA'S NAME IS FOR SUPER MASOCH-IST!
"TONARI NO ATASHI" RAN TO TEN COMPLETE VOLUMES. ♡
ATSUKO NANBA TALKS
OH, BOY.
IN THOSE SITUATIONS, I WOULDN'T KNOW WHAT DO DO WITH MYSELF.
USUALLY I'M THE FIRST TO APOLO-GIZE.
BECAUSE I'M AFRAID TO GO AGAINST MY WIFE'S OPINION.
I REALLY CAN'T EVEN IMAGINE WHAT IT'S LIKE BEING A POPULAR GUY!
Ha ha ha!
EDITOR M'DA
A PURE MASOCHIST MAN

And with that, I hope to try my best here, too.
Recently, I bought one of those robotic vacuums, which I've wanted for years. I couldn't resist the passionate sales pitch the young man at the electronics store gave me. But! This thing's actually a lot busier than I thought it'd be. I've taken to just sitting and watching it whirl around my room. It makes my heart soar.

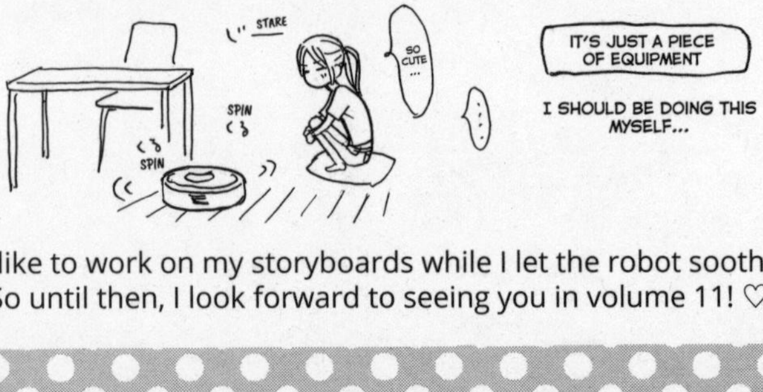
IT'S JUST A PIECE OF EQUIPMENT
I SHOULD BE DOING THIS MYSELF...
SO CUTE ...
STARE
SPIN
SPIN

I think I'd like to work on my storyboards while I let the robot soothe my soul. So until then, I look forward to seeing you in volume 11! ♡

Everyday Essentials, Item 10
Good Luck Charm

This is a homemade good luck charm that
I received some years back from a reader.
It's supposed to grant me a big hit.
I always keep it on my desk.
On the back, it's embroidered with the
words "super popular"... I could cry.
My readers give me lots of power.
Thank you.

"I'm pleasantly surprised to find modern shojo using cross-dressing as a dramatic device to deliver social commentary... Recommended."

-Otaku USA Magazine

The prince in his dark days

By **Hico Yamanaka**

A drunkard for a father, a household of poverty... For 17-year-old Atsuko, misfortune is all she knows and believes in. Until one day, a chance encounter with Itaru-the wealthy heir of a huge corporation-changes everything. The two look identical, uncannily so. When Itaru curiously goes missing, Atsuko is roped into being his stand-in. There, in his shoes, Atsuko must parade like a prince in a palace. She encounters many new experiences, but at what cost...?

"*Parasyte* fans should get a kick out of the chance to revisit Iwaaki's weird, violent, strangely affecting universe. Recommended." -Otaku USA Magazine

"A great anthology containing an excellent variety of genres and styles." -Manga Bookshelf

Based on the critically acclaimed classic horror manga

The first new *Parasyte* manga in over 20 years!

NEO PARASYTE f

BY **ASUMIKO NAKAMURA, EMA TOYAMA, MIKI RINNO, LALAKO KOJIMA, KAORI YUKI, BANKO KUZE, YUUKI OBATA, KASHIO, YUI KUROE, ASIA WATANABE, MIKIMAKI, HIKARU SURUGA, HAJIME SHINJO, RENJURO KINDAICHI, AND YURI NARUSHIMA**

A collection of chilling new *Parasyte* stories from Japan's top shojo artists!

Parasites: shape-shifting aliens whose only purpose is to assimilate with and consume the human race... but do these monsters have a different side? A parasite becomes a prince to save his romance-obsessed female host from a dangerous stalker. Another hosts a cooking show, in which the real monsters are revealed. These and 13 more stories, from some of the greatest shojo manga artists alive today, together make up a chilling, funny, and entertaining tribute to one of manga's horror classics!

The award-winning manga about what happens inside you!

"Far more entertaining than it ought to be... what kid doesn't want to think that every time they sneeze a torpedo shoots out their nose?"
—Anime News Network

Strep throat! Hay fever! Influenza! The world is a dangerous place for a red blood cell just trying to get her deliveries finished. Fortunately, she's not alone...she's got a whole human body's worth of cells ready to help out! The mysterious white blood cells, the buff and brash killer T cells, even the cute little platelets— everyone's got to come together if they want to keep you healthy!

Cells at Work!

By Akane Shimizu

"An emotional and artistic tour de force! We see incredible triumph, and crushing defeat... each panel [is] a thrill!"
—Anitay

"A journey that's instantly compelling."
—Anime News Network

WELCOME TO THE BALLROOM

By Tomo Takeuchi

Feckless high school student Tatara Fujita wants to be good at something—anything. Unfortunately, he's about as average as a slouchy teen can be. The local bullies know this, and make it a habit to hit him up for cash, but all that changes when the debonair Kaname Sengoku sends them packing. Sengoku's not the neighborhood watch, though. He's a professional ballroom dancer. And once Tatara Fujita gets pulled into the world of ballroom, his life will never be the same.

KC
KODANSHA
COMICS

KC
KODANSHA
COMICS

A new
series
from the
creator
of *Soul
Eater*, the
megahit
manga and
anime seen
on Toonami!

"Fun and lively...
a great start!"
-Adventures in
Poor Taste

FIRE FORCE

By Atsushi Ohkubo

The city of Tokyo is plagued by a deadly phenomenon: spontaneous human combustion! Luckily, a special team is there to quench the inferno: The Fire Force! The fire soldiers at Special Fire Cathedral 8 are about to get a unique addition. Enter Shinra, a boy who possesses the power to run at the speed of a rocket, leaving behind the famous "devil's footprints" (and destroying his shoes in the process). Can Shinra and his colleagues discover the source of this strange epidemic before the city burns to ashes?

Having lost his wife, high school teacher Kōhei Inuzuka is doing his best to raise his young daughter Tsumugi as a single father. He's pretty bad at cooking and doesn't have a huge appetite to begin with, but chance brings his little family together with one of his students, the lonely Kotori. The three of them are anything but comfortable in the kitchen, but the healing power of home cooking might just work on their grieving hearts.

"This season's number-one feel-good anime!" —Anime News Network

"A beautifully-drawn story about comfort food and family and grief. Recommended." —Otaku USA Magazine

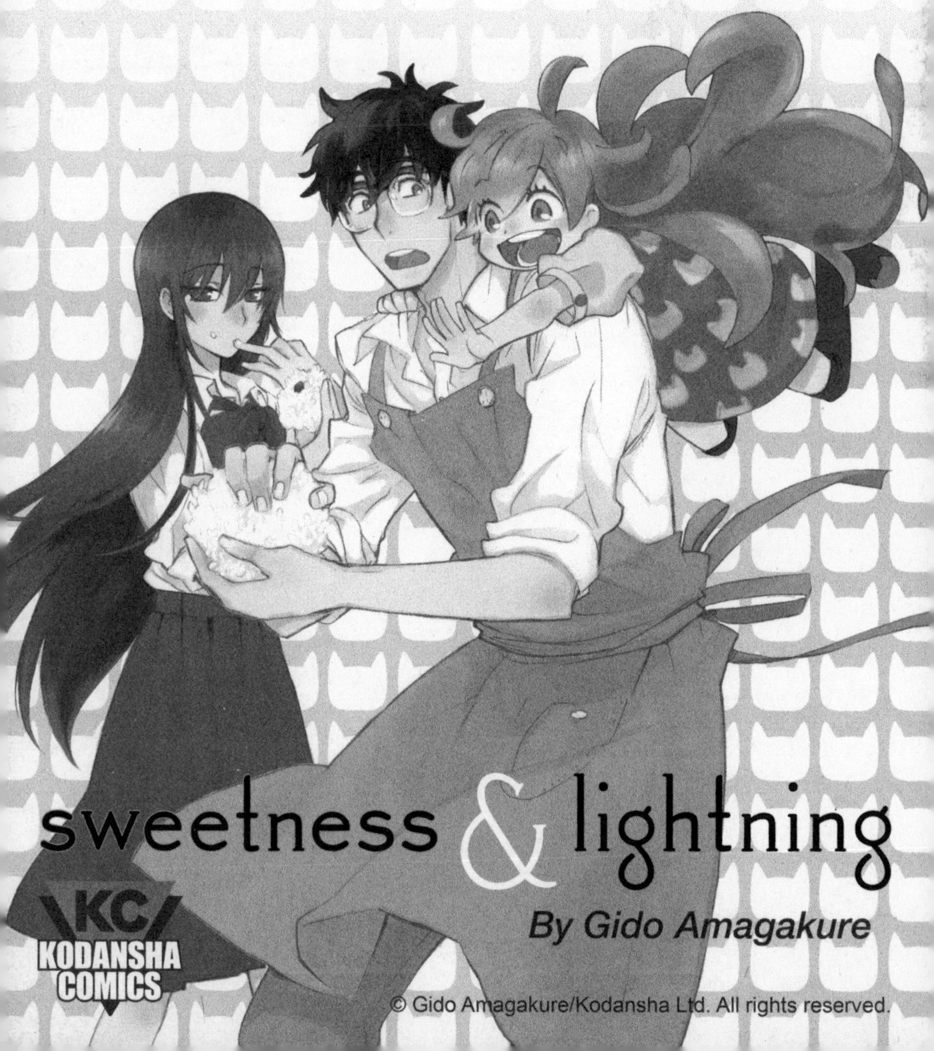
sweetness & lightning
By Gido Amagakure
KC
KODANSHA COMICS

KC
KODANSHA
COMICS

New action series from Hiroyuki Takei, creator of the classic shonen franchise Shaman King!

In medieval Japan, a bell hanging on the collar is a sign that a cat has a master. Norachiyo's bell hangs from his katana sheath, but he is nonetheless a stray — a ronin. This one-eyed cat samurai travels across a dishonest world, cutting through pretense and deception with his blade.

Nekogahara

STRAY CAT SAMURAI

By
Hiroyuki Takei

Japan's most powerful spirit medium delves into the ghost world's greatest mysteries!

Story by Kyo Shirodaira, famed author of mystery fiction and creator of *Spiral*, *Blast of Tempest*, and *The Record of a Fallen Vampire*.

Both touched by spirits called yôkai, Kotoko and Kurô have gained unique superhuman powers. But to gain her powers Kotoko has given up an eye and a leg, and Kurô's personal life is in shambles. So when Kotoko suggests they team up to deal with renegades from the spirit world, Kurô doesn't have many other choices, but Kotoko might just have a few ulterior motives...

IN/SPECTRE

STORY BY **KYO SHIRODAIRA**
ART BY **CHASHIBA KATASE**

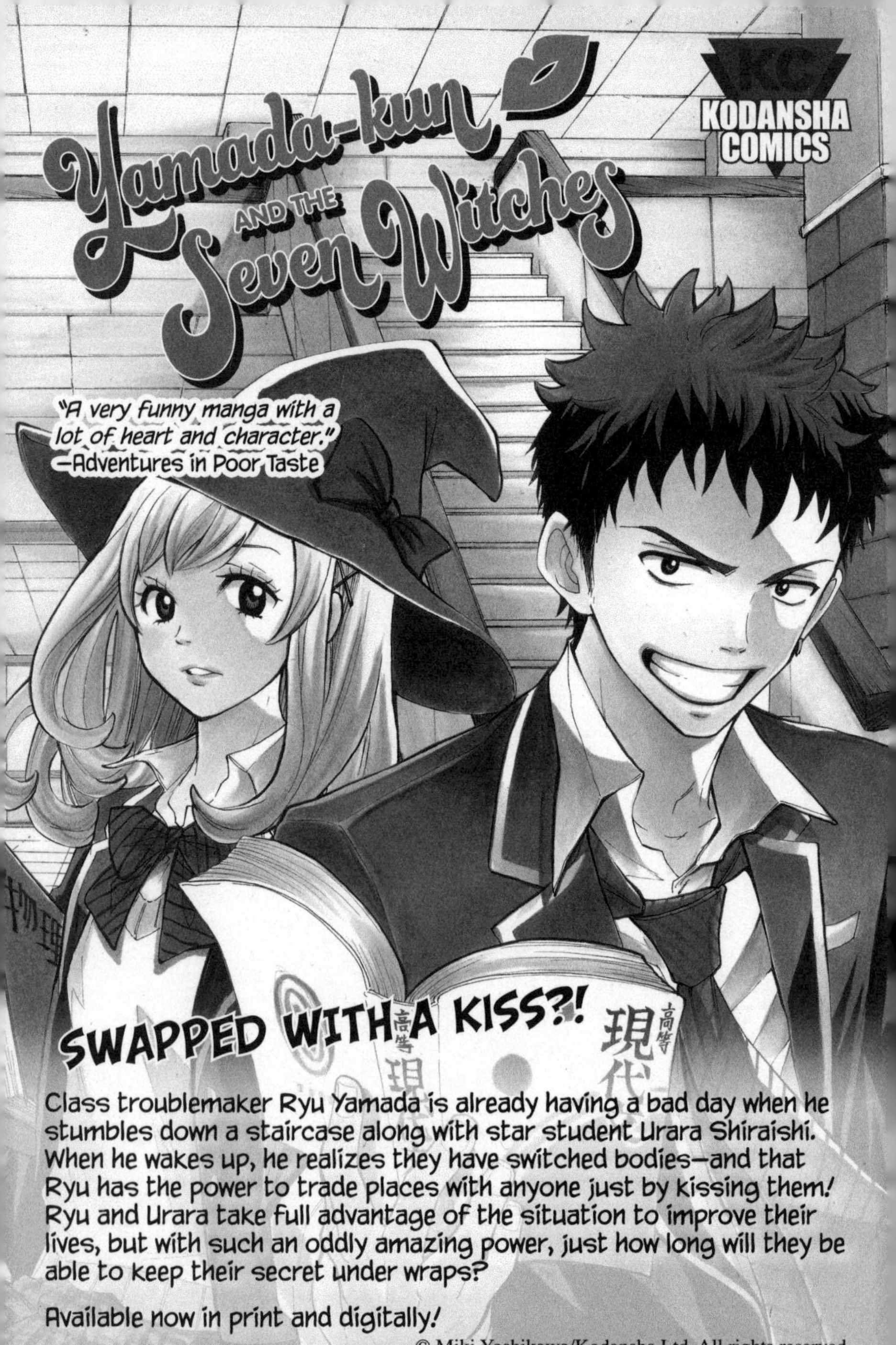
Yamada-kun and the Seven Witches
KODANSHA COMICS
"A very funny manga with a lot of heart and character." —Adventures in Poor Taste
SWAPPED WITH A KISS?!
Class troublemaker Ryu Yamada is already having a bad day when he stumbles down a staircase along with star student Urara Shiraishi. When he wakes up, he realizes they have switched bodies—and that Ryu has the power to trade places with anyone just by kissing them! Ryu and Urara take full advantage of the situation to improve their lives, but with such an oddly amazing power, just how long will they be able to keep their secret under wraps?
Available now in print and digitally!

KC
KODANSHA
COMICS

A new series from the creator of *Soul Eater*, the megahit manga and anime seen on Toonami!

"Fun and lively... a great start!"
-Adventures in Poor Taste

FIRE FORCE

By Atsushi Ohkubo

The city of Tokyo is plagued by a deadly phenomenon: spontaneous human combustion! Luckily, a special team is there to quench the inferno: The Fire Force! The fire soldiers at Special Fire Cathedral 8 are about to get a unique addition. Enter Shinra, a boy who possesses the power to run at the speed of a rocket, leaving behind the famous "devil's footprints" (and destroying his shoes in the process). Can Shinra and his colleagues discover the source of this strange epidemic before the city burns to ashes?

A Kodansha Comics Trade Paperback Original.

LDK volume 10 copyright © 2012 Ayu Watanabe
English translation copyright © 2017 Ayu Watanabe

Published in the United States by Kodansha Comics, an imprint of Kodansha USA Publishing, LLC, New York.

Publication rights for this English edition arranged through Kodansha Ltd., Tokyo.

First published in Japan in 2012 by Kodansha Ltd., Tokyo, as *L♡DK*, volume 10.

ISBN 978-1-63236-163-9

Printed in the United States of America.

www.kodanshacomics.com

9 8 7 6 5 4 3 2 1

Translation: Christine Dashiell
Lettering: Sara Linsley
Editing: Haruko Hashimoto
Kodansha Comics Edition Cover Design: Phil Balsman